SEXUAL DEVIANCY AND SOCIAL PROSCRIPTION

SEXUAL DEVIANCY AND SOCIAL PROSCRIPTION
The Social Context of Carnal Behavior

Clifton D. Bryant, Ph.D.
Virginia Polytechnic Institute and State University

 **HUMAN SCIENCES PRESS,INC.**
72 FIFTH AVENUE,
NEW YORK. N.Y. 10011

Printed in the United States of America
23456789 987654321

Library of Congress Cataloging in Publication Data

Bryant, Clifton D., 1932-
   Sexual deviancy and social proscription.

   Bibliography: p. 385
   Includes index.
   1. Sexual deviation.   2. Social control.   I. Title.
HQ71.B73   306.7   LC81-6216
ISBN 0-89885-024-X   AACR2
ISBN 0-89885-094-0 (pbk.)

CONTENTS

PREFACE

When someone writes a Preface, he or she must, of necessity, consider the audience of readers to which the book is addressed. That makes *Sexual Deviancy and Social Proscription*, by Clifton D. Bryant, a difficult book for which to write a preface.

With the plethora of sex books being published, there is the temptation to ask, is this simply another volume of the "everything you've ever wanted to know about sex" genre? In the instance of this book, such is definitely not the case. This is an important book. It is important for some of the reasons put forth by Professor Bryant in his own Preface that follows and for some reasons that he does not specify and with which he might not agree.

In this volume, Professor Bryant incorporates a broad, eclectic theoretical view of sexual deviance and social control. If he favors any theoretical orientation, it is labeling theory and a sort of symbolic interactionist perspective emphasizing the importance of meaning and motive in situational contexts. I do not believe it could be accurately said that this book significantly advances theories of deviance, sexual or otherwise. But it can readily be said that Professor Bryant ambitiously and successfully synthesizes an extraordinarily wide array of legal, medical, and behavioral science literature on the topic, and adds to that synthesis with his own observations, interpretations, and analyses. The chapter divisions in the book, each one representing a different social "context" of sexual behavior, promise to have a constructive, useful and heuristic scholarly impact on the field. Considering sexual deviancy as spurious, vicarious, verbal, symbolic, imitative, counterfeit, superficial, symbiotic, disparate and violent will be useful not only for further theoretical and empirical work, but pedagogically as well.

Let me turn for a moment to the book's pedagogical usefulness. I believe it will start intellectual fights in many classrooms—productive and animated discussions about what is sexually deviant and what is not, about what sexual behaviors ought be "controlled" and what ones should not, and about what, if any, value the sociological analysis of sexual behavior might have for individuals and society. The concepts of "conservatism" and "liberalism" in sexual behavior, and the ideological substrates of those interpretations, will be brought to the fore by this book. It will surface differing perceptions of sexual behavior held by men and women.

Professor Bryant has written several books about deviance. I have read all of them. Frankly, I believe he had more fun writing this book. The narrative is salted with a wry sense of humor.

He has rather strong preferences in his interpretations of sexual deviance, and they are manifest in this book. But Bryant has been penetratively insightful about sexual behavior (for example, the hypocrisy of sexual mores in the 1950s). Sometimes, he seems to have been, at least implicitly, unduly negatively judgmental (for example, his categorizing of homosexual behavior as "counterfeit" sex). Sometimes, he seems to be a bit off track in his interpretations (for example, the difference between sexual liberation and sexual deviance among contemporary women). But he has been consistently *honest* in this book. This makes this book refreshing, and especially useful professionally as well as in the classroom.

The author sent me, as is typical, a pre-publication manuscript which I could read in order to prepare this Preface. Because of time constraints, however, untypically, the copy of the manuscript I received included the comments, queries, suggestions, objections and recommendations of the publisher's editorial advisor. There were a number of such editorial reactions and comments from this editor who obviously was extremely well informed not only about manuscript style and format but substantively about the sociology of sexual behavior. Though I know it's not feasible, I wish that the editorial consultant's comments, and Professor Bryant's rejoinders, could be included in the book as a running commentary. Many of the editorial consultant's comments, of course, were addressed by Professor Bryant in his revision of the manuscript, often with attendant lengthy expository responses. But the written exchanges between him and the editorial consultant constitute an intriguing debate on the perspectives, interpretations, and analyses which run throughout the volume. Sometimes I found myself agreeing more with the editorial consultant; other times, more with Professor Bryant. I am certain that readers, whether students or professional sociologists, no less will be stimulated to debate.

Since sociology, particularly the sociology of sexual behavior, is by no means an exact science, what more can an author expect than that his or her book causes people creatively to consider important social issues. *Sexual Deviancy and Social Proscription* will do precisely that.

> Louis A. Zurcher, Ph.D.
> Acting Dean
> School of Social Work
> The University of Texas at Austin
> June, 1981

AUTHOR'S PREFACE

No forms of human behavior are more potentially disruptive to the social order than those attendant to sexual gratification. The sexual urge is a powerful component in physiological motivation and plays an equally intense role in the shaping of the social configurations which accomplish to externalize carnal desire and provide for its satisfaction through institutionalized behavioral means. The carnal urge can also be, and often is, equally cohesive, in affecting social solidarity through sexual bonding and concerted efforts to facilitate and routinize opportunities for sexual gratification. Sexual behavior does not occur within a social vacuum, however, and must accordingly, be socially monitored, channeled, and controlled in an effort to direct it toward socially constructive purposes and away from more disruptive courses. A not inconsiderable amount of societal effort is exerted toward the containment and control of human sexual behavior.

Inasmuch as the social behaviors that bring about carnal gratification are widely varied, complex, and often socially convoluted, the societal efforts aimed at the containment and control of such sexual activities are usually equally elaborate and involved. There are, for example, numerous social proscriptions and prescriptions that speak to the appropriate circumstances, conditions, and participants constituent to numerous varieties of sexual expression and carnal gratifi-

11

cation. Sexual deviancy, like all forms of deviant behavior is relative, however, and there is infrequent consensus on the labeling of particular sexual behavior. What is normative and prescribed in one context is often deviant and socially proscribed in another. Such situational discensus and variability may often be a discordant element in the social order. Our comments in this book treat sexual expression and carnal behavior against a backdrop of social context and variable meaning. It is our purpose to show that sexual behavior that is labeled deviant is not an absolute phenomenon but is subject to great variation in interpretation and social reaction depending on the circumstances of its commission.

Deviant sexual behavior has been addressed from the perspective of numerous disciplines and vocations including the law, medicine, psychiatry, sociology, psychology, and law enforcement, to name several, and a resultant diverse and scattered literature has developed. Inasmuch as the findings and observations from this varied literature have all made contributions to a better understanding of such behavior, this exposition draws on selected examples of research and commentary from all of these disciplines and points of view. There has not been significant theoretical convergence in regard to the definitive etiology of specific modes of sexual deviancy within a given discipline, much less between and among disciplines. Accordingly, if an appropriate understanding is to be obtained of the vagaries of social cognition and definition surrounding carnal behavior, and subtleties of interpretive nuance attendant to the context of sexual deviance are to be appreciated, a multidisciplinary exploration would seem indicated. Deviant sexual behavior can be viewed from many intellectual vantage points, and a pluralistic set of observations and insights often afford the most effective grasp and understanding of the phenomenon.

Traditionally, sexual deviancy has often been addressed in terms of relatively simplistic and direct classificational efforts, most commonly looking at the type of sexual deviancy in terms of the specification of the sexual act involved. Thus, sexual deviancy may have been viewed and explored as rape, exhibitionism, or prostitution, for example, but always the object of focus is the sexual act itself. Other similarly simplistic, categorical frameworks for the examination of deviant sexual behavior have probed such dimensions as the degree of social reprehensibility of the offense, the degree of encroachment on the legal normative order, the statistical frequency or modal occurrences of the sexual offenses, or the extent of victimization involved in such behavior. The discussion in this book, however, is based on a somewhat different conceptualization of sexual deviancy. As mentioned earlier, sexual behavior occurs within a social context and is, accordingly, subject to collective interpretation and cultural meaning. Such behavior may then be judged as either normative or deviant. In this sense, sexual deviancy is relative to time, place, circumstances, and audience. But, not only is deviant sexual behavior a function of interpretive context and the perceived meaning to the audience or observers, it is also a function of the meaning and symbolism to the actor, as well as the need and purpose which the carnal behavior fulfills. Toward this end, the discussion attempts to articulate a set of conceptual categories of sexual deviancy along a continuum of interactional intensity ranging from the imaginary and symbolic at one end, to superficial, symbiotic, and violent at the other.

The interpretive context and attendant social meanings to actors and audience dictate the level of interactional intensity. Within such an analytical paradigm, the same sexual act might appropriately be included within several conceptual categories, depending on its meaning to those involved. Sexual intercourse might be a meaningful emotional involvement, albeit deviant if adulterous, a superficial mechanism of orgasm, and, thus, carnal gratification only, or an externalization of neurotic hostility and aggression. A visit to a massage parlor for masturbatory services might, on the one hand, serve as an emotional as well as physical substitute for genital heterosexual activity or simply as a device for casual orgasm and thus, relief from sexual tension. Generally speaking, specific forms of sexual activity are constituent to the particular modes of sexual deviancy discussed in this book, but in some instances, the same sex act may be included in several categories depending on meaning and interpretation. The thrust of this exposition, then, is to set sexual expression within an appropriate historical and cultural setting and to explore the social dimensions of its commission, context, and the participants of such behavior. The author hopes the student of deviant sexual behavior will derive an enhanced insight into the mechanisms of social control, as well as the socially convoluted configurations of carnal expression, which they attempt to proscribe and prescribe.

A number of my colleagues here at Virginia Polytechnic Institute and State University are to be thanked for their advice and critique on various parts of the manuscript. Tim Carter, C. Jack Dudley, John Edwards, William McWhorter, Donald Shoemaker,

Jim Skipper, and William Snizek all offered valuable suggestions and comments. Susan Twaddle, one of my graduate assistants, did an excellent job in preparing the index. Ms. Twaddle, along with my other graduate assistants, Kathy Shiflet, and Deborah Brooks worked tirelessly in doing library research and bibliographic work for the book. I am indebted to my secretaries, Christina Hocksstein, Loretta Turpin, Cindy Crawford, Debbie Rhea and Pat Baker, for their energetic and meticulous clerical work in preparing the manuscript. A very special thanks goes to Lou Zurcher for taking the time from a busy schedule to prepare his excellent preface for this volume.

Clifton D. Bryant, Ph.D.
Blacksburg, Virginia

Chapter 1

CARNAL BEHAVIOR AND SOCIAL PROSCRIPTION

A Conceptual Overview of the Social and Interpretive Context of Sexual Deviancy

Sexual behavior, like all human behavior with social importance, is subject to societal control. Because of the intensity of the sexual drive and the volatile implications for the equilibrium of the collective enterprise, these behavioral configurations attendant to the obtaining of sexual gratification—carnal behavior, as it were—are the object of particular social concern and concomitant efforts toward sanctionative regulation and direction. The externalization of carnal desire is basic to human interaction although much societal effort to channel and control it is concerned with directing the sexual drive toward socially cohesive and constructive goals. Within the framework of institutional structure, significant energies and resources are expended in addressing or redressing the problems of normative violations of sexual prescriptions and proscriptions.

Human activity involving sexual gratification is broad in form and variety and rich in social complexity and meaning. Accordingly, in our society as in many, there is a lack of consensus and conviction concerning the social significance and cultural disruptiveness of much carnal behavior. There is controversy, depending on perspective, surrounding carnal activity and the degree to which particular forms of sexual expression may threaten the continuity of cultural ideology and the maintenance of social convention. Similarly, there is discensus, if not dispute, in regard to the various social mechanisms and cultural rationales, by which behavioral configurations, of sexual motivation, are labeled as deviant, and toward which sanctioning efforts are effected or attempted. Carnal behavior, and its social control, is clearly a discordant element in contemporary society, as witness the "gay rights" controversy in Miami in 1977 which saw the repeal of the gay rights ordinance there, and the subsequent other anti-gay efforts and protest demonstrations by gays, throughout the country for the next several years. Other discordant elements have included the legal skirmishing in the area of pornography, and the wide divergence of social opinion and support on such issues as the decriminalization of prostitution, rape, adultery, and surgery to accomplish sex reassignment. In the face of rapidly changing social values and attitudes, and especially the liberalized posture in regard to sexual behavior among consenting adults, as well as the trend toward cultural pluralism which is strongly asserting itself recently, it is likely that the question of appropriate social preoccupation and concern with sexual deviancy will assume an even greater magnitude in terms of societal controversy and conflict in the future. In this regard, an adequate understanding of the broader dimensions of deviant sexual behavior, which should include an examination of the vagaries of human activity concomitant to carnal gratification, seems indicated, and necessary for thoughtful involvement in the social controversy surrounding such behavior, and its meaningful resolution. Such an examination should yield a more sensitive insight into the convoluted structure of carnal behavior and a deeper awareness of the interrelated nature of sexual expression and the larger social systems of behavior.

The broad range of behaviors sometimes labeled as "deviant" dictates the need for some type of categorical differentiation in order to effectively examine and understand such behavior. The use of such a classification scheme or conceptual paradigm facilitates the analytical perspective and aids in obtaining a more sensitive insight into the social interaction attendant to carnal fulfillment. Most treatments of deviant sexual behavior have tended to address the phenomena within mutually exclusive, typological, or classification frameworks. Such conceptualizations have attempted to articulate ordered hierarchies of assumed individual motivation, degree of social reprehensibility, extent of legal applicability, or severity of sanction, among other social assessments, and reactions that may attend violation of the norms of sexual conformity. Such expositions are not without inductive value, but, unfortunately, tend to present an overly idealized, and, therefore, rigid conceptualization of sexual behavior. Sexual behavior is situational in that it occurs within a social context, and is, therefore, subject to the vagaries of collective interpretation and cultural meaning. Sexual behavior labeled "deviant," like all deviant behavior, is relative in its violation of social norm and proscription and in the reception and reaction it engenders from the public. It should, therefore, be viewed within a framework of social meaning and import.

In this respect, sexual deviancy cannot always be appropriately cataloged within mutually exclusive categories. The same sexual behavior, in one situation, may constitute a romantic expression of affection and tenderness, but yet, within a different set of circumstances or within another social definitional context, may represent the depraved and illegal manifestation of lascivious, carnal excesses. Likewise, sexual activity of similar mechanical mode and interactional configuration may appear to be superficially the same in terms of carnal expression, but may represent quite different behavior from the standpoint of symbolic meaning to the individual, interpretive context, and social labeling, and reaction. Thus, the raincoated, "flasher" on the boulevard, and the featured "ecdysiast" in the nightclub both engage in the seemingly same carnal act—that of exposing their anatomy to others. In the instance of the former, such exhibitionism, may provide sexual gratification, or even orgasm to the individual, but not infrequently, is traumatically shocking and offensive to the viewers. Such behavior is viewed as illegal, aberrant, and a manifestation of psychological pathology. In the latter case, the individual receives little, if any carnal gratification, generally being relatively inured to the erotic dimension of her behavior, but provides such gratification to her viewers by virtue of her symbolic sexual activity. Such behavior is usually legal, a normal vocational routine, and is seen as simply an entertaining art form, albeit improprietous form of artistic expression. Beyond the dimension of different sexual gender in the two cases, perhaps a better illustration of differential interpretation and meaning might exist in the nudist seeking epidermal freedom and sunshine and the sidewalk flasher seeking reaffirmation of his maleness.

Masturbation may serve as another illustration of sexual deviancy in differential interpretative context. The pubescent adolescent secretly masturbating in way of carnal exploration is quite different in qualitative interpretation from the individual who calls telephone counseling services in order to be able to interact verbally with a female, and, thus, enhance his sexual fantasies while masturbating during his telephone conversation. Both instances are, in turn, interpretatively different from the businessman away from hearth, home, and spouse, who visits a massage parlor near his motel in way of erotic respite, to receive narcistic reverie and orgasmic relief via the mastabatory services offered by masseuses. Even the erotic courtship behavior of teenagers replete with anatomical exploration and mutual masturbation represents a yet different carnal context. Manual manipulation of the genitals to orgasm may assume a number of erotic meanings and elicit differential social reaction depending on the symbolic interpretation. Similarly, other forms of carnal expression including sexually suggestive language and behavior, homosexual activity, bestiality, prostitution, sexual violence, and coitus, to name some, may be viewed and understood quite differently by participants and public alike, and the subsequent meaning and definition of such carnal behavior may assume widely varying consequence and response.

Thus, depending on the interpretive context, some sexual behavior may be classified within several deviant categories. It is the exacerbating and mitigating conditions and circumstances bearing on the interpretive social context of sexual deviancy that are important to study and understand.

This frame of reference includes an additional perspective by bifurcating carnal deviancy into that behavior which is essentially private and affective in orientation, and that which is commercial and economically instrumental in nature. This book examines an array of carnally motivated behaviors and erotic expressions within a framework that focuses on the sexual modes of deviantly labeled individual behavior, and the more institutionalized, and often more tolerated, collective carnal activities. Although the private pattern may be frequently viewed as aberrant or pathological behavior, the collective mode may take on commercial or recreational dimensions, and although still formally considered as a deviant manifestation of carnal expression, may be tacitly accepted and conceptualized as functional, if not culturally appropriate in selected circumstances. It is important to understand the social considerations involved in the differential conceptualizations of carnal behavior and the attendant cultural response. The individual who departs from the norms of sexual conformity in obtaining carnal satisfaction represents a vagrancy from the social contract and, thus, a threat to the collective interest, in the manifestation of his or her private patterns of sexual deviancy. The economic exploitation of carnal appetites as demonstrated in the commercial configurations of deviancy is, on the other hand, often seen as merely a subversion of the sexual exchange process and a necessary concession to the maintenance of social equilibrium. Thus, viewing the social context as the appropriate matrix for understanding the etiology and import of sexual expression, the focus includes both the level of social intensity and the element of social exclusivity.

There is no definitive or exhaustive inventory of social contexts in regard to sexual deviancy, inasmuch as the myriad combinations and permutations of constituent elements that alter motivation, perceptions, and reactions attendant to sexual deviancy result in a panoramic variety of contextual situations. Such situations range from the ludicrous to the tragic and from fantasy to stark reality. They encompass carnal behavior at every behavioral level from the subjective, to the symbolic, to the physically aggressive. Subsequent chapters of this book discuss the social contexts of some representative modes of sexual deviancy and the interpretive dimensions of social importance attendant to such a behavior. A total of 10 such representative modes of sexual deviancy and their social contexts are addressed. The exposition describes a continuum of sexual expression ranging from fictive to violent, and explores the parameters of, and participants in, such acts, within the context of contemporary social life.

CARNAL BEHAVIOR IN SPURIOUS CONTEXT

Sexual deviancy not only occurs in the realm of physical behavior; it also occurs in the mind. In some instances, for example, a person or persons may believe that another individual (or individuals) is involved in some type of sexual activity that violates normative societal dictates, even though this presumption may be completely without foundation. In such cases, the deviant sexual activity is delusional in that it exists exclusively in the mind of the beholder and is, thus, spurious. The absence of genuine guilt, however, may not dilute the social import of even spurious, but believed deviant behavior. Today's rationality persuades us that the so-called "witches" of seventeenth-century Salem could not possibly be guilty of the crimes of which they were accused, yet the presumption of crime, even though spurious, did in fact lead to their death as punishment. Many persons experience the consequences of sexual deviancy, even if spurious, projected on them by others of suspicious bent. Deviant labeling is very real, socially speaking, even if the process lacks valid foundation.

Although deviant sexual labeling can occur with isolated individuals where offending behavior is perceived or believed, it more likely attends an associational mechanism involving the stereotyping of behavior and proclivities on the part of categories of persons. Some categories of persons, and for that matter even places and things, can be assigned an identity as "sexually deviant" because of stereotypical association based on reputation, and/or carnally suspect behavior. Individuals in certain occupations, of particular age levels, race, or religious persuasions, or even of specific marital status can be more prone than most, to be identified with, or accused of, sexual misconduct. Because such a labeling process is often pervasive, persons in these categories may become defensive about such ascriptive deviancy, just as the public or a segment of it, can become cynical, if not offensive, in reacting to the fictive carnal tendencies of the category of people in question. On the assumption that a regular routine of sexual gratification is habit forming, and that its absence produces tormenting sexual frustration, widows and divorcees, for example, are frequently perceived as sexual libertines burning with licentious passions. Such women, often aware that they are categorically viewed as libidinousness and likely of easy virtue, may avoid dating situations because of their stereotypical image. Similarly, the mere fact of an elderly male even caressing a child can be perceived by some, as the thinly disguised, carnal degeneracy of a "dirty old man." As the Florida political campaign of the late 1970's vividly pointed out, homosexuals, already social pariahs because of their sexual persuasion, are also often believed to be enamored of all types of carnal excesses, ranging from child molestation to sexual violence. Even lifestyle may carry the spurious presumption of sexual deviancy, inasmuch as being avant-garde, even in seemingly innocuous ways, might, in some situations, give rise to speculation about the innovativeness or unorthodoxy of one's sexual activity. The mere ownership of a bidet, for example, is to many, so blatantly redolent of latent sexuality in decadent variety, as to indicate a patently sexually depraved existence.

As a social context, spurious deviancy can involve the full spectrum of sexual modes, and accordingly as a category, has no claim to mutual exclusivity on the basis of sexual technique. Similarly, this spurious context shares the property of mental sexual activity with other contextual categories to be discussed in this book. The distinguishing feature of this conceptual context is the presence of an erroneous or fictive presumption concerning the sexual activities or tendencies of others, and which frequently precipitates behavior oriented toward, or in response to, the spurious deviancy.

Inasmuch as within this context, some persons, in effect, manufacture deviancy in their mind, they can often collaborate in their own swindle by becoming eager participants in would-be commercial carnal enterprises as a result of their own distorted images of the availability of sexual gratification. Such enterprises may promise much by innuendo in terms of sexual gratification, but in actuality, offer pitifully little in comparison to the elaborate sexual scenario woven from the threads of the sucker's fantasies. As a result, some persons are even lured into involvement in situations of embarrassment, and occasionally financial or personal exploitation, as a result of their erotic appetites in regard to the illusionary carnal opportunities.

Because spurious deviancy is often real in its consequences and importance for the suspected party, it must be taken into account as a significant contextual category of proscribed sexual activity. Where sexual deviancy is inferred or erroneously perceived, it also has social importance for those who make the inference, and thus mentally, at least, become accusers. In a social sense, reality is created by our perceptions and definition of the situation, and our subsequent reactions to this collective definition. Just as physicians must recognize and appreciate imaginary illnesses as a valid category of human medical disorder, spurious sexual deviancy must also be addressed as a socially important variety of deviant behavior, and should be examined for many of the same reasons that one studies prejudice. It is desirable to understand the circumstances under which fictive deviancy is perceived, as well as the mechanisms of ascription themselves. Interestingly, it appears that the fact of a more enlightened and sophisticated populace in recent times, has not particularly tended to dilute the inclination to sexual stereotyping of various categories of persons. In the final analysis, it would seem that many see in others those sexual persuasions which either most sharply contrast with their own posture or normative conformity, represent the inclination of carnality which they most fear in themselves, and thus resent in others, or best complement their own sexual fantasies.

CARNAL BEHAVIOR IN VICARIOUS CONTEXT

Mental sexual activity is not always the spurious product of delusion and projection. It may well be a contrived substitute for, or even adjunct to, if not constituent part of, physical carnal gratification. Unlike the lower animals, for whom sexual arousal is based largely on the stimulation of the physical sensory system, humans with their well-developed capacity for the mental manipulation of complex symbols, are able to generate fantasy activity in connection with sexual arousal and carnal gratification.

Mental sexual activity may aid or accelerate sexual arousal, inasmuch as it represents a means of anticipating or vicariously sampling, as it were, subsequent physical sexual behavior. Vicarious sex then is a kind of reality testing, and thus serves as a guide for evaluating and reinforcing, or modifying physical sexual behavior. Sexual fantasy may also enrich, embellish, enhance, intensify or facilitate the physical sexual experience, and may accordingly be a significant component in carnal gratification. Mental fantasy is often more potent in precipitating sexual activity than are physical stimuli.

Perhaps, an even more important function of sexual fantasy, however, is its ability to serve as an effective symbolic substitute or replacement for physical sexual fulfillment. In this regard, it can sometimes represent a socially acceptable, or at least socially tolerated, surrogate form of carnal gratification. Sexual fantasy may well depend on visual or other cues, and this requirement may cause vicarious carnal activity to impinge on conventional physical modes of social behavior, attendant personal perogatives, and interpersonal relationships. It is this social significance of fantasy and vicarious carnal fantasy that renders it subject to collective concern and social control, for even the acceptance or toleration of vicarious sexual activity is component to a larger system of normative regulation and proscription. The proscriptive element of vicarious sexual activity, not infrequently, addresses itself to the degree to which sexual fantasy and the attendant carnal diversion tend to invade the physical and emotional privacy of others.

To depend on sexual fantasy for vicarious carnal gratification may require the observation of the nude or semi-nude body of a person of the opposite sex, or even a couple involved in the act of sex itself. For some, the observation of other behavioral phenomena, perhaps only marginally related to nudity or sexual behavior, can produce the impedus for sexual fantasy. In the absence of commercial or artistic opportunities for such observations, the individual who seeks such stimuli may turn to unauthorized and clandestine observations of others while nude or involved in intimate personal behavior. In so doing, the observer invades the privacy, and transgresses the prerogatives, of those being observed. Such observations, labeled as "peeping" or voyeurism, can provide an element of salacious gratification based on the clandestine and forbidden nature of the observational context as well as the actual anatomy or activity viewed. An occasional or inadvertent glimpse of tabooed anatomy may constitute only a minor breach of etiquette or comportment. Such persons, however, become preoccupied with, and dependent on, peeping (or otherwise monitoring) at the private and hopefully nude, behavior of others for their sexual fulfillment. Voyeurism, accordingly, may be conceptualized as deviant carnal behavior within a vicarious context inasmuch as it violates the privacy of others, and, secondarily, because it represents a socially defined "unnatural," and thus pathological sexual preoccupation.

The sanctity of the privacy of others, notwithstanding, vicarious sexual activity may represent social deviancy in other ways. Thought, like physical behavior, is subject to cultural norm and social control. To exceed the social limits is to commit a kind of "crime-think" so to speak. A degree of vicarious sexual titilation may only constitute romantic eroticism, but preoccupation with mental sexual scenarios, and the observations requisite to such vicarious activities, would represent a sexually "degenerate" orientation, socially speaking and would probably be classified as deviant behavior.

There are alternative mechanisms, however, to that of voyeurism for obtaining appropriate visual stimuli for vicarious sexual activity. A variety of commercial modes ranging from professional strippers to topless barmaids, and from "girlie" or "skin" periodicals to stag movies, and porno arcade viewing machines, all intentionally attempt to provide sexual or erotic stimuli and thus facilitate and enhance vicarious carnal fulfillment. Again, the patrons or customers of such commercial services, by virtue of the socially conceptualized degenerate and depraved nature of their preoccupation with such blatant exotic phenomena and the perceived nature of their vicarious carnal fulfillment, are frequently labeled "socially deviant," and may be sanctioned as such. The providing of such sexually stimulating services may well also represent sexual deviancy, but the process of obtaining carnal gratification from intensive exposure to sexual stimuli which promotes vicarious activity, is, in and of itself, often in violation of social norm and customary standards of proprietous behavior, and should be viewed as deviancy within a vicarious context.

To many persons, a preoccupation with visual sexual stimuli, and carnal fantasy, may also be redolent of other carnal propensities and deviant sexual persuasions, and suggest a potential sexual danger. In some instances, the individual known for voyeuristic behavior and/or a preoccupation with vicarious sexual activities may be stereotyped as a "sex nut" or "pervert." Such attribution does invoke elements of the spurious context, but, in general, the tendency to rely on vicarious carnal gratification is seen, in and of itself, as deviant inasmuch as it is conceptualized as reflecting indolence and a depraved and degenerate mental appetite, as well as often violating the privacy boundaries of others.

CARNAL BEHAVIOR IN VERBAL CONTEXT

Language, symbolically speaking, is the foundation of thought. It also represents the manifestation or externalization of thought. It is often the antecedent, and/or adjunct of behavior. As symbolic interaction, it is behavior itself. As with thought and behavior, language is also subject to the dictates of normative cultural regulation that seeks to channelize and control it, in directions deemed relevant and appropriate to the needs of society. Such cultural regulation and the attendant societal monitoring is especially evident in regard to sexually oriented language. The centrality of sex in our lives gives it a significant prominence in our language interaction and communicative concern. It is possible to write and talk about sex, in some instances as a constituent element of sexual activity itself, as a facilitative device for generating sexual fantasy, and, thus, as a kind of sexual substitute, or even as a symbolic mode of sexual interaction. Sexual interaction, in all of its vagaries, not infrequently occurs within a verbal context—in this instance verbal referring to words and language, written or spoken—and, as in the instance of other cultural contexts, is subject to a variety of cultural prescriptions and proscriptions within this contextual setting as well. In spite of the mechanisms of social control bearing on the verbal context and the attendant social sanctions, there are widespread violations of sexual language norms that are consequently labeled "deviant behavior."

Tabooed words or obscenity include a wide range of anatomical and physiological terms as well as other kinds of words with a sexual reference. Beyond the use of selected words themselves, other social norms may dictate the circumstances under which some words can be used or even be appropriate to use. Some "dirty" words or sex talk may be more permissible and tolerated among certain groups or categories of people than others. Examples here might include all male groups, or groups of young married couples, or even between "joking" (as defined by anthropologists) relatives. Some such words may be taboo in public but appropriate in some circumstances between lovers or spouses. Some taboo words with sexual references may be made more socially acceptable when clothed in Latin or scientific phraseology, or in literary similies or euphemisms. Obscene words are perhaps rendered most objectionable when uttered in Anglo-Saxon forms.

The use of obscene or sexual words in a public place, in the presence of an inappropriate person—an individual especially likely to be offended or a person who cannot identify the user of the tabooed language—is considered to be particularly offensive and subject to legal sanction. The blatant user of obscenity may find himself a social pariah, and obscene verbal abuse may precipitate fights, lawsuits, or warrants for arrest. The use of profanity in a public place may lead to ejection, if not arrest and fine, and the anonymous obscene telephone caller may even face jail if apprehended. The obscene telephone caller—an endemic nuisance in contemporary society—is often sexually stimulated by his verbal invasion of his victim's privacy, and her attendant verbal response. The caller may derive considerable carnal gratification from such clandestine verbal activity and the presumed sexual fantasies that is generated in conjunction with it. Some obscene callers may even masturbate while talking with the victim, thus, combining auto-erotic and vicarious gratification while involving the victim as a participant in his carnal scenario.

Obscenity or sexually explicit language can provide carnal gratification to either those uttering it, or those hearing it—or both. Yet, others derive salacious enjoyment from the mutual use of sexual words with a person of the opposite sex. For many, some use of sexual language may enhance the sexual encounter by promoting vicarious sexual imagery and, thus, embellish the anticipation of sexual gratification. Patrons of prostitutes not infrequently may even request that the prostitute direct obscenities at them. A business was initiated recently in Japan that offers a telephone recording of a female voice simulating cries and moans during coitus, and other erotic content. Even though many persons may be sexually stimulated by such language, its excessive use, and especially a preoccupation with "dirty" talk or sexual topics can be viewed as symptomatic of emotional disturbance or mental pathology, if not a manifestation of sexual depravity. The loss of self-control, which may result from mental disorder, head injury, or senility, not infrequently is accompanied by an increased use of obscene and sexually explicit language. In some persons, such as young children, such behavior is viewed as particularly pathological.

Although private use of sexual obscenities can only have narrow social latitude for expression, there appears to be greater (albeit not unlimited) social toleration of some forms of commercial sexual communication. Perhaps the most classic form of such sexual language, however, is pornography, which ranges from the intellectually suggestive to the more explicit "hard core" variety. Pornography can assume the form of comic books depicting sexually perverted activities with minimal verbal commentary or crudely written fictional accounts of sexual vagaries mass produced in "porno factories." It may also exist as elegantly composed fictional expositions of superb literary style and structure, but with salacious content, and even as sexual technique manuals that provide instructions for sexual variations of the most catholic persuasion. For persons who prefer the spoken word in preference to the written, the "blue" nightclub comics exist, as a carnal cheerleader relating ribald stories, telling jokes with sexual themes, and uttering obscenities, all for the salacious appetites and sexual stimulation of his audience to facilitate their vicarious carnal imagery and gratifications. Pornography, written or oral, is often only tolerated to a degree, however, and the deviant violation of social limits may bring legal retaliation as witness the famous conviction of Ralph Ginsburg in the case of *Eros* magazine (Ginsburg v. United States, 383 U.S. 463 (1966)), and the obscenity trial of comedian Lenny Bruce in 1964.

CARNAL BEHAVIOR IN SYMBOLIC DEVIANCY

The naked anatomy of the opposite sex, or the sight of others engaged in sexual activity is capable of affording sexual stimulation and carnal gratification to the observer. There is a strong element of sexuality in nudity and the very fact of the genitals being uncovered suggests symbolically that they are more accessible. Nudity, then, at a symbolic level, represents the facilitation of, and receptivity to, potential sexual behavior. Thus, there is more of a possibility as well as probability of sexual interaction. Accordingly, nudity is a powerful factor in generating sexual fantasy, as well as precipitating other kinds of more overt carnal behavior.

Because of the sexual significance of nudity there are elaborate cultural normative and value systems surrounding the naked body and the degree to, and circumstances in, which it may be exposed to others. In most instances, it is a social offense to expose one's own nakedness to others, and when it does occur, it is labeled "sexually deviant" behavior. Attitudes and values surrounding nudity and anatomical privacy, although constituent to all cultures, are subject to considerable variation from society to society. Such attitudes and values usually coalesce as modesty norms, which, generally speaking, address themselves to the appropriate covering and coverage of the genital, and other sexually related, parts of the body. The application of modesty norms, however, are usually subject to further variation based on such factors as age, sex, time, circumstances, and occasion. Numerous cultural rationale and justifications may be offered as explanation for the normative concern with modesty, but underlying such rationalizations would seem to be a concern with anatomical exposure as a potentially volatile social element in sexual behavior. Accordingly, complete or partial nakedness is subjected to social regulation, proscription, and sanction. In effect, anatomicaly exposure must be socially monitored and controlled least it ignite carnal behavior of larger social importance.

In our society, some degree of nudity may be tolerated, even encouraged or mandated, under some circumstances. Some persons may totally or partially exhibit their bare anatomy for a variety of non-sexual reasons including economic considerations, pride, as an act of defiance, or assertion of nonconformity, to be more comfortable, or for reasons or dictates of fashion. Partial or total nudity may even be necessary concessions to effective medical care. Where, at an earlier time in history, upper class Chinese women, for example, would not permit a physician to see or touch any part of their anatomy that was normally clothed (this dilemma is described in more detail in Chapter 2), today in most, if not all of the modern world, it is expected that patients partially or completely disrobe in order for a physician of either sex to examine them. In some parts of Europe, such as Hungary, in the eighteenth and nineteenth century, the norms of modesty were such that it was not only unseemly but even illegal for doctors to attend women in childbirth because they might have to see the genital area of their patients. Even midwives were constrained to deliver babies from women without lifting the skirts or petticoats from them, all of their manual activities being accomplished under the dresses of their patients. The norms of modesty, have in modern times, of course, been much moderated in the interest of medical efficiency and the more practical delivery of health services. Depending on the social context, anatomical exposure may be conceptualized as artistic, functional, healthful, or even "cute." Nudity more generally, however, reflects or symbolizes sexuality. In certain circumstances, and under certain conditions, partial or total nudity as an element of eroticism, may be socially acceptable. In some company, for example, the bikini bathing suit, an extremely low-cut dress which permits prominent exposure of female breasts, the see-through net dress, or other items of female apparel that emphasize bare anatomy, while patently erotic, and designed to sexually stimulate, may simply be labeled and treated as glamorous or "seductive." Similarly, paintings and sculptures of nudes (of either sex), are usually viewed as examples of artistic expression.

Anatomical exposure, within other social contexts, can be defined and labeled "pathological," "perverted," and/or "criminal." An example of such behavior, seen as socially reprehensible, and, thus, as a deviant form of nudity is the instance of a male deliberately exposing his genitals to others and especially females. Exhibitionism, as it is known, is viewed as a particularly depraved and dangerous form of deviant sexual behavior and is often severely punished. Females also, although far less frequently, can, too, expose their nude anatomy. Individuals may exhibit portions of their bodies as a means of sexually arousing themselves or to attempt to arouse or interest, even frighten, members of the opposite sex. Many otherwise normal males, young and old, may succumb to stress, or the temptation to be promiscuous or erotic with the opposite sex and impulsively expose their genitals. For some individuals, exposing themselves can simply be an act of poor judgment, or lack of appropriate internalized control when coupled with the enthusiasm of adolescent sexuality. It is widely believed that the exhibitionist is an oversexed individual. Studies of exhibitionists, however, suggest that they are, in actuality, undersexed, and even if married, often enjoy a less than satisfactory sexual adjustment with their spouses. Exhibitionism may often constitute a compulsive, and, thus, neurotic syndrome. Whether compulsive, or impulsive, some men deliberately exhibit their genitals to females as a symbolic means of asserting their masculinity, and, thus, sexually relating to them. More men are arrested for the crime of exhibiting their genitals to females than other sexual offenses.

The deviant exposure of naked anatomy is not always a case of personal pathology. Sometimes the motivation is economic, and the function, obstensibly entertainment. The night club stripper or ecdysiast, as she is more politely labeled, represents an example of such a commercial configuration of deviant nudity. The stripper, by removing her clothes and engaging in sexually suggestive behavior, provides erotic entertainment and vicarious sexual gratification for her patrons who seek visual sex as a substitute and salacious supplement to genuine sex—for a price. Similar to the stripper and the symbolic sexuality that she offers, are the topless employees in restaurants and bars, and the erotic dancers and performers who offer simulated sexual activity rather than naked anatomy. Not all commercial nudity is "live," however. The females who pose for "cheesecake" and "pinup" nude calendar and periodical pictures offer only the image of naked anatomy, and symbolic sex in the truest sense of the word, for the carnal gratification of those who can appreciate the visual representation of nudeness second hand, rather than "in the flesh."

As a category of deviant carnal behavior, symbolic behavior may encompass a wide spectrum of sexual expression including both manifestations of homosexual, as well as heterosexual inclination. Similarly, the motivation for symbolic sexual activity may range from love to hate, and from simple ennui, to complex forms of compulsive neurosis. It might be argued that symbolic sexual behavior should appropriately be treated within the vicarious context, inasmuch as such behavior is obviously a reflection, or manifestation, of sexual fantasy. Symbolic sex, in many instances, facilitates or reinforces fantasy, and is often intended to precipitate or accomplish vicarious carnal stimulation. Certainly, there is spillover from one category to another, but, nevertheless, there is a subtle distinction mandating a conceptual differentiation. In the instance of sexual activity classified within the vicarious contextual category, it is the perception of sexual phenomena, and the carnal subsequences that is deemed deviant, rather than the antecedent sexual phenomena itself, which is considered to be intentionally unoffensive, if not relatively innocent. It is the precipitant sexual activity within the symbolic contextual category, however, that is deemed deviant by social standards. The conceptual distinction, then, revolves around the relative emphasis on carnal activity representing either agent or result, as it were.

CARNAL BEHAVIOR IN IMITATIVE CONTEXT

Sexual stimulation, orgasm, or fulfillment in general, obviously does not depend on heterosexual intercourse. Manual self-stimulation, or stimulation by another, of the genitals will effect orgasm and afford sexual satisfaction. Sometimes defined only as autoerotic sexual gratification, masturbation can, for purposes of this paradigmatic discussion, also include other configurations of genital stimulation by another person, other than by penis-vaginal intercourse. Masturbation, while mechanically efficient in this regard, has traditionally been conceptualized as deviant sexual behavior, and frequently sanctioned as such. Inasmuch as our society has tended to ethnocentrically view, and culturally prescribe, heterosexual, inter-genital stimulation as the appropriate mode of obtaining orgasm, masturbation has been seen as a kind of "imitation" sexual gratification, as well as deviant, because it departs from the more "genuine," "normal," and "natural" heterosexual mode. The fact that it is often employed to obtain orgasm in the absence of heterosexual outlets, serves to reinforce its image as "imitative."

Masturbation is a universal form of sexual stimulation and fulfillment, especially among children and adolescents, but is subject to a wide variety of injunctions and constraints in many societies inasmuch as it is viewed as an impediment to the channelization of the sexual drive into more adult heterosexual modes, and, thus, can delay the transition of maturity and the assumption of an adult behavioral posture. In Western societies, masturbation has traditionally been proscribed and discouraged because of strong moral values and medical contradictions, as opposed to only the concern with the breaking of juvenile patterns found in non-industrial societies. The moral objections to masturbation grew out of the general early Christian ideological posture (and particularly the teachings of Saint Augustine) that sex was a necessary evil, and that accordingly was only justified as a means of procreation. Interestingly, masturbation is perhaps the only form of sexual deviancy, where social objection, at least partially, was founded on medical rationale. During the eighteenth, nineteenth, and into the early part of the twentieth century, masturbation was additionally condemned because of the belief that it was medically deleterious. The practice was identified as a causal agent in a wide variety of physiological, neurological, and neuro-psychiatric diseases. So serious were the medical concerns about masturbation that numerous "sexual" harnesses, chastity belts, and other devices that forestalled masturbation were devised and widely prescribed by physicians. The treatment for masturbation, including surgical techniques that often resulted in impotence or sterility, was more feared than the prevention devices, however. In more recent times, medical condemnation of masturbation moderated but it residually continued to be socially conceptualized as unwholesome and a "problem," and, in some instances, contributing to premature ejaculation in males. Many persons still consider masturbation to be the manifestation of an infantile level of psychosocial development and gratification.

In spite of social values, norms and sanctions to the contrary, masturbation has been a common practice among males, and relatively common among females. More recent research has suggested that masturbation is becoming more common, and more frequent, among both sexes, and is occurring at a younger age, as well as continuing later in life, even among married persons. In some instances today, masturbation is even being recommended by medical and psychiatric authorities as a means of achieving orgasm and to enhance adjustment to sexual intercourse. Even vibrators are being prescribed to women to facilitate their masturbation. Various sexual manuals have recommended masturbation to both sexes as training, for release from tension, and for fun and recreation. Thus, masturbation has, in recent years, been seen more as an aid to orgasmic efficiency and/or a physical activity affording simple hedonistic pleasure. Petting to orgasm, involving mutual masturbation, has also traditionally been a means of sexual gratification while preserving technical virginity for young people, especially those of middle or upper-middle class background, although some couples are now progressing on more rapidly to actual intercourse than was the case in the past. In spite of the lessened moral and medical constraints concerning masturbation, and increased social permissiveness about the practice, it is still widely viewed as inappropriate or socially deviant, whether as compromise sexual interaction in dating, or private mode of carnal gratification.

In any event, masturbation is considered to be very much a private activity and public masturbation is severely sanctioned although it has occasionally occurred in some public entertainment situations. It is also viewed as pathological in those instances where anonymous males call females on the telephone and masturbate while talking to the stranger on the other end of the line. The offender uses the telephone conversation with the unknown female as the basis for sexual fantasy and vicarious carnal stimulation. Deemed particularly pathological, also, is masturbation that involves the use of vinyl, life-sized sex dolls with vibrating hands, mouths, and vaginas for persons who lack opportunities for heterosexual encounters. Masturbation has also gone commercial, however, as in the case of the ubiquitous massage parlor that offers clandestine, and often illegal masturbratory services, and erotic context, to facilitate sexual fantasy and carnal gratification, while disguised as dispensers of health ministrations. Although often offering only penis manipulations to orgasm rather than the complete range of sexual gratifications found in most brothels, the massage parlors may often be preferred. Aside from affording the advantages of less danger from venereal diseases or public raids and arrest, as well as less social stigma attached to their patronage, the parlors offer an even more important hedonistic benefit. In keeping with the service-oriented society of today, the customer simply lies there, wrapped in erotic reverie and totally indulges his narcissistic hedonism while ostensibly sensual females minister anatomically to his sexual appetites. Commercial masturbation, although seemingly relatively innocuous in comparison with some other modes of socially defined sexual deviancy, nevertheless, is also subject to social condemnation and subsequent legal harassment and sanctions, as an objectionable and degenerate form of carnal behavior.

CARNAL BEHAVIOR IN COUNTERFEIT CONTEXT

Of all the variations of sexual expression socially labeled "deviant," perhaps none has traditionally tended to elicit more controversy than has homosexuality. Nor has this controversy tended to abate in recent years. If anything, the dialogue concerning homosexual carnal gratification as a legitimate sexual mode has remained at emotional pitch. Our own society, like most others, has tended to retain a rigid ethnocentric posture in regard to culturally-approved patterns of sexual behavior. Seminal to this cultural ideological stance on sexual behavior is the conceptualization of intergenital, heterosexual activity as the fundamental and appropriate form of carnal fulfillment. In spite of contemporary tendencies to negate or mitigate the traditional norms of sexual comportment, homosexual gratification is still viewed by a substantial portion of the population, and especially that portion of the population in a position to enforce their conception of sexual normality, as significantly at variance from the prescribed heterosexual and genital mode, and, thus, abnormal, unnatural, and deviant. Inasmuch as heterosexual coitus is viewed as "real" or "genuine" sex, homosexual behavior conversely is considered by many to be inauthentic or "counterfeit," because it affords carnal fulfillment outside of the conventional mode and attempts to substitute the gender of the participants and the techniques of sexual gratification. "Counterfeit" sex, as with other forms of sexual deviancy, is often subject to severe social sanctions. Since there is wide divergence in public opinion concerning the significance and reprehensibility of homosexuality, there is an uneven, if not erratic, pattern of social sanction for such behavior. It may be tolerated and even widely countenanced in some situations, and punished as social degeneracy in others. Interestingly, it is considered sufficiently pathological in some quarters, that the offender may be encouraged, if not forced, to seek psychiatric treatment, even though he does not see himself in this same light. In the case of other kinds of sexual deviancy, the offender may recognize the existence of his own pathological persuasion and seek professional help. In some cases, the sexual deviant may be considered criminal but not necessarily a victim of mental pathology. The categorization of homosexuality as counterfeit rests on two bases. The first is the aforementioned deviation from the normatively prescribed heterosexual pattern, with the resulting "inauthenticity" of this sexual mode. The second foundation for the labeling arises out of the fact that persons of homosexual persuasion not infrequently are compelled to disguise the fact, then engage in mechanisms of concealment, including role falsification, and a kind of "counterfeit" lifestyle involving sexual expression and gratification. Heterosexual role falsification often results in tragic family situations, and considerable mental anguish and anxiety for the individual homosexual. If his ruse is discovered, there may be severe social, if not legal, sanctions, and often the disruption, if not disintegration, of his social and familial ties.

Homosexuality, the subject of traditional controversy, has been attributed to a variety of etiological factors including glandular imbalance, mental disorder, traumatic personal experiences, organic disease, and inappropriate socialization among others. There is disagreement, as it were, as to whether homosexuals are born or made. It has been suggested that the psychoanalytic labeling of homosexuality as "perverted," is in fact, the result of a strong, residual, religious bias.

Homosexuality would appear to be the object of social condemnation because of several reasons. There is obvious disapproval of romance and/or sexual bonding of two persons of the same sex because it runs counter to the historical division of social labor between sexes. The homosexual couple also is in violation of the cultural mandate to perpetuate the species, and because their sexual interaction only affords carnal gratification, not offspring. (This rationale of condemnation has perhaps been negated somewhat in recent years, by virtue of the large number of married heterosexual couples who have elected to postpone or forego children. According to traditional norms, however, childlessness, even if voluntary, represents a vagrancy from social expectations, and a kind of "deviant" ancillary marital status, albeit anacronistic, i.e. "the childless couple"). Then, too, homosexual couples must rely on manual and oral sexual stimulation, and/or anal intercourse. Oral and anal sex, as sodomy, are particularly condemned as "unnatural" sex acts and severely sanctioned, whether occurring within a heterosexual or homosexual union. Finally, homosexuals are socially disapproved because they are "different" in terms of variant life styles and contrasting patterns of behavior. There is widespread disapproval of homosexuals, and they often experience social discrimination and physical abuse as a result.

In recent years, the public posture toward homosexuality has changed considerably in the direction of more toleration, if not permissiveness. Many homosexuals are publicly admitting their sexual persuasion, and social discrimination is eroding informally, as well as formally. Homosexuals have organized churches, businesses, and lobby organizations and are increasingly assaulting various legal barriers that have hitherto prevented their full cultural participation. Coping with residual hostile public response is still traumatic for many homosexuals, however. With increasing social ecumenicalism in terms of sexual activity, homosexuality is becoming more accepted as an alternate sexual mode, and in this connection, bisexuality is becoming relatively prevalent and even "chic," in some sexual *avant-garde* circles.

Homosexuality is not the only variant of sexual behavior that may occur within a counterfeit context. Transsexuality also represents the counterfeiting of more conventional sex. Significant numbers of individuals are disaffected by the fact of the gender of their sex, and for various reasons, psychological, social, and physical, think of themselves as more appropriately members of the opposite sex. In effect, they become males locked inside female bodies or vice versa. Traditionally, there was no absolute remedy for such a gender dilemma. Some such persons with a milder disaffection for their own sex, usually referred to as transvestites, feel compelled to "cross dress" and wear the apparel of the opposite sex. Such a propensity may go no further than occasionally wearing the undergarments of the opposite sex, although other individuals are inclined to indulge in a more elaborate charade, perhaps dressing completely like a person of the opposite sex, even to the extent of trying to fool persons of their own sex.

For some persons, the gender dilemma is more intense and painful, and these individuals, known as transsexuals, sometimes are motivated to acquire the physical sex of their orientation. Recent years have seen advances in surgery and hormone therapy that make physical changes of sex possible, at least cosmetically speaking. The process of conversion, or "sex reassignment" as it is known, involves not only surgery but also hormone therapy, and in some instances psychiatric therapy as well.

Although "sexual reassignment" for transsexuals is becoming more public and more publically tolerated, as are transvestites and homosexuals, all such variations from the more conventional and traditional forms of carnal expression and comportment, continue to be widely viewed and treated as instances of sexual deviancy, even if the former sanctions are informal rather than legal. "Counterfeit" sex, as the public sees it, departs from the biological and social scenario, and thus should only elicit pity and repugnance, if not hostility.

CARNAL BEHAVIOR IN SUPERFICIAL CONTEXT

Sexual consummation is, according to cultural ideal and norm, supposed to occur only within the relationship of marriage. Additionally, Judeo-Christian philosophy specifies coitus essentially for procreation, as well as a mutual expression of affection and tender emotion, the exercise of marital obligation, and as a reinforcing mechanism for the cohesive bonds of matrimony. Sexual fulfillment occurs outside of marriage as well as within, however. Where it occurs constituent to courtship, it is technically a violation of social proscription, but where the ultimate outcome of the dating interaction is marriage and the establishment of a family, there tends to be a mitigating interpretation of the sexual deviancy.

Carnal activity is not always a reflection of love or profound emotion, mutual obligation, solidifier of marital ties, or even a step in intimacy prior to marriage. Sexual behavior may also be a manifestation of aggression, hostility, or even brutality. It may also be a commodity, bought and sold. Sexual gratification may also be part of an elaborate and abstruse non-monetary exchange relationship. It can also, in some instances, and especially outside of marriage, represent little more than a mere superficial mode of human carnal interaction. Superficial sex is casual sex and, thus, in general, unemotional sex. It involves immediate gratification that neither reinforces, nor is reinforced by, more pervasive and persistent ties of love or attachment. Superficial sex is essentially without purpose or goal beyond the immediate gratification of carnal appetite. Such carnal activity is simply sex for entertainment, after the fashion of that espoused by an early advocate of birth control, Margaret Sanger, who demonstrated for contraception with the motto of "coition for recreation only."

Sexual activity attendant to dating is often particularly characterized by superficial sexual interaction. In our society, dating does not necessarily lead to marriage, and in fact, much dating, even with certain patterns of sexual activity such as heavy "petting," and even coitus, may be defined and occur largely within a recreational context. Although it is true that petting was often rationalized as compromise sexual gratification between persons with an emotional attachment, it has also often involved a kind of sexual game between the sexes with the male trying to "score" or "make out," while the female tries to withhold the more intimate sexual favors as long as possible. In this connection, sexual exploitation by males to the point of violence, has been reported by some researchers. In recent years, especially where young people are more frequently rejecting marriage, sexual activity in dating would seem increasingly to serve recreational and carnal functions rather than romantic. Promiscuous sex, without emotional involvement, and principally for purposes of entertainment, represents a violation of both proscription against premarital sexual activity as well as a subversion of societal values concerning the function of courtship.

Casual and recreational sexual intercourse, almost to the point of impersonality, would seem to be especially constituent to the new "swinging singles" culture. Single adults, often divorced and/or committed to the single matrimony state, sometimes because of cynicism or dissaffection, engage in a seemingly endless round of social activities with other singles of the opposite sex, primarily for the purpose of pairing off in dyads, on a non-romantic basis in order to engage in sexual relationships on short term bases. These contrived patterns of pseudo-courtship and the attendant casual and superficial sexual encounters are recreational, but also in some instances, apparently represent a coping mechanism for dealing with a painful existential reality. Again, such sexual activities of shallow emotional dimensions represent a deviant lifestyle of carnal excesses, debauchery, and decadence, by many of traditional morality and convention.

Superficial sexual gratification is also available in commercial configuration. For those persons who are away from acquaintances of the opposite sex or have limited opportunities for dating, it is now even possible to rent a female (or male) to act as a date or escort and provide instant and temporary contrived companionship and afford, or share in, recreational activities for a price. Often for a higher price, the companions will also render sexual services on an equally casual, superficial, and presumably recreational basis. The customer receives superficial social interaction with a person of the opposite sex, and on occasion, recreational sexual gratification with a pseudo-lover. There are a variety of other superficial modes of obtaining carnal gratification. The ubiquitous "executive" massage parlor is one example of prostituted sex with superficiality as a significant characteristic. The patron drops in a convenient parlor, selects a masseuse from the "meat display," purchases massage services, but also obtains masturbatory sexual gratification as a residual service that is provided impersonally, but within a context which allows the fullest freedom of narcistic reverie and sensate preoccupation. Superficial sexual gratification may also encompass homosexual activities where some individuals stop off in public restrooms to be fellated by strangers in a totally impersonal context which is even largely devoid of verbal interaction.

Superficial sex represents more than the inherent violation of various social proscriptions concerning the modes of sexual activity.

Inasmuch as it involves the obtaining of sexual gratification for sensate, and, thus, hedonistic, purposes per se, it represents the deviant epitome of carnality, and thus symbolizes to many a kind of social satyriasis (on the part of both sexes).

CARNAL BEHAVIOR IN SYMBIOTIC CONTEXT

Marriage, as a structural dyadic relationship, involves a variety of reciprocal ties and obligations including economic, emotional, and sexual. In this sense, it can be thought of as an exchange mechanism. The privileges of sexual gratification are tied in other reciprocal obligations of the marriage contract including those of loyalty and sexual exclusiveness. Marriage, then, because of the constituent exchange processes, may be viewed as a kind of social symbiotic relationship between a man and a woman.

The societal normative elements associated with the sexual aspect of this symbiotic relationship include the opportunity for sexual gratification on the part of both marital partners as well as the cultural theoretical mandate of restricting sexual gratification only to inter-genital sexual intercourse, undertaken in the prescribed "normal" coital position, and exclusively for the purpose of procreation only. In recent years, however, attendant to the various waves of sexual emancipation, and encouraged by the erotic element in the mass media, sexual exploration within marriage has increased with the goal of maximizing sexual gratification. Such exploration has encompassed such socially (and legally) condemned, sexually deviant practices as oral and anal sexual gratification, innovative coital positions, the use of devices such as vibrators to "enhance" the sexual experience, as well as a wide variety of unusual practices designed to increase sexual stimulation ranging from clothing fetishes to "light-hearted bondage." In spite of many such practices, while perhaps being accepted as functional, if not engaging variations of sexual expression and widely practiced, among certain sophisticated elements of the population, the fact remains that for the larger and more traditional portion of society—those of less catholic sexual persuasions—the widening horizons of sexual gratification are at best "kinky," and at worst, licentious carnal debauchery. Certainly, legal sanctions are still occasionally applied, even if erratically, to some couples who violate the canons of more conventional sexual conformity.

In spite of an apparent dramatic change in social values concerning sexual variation, and especially within marriage, many individuals have apparently found the opportunities for sexual gratification attendant to the symbiotic relationship of matrimony, to either be inadequate or inappropriate; in their sexual disaffection, they have sought alternate outlets for carnal gratification. Such alternate adulterous outlets have included both casual affairs and more enduring mistress/paramour relations. Such arrangements often have symbiotic dimensions not dissimilar to those of marriage. Where such semipermanent symbiotic sexual relationships also do not satisfactorily provide for carnal needs, real or fantasy, the individual may have to enlarge the circle of persons in the symbiotic sexual network in order to afford an even wider array of carnal outlets. Such a variety of extramarital deviancy of recent times is "swinging" or wife swapping. Swinging is, in effect, consensual adultery. It involves more than simple exchange of sexual gratification. It also involves the reciprocal and symbiotic exchange of appropriate physical and emotional gratification as well in the effort to satisfy carnal and other needs within the context of a contrived social system. Ongoing sexual relationships with mistresses or paramours, regardless of the obvious psychological, economic, or carnal needs reciprocally served, continue to be condemned as a breach of legal and social norms attendant to the marriage contract. As well, they are often a manifestation of unbridled carnal lust. Swinging, even to most persons of considerable sexual liberalism, represents carnal degeneracy of a pathological variety.

Sexual gratification, outside of marriage is also sought through formal economic exchange, in commercial relationships that are devoid of mutual affective interaction or emotional support. Commercialized sex or prostitution is much more than the simple act of permitting the male (or female) customer the use of her (or his) sexual organs temporarily (or whatever service is rendered) for a fee. Prostitution, although seemingly to provide only economic sustenance to the practitioners, also affords a variety of psychological, albeit pathological satisfactions and benefits. Some prostitutes enjoy the attention they receive from men. Others derive pleasure from the fact that they can express contempt or avenge themselves on men through their lack of sexual response. Some are acting out neurotic motivations, and others find excitement or even glamour in their work. This is especially the case with prostitutes who have a clientele of men of high prestige, or even celebrities. The prostitute also delivers more than sexual gratification. She offers sexual variety, simulated companionship and conversation, and facilitates sexual fantasy. Some even conceptualize themselves as affording "therapy" to disaffected married men. Prostitutes also sometimes support and facilitate business transactions by providing added inducements. Male prostitution for the carnal gratification of homosexuals seems to be much more evident than in the past suggesting a more urgent search for sexual outlets. Whether male or female, however, the prostitute and her/his client enjoy a sexually symbiotic relationship with value, sexual or otherwise, given and received in reciprocal fashion.

Prostitution, like other forms of extramarital sexual gratification, continues to be conceptualized as both deviant and criminal, although there have been vigorous efforts in recent years to decriminalize such sexual exchange behavior. Interestingly, some law enforcement agencies are now attempting to wipe out prostitution by concentrating their arrest and conviction efforts on the patrons of prostitution. This is not an entirely new sanctitive posture, however, inasmuch as the patrons of prostitutes have traditionally been negatively and deviantly labeled as "whore mongers," and accordingly have had to bear the burden of social stigma and informal sanction, along with the "harlot" practitioners who also have had to endure legal punishment for their carnal commercialism.

CARNAL BEHAVIOR IN DISPARATE CONTEXT

Seminal to the cultural conceptualization of specifications of prescribed social characteristics of sexual partners in most societies, is the articulation of appropriate age variation. Social norms concerning the range of tolerated age discrepancy may, in some instances, be physiologically functional. Persons of pre-sexual maturity might suffer physical harm or permanent handicap if used for sexual gratification by adults. In general, however, there would be no anatomical or physiological impediment to young persons engaging in sexual intercourse, siring and bearing children, or entering into marriage after sexual puberty. Thus, while there is clearly physiological rationale for proscribing sexual intercourse with persons below certain ages of genital maturity, many of the norms proscribing and regulating the age diversity in sexual partners are more social than physiological in rationale. Accordingly, in our society since there are serious social concerns about the social maturity and ability of a young couple to effect a successful cohabitational union and to be economically self-supporting, there are minimum age requirements for marriage based on these concerns.

Similarly, there are minimum age prescriptions for engaging in coitus, usually (but not always) pertaining to the female in the sexual dyad. Such age requirements are based on the assumption that a female below a certain chronological level of maturity may not necessarily be completely aware of the possible consequences and social importance of engaging in sexual intercourse. She may not fully understand the intricacies of conception, or the social consequences of pregnancy and bearing an illegitimate baby. Perhaps more importantly, she may not realize the full social importance of losing her virginal status in a society which has traditionally placed extremely high value on female chastity before marriage. Because society takes such umbrage at the dilemma and social problem of the illegitimate child, and because virginity has retained such a high social value, the violation of the age restriction on coitus is viewed as an extremely serious form of sexual deviancy, and usually sanctioned accordingly. The actual age specification of statutory rape, as such sexual offenses are known, varies from state to state as do the punishments. In the face of much moderated views on sexual chastity and increased sexual activity between young people, statutory rape is becoming somewhat eroded in terms of the severity with which it is viewed and punished.

Still extremely reprehensible, however, is the act of coitus or other sexual activity, with a prepubescent child of either sex. Child molestation is considered to be among the most socially detestable crimes because of the vulnerability, and helplessness of the child, and the presumed physical and psychological trauma which they experience as a result of the sexual interaction. Where the child offender or statutory rapist is a parent or close relative, and thus commits incest in the process of engaging in sexual activities with the child or youth, the severity of the crime is compounded. This results from the traditional societal revulsion of incest and from the fact that there is supposed to be a special relationship of trust and affection between parent or relative and child. There is also a special obligation of protection bearing on the adult, all of which renders the violation of the sexual norm involved particularly despicable and depraved from the standpoint of society.

Various modes of child molesting are not uncommon, however,

although public reaction to child molesting is so negative and the legal sanctions so severe, that many offenders, when apprehended, are reluctant to accept and admit the "deviant" label. Rather than being the complete victim of sex offenses, some children are passive participants, others may even precipitate or respond positively to the sexual activity, and some children have been known to initiate sexual activity with adults, seducing them, as it were. In spite of the fact that it is considered a pathological perversion, some offenders do not wish to get rid of their pedophilia, finding such a mode of sexual gratification to be preferable to others.

Even where legal, significant disparate differences in age between a married couple or a couple engaged in sexual activity is considered inappropriate and socially deviant to a degree. Examples here might be the old husband and his "child bride," or the older woman who is viewed as "robbing the cradle" because of her youthful paramour. The societal concern with the disparate age of persons involved in sexual interaction causes special attention to be given to the older perpetrator of sexual deviancy as well as the younger victim. In this connection elderly persons, in general, are often conceptualized as asexual. When they do manifest sexual desires, they are often viewed as "dirty old men" or sexual degenerates. It appears that some older men are especially vulnerable to charges of sexual deviancy because of the public predisposition to judge the sexual impulse in the elderly as deviant. Their proclivities to seek affection and response from younger persons, and especially children, may be misconstrued. Older females may be able to hug and fondle children because it is more "natural" for them to do so. For the older male, however, any similar behavior on their part may be viewed as an attempt to sexually molest the child and accordingly derive carnal gratification. There would seem to be evidence of a prejudicial attitude toward older people in our society, and this may result in a tendency to overreact to the older person's deviancy. In any event, the "geriatric" sex offender is particularly offensive to societal standards of morality and proprietous sexual behavior.

Age disparity in sexual interaction may even, in some instances, be commercially exploited as in the case of the young male "gigolo" who economically panders to the romantic and carnal needs of older women, or child prostitutes of both sexes who sell sexual services for high fees to some adults who eagerly pay the price in spite of the severe societal condemnation of such a practice. For those of more catholic sexual persuasions, the younger purveyors of sex are particularly tempting, but the risks are high inasmuch as society often reacts in a most negative fashion to even consensual sex involving children, regardless of whether it is bought and paid for or not. In our society, those persons who financially exploit the sexual favors of children are particularly repugnant to the general norms of community morality. Still, where there is demand there is supply regardless of the risk, and the child prostitutes will undoubtedly continue to be made available to those of debauched sexual appetites in the face of public condemnation and severe social sanction.

CARNAL BEHAVIOR IN VIOLENT CONTEXT

Just as love and hate are said to be but different dimensions of the same emotional posture, sexual activity and violence, similarly, are often inextricably interrelated. At the more biological level (and especially in the instance of non-human animals), this relationship grows out of the territorial imperative of most species, the mating instinct, and its linkage with the domination drive. At a more biologically advanced and socially mature level, the emotions of love and hate are linked in various ways.

Aggressive behavior and violence may occur attendant to competition for members of the opposite sex. Courtship, like animal mating behavior, can be competitive and lead to violence between male competitors. Similarly, sexual jealousy of both heterosexual and homosexual variety has often led to violence and even murder in some instances. The competition in courtship may also, however, entail attempting to maximize opportunity for sexual gratification; in some instances, research has shown that male suitors may resort to coersion and offensive force to the point of violence directed at the persons they are dating in their efforts to obtain sexual access. The violence that sometimes attends male attempts at sexual exploitation may, on occasion, become mutual. In courtship, sexual conflict, real or symbolic, is often intermixed with love, affection, and lust; "lovers' quarrels" not infrequently result in physical violence.

Sexual aggression and violence does not necessarily end with marriage, however. Wifebeating (and husbandbeating, for that matter), in addition to more generalized mutual hostility and violence, is frequently related directly or indirectly to sex. In some instances, wifebeating grows out of a marital pattern where the wife plays a dominant and assertive role and the husband is usually submissive, except when he becomes drunk. In that situation, the spouses may effect a role reversal, and the husband may beat the wife when she rejects his sexual advances. A similar kind of role reversal may occur in those instances of husbands assaulting their wives with an intent to kill. The wives might withhold sex from their passive husbands, who in turn would hold their hostility in check as long as possible; when they could not do so any longer, they would react with aggressive outbursts.

For some persons of both sex, carnal gratification can only be accomplished and enjoyed within the framework of violence. Some individuals are only sexually aroused, or at least have their sexual gratification enhanced, when they are bound and/or experience violence and pain inflicted by others, while other individuals of more sadistic bent derive carnal gratification from the infliction of pain on others, even if symbolically. There are men who beat their wives because they themselves are sexually aroused in the process. There are also those men who are carnally stimulated or gratified when they are beaten or subjected to humiliation, and if they have no wife or lover who will oblige them, may have to pay a prostitute to administer this service. Accordingly, some brothels and prostitutes cater to such catholic sexual tastes, and some businesses exist to merchandise the necessary equipment. Some mild degree of sadomasochistic sexual activity, such as "light-hearted bondage," is not uncommon with some married couples, and some recent sex manuals even encourage such sexual experimentation as a means of added erotic enhancement to their carnal fantasies and sexual titilation.

Sometimes, of course, sexual violence may reach the level of brutality, even death. So-called crimes of "sexual passion" involving rape, murder, and even dismemberment occur with some frequency in our society, although those of the more sensational variety often receive publicity out of proportion to the frequency of their occurrence. Such crimes of sexual violence can encompass heterosexual or homosexual offenses against the victims who may be either male or female. Although violent sexual crimes may have neurotic or psychotic motivation reaching far beyond the desire for mere sexual gratification, nevertheless there is often some intimate linkage between the carnal stimulation of the perpetrator, and the sexual abuse and violence visited on the victim.

The most prevalent of all sexual crimes of violence (and perhaps the most underpublicized offense) is rape. It has been asserted that the majority of all rapes are not even reported because the victim fears the publicity, rejection of her boyfriend or husband, or seeks to avoid the ordeal of police investigation and trial. The rapist is not infrequently a person known to the victim, including ex-spouse, relative, neighbor, or even boyfriend, and for this reason she may be reluctant to report the crime. Rape, even when reported, is often not cleared by arrest, and is a difficult crime to prosecute and to obtain a conviction. Rape is allegedly not a crime growing out of sexual deprivation or perpetrated by "over-sexed" individuals, or even necessarily a crime motivated by sexual desire alone. Rather, it is a sexual act of far more complex dimensions characterized by aggression and hostility toward the victim personally, a category of persons such as white women, or perhaps females in general. Some rapists simply need to express their sexuality through violence and sadism. Where sexual motivation appears to be a primary incentive, the rapist is often a person who cannot relate to women in a sexually normal fashion. Rape, it has been asserted, in some instances, encompasses a degree of victim precipitation, although this question is still a matter of professional debate among behavioral scientists. Rape may be an endemic offense to some social situations such as wartime where, according to some writers, it becomes a political act of suppression, as well as creating a context for some males to act in an exaggerated masculine fashion involving violence and sexual dominance. Rape is a singular criminal offense in that, according to the social context and one's perspective, may be either economic, personal, or political crime, or all three at once.

Males may be victims of homosexual rape, just as women are victims of heterosexual rape. In prisons and jails, rape of the weak and helpless may become routine and frequent, often arising out of an attempt to create a structure of dominance as well as to obtain carnal gratification even where not normally available. The pattern of sexual exploitation of young and weak prisoners is a common one in the institutionalized context of today's society. There are instances where guards and block wardens have "rewarded" groups of inmates by giving them a young prisoner for homosexual purposes. In other cases, such young prisoners have even been "sold" to particular sets of inmates. In order to survive, some young prisoners have had to voluntarily become the habitual victim of sodomy by one individual inmate who would then undertake to protect him from the other inmates. The institutional context of prison, with its often endemic violence and homosexual abuse, cannot help but dehumanize both rape offender and victim, alienating them further from conventional society. In the instance of the offender, he becomes programmed, as it were, to derive carnal gratification and to vent aggressions and hostilities through the exercise of sexual violence. The victim on the other hand, in experiencing such abuse, is forced to accept the fate of victimization as an inescapable fact of the exigencies of carnal behavior.

SUMMARY

The vagaries of carnal motivation and sexual interaction in our society give rise to myriad interpretive contexts and elicit a range and multiplicity of social responses, often themselves more situational than fixed. Sexual behavior cannot profitably be viewed simply in terms of categories of manifest structure and theme; rather, it must be addressed at the level of function and meaning within a larger cultural complex of carnal gratification. It is the reality of the individuals involved and the public perceptions of the activity which give substance and social content to sexual interaction. Carnal behavior is symbolically operating at various levels of social functionality and institutionalized mode. In this regard, the discrepancy in social toleration and the attendant application of social sanctions between private patterns of behavior concomitant to sexual gratification and the more publicly commercialized configurations of carnal activity is particularly evident. The individual who marches to the beat of a different sexual drummer in a singular fashion may well be labeled as aberrant and dysfunctional to the social enterprise, but the various instances of institutionalized collective carnality that encompass economic parameters are often conceptualized in a somewhat more exigent, if not functional, fashion. In the final analysis, sexual deviancy must necessarily be viewed against the backdrop of cultural utility and the practical limits of social suppression and control.

Chapter 2

ATTRIBUTIVE AND ILLUSIONARY CARNALITY

Sexual Deviancy in Spurious Context

More sexual deviancy occurs in the mind—of the public—than in reality. It is perceived and believed, but cannot be demonstrated, and is, thus, spurious. Spurious sexual deviancy, like genuine sexual deviancy, may repel, or invite or attract, the perceiver to personal involvement. Thus, the person who conceptualizes the non-existent misconduct may react either positively or negatively to that which he imagines.

The American mentality, heir to the legacy of puritan ethic, still imbued with the residue of Victorian propriety, and subject to the ethnocentric bias of cultural conformity, not infrequently perceives deviancy, and especially sexual deviancy, where there is none.[1] The middle class American, most prone of all to distorted perception of the conduct he encounters, perhaps because of his own frustration, born of behavioral rigidity, may be inclined to project his sexual fantasies, fears, and distortions upon the activities of others. Such projection mechanisms may be triggered by unusual combinations and permutations of situational elements and cues, in conjunction with personal experiences and stereotypical associations, and the beholder may then proceed to weave the richly embellished fabric of imagination with which to fashion the spurious behavior. Even the most minutely perceived indicator or dubious association can serve as the inductive progenitor of either tantalizing or repulsive mental scenarios; the individual may either attempt to become a participant in his own dramaturgical product, or on the other hand be disaffected or repulsed by the reality he perceives and reject it and all involved.

CATEGORICAL SETS AND SEXUAL STIGMATIZATION

Interestingly, the perception machinations attendant on creating fictive sexual deviancy, not infrequently manipulate *categories* of persons, places, or things, rather than actual entities or situations. As in the instance of all stereotyping processes, the guilt by association attaches itself to the social category, and the individual or situation bears the brunt of stigma by sexual impropriety or offense. In this connection there is great variety to the range of social categories which bear the stigma of deviant sexual behavior in our society. Such categories include occupation, age, race, nationality, religion, location, and lifestyle, to name a few, and in monitoring the social enterprise, many citizens inductively link deviant sexual parameters, even if spurious, with the merest sampling of unorthodoxy in regard to preconceived notions of conformity.

SEXUAL STATUS AND SEXUAL DEVIANCY

Perhaps most basic and universal of sexual deviancy stereotyping is the tendency to ascribe sexual tendencies, proclivities, and postures to one or the other sex. The male sex is characterized as animalistic, sexually selfish, insensitive, narcistic, and sexually exploitative. According to the saying, "men are only after one thing," and accordingly, there is the widely-held view that men, in the absence of appropriate social controls, constraints, and restraints, are lechers, would-be rapists, or blatant seducers, at the least.

It is the female, however, that enjoys the blackest reputation in terms of sexual inclination and, thus, deviancy, on a cross-cultural basis. In some Arab societies, women are, for example, called "the cows of satan," and "the devil's nets" suggesting that they are the "initiators of evil."[2] In Judeo-Christian tradition, of course, it was woman, personified by Eve, who because of succumbing to temptation, caused the downfall of man. There is an old Arabic saying, "the straightest woman is as twisted as a sickle."[3] According to some scholars, it is because of concern about maintaining and enforcing the "propriety of female sexual behavior in intersexual contact situations" that there are such elaborate protective and confinement normative configurations for females, such as chaperoning.[4] As Fox describes this concern:

> ... Because women are viewed as creatures of insatiable sexuality who cannot be trusted to control themselves (and guard the honor of the family themselves), they must be carefully protected within or secluded from the world of strange men outside their homes.[5]

Thus, early marriage is viewed as a device for putting a potentially sexually deviant female "under the beneficial protection of man" as quickly as possible. Again the Arabs speak of "shame is a young girl," but term the son-in-law, "the veil cast over shame."[6] Even in the United States, early marriage for females may be encouraged as a means of protecting them from their own sexually deviant proclivities. Again, as Fox phrases it:

> ... The shorter the length of time a young woman is exposed to the possibility of premarital sexual activity, the less likely she will be to "get caught" in such activity. Thus, the young ages at marriage that characterize nuptiality patterns in America may be in part a response to the "nice girl" pattern of social control.[7]

Women then, at best, are often stereotyped as persons with strong and, thus, deviant, potential. Where the female steps out of this protective social pattern, she opens herself for ascription of even more blatant sexual deviancy. Thus, a female that goes out alone, particularly at night, is either "asking for trouble" or "looking for it." Women who go to bars or similar public places may then, accordingly, be morally suspect. So, too, many women who dress in an overly provocative fashion, go to the "wrong kinds of places," run around with the "wrong kind of people," "late date" or engage in other unconventional patterns of association with persons of the opposite sex, such as going on trips together unchaperoned. For a female to hitchhike is to, in effect, advertise that she is sexually available.[8] Hitchhiking women who have subsequently been assaulted or raped not infrequently receive little sympathy from juries and judges and there have been acquittals based essentially on the fact of the victim having been a hitchhiker.[9]

Thus, the narrowly circumscribed parameters of the "nice girl" role in American society (and most others) essentially means that even a minor transgression of the normative boundaries is to invite severe social stereotyping and the attendant ascription of sexual delinquency.

OCCUPATIONAL CATEGORY AND SPURIOUS SEXUAL DEVIANCY

Occupational specialties, reputationally speaking, often carry a connotation of sexuality, either inherently, or in terms of certain elements that may be present or absent within the occupational context. Persons who occupy the various categories of work in the division of labor, may be adjudged sexually deviant more by virtue of their stereotypical reputation than by deed. Servicemen, for example, of all branches of the armed forces are notorious for their alleged libidinous over-zealousness, but the sailor, above all, has the reputation of being amorous to the point of lechery. Many male occupations, particularly those that exude a virile image, also project an image of sexual abandon along with the masculine *élan*. Professional athletes, according to popular belief, are traditional womanizers and "hell-benders." It was, therefore, quite a shattering experience to the American public when they experienced the disclosure that a number of prominent athletes were, in fact, of gay persuasion. The sexual stereotype of male hair stylists, dress designers, or any other traditionally female occupation, is frequently that of homosexual, and, thus, deviant even though in "real life" they may actually be married (to a female) or at least "straight," even if single. Actors, and even those who normally assume *macho* roles, are frequently troubled by the less-than-masculine image that the public holds of male thespians. In fact, people in show business generally complain that the public image of members of their industry as swingers, debauchers, and perverts, is largely illusionary, based on only a few notorious episodes, and overlooks the absolutely conventional lives that most of them live. The sexual revelations of Washington came as no real surprise to many people, since they already believed that most politicians were probably guilty of wanton lasciviousness as well as malfeasance. It is the sexual temptations constituent to many occupational settings that often give rise to public speculation about the sexual misbehavior that many believe must surely attend the temptations, occupational practitioners being only mortal, so to speak. There is, in fact, a very real opportunity structure for sexual activity in many occupational settings because of the intimate presence of clientele, colleagues, or co-workers of the opposite sex, and the public along with the practitioner is often very much aware of it.

If the artist paints pictures using nude models, he may well be overcome by lust and abandon behavioral propriety, if not sexual continence, according to some popular belief. The physician, generally conceded to be among the nobler vocations is also suspected to be subject to temptations. A practitioner in the course of his daily routine may examine scores of naked female bodies, scrutinizing and handling, as it were, their most intimate parts. In the face of such sexually volatile encounters, systems of checks and balances must be established in order to insure and sanction behavior equilibrium. Elaborate dramaturgical procedures, for example, must attend the gynecological examination so as to compartmentalize the anatomical scrutiny.[10] The genital area can only be examined with routinized draping of the body with a sheet, and even the perfunctory breast examination may entail the placing of a gauze pad over each nipple in order that they may be lifted only one-at-a-time by the physician for his routine manipulation of tissue. The essential thing is that the physician not behold his female patient in a *gestalt* and, thus, more potentially lustful, fashion. Traditional Chinese wives (and no doubt their husbands) were so apprehensive about the sexual impropriety of being intimately examined by a male physician, that it was customary, when ill, not to even visit the doctor, but instead to send a servant to the practitioner with a small ivory nude doll. The servant would simply point to the part of the doll's anatomy, corresponding to that of her mistress, and, thus, describe the lady's symptoms. The doctor would accordingly prescribe, and both sexual decorum and safety were appropriately observed. Professional ethics, some state laws, and good common sense also dictate that a physician have a female nurse or attendant present during a female examination. Thus, dramaturgics, anatomical compartmentalization, depersonalization, and a chaperone would all seem requisite to the maintenance of sexual propriety and comportment between doctor and female patient. Of course, public belief is also cognizant of the close working proximity of doctors and nurses, and some degree of sexual license is neither unexpected nor unrumored by the public.

Female occupational specialties would appear to suffer the burden of sexual rumor more than male, however. Female performers and especially those that appear partially or completely disrobed are particularly susceptible to sexual innuendo and attribution of sexual deviancy. A number of researchers have pointed out that strippers are frequently thought of, and treated as, prostitutes regardless of the comportment of their personal lives. As Boles and Garbin describe it, "The men who go to strip clubs believe that a vast majority of the strippers are prostitutes. As such, the girls are propositioned indiscriminately."[11]

Salutin, makes a similar observation when she comments that:

> . . . For one thing, the general public regards all strippers as prostitutes anyway, and for another, strippers are always being propositioned.

> Nevertheless strippers much resent being labeled a prostitute. One woman said, "I hate clubs, especially small ones in northern Ontario. They'll treat you like a prostitute whether you are one or not just because most of them have been who were here before you . . . When you finish the show, you never know what drunk is going to be waiting for you at the top of the stairs.[12]

Go-go dancers, chorus girls, topless waitresses, and other female performers who display partial nudity, or women who perform intimate services for men, such as masseuses in massage parlors, may also enjoy a similar negative public stereotype. The negative images involved range all the way from simple promiscuousness to prostitution to lesbianism. Although it is true that there are some such females who are also prostitutes, or lesbians, the fact of the matter is that many of them are married, have children, are heterosexual, and generally moral and legal in their everyday behavior. The women in these occupations are stigmatized as deviants, however, because of the social milieu in which they must work, and the people with whom they are thrown into contact. Also, these performers by exhibiting their bodies and performing in an obscene manner, are in violation of community standards of proprietous comportment and "good taste."[13] Because they exploit their bodies and their sexuality, they become, in the eyes of the public, a kind of symbolic prostitute, and, thus, the image of a real prostitute, spurious or not, attaches itself.

Many other, far less exotic and erotic, female occupations, however, are also subject to sexual stereotyping and stigma. The airline stewardess, for example, long a cherished occupational ambition of many teenage girls has in recent years, become more a sex symbol. Much of this sex symbolism derives from deliberate efforts on the part of airline advertising campaigns designed to lure more male customers on board. Advertisements such as, "Make You Feel Good All Over," "Fly Me—I'm Cheryl," or "Almost Anything," apparently tended to fuel the fires of sexual fantasies if not lust, especially in the minds of male passengers. The seed of sexuality, perhaps planted by public suspicion, especially after the suggestive advertising campaigns, was no doubt nourished by various erotic movies in recent years about stewardesses, such as *The Swinging Stewardesses,* and *Come Fly With Me,* and *exposé* books about work in the sky (and leisure on the ground) like *Coffee, Tea, or Me,* or *How To Make a Good Stewardess.*[14]

The advertising slogan introduced by Continental Airlines in 1974, really reinforced the sex object public image. The slogan simply read, "We really move our tails for you." With the help of Madison Avenue, and company policies that sometimes called for hot pants or miniskirts as uniforms, the public image of stewardesses, at least for some, included sexual promiscuousness. Attendant to this image, some stewardesses have reported being pinched, patted, and fondled by passengers. Others have accused passengers of putting their hand up their skirts, trying to kiss them, and sexually propositioning them. One stewardess reported that when she sat next to a male passenger during some turbulence on a night flight, he forced her to masturbate him.[15] Accounts of such sexual harrassment have been more prevalent in recent years, suggesting perhaps that some male passengers have become more sexually emboldened by the suggestive advertising campaigns of the airlines, or that the stewardesses have simply become less constrained about revealing such episodes. Perhaps, however, the negative image of stewardesses held by some of the public can best be summed up by one male passenger. A stewardess had rebuffed a particularly aggressive passenger, and when he grabbed her, she pulled away. At this the passenger shouted out, "You're all goddamn whores anyway."[16] For such men, stewardesses were viewed as being immoral women, anyway, and were, thus, particularly annoyed when the women would not participate in the sexual escapades produced by their fantasies. The spurious deviancy of stewardesses becomes very real in the minds of some. Just as high school boys (and grown men) are often assured that all female car-hops and mini-skirted cocktail waitresses will "do the deed," many persons are secure in the erotic knowledge that "nurses make good dates," and of course, perhaps the majority of us are completely assured that "blondes have more fun."

Perhaps, however, the epitome of occupational stereotyping linked to sexual stigmatization is the instance of the Japanese *geisha*. The *geisha* is historically and traditionally an honorable vocation that encompasses a wide range of occupational responsibilities including some of those associated with waitress, companion, B-girl, and entertainer. The *geisha* attends the male patron while he enjoys a meal and during the meal, she might sing or play instruments, talk or joke with the patron, and even feed him. She is hostess, companion, and a kind of social director, on a miniature scale, as it were. She traditionally has not rendered sexual services to the patron. Training to be a *geisha* is long and arduous and to succeed is to attain genuine occupational success. The bill, at today's inflated prices, for several men going to a *geisha* house for a meal, might be in excess of several thousand dollars. To the American public, however, and especially in years past, the word *geisha* was essentially synonymous with the word prostitute. It has long been assumed, by many, that *geisha* houses were brothels. After World War II during the U.S. occupation, and later during the Korean War, many servicemen went in search of *geisha* houses in the firm belief that they were establishments that provided sexual gratification, for a price. While it is to be admitted that having a *geisha* attend one at a dinner might well afford one a modicum of vicarious carnal gratification, the G.I.s were disappointed when they learned the true nature of the vocation. Similarly, many American tourists and businessmen have discovered that they held a most distorted perception of the services offered by a *geisha*. In spite of contemporary public enlightenment, there is still a persistent belief, in the minds of many, that in spite of all information to the contrary, *geisha* are likely women of questionable morals who are not above dispensing sex on a commercial basis.

RACE, NATIONALITY, RELIGION, AND SPURIOUS DEVIANCY

Racial stereotypes are numerous, pervasive, and usually irrational. Orientals are crafty and inscrutable; blacks have rhythm and thick skulls. Blacks are also animalistic, according to myth, and are imbued with an insatiable sexual appetite. The coital enthusiasm of black females, and the inordinate size of black male genitalia are part of the constituent "woof and warp" of the fabric of our national myth system. From such cultural distortions come the widespread beliefs that the daily lives of many blacks are little more than an ongoing bacchanalian orgy. As evidence in the belief, especially on the part of whites, of extensive sexual deviancy and degeneracy on the part of blacks, it should be recalled that on many instances in the past, black men in this country were jailed, assaulted, or even killed for relatively innocuous behavior that had sexual connotation or overtone. A wolf whistle at a white female may have brought massive retaliation because of the while mental preoccupation with the probable existence of black sexual intent. The classic case of this, however, was the widely reported episode of some years back, of a black farmer in South Carolina who was arrested and indicted for "leering" at a white woman. It was believed, apparently, that the leering had salacious intent, and, therefore, probably presaged aggressive sexual misconduct.

Nationality is sometimes strongly redolent of deviancy, even if spurious. The sexual liberation that transpired in Scandanavia before it made its presence known in the United States, generated the belief in the minds of many Americans that the populations of the various Scandinavian countries, and especially Sweden, were also totally without sexual constraint; the result was that women were promiscuous to the point of near nymphomania. In the minds of many persons in the United States, Sweden became almost sexually synonymous with Sodom and Gomorrah. Evidence that there was belief that this sexual deviancy was endemic in Sweden, even if spurious, can be found in the fact that it was widely reported that some male students attending colleges and universities in Sweden often were considered as boors and uncouth, and some made complete fools of themselves by practically assaulting Swedish girls in the mistaken belief that the girls were carnally inclined to an almost uncontrollable degree.

Latin American and Italian men have the reputation of being great lovers, but the reports of their wives (and girlfriends) frequently contradict such reports. Many G.I.s who were stationed in Germany during the occupation found that the German *fräuleins* did not live up to the Marlene Dietrich image of sexual sophistication, nor were they even necessarily "loose." Where they did encounter promiscuity the motivation was more often economic (for survival purposes) rather than lust, and many simply encountered sturdy peasant stock who were more interested in marriage than sexual abandonment. If the Scandinavians in general, and Swedes in particular, however, were viewed as the prototype of sexual license, the French were traditionally perceived as the real sexual sophisticates. The French catholicy of sexual taste is legendary, and the very national label itself is synonymous with sexual variation. "Deep" or "tongue" kissing is known in the vernacular as French kissing, and the idiomatic expression for fellatio, especially when a prostitute is involved is a "French Date," or "Frenching." France has also been synonymous with dirty postcards, literary pornography, and prostitutes and pimps, as in "dressed like a French whore" or "French pimp." Henry Miller, and the Doughboys of the AEF in World War I may have contributed to the public wicked image of French deviancy and debauchery, but in any event, jokes that invoke French phraseology such as *"menage a trois,"* French numerology like *soixante-neuf,* or even *double entendre* references to the geography of France such as the "southern coast of France" are part and parcel of the lewd *repertoire* of most blue comics. In view of the well-ingrained image of Gallic sexual deviancy, it might have been something of a shock, if not genuine letdown for many people, when they read recently of a national sex survey conducted in France that polled the sexual patterns and persuasions of French men and women. Gallic sex-life, it seems is no more diversified or sophisticated than in the United States.[17]

As for religion and alleged deviancy, it should be recalled that the anti-Catholic movement of the early nineteenth century in the United States generated some extremely vitriolic prejudice toward Catholics and Catholic institutions such as the convent.[18] This prejudice fueled a variety of distorted public beliefs and persuasions such as the ridiculous notion that Catholic convents were little more than fronts for flagrant debauchery among nuns and priests. A number of books were published that purported to provide an exposé of such carnal behavior and some such books were dramatically convincing to some segments of the unsophisticated public of the day. An example of a book of this genre was Scipio de Ricci's tract, *Female Convents: The Secrets of Nunneries Disclosed,* with its lurid allegations of sexual misconduct among nuns and priests.[19] Additionally, there were persistent rumors that the bones and skulls of infants had been found in some convents, suggesting the possibility of nefarious Satanic rites and ritualistic infanticide in addition to sexual licentiousness. So strong was the belief that the nunneries harbored sexual deviancy, if not worse, that in 1834, a convent in Charlestown, Mass. that maintained a boarding school for girls, was attacked by a mob intent on freeing the girls believed held prisoners there. The mob subsequently burned and looted the convent, as the nuns and the girls escaped by a back door.[20] Religious prejudice thrives on spurious deviancy, and even today, some of the exotic religious persuasions are occasionally linked in rumor with inappropriate sexual activity.

Marital Status, and Spurious Sexual Deviancy

There is an old rural truism that "You can't court a widow too much;" the implication, of course, being that a woman who has enjoyed a rich carnal life in marriage is quite likely to have retained her sexual appetite. Even more sexual innuendo attaches itself, however, to the "grass widow"—the divorcee. There are still some business establishments, and some institutional agencies that until recently, at least, would not hire divorced persons, and especially divorced women. Many rural school systems in years past were not favorably disposed toward hiring divorced women in the belief that they would set a bad example for their students, and would probably become involved in sexual misconduct, anyway. It is often upsetting to wives to have a divorcee move in next door out of fear that the divorcee, with her carnal appetite, will probably try to vamp their own husbands. Landlords sometimes are reluctant to rent apartments to divorcees because of the sexual debauchery that might likely come to pass in their apartments. The American image of the female divorcee is essentially one of a libertine bent on sexual conquest and an amoral lifestyle. Many divorced women complain bitterly that the public, and especially men, tend to assume that they are sexually frustrated, and that accordingly they are easy targets for seduction, if in fact they are not already living a carnal life. Morton Hunt, in his study of formerly married persons reported that many of the divorced women he interviewed told of the men they dated making a sexual "pass—verbal or physical, jestingly or seriously," either on the first date, or at least within the first few dates.[21] Such sexually aggressive behavior was not without its impact on the women involved. One woman, for example, told Hunt:

It's kind of horrible. They're a bunch of nuts, all trying to prove something. After my first few dates, I wouldn't go out with anyone new for a long while—I just didn't want to have to face that inevitable try and the inevitable anger that my refusal produced.[22]

After a while, however, many divorcees apparently adjust to such advances. Another woman interviewed said that the first time it happened, she was shocked and cried, the second time she became angry, and the third time when she was ready for the sexual overture, she became giggly! In some instances, Hunt reported that divorced women, sometimes even on their first date, were asked out again, but only if they lived up to their part of the bargain—going to bed with their date. One woman apparently was particularly shocked when the man she was dating for only the second time, started talking about sex after only half an hour, and then inquired, "How about it?" Other men she dated for the first time were more parsimonious in their verbal efforts, and after an hour or so would simply inquire, "Yes or no?"[23] Such behavior, according to Hunt, makes some divorced women believe that their dates must think them to be whores, who "should 'turn a trick' for her dinner."[24] So strong is the social mandate to marry in our society that a middle-aged bachelor or old maid may be considered "odd" or "strange" and not infrequently, are suspected of having homosexual tendencies.

Men have trouble with marital status and the association of sexual deviancy, as well as women. Charles Merrill Smith, in his tongue-in-cheek guidebook, *How to Become a Bishop Without Being Religious,* points out that church congregations are not prone to tolerate unmarried clergymen for several reasons including some practical reasons, but also because they find it behaviorally inappropriate. As he puts it:

> First, a clergyman who remains unmarried for more than a year after graduation from seminary is suspected of being abnormal, immoral or chicken.[25]

In some parts of the world, and especially in Latin America and the Mediterranean countries, young unmarried girls are rigidly chaperoned, in the belief that not to do so would be to invite swift and sure sexual involvement with a young man because of the unbridled passions of both. In such countries, as was also the case here in earlier times, for a female simply to be alone with a man while not chaperoned would effectively compromise her reputation and purity. Even today, for a male and female to spend the night together in the same house or room, if not chaperoned, is *prima facie* evidence of coital activity, regardless of whether the couple was completely chaste in their interpersonal interaction. Many a divorce case is granted on the basis of assumed sexual deviancy, simply because the erring spouse was in unsupervised proximity to a person of the opposite sex.

AGE AND SPURIOUS SEXUAL DEVIANCY

Age, of course, also has its association with spurious deviance. Elderly men, perhaps more than any other single age status, are linked in the public mind with sexual deviancy. Such deviancy may range from molesting children to patronizing prostitutes, and from voyeurism to exhibitionism. In many cases, an innocent act of play involvement with children may elicit a charge of child molesting, and an absent-minded act of forgetting to zip up the fly on their trousers may generate a complaint of exhibitionism. Relatively simple and innocuous acts are often interpreted as having a sexual, and sexual deviant context. One researcher reported that in a geriatric hospital, an (elderly male) "patient makes offensive remarks to the female personnel," and later, "when the ladies of the staff are questioned they often quite indignantly describe how the patient made suggestive remarks to the effect that he found them sexually appealing."[26] In a sense, the public is overly ready to perceive sexual deviancy in some behavior of elderly men, whether it exists or not. As Frederick E. Whiskin puts it:

> Finally, regarding abnormal sexuality, when an older person commits an unnatural sexual act, society over-reacts in terms of energies derived from attitudes which are built it, lying in wait for the triggering event.[27]

Much of this tendency to link spurious sexual deviancy to the aged male arises out of our conceptualization of old age as a desexualized period of life, and social status. Again, according to Whiskin:

> In our culture there is, without doubt, less tolerance of overt, or even covert, expression of sexual interest toward the opposite sex in the elderly than in younger people. It is as if sexuality becomes progressively more *verboten* as one ages beyond a certain point. The expression, "dirty old man," probably finds its origin in these cultural attitudes.[28]

Because even normal sexual activity is generally viewed as incongruent and, thus, inappropriate, conduct in the aged, even behavioral tendencies in this direction by the elderly, are not infrequently labeled as pathological.[29] Given this type of societal predisposition toward condemning expressions of sexuality in the elderly, it is perhaps not surprising that various kinds of sexual deviancy, or at least the potential for such behavior, is often attributed to older individuals.

URBANISM AND SPURIOUS SEXUAL DEVIANCY

It is a cultural truism, even if not necessarily valid, that the city is more wicked than the country. Since the Biblical account of Sodom and Gomorrah being destroyed for sin, the urban place has been inextricably linked with hedonism, immorality, and carnality in human behavior (even the name Sodom gave rise to sexually deviant labels such as Sodomite, and sodomy). Even in these enlightened times, young people, upon the approach of adulthood, lemming-like, still mass migrate to the cities in search of their fortunes, and to sow wild oats and pay reverence to the god Báal. Similarly, the visiting big butter and egg man from the Midwest, and the conventioneer Shriner from small town, U.S.A., both tingle with salacious anticipation of the wickedness and sexual licentiousness, of which they hope to partake by the time they reach the city limits of the big city. The myth and lore of our society is ripe with references to the sexual naiveté of the rural dweller and the carnal sophistication of the urbanite. In spite of the obvious defect in logic, the farmer's daughter is invariably seduced by the sexually guileful "city-slicker." Incest, bestiality, and other sexual diversity and deviancy, may be more characteristic of rural than of urban areas, but the belief lingers on, that the city, not the country, is in fact, the meeting place of flesh and the devil. Sexual connotations may even attend particular areas of towns such as Soho in London or Greenwich Village in New York, inasmuch as they are the places "where the action is."

LIFESTYLE AND SPURIOUS SEXUAL DEVIANCY

Spurious sexual deviancy, however, even attaches itself to lifestyle including décor, activities, and belongings. A young couple of my acquaintance in college, had acquired a well-done oil painting of a nude while they were in graduate school. Much as they liked the painting, they elected to sell it upon graduation before moving back to their own small hometown. The painting was, as they put it, "too nude." In the small town in which they would live, the mere ownership of such a decadent artifact would imply immorality and sexual hedonism. Another acquaintance took a high administrative post at another university, and the job included a house. He and his wife were much embarrassed and dismayed to discover that in the master bedroom of the house, the walls were covered with purple flocked wallpaper and the entire ceiling was mirrored! Needless to say, they continue to be the butt of lewd jokes. The possession of erotic books, a subscription to *Playboy,* the keeping of unusual hours, the ownership of black bedsheets, the wearing of too revealing clothing, or the purchase at a local store of a vibrator for the relief of strained back muscles, might all, in some social contexts, give rise to public speculation of sexual deviance.

Perhaps no sexual stigma is more bizarre, however, than that attaching itself to the ownership of a highly functional plumbing fixture. It would appear that the ownership of a bidet, the "scarlet plumbing fixture," as it were, regardless of its hygienic efficacy, may cause an entire family to be conceptualized as un-American, carnal, weird, and perverted. The bidet, and its intended function, is apparently so alien to the plumbing ethnocentrism of many Americans that their minds boggle—and then work overtime to generate convoluted sexual fantasies about the deviant activity that must surely attend that enigmatic and erotic apparatus with which the tainted perform their perineal ablutions. The bidet, although relatively common in some countries of Europe, and to a somewhat lesser degree in Latin America and Southeast Asia, is almost unknown in the United States, except perhaps in terms of the most superficial acquaintance or knowledge, often with attendant distorted understandings of its function and social import. A recent study of students at a large Eastern landgrant university, for example, revealed some of the most incredibly perverse and contorted attitudes and views about bidet owners and their spurious sexual activities.[30] A majority of the students had never heard of the bidet and only a very small percentage knew someone, or knew of someone who owned one. Only one student out of several hundred queried reported a bidet in their home. Those students who had never heard of this bathroom appliance were provided with a definition. Then, all of the students were asked to assign priorities to various water related household appliances including the bidet, which they might desire in their own ultimate home. The great majority of the respondents (80 percent) indicated that they had no desire to have a bidet in their eventual home. When asked to provide their perceptions of families who might own a bidet, their replies were startling, if not amusing. Only 40 percent of the students in the study provided a positive description of the family owning a bidet, and 22 percent gave a response coded as "deviant." The actual comments concerning the stereotypical bidet-owning family are prejudiced to the point of being ludicrous. Members of such families were characterized as "foreign," "lazy," "status-seekers," "eccentric," "health nuts," "weird," "crazy," "nuts," "perverts," "probably sexually neurotic," and "[getting] sexual pleasure out of the device." The classic comment of one student respondent was vehement, if not downright rabid in his moral denunciation of a family perceived as brazen enough to possess such an instrument of obvious degeneration. As the respondent put it, a bidet-owning family is, "a bunch of append-ageless perverts who have never bathed. [The bidet is] totally useless insofar as offering something not readily available. Their income is probably above average and their home a *whorehouse* [italics ours]." Note that from this description, one could infer that the owners are emasculated, filthy, foolish in their total lack of utilitarian sensitivity, affluent, and harborers, if not purveyors, of harlotry. There would seem to be little doubt that, at least in the minds of some young people, the bidet has a decided mental and moral stigma. It is fascinating to contemplate, that in the minds of some, the mere ownership of such a plumbing device is synonymous with degeneracy and perversion. Considering the fact of our eminent entry into the final quarter of the twentieth century, it is odd that, for these permissive, if not enlightened times, the middle class should hold morally suspect the members of any family that might desire to wash their bottoms on a frequent basis; that by virtue of possessing a device patently contributory to fastidiousness, such a family should have to bear the social burden of sexual stigmatization as a result of being the owner of a "scarlet plumbing fixture."

In the final analysis, sexual deviancy, even if illusionary, is often attributed through no action or omission on the part of the alleged deviant. Like other attributed statuses, the spurious sexual misreant, rather, is subject to the contingencies of contextual interpretation and is thus victim to the mental machinations of his accusors, and their salacious thoughts.

CONTRIVED SPURIOUS DEVIANCY

In not all cases of spurious sexual deviancy is the victim perpetrator necessarily innocent. In some instances, it is that person who becomes involved in a misadventure of his own making. It is said that only a crook at heart can be "crooked," and that only the greedy can be suckered into a confidence game in an attempt to con someone else. It may well be that only the carnal at heart can become the victims of carnal hoaxes. In such instances it is the victim himself who generates the fantasy of sexual deviancy, and then sometimes discovers that his wickedest hopes are spurious.

Many an individual has bought a "dirty" book only to discover that its contents do not live up to his levels of mental salaciousness. Carnival girlie shows are built on a foundation of the patron's own sexual fantasy, and once inside, lured by promises of scandalous revelations, and blatant genital exposure, the sucker than discovers that he sees or hears little more than he might at a GP-rated movie. The carnival, however, offers one last chance to fantasize and invites the mark (patron) to the "real," inside show, *after* the regular show, where nothing is held back and all is revealed—for an additional price! Again, the individual can enjoy the delicious fantasies of complete sexual debauchery, only to discover that the after-show show —the blowoff—as it is affectionately termed in the carnival industry, offers little in the way of even vicarious sexual gratification for the stiff price of admission.

Many confidence swindles, such as the traditional "badger game," have been built on the lustful appetite, and the prolific sexual imagination of the sucker. A particularly hoary con game in the carnival business is the old dodge of selling the key to the girl's room. A particularly attractive female and her male assistant work a midway concession. With the help of the male assistant, the patrons of the concession would be given to understand that the attractive female was sexually available if someone would only come to her room at the hotel after the show closed. The male assistant would set the stage and sell the sucker the key to the girl's room. The sucker would do the rest, and would mentally conjure up a sexual scenario of X-rated quality. The assistant would sell the key to the girl's room to dozens, if not hundreds of suckers. When the show closed, the stairs and halls of the hotel would be as crowded as a California freeway, but the carnie couple would be far away and laughing, and the sucker probably would not have enjoyed his spurious deviancy![31]

An interesting recent manifestation of economic exploitation of spurious sexual deviancy is the "Glo-Worm Society."[32] Between January and July, 1979, almost one million "sexually suggestive" letters were sent to both males and females, across the country, offering membership in a "private society started by 'fun-loving young ladies.'" In the solicitation letters, the club is described as an:

> ... exclusive private society; an organization that was started by a group of fun-loving young ladies who are dedicated to the proposition that men and women were put on this earth for one reason—to enjoy each other.

Even though prospective members had been assured that they could have their money "cheerfully refunded" if they joined and were not satisfied, when they did join and were not satisfied with what they received from Glo-Worm, the refunds were not forthcoming. In the face of innumerable complaints from less than satisfied customers, the U.S. Postal Service, the Florida Attorney General, and the Orlando Chamber of Commerce all undertook to investigate the scheme.

A similar but more ambitious exploitation scheme using spurious sex as bait was the recently exposed arrangement whereby advertisements in Germany offer "Three weeks in Thailand . . . The wife of your choice . . . An unforgettable marriage ceremony . . . All for $3,000."[33] The German men who were taken in would pay their money, fly to Thailand on an air charter flight, be introduced to an attractive Thai girl who would appear to be "innocent, faithful and obedient," marry her and return to Germany, with the promise of the girl to join him, and would go through the same routine with the next customer from Germany. It turned out that the girls were prostitutes and were part of a large racket that were swindling the gullible German men. The men were simply being separated from their money with the promise of marriage and sex that was spurious.

Times have changed, but suckers have not. In these times of apparent sexual liberation and unfettered hedonism, the individual with more carnal imagination than rational judgment may well find himself victimized by spurious sexual deviancy. In spite of the presumed sophistication of much of our adult male population today, it is surprising, (and perhaps amusing) to learn that sexual con-games of near transparent intent are still successful in separating the naive from their money. In this connection, some interesting new commercial configurations based on spurious deviancy have recently appeared in some areas. In these commercial situations the sucker is conned by his own depraved imagination. One recent report on such nefarious activities, for example, detailed the establishment of numerous sham sexual service "shops" in some large cities such as Los Angeles.[34] In this particular article, the authors describe such shops including some typical examples with business names such as "Oral Intercourse Center," "House of Oral Sex," or "Institute of Oral Love." Often newly in town looking for "action," the individual is confronted by a proliferation of commercial establishments offering nothing specific, but a powerful innuendo of sex of diverse variety. The advertising on the front provides the theme, the establishment itself provides the stage setting, the props, and the supporting actresses. The sucker provides the lead part, and the scenario manufactured from his own sexual fantasies. The customer presumably accepts the business labeling as completely valid and goes into the shop to avail himself of the sexual services he believes available. The establishment promises nothing, rather, the mark provides the mental answers to his own questions. The only sexual deviancy that will transpire is within the context of the mark's dramaturgical creations. It is only after he has paid for the sexual pleasures he envisaged, that he discovered how ephemeral and spurious the deviancy he imagined was. Once escorted into a private room with a female attendant, the customer is startled out of his sexual reverie and has his carnal expectations dashed, when she proceeds to provide him with "oral sex" in the form of asking him questions about his sexual attitudes and persuasions, or only simply *talking* about sex. The sucker realizes he has been taken and either leaves quietly, or if he wishes to be argumentative about the sexual misrepresentation, either the female points out that the rendering of other sexual service would be illegal, or if he persists in his complaints, he may be assisted in leaving by a husky male manager.

SUMMARY

Much sexual deviancy is illusionary, and thus, mental and imaginative, and accordingly, spurious. Sexual deviancy may be perceived and believed where it does not exist. Perception is often distorted, particularly in regard to sexual contexts and activities. Constrained by a variety of restrictive and repressive sexual value systems such as the Puritan ethic, a sense of Victorian propriety, and middle-class morality, the average American may be prone to project his sexual fantasies, fears, and distortions on the activities of others. Facilitated by chance situational cues, idiosyncratic personal experiences, and stereotypical associations, the individual may perceive the merest element of possible deviant behavior, richly embellish the possibility with his imagination, and either be repelled or attracted by the sexual scenario to the point of involvement or participation in his own dramaturgical product.

Creating such sexual fiction frequently involves a stereotyping process, and accordingly, the manipulation of categories of persons, places, or things, rather than actual entities or situations. By the mechanism of guilt by association, the stigma of deviant sexual behavior attaches itself to a wide variety of social categories including instances of sex, occupation, age, race, nationality, religion, location, and lifestyle, to name but a few. Even the smallest trace of unorthodoxy might generate notions of elaborate configurations of sexual deviancy, albeit spurious.

Even sexual status may carry the suggestion of indication of deviant sexual inclination. Although males are traditionally known to be after "only one thing," it is the female who is almost universally perceived as being "creatures of insatiable sexuality" who must be protected from their own carnal appetites, even if this means restrictive social protection patterns such as chaperoning, isolation, or even early marriage as a means of "not getting caught" in permarital sexual activity.

Occupational categories, however, may well carry the most blatant suggestion of sexual association, even if fictional. Many persons may carry the suspicion of carnal deviancy simply by virtue of their stereotypical reputation than by deed. Sailors are often viewed as "wolves," professional athletes as "womanizers," entertainers and politicians are swingers and debauchers as are airline stewardesses, and strippers and topless go-go dancers are often considered to be "loose women," if not prostitutes. None of these associations are necessarily valid, and may be simply the spurious product of someone's overly-active stereotypical imagination.

Even race, ethnic background, or nationality have stereotypical sexual attributes. Black men, it is widely believed, have extraordinarily large penises, and blacks of both sexes are alleged to have insatiable, animalistic sexual appetites, not to mention the black male's inordinate lust for white women. Such spurious allegations and assertions were often behind the racial abuse of black men in many instances in the past, sometimes even resulting in beatings, jailings, or lynchings.

Many persons believe that Swedish women are essentially carnal in motivation, promiscuous, and sexually amoral. They also believe that Latin and Mediterranean men are great lovers, that German women are particularly amorous, and that the French of both sexes are particularly sophisticated and catholic in their repertoire of sexual technique. As cited earlier in the discussion, during the nineteenth century, the Catholic religion was spuriously alleged by some prejudiced writers, to incorporate satanic religious rites and to countenance sexual license and debauchery among its nuns and priests. Such bigotry and distorted mental machinations, in some instances, even resulted in the persecution of Catholics, and the destruction of churches and convents.

Previously married females, widowed or divorced, are often spuriously considered to experience discomforting and frustrating sexual deprivation as a result of the interruption of the rich carnal life they allegedly enjoyed in marriage. Widows and divorcees "can't be courted too much," and have a strong latent tendency to sexual excesses, according to belief. As a result, many such women have experienced job discrimination, difficulty in obtaining housing, and when they meet and date men, their escorts not infrequently are often sexually brusque and assertive to the point of offensiveness by "making passes" or bluntly inquiring if they will engage in sexual intercourse with them, sometimes on the first date or even shortly after meeting them. It is true that some never-married women may have encountered similar difficulties and unpleasant episodes because of spuriously attributed sexual tendencies, but the previously married individual would seem to be the more frequent victim of such labeling. The notion that once a female has experienced sex on a routine basis for a period of time, such as in a marriage, she cannot break the habit, is so firmly entrenched as a stereotypical cultural assumption, that many men react to such females in an almost reflexive, sexually aggressive fashion.

Of course, men, too, sometimes have stereotypical problems in terms of the ascription of spurious sexual deviancy, such as a middle-aged bachelor who may be viewed as "odd" or even homosexual as a result of not being married. Similarly, middle-aged, unmarried females are sometimes seen as "queer old maids," or individuals who cannot properly relate to men or appropriately adjust to sex.

Age, too, may also carry the connotation of inclination to sexual deviancy, even if a spurious propensity. The elderly male particularly may be so stereotyped and even an innocent act of endearment to a child, or forgetting to zip the fly on his trousers may result in the appelation of "dirty old man," or the belief, or even charge, that he is in fact guilty of child molesting or exhibitionism. In our society, the aged, according to our value system, are supposed to be asexual. Where they do manifest sexuality, or even appear to do so, the assumption is often made that such tendencies are pathological and that they are sexually deviant, even though such an ascription is likely spurious in fact.

The city has historically been viewed as a place of wickedness, carnal hedonism, sexual license, or corruption. In actual fact, the urban setting may be no more conducive or facilitative to sexual deviancy than the rural context, but with the distorted perception afforded by our cultural biases, it is the city that more often bears the stigma of carnal excesses and sexual deviancy.

One must carefully observe the letter and spirit of community propriety and social conformity in terms of circumspect comportment and lifestyle, for in the same manner as with certain social statuses, an unorthodox lifestyle or possession may precipitate a social image of licentiousness and public speculation about possible sexual deviance.

No possession is more blatantly redolent of decadence, immorality, and sexual degeneracy, even if illusionary, than the bidet—the "scarlet plumbing fixture," as it were. Research has revealed that the bidet and its intended function is so alien to the untutored mentality, that many persons develop elaborate and convoluted sexual fantasies concerning the deviant carnal activities that must surely attend the ownership and use of such a tainted plumbing apparatus. Many persons simply hold the families who own bidets morally suspect, and sometimes refer to them as "weird," "perverts," [getting] "sexual pleasure out of the device," or worse. Thus, even the ownership of a socially vagrant plumbing fixture may invite salacious interpretation and the attribution of sexual miscreance, even if spurious.

Sometimes, the attribution of sexual deviancy is invited and a social context suggestive of carnal opportunity is contrived. Many confidence games, and exploitive business and economic enterprises operate to portray the illusion of sexual activity or potential and, thus, are built on the lustful appetite, and the prolific sexual imagination of the sucker. Various kinds of sexual scams and emporiums have accomplished to let the customer or patron develop his own sexual scenarios about the goods and services they offer, and then can more readily separate the mark from his money inasmuch as his perceptions are built on a foundation of spurious reality and he has more carnal imagination than rational judgment.

Chapter 3

VISUAL EROTIC STIMULATION AND MENTAL IMAGERY

Sexual Deviancy in Vicarious Context

Attendant to man's position on the phylogenic ladder has been his dulled sense of olfactory perception, and his upright position, which has, among other things, tended to obscure and mystify, as it were, the female genitalia.[35] Unlike the lower mammals who depend to some degree on the exposure of, and various sensual and other cues related to, the female genitals, man is necessarily more moved to sexual activity by mental, rather than physical, stimuli. Furthermore, with their elaborate capacity for the manipulation of complex symbol systems, humans are the only animals capable of a rich fantasy life. Human existence, itself, depends on the mental scenarios that one is capable of creating, and from among which one can select options, managing and reassembling the mentally contrived, before using the product as a guide for behavior. Vicarious behavior then, is a means of testing reality and planning and evaluating behavior, as it were. In no area of human activity is vicarious behavior perhaps more significant than in the realm of sex. Sexual activity, and ancillary related behavior such as going partially or totally naked, is subject to an intricate system of constraints and prescriptions, and the attendant normative complexity requires an ordered mental manipulation of alternatives. Vicarious sexual imagery serves, thus, as a means of reality testing and the refinement of alternative selection.

Vicarious sexual gratification as a symbolic replacement for physical sexual fulfillment represents a socially acceptable substitute. Vicarious sexual imagery is an important adjunct and supplement to carnal gratification both enhancing and facilitating sexual interaction between individuals. Because of its emotional capriciousness and its social import, vicarious sexual indulgence is also subject, to some degree, to social norm, especially in terms of the presence of stimuli that can precipitate it, and the degree to which it impinges on the prerogatives of others. Vicarious carnal diversion may be an essentially private activity, but its social toleration is especially sensitive to the degree to which its exercise tends to invade the privacy and emotional equilibrium of others.

PHYSICAL AND SEXUAL PRIVACY

In our society, considerable stress is placed on the individual right of physical privacy. Additionally, the individual is constrained to avoid nakedness except when alone or in the presence of the most intimately related persons such as a spouse, and to perform bodily eliminative functions such as urination and defecation in solitude or only in carefully sequestered and designated areas, such as stalls in public restrooms otherwise. Similarly, sexual activity of any variety is considered patently inappropriate except when carried out in seclusion.[36] In spite of the penchant for insuring modesty, and protecting the privacy of sexual conduct, with attendant mechanisms of social control and sanctions for the violation of such boundaries of privacy, there would also appear to be a preoccupation with some persons to intrude on the bodily privacy of others and to derive satisfaction and especially vicarious sexual gratification, from unauthorized and clandestine observation.

Unauthorized observation of personal anatomy, or sexual activities, occurs at varying levels of intent and intensity and in the face of differential barriers that attempt to insure that sexual modesty, decorum, and privacy are insured. To some degree, it may be that unauthorized observation for purposes of salacious gratification, even if relatively innocuous in import, is behaviorally endemic to our population.

Peeping or voyeurism may be something of a national pastime in various unstructured forms and conceptualized as innocent, even if lacking in dignity and/or propriety. In other forms, it may be viewed as pathological, or even criminal and may elicit severe sanctions and sexual labeling of the transgressor. Interestingly, not all societies countenance the invasion of anatomical or sexual privacy, even tacitly, like our own. In Bali, for example, the women traditionally went bare-breasted. Although the female breast is anatomically desexualized to a considerable degree in comparison with the United States, it is not without some sexual symbolism or lacking in aesthetic appeal. Nevertheless, there was an almost total absence of leering or staring at the naked torsos.[37] Furthermore, women (and men) often bathed naked in groups in streams by the side of the road. If a man or men walked past the naked females while they were bathing, the men would avert their eyes or discreetly pretend not to notice. The Balinese put the very highest cultural priority on personal, including anatomical privacy, and if walking with a foreigner past the naked bathers, might be inclined to inform the outsider that they should avert their eyes since "your eyes should not go where they are not welcome."[38] A clandestine voyeur would be subject to greater social scorn than even a public starer, and even more importantly, most Balinese would have great discomfort with the impropriety of a self-image of one who intrudes on the anatomical or sexual privacy of others.

In the United States, persons walking through a city park might glimpse a young couple locked in a passionate embrace, perhaps involved in relatively intimate exploration of each other's body. Persons in Bali might totally ignore the scene, individuals in France might seemingly ignore it or dismiss it with a shrug.[39] The U.S. strollers, however, would probably be more inclined to stare, perhaps even stop to observe and even call it to the attention of their fellow strollers. In some places, they might even seek a policeman to have the overly romantic couple arrested for creating a public nuisance. Often, young females may retreat to rooftops or isolated stretches of beach seeking the privacy that will permit them to sunbathe *sans* swimsuit, topless, or at least in an overly revealing bikini. Not infrequently, however, pilots in small planes, seeing the sunbathers, may purposely fly low back and forth over the spectacle of tanning flesh in an effort to get a better look. If not pilots in small planes, then male occupants of higher floors in the adjoining buildings may strain their necks "observing" the sunbathers from their vantage point.

Peeping Versus Voyeurism

Edward Sagarin in his discussion of observation and privacy underscored the distinction previously made by Paul Gephard and his colleagues at the Institute for Sex Research between voyeurs and peepers.[40] According to Sagarin, voyeurs are observers who may occasionally look with salacious intent but seldom go beyond this point in their observational activity. The peeper, on the other hand, may be compulsive and regular, perhaps even to the extent of highly institutionalized routines of clandestine observation of other persons when they are disrobed or engaged in sexual activity. The true peeper may (but not necessarily) move on to other and more serious sexually gratifying activities. Under this dichotomy, voyeurism is a relatively common and innocent pastime, satisfying curiosity, and providing momentary carnal gratification, while peeping is more intense, regularized and pathological, affording satisfactions for more deep-seated pathological socio-psychological needs. As Sagarian views it, "Yes, we are all voyeurs to some extent, but that does not make us all peepers."[41]

The *boulevardier,* leaning against the parking meter, surveying the sidewalk parade of feminine pultritude, and especially attentive to the undulating *derriere* of the blonde in the tight mini-skirt just passing, may be mentally undressing her and imagining her anatomical movements in a horizontal rather than vertical position and enjoying every salacious, vicarious moment of his carnal fantasy.[42] Such a person is a voyeur, but inasmuch as the blonde in the tight skirt is displaying the abundance of her physical endowments publicly, the staring male can hardly be said to be invading her anatomical privacy, and in fact, she may not even know, much less object, to being stared at. The 35-year-old spinster at the beach, who devotes considerable attention to the young, virile-looking lifeguard and his bulging biceps and strong loins, imagining herself locked in his powerful embrace, crazed with lust, is also something of a voyeur. In both cases, however, these are essentially innocuous sexual diversions—a moment of innocent but tantalizing fantasy and vicarious carnal gratification. Such instances of sexually motivated observation are quite different from those often indulged in by the compulsive peeper.

Sagarin relates the account of a husband and wife in Gilford, N.H. in 1964, who discovered that their rented house had its master bedroom wired for eavesdropping. Hidden microphones and wires carried sounds from the bedroom to the landlord's nearby house.[43] Clearly, the landlord had carefully conspired to listen in on the couple's pillow talk. When the couple made the discovery, they were less than pleased about their landlord's avocation, and subsequently sued him and won. It was also reported a short time back that some single females renting an apartment heard noises in the wall and came to discover that their landlord had constructed carpeted crawl spaces and passages in the walls of their apartment and spent his idle hours peering at them from peepholes in the secret passageways.

The term "peeping," for many, often brings to mind the legend of Lady Godiva, the wife of a Saxon nobleman who allegedly rode naked through the streets of Coventry as a condition of her husband relieving his vassals of a particularly oppressive tax. The grateful townspeople, so the story goes on, voluntarily shuttered their windows and refused to look at the lady's nakedness. One citizen of the town, Tom the tailor, however, did with salacious intent, peep at Lady Godiva and was either struck blind, or blinded by the townspeople for his wicked vicarious debauchery, depending on the version of the legend. Peepers or voyeurs have often been labeled as "Peeping Toms" as a result of the legend, which incidently, has been branded as a complete fabrication.[44]

PEEPING AND VOYEURISM IN ART AND LITERATURE

Peeping and voyeurism has often been a theme in American literature and art. Thomas Hart Benton, for example, painted several canvases depicting a peeping scene. In his *Persephone* completed in 1939, he draws on the Greek legend of the goddess of fertility, Persephone, who was abducted by the lord of the underworld, Hades. He chose to illustrate this legend in a dreamlike painting that shows a naked Persephone, languidly reclining under a tree by a quiet stream. Hades is shown as an old and wrinkled farmer, hiding behind the tree, his attention fixed on the body of the young, naked woman.[45] Earlier in 1938, Benton had also painted *Susanna and the Elders.* In this canvass he took his theme and the name of the painting from the Biblical story. He shows a nude Susanna sitting on the banks of a stream about to lower herself into the water to bathe. In the background, hidden behind a tree, two Ozark rednecks watch the naked Susanna.[46] A movie of recent years, *The Marriage of a*

Young Stockbroker, starring Richard Benjamin, concerns the trials and tribulations of a young man who is a voyeur or Peeping Tom. Even after his marriage, he is more aroused by looking in his neighbors' windows than by his new wife. Almost the entire movie addresses itself to his voyeuristic adventures, but at the end of the movie he apparently has become adjusted to the more conventional modes of sexual gratification. Various popular songs, such as the previously mentioned "Standing on the Corner," tell of the vicarious pleasures of girl watching, and keyhole and door-transom peeking has been a near ubiquitous component or theme in many movie, stage, and television comedy skits. In James Gould Cozzens' Pulitzer Prize-winning novel, *Guard of Honor,* dealing with an Army Air Force base in Florida in 1943, the author has the commanding officer of the WAC Detachment complain to the Base Commander that when the enlisted WACs go to the base hospital for treatment or examinations, they are peeped at.[47] Cozzens has her report that:

> In general, we are not very well satisfied with the arrangements the Base Hospital makes for the regulation physical inspections of enlisted women. It isn't convenient, having to send them all over there; but I quite understand that until the infirmary here in the Area is finished, those are the nearest adequate facilities. Though, of course, they aren't adequate, either, Colonel. The girls reporting have no proper place to undress. It is right next to an orderly room, or something of the sort, used by male enlisted personnel. Though I think disciplinary action was taken in one case, some of the men continue to make little holes or openings through the walls so they can see in, and the girls know that, and I think if they can't stop the men from doing it, then they must give them a different room. I brought the matter up with Major McCreery, but he said there was no other room, and anyway, a thorough inspection did not disclose any such holes now. There had been some, but they had been stopped in such a way that they can be, and are, reopened whenever the girls are undressing, and then covered up, so anyone inspecting doesn't find them.[48]

Peeping and voyeurism is sufficiently constituent to our sexual culture that it is not infrequently depicted in all of the various media. Interestingly, peeping and voyeurism in art, literature, or the movies is not usually portrayed as pathological behavior or a perversion, rather it is presented more as simply an expression of idiosyncratic sexual activity or as in the Cozzens' novel as a game-like form of vicarious sexual gratification. Cozzens' episode, although fictional, is not without valid foundation. Many years ago, as a Lieutenant of

Military Police in the "old brown shoe army," the author encountered a somewhat similar case. In this particular instance, the military base housed a United States Disciplinary Barracks. The "trusty" inmates had various work assignments around the post including filling and maintaining the coal-fired furnaces in all the buildings. In this connection, they were relatively unsupervised and came and went as they pleased. Even the WAC BOQ (Bachelor Officers' Quarters) Building had a coal furnace tended by "trusty" USDB inmates. The inmates, apparently frustrated by ennui, sought diversion by burning peepholes through the walls between the furnace room and the WAC officers' rooms, with the hot poker they used to stoke the coal. They might have enjoyed the vicarious stimulation that their avocation afforded almost indefinitely had not one overly eager inmate made the mistake of pushing the hot poker through a wall without first checking to be sure there were no WAC occupants on the other side. As it turned out, there were several WAC officers sitting around in the room talking when suddenly a sizzling hot poker end thrust itself out of the wall, practically under the very nose of one of the startled women. Needless to say, the inmates' gratifying pastime was involuntarily terminated shortly thereafter.

SCIENTIFIC VOYEURISM

Voyeurism is, in large measure, situational, inasmuch as it may be viewed as innocent pastime, pathological sexual pursuit, or even research mechanism, depending on the persons, situations, and circumstances involved. One writer, some years ago, reported that a group of behavioral science researchers at one university undertook a study of the sexual talk, and other details of their lovemaking, of married couples. In this connection, they concealed tiny microphone-transmitters in the bedrooms of couples who lived in a college housing project on campus. The hidden devices transmitted the sexual sounds and talk of the young people and the researchers subsequently advised the couples about the project, promised anonymity and requested their permission to use the recorded material in their research. According to the writer, not one couple refused permission.[49] In this particular instance, presumably all scientific safeguards were employed to protect the anonymity of the couples and their recorded sounds. Nevertheless, it is difficult to forget the instance of the attorney who worked for the Congressional Committee that was investigating the Nixon tapes, who for a lark, took one of the tapes to which he had access to a party and played it for the titillation of the guests. In recent years, the published results of sex research conducted by social scientists and others have often been public best sellers. It would appear that the published accounts of such sex research serve curiosity, if not voyeuristic, needs that exist in many people. People want to know what other people are doing sexually. They may simply seek a modal, and, thus, presumably normative, yardstick by which to gauge their own sexual activities. In effect, some persons seek legitimation of their own variants of sexual behavior, in the findings of sexual researchers. Other readers of sex research data may wish to be educated—to learn what directions their sexual proclivities may and can take. The modal results of sex research becomes a kind of guide book, as it were. Yet, others who avidly absorb the findings of sexologists may use the insights they obtain as verification of the abnormality, if not perversions, of the sexual behavior of others, thus allowing themselves the assurance and security of super-normality. For whatever the various reasons, insights into the sexual persuasions and activities of others provide rich vicarious fare for many people, and both the original reports themselves such as those published on the work of Kinsey *et al.,* Masters and Johnson, Sorensen, and others, as well as the secondary commentaries and critiques of such reports have usually become best sellers. Even fictional accounts of sex research such as *The Harrad Experiment, Venus Unmasked,* and *The Experiment* have also enjoyed an appreciative public reception.

Sex research has traditionally relied on the sampling of attitudes and opinions and on the recall of details of sexual activities. More recently, however, sex research has, in some instances, become very much observational in nature. In much of the research of Masters and Johnson, laboratory observation of actual masturbation, machine-simulated coitus, and heterosexual coitus between couples, married or otherwise, was the principal means of generating data. The research team became, in effect, objective voyeurs, observing the sexual performers from behind two-way mirrors.[50] The invasion of anatomical privacy, however, has long been sanctioned, for functional purposes, by appropriate professionals. Physicians routinely examine the naked bodies and manipulate the most intimate portions of the anatomy of patients of the opposite sex. As professionals, physicians are supposed to affect a detached, depersonalized and desexualized approach to the naked body of the patient. The male physician, for example, does not conceptualize the female patient as a sex object, or view her anatomy *gestalt* or piecemeal, within an erotic context. Her body instead, theoretically, becomes merely a malfunctioning organic machine, as it were. Nevertheless, some doctors tell interesting and humorous stories about their examinations of particularly attractive female patients. One physician's biographical account of his intern period in a large hospital recalled a young female patient with especially well-endowed breasts who found herself being examined by several residents and physicians after they heard she came to have her fractured shoulder checked and was wearing nothing on top underneath her coat.[51] A similar incident was related by another physician who had taken his residency at a large and renowned teaching hospital in a southern city several years ago. He told of a well-known exotic dancer and stripper, noted for the size of her breasts, who had been admitted to the hospital for minor surgery. When she was taken to the operating room for the surgery, the word went out around the hospital, and a substantial number of the residents and interns gathered in the operating room observation amphitheater for a distant glimpse. Others more strategically located in the operating room itself, were afforded the opportunity for a leisurely and detailed, if not salacious, view of the dancer's imposing hypermammary development.

Voyeurism as Curiosity

As suggested above, there is apparently a strong curiosity element in voyeurism and especially among young males. Young children are prone to peek and spy on adults as well as other children, motivated essentially by an anatomical curiosity. Young boys may attempt to peep at their mothers or sisters when they are dressing or in the bathroom. Young children of both sexes often are caught "inspecting" the genitalia of even younger children and playing "doctor and nurse," a game which usually involves looking, if not touching, each other's genitals. It is a relatively common exercise in satisfying anatomical curiosity among many youngsters. In this connection, Chilman has commented:

> ... It is further observed that little children, through social learning, generally acquire the idea that all matters pertaining to sex have a special aura of forbidden pleasures. Seeing others nude and exposing

the self (especially when the opposite sex is involved) take on exciting, erotic meanings. Throughout childhood probably most children engage in these activities—ah! the joy of "playing doctor."[52]

Chilman goes on to say that:

> ... Sex play, consisting of exhibitionism, voyeurism and mutual mas-
> turbation occurs fairly frequently in groups of boys between the ages
> of 8 and 13.[53]

Voyeuristic activities may sometimes continue into adolescence, often also motivated largely by curiosity, and if the youth is discovered or apprehended while peeping he may be labeled or described as a criminal. Adolescents who are brought in for treatment are almost always male.[54] There appears to be something of a double standard operating in regard to social norms that sanction voyeurism or exhibitionism, for that matter. If a male even accidently observes a female while undressed he risks being labeled a peeper. If, on the other hand, a female observes a male while undressed, she may be viewed as the victim and the nude male may even be defined as an exhibitionist and, thus, possibly a criminal.[55] Adolescent voyeurism may be compulsive and, thus, defined as pathological, but in many instances, the voyeuristic episode may have been an isolated incident, perhaps even accidental. In the instance of the former, Chilman has asserted that:

> Those adolescents who continue to express sexual interests on a direct,
> childish level of overt and compulsive voyeuristic or exhibitionistic
> behavior are thought, by many students of the subject, to be displaying
> psychological problems.[56]

As she goes on to say, boys are less likely to receive sex information from parents or teachers than are girls, but are socialized to think that they should be more expert on the topic of sex than are girls. From such a premise, it might be possible to conclude that boys are under more pressure to acquire sex information—through clandestine and proscribed means such as voyeurism, if necessary.[57] Some such peeping incidents may involve a group of boys, and the deviant activity may be precipitated from a dare. Presumably, some male adolescents do have a genuine curiosity about female nudity or sexual intercourse that impels them to run the risks attendant to peeping in the windows of others. For some youngsters peeping probably has a dimension of thrill devoid of erotic content. It involves stealth, cunning, danger, and above all, excitement. In this sense, peeping would not be unlike "swiping" watermelons or some similar prank. For some adolescent males, however, peeping may be an emotional respite from stress or fatigue (such as during examinations) and such adolescents may enjoy normal relationships with females of their own age.[58] The voyeuristic activities provide vicarious sexual gratification and, in addition to the carnal catharsis, also serve as an emotional bridge, as it were, spanning the periods of strain and emotional disequilibrium between times of stable heterosexual relationships with females of the same age.

If young children and especially young boys are curious about sex and sex organs, so, too, are men. American adults in general, in spite of their increasing liberal attitudes regarding sexual behavior, would appear to remain decidedly unsophisticated about the physiology of sex. The enormous sale of sex manuals, marital happiness books, and various semi-scientific treatises that define the rudiments of sexual anatomy and processes, often ordered through the mail and not infrequently delivered in a "plain brown envelope," would seem to testify to the gnawing curiosity and yearning to learn about the myriad mysteries of sex. The profusion of sexual therapy clinics that have sprung up around the country to spread the Masters and Johnson gospel often have to devote much of their therapist staff's time to simple educational efforts with their patients. These efforts may include an indoctrination into post-elementary sexual techniques, familiarization with a fuller repertoire of coital positions, and instruction in facilitative procedures for producing multiple orgasms in the female. In some instances, however, the sexual therapy may have to begin with a basic lesson in sexual anatomy of the opposite sex—a kind of sexual organ "show and tell," as it were. A purported former sexual therapist wrote that she frequently afforded her patients the opportunity to satisfy their curiosity (and also increase their quotient of sexual knowledge) by letting them inspect her genitalia. To this end, she often supplied the patient with a gynecological speculum and a magnifying mirror. As the patient devoted his clinical attention to her perineal area, she maintained a lecture-like running commentary on the functions of, and physiological processes attendant to, the various portions of her genital anatomy.[59] It is difficult to assess the literary validity of reports such as those offered by sex therapists writing their memoirs for the salacious book trade. It is perhaps somewhat easier to document the clinical anatomy demonstrations offered by some carnival strippers. Most traveling carnivals have a "girlie" show or "musical review," as it is sometime euphemistically called, among their standard attractions. Most carnie girlie shows have performers with more gymnastic enthusiasm than musical talent. As a result, while music is played during the show, the girl performers, sometimes even tone deaf and ignorant of any real dance steps, entertain the audience with a mixture of bumps and grinds, lots of bare flesh, and an assortment of physical gyrations intended to simulate the passion of orgasm, if not coitus itself. The girls may be labeled as strippers, but in the parlance of the carnival business, their particular brand of exotic dancing and stripping is known as "kootch."[60] Some carnivals catering more to the family trade pride themselves on the high level of propriety that they project. Such carnivals are known as "Sunday School Shows." In Sunday School Shows, there are no crooked gambling games and the girls in the musical reviews don't take *everything* off. Some carnivals, however, are not Sunday School shows, and the girlie shows in such carnivals are often referred to as "strong." In a "strong" kootch show, the vicarious imagery and sexual stimulation is facilitated as much as possible. Such strong acts involve stripping totally naked, particularly lewd gyrations and gymnastics, considerable simulation of coitus (such as working to a "snorting" pole, a large pole on stage that symbolically represents a man or even more symbolically, his penis. The performer does her bumps and grinds against the pole and ultimately pretends to have an orgasm) and unusual feats of anatomical prowess. One carnival "kootch" show operator, for example, provided some examples of such anatomical prowess and related that:

> . . . In Kutztown, Pa., where I worked, we had a girl whose twat was so big she could get five ping-pong balls up it and then bounce them out one by one. Lots of girls know how to blow a smoke ring. One kid I know has an act where she uses a fluorescent light which you can see lit up inside.[61]

"Strong" kootch shows also cater to audiences who apparently have only minimal powers of visual sexual imagery. Vicarious gratification requires a heavy assist of genuine tactile sensory input. For such audiences, some strong kootch shows feature what is known in the trade as "audience participation night." On such occasions, the spectators are allowed to crowd close to the stage and are permitted or encouraged to touch and handle the genital area of the girl performer. The girls often spread their legs to accommodate and encourage the men in the audience. Such strong acts are sometimes not without hazards for the girls, however. Kootch dancers have to be careful not to get too close to the audiences lest they lose control of them and become hurt. Naked kootch dancers have even been carried off the stage bodily by an excited audience, and one dancer reported that a middle-aged, well-dressed man who followed her show from town to town, and always stood close to the platform with his elbows resting on the stage, got so excited at one performance that he leaped up and bit the performer on her vagina, which then required several stitches.[62] In addition to providing vicarious sexual gratification, however, carnival kootch shows also satisfy the anatomical curiosity of some of the audience, and have considerable educational value in this regard. In many shows, for example, part of the act, and particularly the finale, may involve squatting on the edge of the platform so that the audience can inspect the genitalia area of the performer. In this regard, the girls often insert their thumb and forefinger into their vagina to spread it open for better examination. Some audience members, particularly those who are seasoned kootch show fans may even bring flashlights so that their examination of the girl's genitalia can be more thorough and clinical. According to one writer, this lets the audience members "examine clinically and under laboratory conditions, what they 'couldn't see at home.' "[63] Some kootch performers are particularly well known in some areas, inside and out. In speaking of one kootch dancer, the writer observed that:

> . . . and generations of gentlemen from the Pinetree State of Maine to the Show-Me State of Missouri owe their knowledge of "women's parts" to Peaches La May (a featured dancer for many years in a large carnival).[64]

It would appear that men are not unique in their curiosity concerning genital anatomy and physiology, although they would seem to have been the most active and obvious in their behavioral quest to assuage their anatomical inquisitiveness. Recently, and constituent to the women's liberation movement, various "gynecological self-help clinics" have been established as a means of helping women "to liberate their sexual parts from the tyranny of male gynecologists." In such clinics, it is reported that women may take the opportunity to examine one another anatomically, "as a means of familiarizing themselves with the female genitalia."[65] Participants in these clinics buy a plastic speculum (an instrument for dilating the vagina), and with the assistance of a mirror and flashlight can examine themselves and each other "in depth, gynecologically at least, for the first time." According to the author of this report, "some participants report this as an exhilarating experience, a bringing of light into what has previously been a dark place." The clinics are not only intended to provide better gynecological and anatomical knowledge for women, but also to provide them with more of a sense of identity with their sexual organs. As the author puts it:

> There is no doubt that women have not taken the kind of pride in their genitalia that men have, and there is no reason why they should not. Each has its own felicities of design and neither can prosper without the other.[66]

In effect, the women's liberation movement is making an effort to create a kind of "my vagina is beautiful" ideology in the female vanguard of social change.

If there is human curiosity about sex organs, and the sex act itself, there is also some degree of human curiosity about animal sex. Although Kinsey did report that females are less curious about male genitals, than are males about female sexual anatomy,[67] nevertheless some writers have suggested that girls more than boys are likely to experience sexual excitement upon observing the copulation of animals.[68] Although there may be some debate about the differential preferences of the two sexes for watching animals having sexual intercourse, it would appear that there is considerable interest on the part of many persons. Edward Sagarin, for example, asserts:

> That humans of all ages, and of both sexes would be attracted to the spectacle of animal copulation seems easy to accept, although one must express considerable doubt, for want of validating evidence, that this occurs more frequently in girls than in boys, in women than in men. But, more important, there is some question as to whether the attraction to the spectacle constitutes an arousal.[69]

It is interesting to note that many localities have ordinances which prohibit the breeding of livestock, or pets, within public view, because of the risk of offending the community standards of propriety. During the Nazi regime before and during World War II, it was reported that Hermann Goring, the reichsführer of Germany, would invite guests to his estate outside Berlin, and then have a bull mate with a cow for the entertainment and edification of his guests. At various times in the past, copulating animals were featured as acts in some of the seamier night spots in some large cities around the world, and as a variation, animals copulating with humans would also be included as part of the act. Balboa, Panama, for example, had night clubs that featured a donkey having intercourse with a woman. Presumably the large number of sailors and tourists of diverse nationalities visiting the town seeking diversion required entertainment of the lowest common denominator. In recent years, there have been reports of persons involved in the "swinging" or "swapping" circles arranging animal/human sexual episodes for the stimulation and vicarious sexual gratification of themselves and others in their groups.[70] Perhaps the *pièce de résistance* of animal sex as entertainment, however, was a full length, "underground" movie, shown in some San Francisco adult movie houses a few years back to capacity audiences. The film in question was called *Animal Lovers* and portrayed the female star engaged in coitus with various types of beasts including a dog, donkey, and pig.

Voyeurism and Occupational Opportunity Structure

A significant proportion of all voyeurism takes place on the job. In some vocational settings there is more of an opportunity structure for the observation of something that is sexually stimulating, and vicariously gratifying. In some work the individual may be literally surrounded by partially nude members of the opposite sex, and in yet other occupational settings, the occupational practitioners may simply be strategically located in terms of opportunity of viewing sex or nudity. The surveyor with his telescopic transit may sometimes be privy to a couple making love in the distant glade, just as airplane pilots may see more than their share of nude sunbathing bodies. Persons who work around models such as photographers and persons in some garment plants may have an inordinate opportunity to see bare flesh, but opportunity structure may be based on nothing more than the vantage point of height. Truck drivers, and especially the big trailer rigs sit much higher in their vehicles than do drivers of normal automobiles. Thus, they often can look down into automobiles as they pass and can observe things that the automobile occupants may not be aware of. It is only necessary to listen in briefly to some major highway CB chatter among truckers to obtain some idea of the quantity and quality of their voyeuristic activities. Truckers do like to share, and they are almost compulsive about reporting to their fellow truckers every female driver who hikes her skirt up past her thighs to stay cool, and every couple who undertakes some intimate petting while driving down the interstate.

Occupational voyeurism may also occur within other work contexts, sometimes from less mobile, but perhaps even higher, vantage points than truck cabs. One recent account of "peeping" among construction workers on commercial building projects, details the specifics of such workers "watching the windows" of near-by buildings for diversion and vicarious sexual gratification.[71] The construction tradesmen working on tall buildings have the vantage point of height to help them look in the windows of near-by apartment buildings. Presumably the people in the buildings close by are not used to closing their blinds, and tend to ignore the new construction and the workmen, at least initially. The workmen, thus, have ample opportunity for peeping. It becomes a major diversion and means of coping with the ennui of a monotonous manual job. Peeping is in large part, a collective activity. Workmen are morally obligated to tell each other about interesting (and erotic) things that they see, and to call the sights to the attention of others so they, too, can participate. Skill in peeping is required, and the workmen go to considerable lengths to enhance, and facilitate their opportunities for peeping. Voyeurism of this kind does not appear to be pathological, but, instead, may be functional because of the way in which it serves as an integrating force for the work group and the communicative aspect of the activity magnified the vicarious import of seeing nudity and sexual behavior. In any event, the article does raise the question of whether voyeurism is a much more widely occurring activity than had been suspected.

VICARIOUS SEXUAL GRATIFICATION AND HOSTILITY

As many writers have pointed out, sex is as much in the mind as in the genitals. Both physical and vicarious sexual gratification require fantasy and sexual authorities have long suggested that fantasy is a healthy component of sexual arousal. No matter how unusual or convoluted the sexual fantasy, so such persons asserted, sexual fantasy helped stimulate and embellish sexual excitement and was, thus, functional. In recent years, people have been encouraged to give expression to their sexual fantasy and to explore and expand the parameters of the vicarious carnality, "unless whatever arouses us also alarms us, or leads to bad sexual experiences."[72] At least one scholar has challenged the concept of sexual fantasy being innocent carnal machinations of the mind and memory and, thus, healthy. Sexual fantasy and its latent function may be, in effect, neurotic.[73] Robert J. Stoller, a California psychoanalyst, has contended that, "except for a few rare individuals, human sexual excitement is usually generated by hostility."[74] It has long been recognized that there is a relatively close interface between love and hate, and that there are linkages between sex, aggression, pain, and violence. Love bites and scratching in the heat of passion, sadomasochism, and even rape in some instances all speak to these linkages.[75] Stoller is more explicit in his assertion that "the theme present in (sexual) scripts that produce sexual excitement is the desire to harm someone."[76] In effect, the stuff of which fantasy is made is hostility. The sexual partner is not, however, necessarily the direct object of the vicarious hostility. The hostility may result from some sexual trauma or frustration that the individual experienced in the past, possibly even in childhood. Sexual fantasy, then, is not idle daydream, but carefully structured and coded scripts by which the individual can accommodate and work out these "lingering problems from childhood." Such scripts generally require a victim and the sexual partner is cast in the role of the victim and is a kind of symbolic object of the vicarious hostility. The vicarious scenario permits the individual, hurt as a child, to become victorious and conquer and overcome his residual trauma and frustrations by fantasizing the infliction of pain, trauma, degradation, or indignities on the sexual partner. "Frustration and trauma are converted into triumph."[77] Stoller contends that:

> This dominance of hostility in erotism attempts to undo childhood traumas and frustrations that threaten the development of masculinity and femininity (gender identity). The same sorts of dynamics, though in different mixes and degrees, are found in almost everyone, those labeled perverse and those not so labeled.[78]

Stoller sees a number of mental factors, which are present in perversions, that are also constituent to sexual excitement in general. These factors include, "hostility, mystery, risk, illusion, revenge, reversal of trauma or frustration to triumph, safety factors, and dehumanization (fetishization)."[79] Thus, the individual may vicariously take revenge on the character in which the sexual partner is cast, even to the extent of degrading "him or her into nonhumanness or to the status of part object."[80] In some instances, a fetish, a nonhumanized object, may then be substituted for the nonhuman- ized person and endowed "with the humanity stolen from the person on whom one is to be revenged." Sexual fantasy is, according to Stoller, autobiographically disguised as fiction which hides the sexual conflicts, traumas, and frustration from the individual's past. By working the sexual partner into the scenario as victim, revenge and reversal can be accomplished and hostility can energize the sexual excitement. According to this line of reasoning, then, one's capacity for vicarious carnal gratification may be tied to the effectiveness of the mechanisms of degradation employed in one's sexual fantasy. Some therapists and researchers have, however, taken exception to Stoller's thesis.[81]

THE ETIOLOGY OF VOYEURISM

Even though the vast majority of all voyeuristic activity may be relatively harmless in intent, and inoffensive in importance, some peeping behavior, and especially compulsive peeping, may be symp- tomatic of more serious pathology. Such compulsive voyeurism has been labeled offensive voyeurism by Irvin Yalom who has studied a number of clinical cases, and concluded that some compulsive voyeurs do go on to commit more serious crimes, and spoke of such voyeurs equating looking with destroying, or with punishment.[82] According to Yalom, some voyeurs speak of going on a "safari to seek his prey," and others who stated that "peeping punished women who were careless with their nudity."[83] There are some voyeurs who conceptualize their unauthorized viewing as getting a kind of psychological "upper hand" on their victims. They see their victims in a moment of vulnerability but their victims may not even be aware of it. Voyeurism is symbolic seduction. One offender told of peeking at a female as being a means of defying both mother and society by "getting a girl sexually and not having to marry her." Yalom does, however, cite instances of voyeurs who ultimately became more aggressive and committed offenses more serious than merely peeping, such as vandalism, burglary, attempted rape, and arson. It is the sense of the forbidden, the clandestine, and the lack of detection that appeals to the peeper, not just the nudity or the sexual behavior observed. Some voyeurs may even knock on the window or otherwise try to obtain the attention of the victim, but in general, the true compulsive voyeur derives his gratification from the "challenge of the forbidden." Yalom asserts that some voyeurs are almost disinterested in pornography, sexual behavior, and nudity, only enjoying such salacious sights if they can be obtained without detection. Thus, the true compulsive peeper is not so much motivated by sexual curiosity or even the desire for visual stimuli to promote vicarious sexual gratification as in violating the normative prohibitions against the invasion of anatomical and sexual privacy.[84] Yalom even suggests a causal relationship between serious crime and voyeurism. As he conceptualized the relationship:

> The clinical material suggests even a causal relationship between the two acts in the cases where a major crime is committed when the urge to peep is frustrated, where a major crime alternated with voyeurism (each fulfilling the same need), and where the voyeuristic impulse, to quote the patient, is "converted" into a major offense.[85]

As Yalom sees it, then, voyeurism may even act as a latent mechanism that sometimes replaces more violent crime. He suggests that, "it is entirely possible that voyeurism may be used as a defense against aggression in that it is safer to look and destroy unconsciously than to act and destroy literally . . . "[86]

Taking voyeurism a step further and probing another dimension of vicarious carnal gratification is the *frotteur*. Here the individual contrives to accomplish a bodily intimacy through seemingly innocent or accidental means. This usually takes the form of touching, caressing, or brushing against the object of attention. Chesser describes such an encounter and relates:

> Midway between the voyeur and the exhibitionist is the frotteur. He chooses a crowded train or escalator and rubs against the woman in front of him, usually her buttocks. If she protests, he apologizes and assures her that he was pushed from behind. Unless his action is too obvious, he generally avoids trouble, though his victim is not always convinced it was accidental. The buttocks may or may not have any special significance for him. They may be merely the most convenient point of contact. It cannot be said that he does any serious harm. But if we look on all these deviations objectively can we not say the same in most cases? If we candidly examine ourselves, how many people can honestly deny that some of the most *outré* manifestations of sex have been enjoyed in fantasy?[87]

The tactile stimulation produced by touching or rubbing against the victim presumably promotes fantasy and subsequently affords vicarious sexual gratification. Touching, apparently offers more reality than looking and more easily precipitates fantasy.

Smith, in his overview of the literature on voyeurism, offers some insightful findings concerning peepers as opposed to non-peepers based on earlier studies.[88] Children and youth who peep, he says, usually do so in groups. Peepers almost never watch females whom they know well, for they do "not find in known females the satisfaction [that each] seeks." Peepers are likely to be an only child or the youngest child, and report a good relationship with parents but a poor relationship between the parents. Peepers are less likely to have lived in an all-female household, less likely to have had nocturnal emissions, more likely to have had "sadomasochistic, animal, and bizarre" masturbatory fantasies, and more likely to worry over masturbation. Peepers are less likely to have petted and were slow to begin having premarital coitus. A relatively high percentage of peepers have had homosexual experiences that resulted in orgasm, and a relatively high percentage had juvenile court convictions and were more prone to minor criminality. Peepers had less of a tendency to gamble, be an alcoholic or use drugs and were in terms of neuroses and psychoses, more mentally healthy. Peepers as opposed to non-peepers were less likely to be married. In general, peepers do not appear to be prone to serious antisocial behavior, but, according to Smith, some researchers have reported, "a marked tendency to progress from minor to more severe crime among voyeurs." Interestingly, some studies of women's fantasy have suggested that women "do respond with sexual stimulation to sexually explicit visual stimuli, e.g., pictures, films, and live men and women." They also "express voyeuristic interests and have either indulged in such activities or fantasized doing so." One such voyeuristic activity, analogous to the practice of men, "breast watching," is that of "crotch watching," or the "observing of men's trousers in hopes of detecting sexual excitement and to mentally compare attributes of male anatomy." According to Smith, "other more blatant forms of voyeuristic activity are also common."[89]

There has been an attempt to explain voyeurism from a number of different perspectives. Such attempts have included the use of psychoanalytic theory and concluded that voyeurs had fixated a "partial (sexual) impulse" at an infantile level and accordingly it had not been "incorporated into the process of forepleasure" and thus "it became a second drive independent of the sex drive, which retains as its aim copulation." Copulation and voyeurism become two separate means of sexual gratification. As Smith[90] sums it up:

> A person could thus have a seemingly normal heterosexual life whose aim is sexual intercourse, yet at the same time have a drive whose aim is the satisfaction of a partial impulse, e.g., voyeurism.

Other theories of voyeurism have included the idea that they suffer from castration fear and must "search from woman to woman trying to find a woman with a penis," thus proving "that men and women do have penises."[91] Some have suggested that voyeurism results from "one-trial learning" that may have occurred during one "crucial, although possibly accidental, sexual experience." Thus, voyeurism, like other sexual perversions, is said to be explainable in terms of "stimuli, responses, and reinforcements."[92] Modifications of the learning theory approach include social learning and modeling theory. Here, it is believed that sexual deviations, such as voyeurism, occur without actual operant conditioning, but rather by exposure to real-life models who perform certain patterns of behavior which may be imitated by others. As Smith describes it, "thus, behavior can be learned by seeing someone else perform the behavior without having to perform the behavior oneself."[93] The sexual deviancy could then become "self-reinforcing" because of its "tension-reducing effects" in addition to its sexual properties.

Many authorities do not think that voyeurism should be treated as a crime inasmuch as there is no injured party or victim. Others have seen it as a nuisance or victimless crime. Generally speaking, it is treated as a minor crime and may be punished on the basis of an allied offense such as trespassing, or disorderly conduct. The punishment might be light although, in some cases, the penalties might include a heavy fine and a jail sentence. The punishment may well depend on the attitude of the arresting officer, judge, and person observed, as well as the record of the offender and his socio-economic status.[94] Unfortunately, the voyeur may be categorized and residually dealt with as a "sex offender." In California this could mean having to register at the police station or local courthouse in the community of residence as a convicted sex offender. It is necessary to obtain a "Certificate of Rehabilitation" from the state in order to be relieved of this duty.[95] In some countries like England, voyeurism is not treated as a criminal offense but as a civil offense.

Inasmuch as voyeurism is usually viewed as a sexual perversion, it sometimes is treated through counseling or psychotherapy using a variety of techniques and approaches including hypnosis, behavior modification, systematic desensitization, aversion conditioning, and assertiveness training.[96] As Smith warns, however, "sexual enjoyment from looking is a natural instinct and a normal part of sexual behavior," and that the problem is not so much the "elimination of voyeuristic sexual impulses," but rather insuring that those impulses are satisfied through "socially acceptable means."[97]

COMMERCIALIZED VOYEURISM

In spite of the almost limitless opportunities for personalized patterns of voyeurism and peeping, and the attendant vicarious carnal gratification, many persons prefer "store-bought" or commercial voyeuristic encounters. In times past, many brothels, in addition to providing the usual array of physical sexual outlets, also had special viewing rooms where patrons who preferred vicarious sexual thrills, could in fact, watch through a peephole or two-way mirror, and enjoy seeing other customers having sexual intercourse with one of the house prostitutes. Brothels with opportunities for peeping were particularly common in some large cities and especially in Europe.

In some ways, the pornographic theaters and arcades have replaced such brothels. Watching sex on a movie screen, or through the viewing lens of an arcade projector, is presumably not that different, or deficient in erotic quality from watching it through a brothel peephole or neighbor's window. Commercial voyeurism, it is to be admitted, is perhaps not so spontaneous, and it lacks the thrill of clandestine danger, but it is convenient, relatively without social risks, and certainly explicit in its visual stimuli. The porno movies of the large cities offer a temporary carnal, even if imaginary, respite from the loneliness of the urban environment, and the monotony of routine existence.[98] Seated in the darkness of the theater watching the sexual drama larger than life unfold, the spectator is totally immersed in carnal reverie. Sometimes there are females in the theater, but they are usually ignored. As Slade puts it:

> ... The women's reactions range from amusement to terror, and a few argue their companions into leaving. Those who stay are ignored by the men in the audience. The indifference is not hostility; it results, again, from the function of the theater as a place of private fantasy.[99]

All of the carnal thrills are not entirely vicarious, however. Pornographic theaters provide not only mental sexual stimulation, but also offer the opportunity for masturbation. There is even a well-defined ecological patterning to such activity, and a sub-culture that protects the integrity of individual privacy. Again, as Slade observes:

> ... Yes, the seating order is odd, as the newspaper reporters have noticed. At least one seat separates each member of the audience. This territorial imperative is enforced to permit masturbation—The Hudson deserves the sobriquet "Masturbation Emporium" as much as the burlesque houses of Henry Miller's novels—and to allow space for private musings and individual fantasies. . . . [100]

If the pornographic theater serves to provide commercialized voyeuristic opportunities, so, too, do the pornographic arcades. The ubiquitous arcades of many big cities are less expensive than pornographic movies and also provide vicarious sexual gratification in a more convenient and shorter time frame than the movies. The patron can drop in to the arcade, go to the pornography viewing section of the establishment, insert the correct change in the machine of his choice, and enjoy a brief excursion into vicarious carnal fantasy facilitated by sexually suggestive movies viewed through individual projection machines. The films seen through the projection machines provide only the basics of the fantasy, and the viewer must supply the vicarious embellishments. As one study of such arcades and their patrons has pointed out, not only do pornographic arcades offer the opportunity for vicarious carnal gratification delivered by vending machines, they also afford privacy and social detachment to the viewers.[101] As in the pornographic theater, the arcade patron seeks privacy for his vicarious musings and for the opportunity for masturbation as an additional sensory additive and finale for his sexual fantasies. Again, there is ecological patterning to the contrived privacy, and a tacit toleration of the existential carnality of the patrons. Through a variety of dramaturgical adaptations, the patrons can indulge their vicarious appetites and maintain their self and social images as "moral men."

The stereotype of the customer of porno movies, porno arcades, and erotic bookstores is likely that of the "dirty old man," the lower class derelict, or perhaps, occasionally, the adolescent looking for sexual titillation or insight. In actuality, the customers of such establishments are often persons of somewhat different social characteristics. In one study of the customers of an adult bookstore, the researchers reported that the customers in their study were all male, 61 percent were married and almost all were living with their wives. The mean educational level was 14+ years of schooling and the modal frequency was 17+ years of schooling completed. Almost one-half were in business and professional occupations, and another 21 percent were sales and clerical workers. In comparison with the population in which the adult bookstore was located, the customers studied were "older, better educated by three years, of higher incomes working in high status jobs, and approximately the same proportions married."[102] These results agree with earlier studies of adult bookstore customers that suggested that such persons are often Caucasian males, married, middle aged, middle class, who have above average incomes, and who have high status occupations.

Perhaps the individual, inured to the pressures for conformity and homogenity, and dissaffected by the alienation and depersonalization of urban life in an industrial society, seeks the ultimate actualization of self in private sexual fantasy, largely of his own composition. The porno arcades and theaters simply voyeuristically assist in the creation of vicarious sexual experiences more meaningful than those which genuine reality allows. Subjective reality, even for a brief time, becomes preferable to objective reality. As Slade has so aptly phrased it, "the real thing, as always, just doesn't compete with the silver screen."[103]

PORNOGRAPHY AS VOYEURISM

With sexual liberation of recent years, and especially various Supreme Court decisions concerning pornography, popular voyeurism has, to some degree, moved away from the keyhole or the bedroom window to the theater, both movie and legitimate. The permissive posture attendant to the sexual revolution has tended to not only make possible a more open participation in sexual activities of the most diverse persuasion ranging from membership in transvestite clubs to sadomasochism, but has also permitted a much greater freedom of expression of sexual fantasy and the implementation and enhancement of vicarious carnal gratification.[104] Exotic sexual fantasy today tends to be more encouraged by the content of the media, than socially suppressed as abnormal.

The content of many movies in the past several years and especially the so-called "X-rated" (and a good many "R-rated") movies has been essentially a voyeuristic episode focusing on nudity and sexual activities normally conducted only in the most private and secluded circumstances. Such movies permit viewers, in effect, to be voyeurs while sitting in upholstered seats. Similarly, the legitimate stage has hosted many performances of obvious salacious content designed to pique the erotic appetite and stimulate the carnal mental imagery of the spectator.[105] Examples of such theatrical efforts include *Hair, Geese, Futz,* and *Oh Calcutta!* to name some which have featured nudity, homosexuality, bestiality, and masturbation for the benefit of the vicarious sexual gratification of the audience. With simulated coitus giving way to actual coitus on stage and regularly distributed commercial movies from Hollywood explicitly depicting a wider range of sexual interaction and often more vividly, if not greater detailed than "stag" and "underground" films, it would appear that voyeurism as a spectator sport is requiring less and less mental effort on the part of the observer. Of course, literature has always afforded voyeuristic glimpses, even if only through the symbolic medium of the written word, of nudity and the vagaries of human sexual behavior. From Chaucer's *Canterbury Tales,* Boccaccio's *Decameron* and the works of Rabelais, to James Joyce's *Ulysses* and D. H. Lawrence's *Lady Chatterley's Lover,* to contemporary writings such as Philip Roth's *Portnoy's Complaint* and John Updike's *Couples,* to the epic sex novels of Harold Robbins and Jacqueline Susann, we use the literary windows constructed by authors to peep at the sexual escapades of others and to accordingly provide our own mental fantasies with appropriate erotic content to afford vicarious gratification. With the seeming decline of literacy in recent years or at least reading interpretive ability, Americans may be reading less and looking at pictures more. There was a time when *Esquire* provided a single "pin-up" picture, not infrequently a Vargas girl painting usually scantily clothed and often anatomically well endowed. From time to time, a few "cheesecake" photographs might also find their way into such publications as the *Police Gazette,* and others of its *genre.* All in all, much was left to the salacious imagination of the magazine reader. With the coming of *Playboy,* however, a new era in facilitated mental imagery was born. The original centerfold, when it finally reached triple page size, usually portrayed pulchritudinous nudes in awesome, near-human scale, in life-like colors and posed against backgrounds and in positions that encouraged the vicarious involvement of the Playmate and the mental embellishment of the viewer. At first there were curves, than cleavage, then nipples, and most recently pubic hair. Rumor in the periodical publishing business has it that the next photographic trend in regard to the Playmate will be "going pink" (i.e., showing the genital area in sufficient detail that some of the pink tissue inside the genitals will show). In addition to the Playmate centerfold, additional photographic essays showing nude female bodies in suggestive poses and erotic context are usually constituent to each issue. The general tone of the magazine and the collective photographic representation of nudity and often a range of approximated sexual activities, is clearly designed to provide salacious stimulation and afford vicarious carnal experiences with a minimum necessity for literary interpretation. Other "girlie" magazines directed at the male audience are often even more direct in their literary message with earthier photographic inclusions and articles that are designed for readers with limited capability for mental visual imagery. More recently, a new breed of periodical ostensibly intended for the female *bon vivant* and featuring photos of nude men has appeared on the scene, but inasmuch as some research has indicated that females, in general, are less aroused by erotica or less curious about or sexually aroused by the sight of the male genitals[106] than are most males toward female intimate anatomy, there is some reason to believe that such periodicals are more likely providing vicarious sexual exhilaration for males of homosexual persuasion than for females.

In the midst of the sexual revolution of recent years, and the endemic sexual explicitness of today's cultural context, it might be assumed that the population would have become sufficiently inured, if not downright bored, with nudity, the double entendre and salacious presentation of many entertainers, and the sexual suggestiveness, if not actual sexual simulation, so often portrayed in the media. In this connection several years ago, one observer wrote that young males were becoming increasingly disinterested in X-rated movies and other entertainment of that *genre* which featured female nudity, reasoning that, if in fact, they wanted to look at a naked female, they would simply tell their girlfriend to take her clothes off. For some segments of the population, however, such a potential for sexual titilation either does not exist or does not effectively or sufficiently satisfy the need or desire for vicarious carnal gratification. Whether many persons have, in fact, become bored with and inured of, present levels of pornographic salaciousness and, thus, seek more intense vicarious erotic experiences to stimulate their jaded sexual palates, or whether the convoluted social reality of contemporary society simply dictates the need for a more bizarre range of sexual fantasies for escape and erotic stimulation is difficult to determine. It is obvious, however, that the extreme limits of carnal stimulation are being probed in the interest of generating sexual fantasy and intensifying the erotic experience. Some assert that such probes are going beyond the limits of ultimate social toleration, if not rationality itself. The Indianapolis Vice Squad captain, for example, said:

> We're not going to the prosecutors and ask for indictments against nudity. . . . What we're fighting is seeing women in all types of grotesque positions. It's just spread, spread, spread, And there's a lot of violence coming in.[107]

Pornography of the most perverse, if not pathological, variety and mode has become increasingly popular, flagrant in its prurient appeal, and near ubiquitous in its presence. Until it was blacked out a time back, one cable television channel in New York City, for example, offered a television show titled "Midnight Blue" that featured such obscene attractions as a chorus line of naked, undulating, male strippers and a demonstration of a man wearing a product called "candy pants." A woman is shown chewing the spun-sugar underpants off the man who is wearing them.[108] Viewers of the program were able to view an interview conducted by the publisher of *Screw* magazine, Al Goldstein, with porno star Carol Connors who had appeared in *Deep Throat,* a 400-pound stripper, a visit to a tropical fish store staffed by topless salesladies, a performance by an English girl who specialized in fellatio, and a skit involving an attractive leather-clad female whipping a middle-aged Englishman dressed in a skimpy maid's costume.[109] Such porno programs as "Midnight Blue," and other similar offerings have precipitated a controversy between civil libertarians who maintain that interference with porno programs is censorship that interferes with basic freedoms, and critics who assert that pornography of the current *genre* is an offense against public decency and represents a decadence of a pathological nature.

If porno television programs were considered lewd or obscene, some pornography films of recent years even go beyond traditional limits of obscenity. In *The Hottest Show in Town,* a film produced by Drs. Phyllis and Eberhard Kronhauser, two psychologists who have specialized in the study of erotica in much of their scholarship, shows a bizarre array of sexual and/or erotic activities. Included are traditional circus acts performed by nude individuals of both sexes, two dwarfs having intercourse, a herd of horses watching a stallion attempting to mount a mare, and a strongman holding a platform aloft on which a threesome copulates. In one skit, a group of girls are kneeling in a row and clowns insert glowing lightbulbs into their vaginas and anuses.[110]

Pornography appears to be moving in increasingly diverse directions in an attempt to provide erotic fantasy and vicarious sexual gratification for the widest range of carnal tastes and perversions. The peep film arcades that use film loops, provide a kind of market testing mechanism, as it were, in regard to trends and directions in erotic tastes.[111] Pedophilia and sadomasochism films, for example, have enjoyed increased popularity in recent years. Urophilia and urolagnia (urination) theme films are making headway in the "loop" business, but coprophagia (excrement) theme film loops have not.

Some have seen a particularly sinister and pathological bent in the increasing preoccupation of some forms of pornographic media with especially bizarre and convoluted forms of sexual expression and gratification—sadistic sexual violence and pedophilia to name two. In regard to the former, Sachs has commented:

> . . . It is important to recognize that hard core pornography, like *Hustler,* is tremendously and obviously sadistic, masochistic, masturbational, full of defecation and urination as sexual acts, etc. *Hustler* outdoes *Playboy* and *Penthouse* by its accent on sadomasochism, bloodthirstiness, lesbianism, and all kinds of triangular bisexual arrangements.[112]

The appearance of so-called "snuff films" in recent years signals a particularly chilling direction for sexual violence. "Snuff films" are the equivalent of stag films but instead of portraying the usual assortment of sexual high jinks and nudity, they depict a female being tortured or beaten, often quite brutally. These films usually end by allegedly showing the victim being killed or mutilated. It has been said that "snuff films" are contrived and fictional, relying on special effects rather than actual murder enactments. On the other hand, it has been alleged that camera crews are going to third world countries where peasant girls can be easily tricked into performing for the cameras and then are literally being butchered up for the sake of pornographic art. It would be heinous if the latter was valid, but in any event, the fact that "snuff films" are enjoying something of a vogue and are providing vicarious sexual stimulation and carnal gratification for some persons of jaded sexual appetite suggests that our penchant for sexual variety may have passed over the threshold of sanity. Furthermore, the increasing preoccupation with sexual violence in pornography may well portend the increasing manifestation of real sexual violence in the place of vicarious sexual violence. There is now a scientific indication that sex and violence in the media is related to sexual and violent behavior in the individual. According to Eysenck and Nias:

> Our major conclusions are that the evidence strongly indicates that the portrayal of sex and violence in the media does affect the attitudes and behavior of viewers; that these effects are variable, depending on the details of presentation and the personality of the viewers; and that recommendations for action depend in part on a person's value system. Aggressive acts new to the subject's repertoire of responses, as well as acts already well established, can be evoked by violent scenes portrayed on film, TV, or in the theater.... [113]

A particularly, socially offensive trend in pornography is the recent rise of "child porn." The pornography industry has discovered a large and receptive audience for juvenile erotica. There are apparently a significant number of adults who are capable of deriving vicarious carnal gratification from pornographic materials featuring children.[114] "Kiddie porn" material ranges from magazines like *Lollitots* or *Nudist Moppets* which show mostly nude photographs of children to more prurient periodicals such as *Little Girls Together, Young Stud,* or *Chicken Supreme* that depict children engaging in masturbation or homosexual acts, and movies like *Children Love* that portrays boys and girls having sex with each other.[115]

Child porn, appearing in the wake of other accelerating trends in the world of erotica, has triggered off an angry and forceful reaction in many communities both here and abroad. In Great Britain, a Protection of Children Bill has been introduced in Parliament that would attempt to stop the exploitation of children for sexual purposes. Critics fear that such a bill might interfere with the efforts of genuine creative artists who make movies, sculptors, or paint pictures. Lewis Carroll, it should be recalled took nude photographs of his child acquaintances.[116] Public outrage about child porn has led to investigation of the sexual exploitation of children, and as a residual finding has revealed that 60 percent of the perpetrators of child abuse are close friends of the child's family or even members of the child's family. Furthermore, congressmen in probing the sexual abuse of children by adults heard "horror stories about mothers who permitted their daughters to be used by pornographers," and also heard estimates that 25 percent of American women had been sexually abused during their childhood.[117] Legislators, district attorneys, law enforcement officials, and even housewives are waging effective counterattacks against what they perceive as pornography's assault on public decency and community morality. In Memphis, Tennessee, Larry Parrish, an assistant U.S. attorney obtained 60 indictments and scheduled almost a dozen trials "for persons and companies allegedly involved in producing pornography." His "quarry" has included such sexual luminaries as Linda Lovelace, Harry Reems, and Georgina Spelvin.[118] In Georgia, Larry Flynt, the publisher of *Hustler,* was convicted on an obscenity charge, and in Fremont, Calif. pickets appeared in front of the city's massage parlors, and sometimes "marked the license numbers of parlor customers" on their picket signs, and some angry women pickets burst into the parlors looking for their husbands.[119] In Columbus, Ohio, antipornography groups bombed some adult bookstores.[120] In many communities, the town fathers have attempted to at least contain the sexually oriented trade by zoning such business into certain delimited areas of town, such as Boston's "Combat Zone."[121] Even though many civil libertarians have registered concern and distress at the "spill-over" of anti-pornography laws into legitimate areas of social life, nevertheless, some authorities point out that there would seem to be "statistical linkages between high exposure to pornography and promiscuity, deviancy, and affiliation with high criminality groups." Even though they recognize the danger of overly repressive laws that infringe on the constitutional rights of citizens, they still argue "that a line must be drawn" between sexual anarchy and oppressive totalitarian controls.[122] In a similar vein, one writer has asserted:

> ... Seldom does the intensification of an educative stimulus weaken the impact of that stimulus. If that were true, corporations would cease to vie for advertising spots at high moments of TV programs. Again, pornography may initiate and stimulate fantasy rather than merely reflecting it.[123]

SUMMARY

In the final analysis, many of the mechanisms of achieving vicarious carnal gratification—peeping, voyeurism (private or commercial), and pornographic media—must be viewed essentially as efforts to cope with loneliness, and insecurity. It has been asserted that there is voyeurism inherent in most of us. Slade has pointed out, for example, that "in New York, in particular, voyeurism is almost a way of life—witness the binoculars beside apartment windows. Perhaps the isolation of citizens in the city encourages them to violate the privacy of others."[124] In effect, the endemic atomization, alienation, and loneliness of mass society and urban life makes us seek intimate involvement with others even if it is unilateral, furtive, artificial, and deviantly invades their privacy. The voyeur seeks to assuage his curiosity about others where he is denied the opportunity to enjoy meaningful experiences of his own. The voyeur spys on, or listens in on the couple engaged in lovemaking because he experiences sights and sounds, and sexual stimulation he does not otherwise enjoy. Not unlike the child who is not invited to the party but who looks in the window to see what he is missing, the voyeur attempts to vicariously experience that which is not part of his existential existence, or which he believes is not.

The clinical picture of the voyeur is that of an individual who is more lonely and insecure than most, a person who is a kind of victim of social deprivation, as it were. The wallflower, rejected at the dance may escape her situation subjectively by daydreaming of her prince charming. The individual living Thoreau's "life of quiet desperation," may seek stimulation and vitality by spying on the newly-wed couple across the street, or the single working girl in the apartment below. The voyeur (personal or commercial) seeks to know that what he wonders about, and to reassure himself that which he is and does is not inadequate. Again as Slade expresses it:

> One of the functions of pornography is to reassure males threatened by the virile roles expected of them. Literary pornography commonly assuages anxiety by portraying indefatigable males dominating females.[125]

Voyeurism or viewing porno movies may be a respite, an escape from the world of reality, as it were, or the fantasy that it generates may be an adjunct to reality, or to the individual's experience. The social script may need to be "fleshed out" with auxillary fantasy, in effect. In this regard, Slade points out that, "for others it (sex in the films) generates fantasies which can then be grafted on to real sexual experiences or take their place."[126]

Sex is as much cerebral as physical and fantasy is a functional component to actual sexual activity. It is functional in other ways as well. Slade opines that, "fantasy is the rock on which a stable marriage stands, since it permits mental adultery while preserving monogamy."[127] Sexual fantasy and vicarious carnal gratification is wish fulfillment, and therefore narcissistic. It is sexual gratification without social involvement or responsibility. Nevertheless, our world of sexual reality and interaction requires the embellishment of fantasy and vicarious scenario and is, accordingly, a constituent and normative element of our social existence. It becomes deviant and pathological when it supplaces or interferes with reality, becomes compulsive or personally dysfunctional, impinges on the rights of others, or becomes sufficiently convoluted or irrational as to engender an anti-social posture on the part of the individual who employs it.

Pornography, lewd television programs, X-rated movies, "girlie" magazines, and nudity or simulated sex on stage are but a few of the many effective albeit distorted raw materials used to construct sexual fantasy. As cues or backdrops for sustaining fantasy they may serve as functional adjuncts to a meaningful sexual existence. Where they become end as opposed to mean, where their content moves beyond mere sexual stimulation and into the realm of stark depravity and psychotic debauchery, or where they tend to erode the mantel of community civility and equilibrium, they assume the dimensions of a sexual chimera of grotesque proportions.

Chapter 4

OBSCENITY, LEWD LANGUAGE, AND CARNAL COMMUNICATION

Sexual Deviancy in Verbal Context

Language is both behavior and the externalization of thought. Inasmuch as cultural norms seek to control and channelize both thought and behavior in directions deemed appropriate to the needs of society, language is also the object of normative regulation. In this connection, language is conceptualized as having a certain relevancy and appropriateness to time, place, circumstance, participants, and intent. Members of society are constrained to use language appropriate to these instances and situations, and the violation of language norms may be conceptualized as being serious offenses and invoke sanctions as severe as in the case of any behavioral deviancy. Perhaps no topic of language communication is more subject to societal monitoring, and cultural prescription and proscription than that of sex. The centrality of sex in our lives, however, gives it a prominence in our language interaction, and communicative concern. The mechanisms of social control notwithstanding, there are widespread violations of sexual language norms, consequently labeled as deviant behavior, and the subsequent application of attendant social sanctions.

LANGUAGE NORMS AND SOCIAL PROSCRIPTION

Language norms may be concerned with several kinds of tabooed words or obscenity. In general, these categories of forbidden or inappropriate words include words with a religious connotation such as "damn," words that identify parts of the anatomy or bodily functions, and words that have a sexual meaning or reference. Some writers assert that the prevalence of one category of taboo words in a given society may be a function of preoccupation with cultural taboos.[128] As an example, one authority, Dr. Vladimir Piskacek, has pointed out that in certain countries, such as Poland, Austria, and Hungary, which are particularly religious, the use of blasphemous words as obscenities is particularly noticeable.[129] The use of such words with religious connotation is a modal way of expressing rebellion. The same researcher, "who has studied linguistics among various cultures", has asserted that in Germany, where there are high standards of cleanliness, there appears to be a heavy use of excretory words as obscenity—perhaps as a "revolt against this meticulousness."[130] Interestingly, however, in the United States, there is a heavy emphasis on sexual swear-words. Piskacek also contends that the predominance of sexual words in American obscenity may be a reaction to the traditional puritan code of sexual behavior here, and perhaps is "subconscious anger against prudishness."[131]

MODAL OBSCENITY USE BY SOCIAL CATEGORIES

Obscenity is employed by practically all categories of persons in all societies including our own, but there may be a significantly different frequency of use of such taboo words from one category to another. Because of social norms in regard to the use of obscenity, females have traditionally been less inclined to use swear words (or be exposed to them) than have men. In this connection, Ashley Montagu, the noted social anthropologist, has observed that:

> In our society woman is indisputably the "gentler" sex to whom violent activities and vehement expressions of any sort were until very recently forbidden. It wasn't done. Woman was too fragile and sensitive to be exposed to the most refined expressions. She was too tender ... [132]

Adults more frequently use obscenities than children. Even occupational categories may vary in their use of taboo words. One psychologist, for example, reported that 24 percent of the vocabulary used on the job by factory and construction workers were "dirty words." White-collar workers, on the other hand, only used a vocabulary with 1 percent dirty words while at the office, and only 3 percent to 4 percent when at parties.[133] Sailors are reputed to be particularly heavy users of obscenities, thus, the euphemistic phrase "salty language." Mule-skinners, of course, were stereotypically reported to employ a particularly obscene and profane vocabulary in their work (mules, it was said, simply did not respond as effectively to polite language as to obscenities). No occupation seems to be immune from the use of obscene words, even the office of President of the United States. When the Nixon Watergate tapes were transcribed, the President's comments were so laced with obscene words, salacious, scatalogical, and otherwise, that when they were edited out, the phrase "expletive deleted" had become part of the American vernacular.[134]

Children, like adults, use obscene words, and as will be seen later in the chapter, sometimes to the point of perceived pathology. The use of such words by children, however, as with adults, may be functional to a degree. According to one psychiatrist, children use obscenity "to vent hostility," and by employing the words for excrement and bodily functions they "release feelings of sexual excitement."[135]

TABOO WORDS IN CULTURAL CONTEXT

The nature of "dirty words," like other kinds of words, seems to change with time. In the middle of the nineteenth century, especially in England, it was improper to use words, in mixed company (both sexes present) that connoted any part of the human body between the neck and the ankles, with the possible exception of the heart and stomach.[136] A word like chest, belly, abdomen, or thigh was essentially considered to be an obscenity and a violation of the language norms of propriety. Even later in this country similar standards prevailed. H. L. Mencken, in his definitive, *The American Language,* reported that there was a time in this country when a study showed that 40 percent of the co-eds at a southern college "deplored the use of the word 'bull'." Close to 20 percent of the co-eds were "shocked" at the word "leg." (Limb was considered a more preferable word inasmuch as it has less human anatomical connotation.)[137]

In addition to certain words being generally taboo, there are other social norms that can dictate the circumstances under which some words can be used or even be appropriate to use. The use of some obscene words may be tolerated or even encouraged within a group made up of the same sex, and particularly males. "Dirty" words, and sex talk, usually are more tolerated among persons of similar age than individuals of diverse age. Young couples may get together for a party and have occasion to tell ribald stories and sex jokes. The question of kinship and the use of obscene language is particularly complex. In some societies, there are particular sets of kinship relationships that permit and perhaps even mandate a "joking" relationship in terms of interaction. This joking relationship not infrequently includes sexual humor and even sexual horseplay such as genital snatching. It may also include certain anatomical and sexual intimacies as part of this interaction. Margaret Mead told of asking a Manus wife if she permitted her own husband to touch her breasts. The woman indignantly replied, "Of course not; that (privilege) belongs to my cross-cousin (joking relative) only."[138] Just as there are certain kinship relationships that are privileged in terms of sexual humor, sexual horseplay, or the use of obscene words, there are, likewise, some kinship relationships where an avoidance of such topics and interaction is mandated. In the United States, kinship is not highly developed (in comparison with many other societies) and is, accordingly, characterized by patterning of kin relationships and interaction that is relatively "implicit, inconspicuous, and generally 'weak'."[139] This relative lack of obvious patterning includes the joking relationship and the attendant verbal interaction regarding sexual humor and obscene words. Although there may be some kinsmen with whom it may be decidedly inappropriate to use obscene language, in general, in our society, there are no hard and fast norms about with which kinsmen one may be able to be verbally open.

SEXUAL OBSCENITIES AND LOVEMAKING

Sexual obscenities and explicit sexual talk, although normatively prohibited in public and with most categories of persons, may, nevertheless, be uniquely appropriate between lovers or, in some instances, spouses. Although at one point in history a proper and proprietous husband or wife would never even use a word like "sex" with the other, even in the privacy of their bedchambers, it has been pointed out that in recent years some individuals may have a strong desire to hear their lover or spouse use sexually obscene words as a constituent part of sex play. In this regard, Denali Crest has observed:

> One of the long-held taboos about sex concerns what a couple may and may not say to each other when they are making love. Some people accept the notion that partners should limit themselves to words of love and to telling the other how much they enjoy sex with them. They might, however, think odd the desire many couples have to use and hear four-letter (or vulgar) words while making love. Psychologists refer to this desire as *erototalia,* and though few people will talk about this urge outside the bedroom, it seems that many people have it. Informal research done by a number of marriage counselors show that 80 to 85 percent of the couples they helped admitted to using erotic language occasionally, if not regularly, during loveplay.[140]

Some persons derive sexual stimulation and gratification from uttering sexually obscene words and others from hearing them. Yet others derive salacious enjoyment from the mutual use of sexual words with a person of the opposite sex. Many great lovers in history have been reputed to be lavish users of dirty words, and the French author Pierre de Brantome once wrote that "great ladies . . . [are] a hundred times more dissolute and lewd in speech than common women [during lovemaking]."[141] Ingrid Bergman, the famous movie star who left her husband for the then, middle-aged and balding Italian movie director Roberto Rossalini, once confided that one of the appealing charms of her paramour was his combination of tenderness and vulgarity. Explicit sexual talk including sexual obscenities may enhance the sexual encounter by promoting vicarious sexual imagery and thus embellish the anticipation of sexual gratification. As Myron Brenton has put it:

> . . . Words can be a very effective sexual stimulant because talking sex means thinking sex, and thinking sex means fantasizing sex, and fantasizing sex leads to a stirring of erotic impulses.
> In effect words can be not a substitute for foreplay but an integral part of it, as arousing as a caress . . . [142]

Regardless of the fact that some couples today may employ explicit sexual talk in their lovemaking efforts, there was a time in the past when quite the opposite was true. For perhaps the great majority of couples, either because of shyness, rigid conformity to the norms of proprietous comportment, or sexual reticence, lovemaking was conducted in the verbal void or to the accompaniment of simple endearments. Likewise, when not making love, most individuals are probably quite parsimonious with their use of sexual obscenities. It is within this context that many persons are, therefore, quite shocked, if not hurt by the fact of having their illusions shattered, when in some situations, they discover that their spouse, and especially if the wife, has an extensive vocabularly of very sexually explicit four-letter words. Examples of such situations might be the wife getting drunk, developing a mental disorder, while under the influence of anesthesia, with the onset of old age and senility, or when extremely angry or agitated. The use of explicit sexual obscenity is generally not part of the normative structure of verbal interaction between many spouses and in some families it is particularly traumatic when the norms are violated. The apparent increasing use of sex talk by some couples represents a dilution of traditional norms of verbal interaction.

OFFENSIVE LANGUAGE IN COMMON USE

Not all sexually explicit words are necessarily obscene or completely objectionable. In our language, most anatomical parts of the body, bodily functions, and various aspects of the sex act along with related sexual activities, can be adequately described with a number of options, verbally speaking. For some such phenomena, we have appropriate Latin words such as *cunnilingus* or *fellatio;* in the instance of other anatomical or sexual processes we have proper, formal words such as urinate or micturate. There are also various euphemisms or vernacular words for sexual organs or bodily processes. Additionally, there are also many ethnic sexual words in use wider than just their group of origin, such as the Yiddish words *tokus* for genitalia and *tushy* for buttocks, and finally there are the more widely known, but also more *verboten* Anglo-Saxon four-letter "dirty" words. Actually in an earlier time, the so-called four-letter words for bodily processes, sexual intercourse, and related topics were used quite widely by the "common" people, thus, they were vulgar words (the original meaning of vulgar, it will be recalled, was simply "belonging or relating to the common people"). In time, of course, vulgar words became "dirty" words with salacious connotation. The cultural pluralism of our society, and the tendency of different generations to develop their own unique vernacular words and phrases, has tended to give mankind a rich obscene vocabulary.

Words and phrases with sexual or erotic meaning are not always offensive in some societies. In Chinese exotic literature, for example, the penis may be euphemistically referred to as the "jade stem" or the vagina called the "jade gate" or "jade portal." Even coitus may be referred to as "climbing the jade mountain," or the "mountain of joy." As Crest puts it " . . . Chinese erotic literature . . . is splendidly explicit, yet totally pleasant and inoffensive."[143] Although, undoubtedly, some of the puritan colonists had to employ a raw vocabularly, nevertheless, from the earliest days of the country there have often been norms and laws prohibiting the public use of obscene and profane language, and especially words with a salacious or scatalogical connotation. Many municipalities, for example, had (and still do) ordinances prohibiting the use of obscene words. Legal sanctions, in some instances, were relatively severe, considering that the "crime" was only a violation of language norms. At an informal level, additional social sanctions were often brought to bear on persons guilty of using obscenity and especially in a totally inappropriate setting. The taboo against "dirty language" was carefully inculcated into children, using the threat of, and sometimes the punishment of, having their mouth washed out with soap. When "dirty" words appeared in literature, they generally became the center of widespread legal and social controversy. A classic case in point is D. H. Lawrence's famous (or infamous by some standards) novel, *Lady Chatterley's Lover,* in which a refined lady and the gamekeeper on her husband's estate, Mellors, an individual of more plebian background, enjoy a sexual affair. Mellors' language is especially "vulgar" since it is heavily laced with four-letter Anglo-Saxon words. In the scenes where he makes love with Lady Chatterley, his language of endearment is essentially four-letter words, but Lawrence attempts to make the point that Mellors' language is *natural* to him and the situation. Such language between lovers within this situation is not dirty but spontaneous, appropriate to the occasion, and beautiful. Nevertheless, the public was outraged by the explicit sexual language used by the fictional lovers, and found the fact that Lawrence had his characters even give proper names to their penis and vagina—John Thomas and Lady Jane respectively—particularly offensive.[144]

SEXUAL OBSCENITIES AND VICARIOUS CARNAL GRATIFICATION

Some persons use sexual obscenities because they are limited in more appropriate vocabulary, while others may rely on such words because of subcultural or situational norm. Some individuals may use them with a sophisticated flair, in the course of courtship or lovemaking, and yet others may employ sexual language as a mechanism for generating vicarious sexual imagery, or even aiding in obtaining carnal gratification. In some such instances, there may be a pathological element to the use of sexual obscenities, and sexually explicit language. An illustration of such pathology, perhaps, is the obscene phone caller. Each year many persons, and especially women, receive anonymous phone calls from someone, almost always a male, where the caller may either simply breathe heavily into the receiver, in a real or simulated lustful fashion or may utter obscenities or sexually explicit suggestions to the listener. Some obscene phone callers are essentially "thrill-seekers."[145] Many of these callers are juvenile boys. The thrill-seeker usually wastes little time in making an obscene remark or an obscene proposition, usually of a sexual nature. The caller does not really anticipate an affirmative answer from the female listener, but rather enjoys the shock reaction of the listener who may become angry or simply nonplussed. In some instances, the female listener may even direct obscenities back at the caller. In any event, the caller seeks an emotional response. According to Beverley T. Mead, "Such a response gives the caller some feeling of mastery or at least a sense of satisfaction in daring to offend propriety."[146] The thrill-seeker presumably also derives some degree of vicarious carnal gratification from this salacious interaction. Some obscene telephone callers have been labeled as "ingratiating seducers." These persons may introduce themselves on the phone to a female stranger, and then proceed to present some detailed fabricated story designed to convince the female that he is sincere, possibly a friend of one of her friends, and that he seeks the opportunity for a proper personal introduction. Sometimes he may succeed in convincing the woman to meet him but usually he will lead her on until the point she is offended. This type of caller may, or may not, use obscenity or even sexual innuendos. He is essentially a vicarious telephone "seducer." Mead suggests that such a caller "may enjoy a 'masterful' feeling of having lured his victim and perhaps left her feeling intrigued or at least frightened."[147] The vicarious sexual gratification here derives from the symbolic seduction over the telephone. A third type of obscene phone caller is the "trickster." The trickster is a kind of verbal voyeur, who seeks to gain intimate information, not infrequently of a sexual nature, from the listener. This type of caller tries to use cleverness to convince the listener that he is conducting some kind of formal, but confidential, survey or research. The caller may pose as a minister, a doctor, a police officer, or a social scientist, but he will attempt to make the listener disclose intimacies about her sexual habits or preferences, or some similarly related topic. This person does not normally use obscenity but instead derives vicarious thrills and gratification from learning about the sexual activities and attitudes of the female listener.[148]

Obscene phone callers of any of these varieties are not unlike sexual exhibitionists. According to Mead, they are frequently persons who are lonely and frustrated, who may feel sexually inadequate, or even be impotent. She regards them as "unseen exhibitionists," since they are not as daring, so to speak, as real exhibitionists.[149] Obscene phone callers are rarely dangerous, prone to violence, nor do they move on to more serious sexual offenses. They are more of a nuisance than a danger. The legal penalties, if apprehended, however, are relatively severe, and law enforcement agencies, in cooperation with telephone companies, do often manage to identify such callers, particularly if they are persistent in making calls, and especially to the same number.[150]

THE OBSCENE PHONE CALL AS SEXUAL DYAD

Some telephone callers seeking carnal stimulation are not so much inclined to use obscenities or even sexual talk as they are to simply have the opportunity to listen to a female. Several writers have reported that the open-line crisis therapy agencies are encountering the problem of the telephone masturbator.[151] Here, the male calls in and, sexually stimulated by the sound of the female therapist's voice, will engage in masturbation. According to Brockopp and Lester, there seem to be two such types of callers. Some male callers will phone the crisis center and engage the female therapist in conversation, often with some fictional account of a personal problem. He does not inform the listener that he is masturbating. Perhaps after a time the caller may admit what he is doing or the therapist may suspect it and confront him with her suspicions. In these instances, the therapists are often angry because they have been tricked and perhaps "ineffectual." They are sometimes " . . . furious at putting in hard work to no end." The second type of caller does not present any elaborate fabricated story, but may simply breathe heavily and urge the phone therapist to "talk to me," "don't leave me," or "please let me finish." In some cases the caller may even try to get the counselor to encourage him with lewd remarks. Here, the therapists may hang up or be "angry" or "disgusted." Some even complain of being "sexually exploited," or "used." The therapists experience a real dilemma.[152] If they stay on the telephone while the caller is masturbating, they are, in effect, a participant to his fantasy, and perhaps a contributor to his problem. Furthermore, they are often disaffected by the caller's actions and feel as if they are being sexually exploited. They cannot have the telephone calls traced and have the callers arrested since this is contrary to the mission and purpose of telephone counseling services. If they hang up, however, they are denying help and counseling to someone with a problem, and referral is impossible. This, too, is counter to the aims of such counseling services. There is little doubt, however, that the callers are involving the therapists in their carnal gratification or that they are engaged in elaborate vicarious imagery. One caller was reported, for example, who became more verbal as he became more excited, and instructed the therapist listening to him on the telephone to "open your legs."[153] The telephone masturbator is an interesting example of a situation involving verbal sexual deviancy, where the offender is, in effect, victimizing the agency that is available to help him.

OBSCENE LANGUAGE AND SEXUAL ENHANCEMENT

Just as some individuals derive carnal gratification from anonymously uttering sexual obscenities or making fictive sexual propositions on the telephone, other persons apparently are sexually stimulated by obscenities directed at them and by other kinds of verbal interactions. Prostitutes and masseuses in massage parlors often report that some clients expect to be verbally abused. In their study of massage parlors, Bryant and Palmer, for example, related that:

> The masseuses told of encountering a variety of idiosyncratic sexual behavior and requests. One patron arrived with a whip, and several wanted the masseuses to yell at them.[154]

An interesting arrangement that affords verbal sexual stimulation over the telephone to men who seek this type of carnal gratification was recently reported in Japan. An enterprising Japanese business-man named Takeo Kazama has originated a unique telephone ser-vice which has been labeled by at least one newspaper as "dial-a-risque-or-off-color-story."[155] A client after learning about the service, telephones Kazama and hears the sound of a woman's cries and moans simulating orgasm during coitus. The woman's voice is followed by a request for $3.00 and the address to which it is to be sent. When the fee is sent in the new subscriber receives a telephone number to dial which he can call and have the opportunity to listen to a five minute taped program of erotica. The tapes are changed every week. Kazama claims he got the idea after reading about men who make obscene phone calls to strange women. Within two months, Kazama enrolled 40,000 subscribers in Tokyo, Kobe, and other cities. Mr. Kazama has apparently touched a carnal nerve, as it were. As he puts it:

> Since there are such men in the world [obscene phone callers] it oc-curred to me that there must be thousands who would like to have women tell them off-color stories.[156]

OBSCENE LANGUAGE AND SOCIAL LIMITS

Although much obscenity and sexual language is tolerated, and especially in some circumstances, or at least accommodated, it is often defined as deviant and sanctioned accordingly. A person swear-ing loudly in public may be arrested and a man who is too explicit in his sexual innuendos may be rebuffed by the lady he is courting. A child may have his mouth washed out with soap for uttering a "dirty" word, and a politician may lose the confidence of his constit-uents, if not their votes, if it is discovered that he is a habitual user of obscene language. A "foul mouth" girl may not win the boy or get the bid to the coveted sorority. Obscene verbal abuse may precipi-tate fights, lawsuits, or warrants for arrest, and the blatant user of obscenity may find himself a social pariah, if not subject to legal sanction.

Not infrequently, some high school and college students find themselves as the center of controversy as a result of writing an editorial or article for the school paper that contains "strong," offen-sive, or obscene words. Faculty advisors sometimes try and suppress the material, and then the question of freedom of speech and censorship is raised. Court battles sometimes ensue. In a similar instance, a book of poems written by young people was ordered removed from the shelf of a high school library by the School Committee. One of the poems, written by a 15-year-old-girl was considered to be "tasteless, filthy trash" by the committee. In the poem about the city, the girl expressed her disgust at being appraised as a "piece of meat," and describes the situation in the city. She wrote:

> One million horny lip-smacking men
> Screaming for my body.[157]

The school librarian went to court to have the book restored to the shelves.

There have been numerous instances of parents or school officials demanding that various books or periodicals be removed from school libraries because it was felt that they had crossed the limits in terms of public tolerance of obscene language. By today's standards, some of the offending books such as Salinger's *Catcher in the Rye* appear extremely innocuous. For that matter, even previously forbidden books like *Lady Chatterley's Lover* or *Ulysses* seem relatively tame in comparison to some best selling novels today.

The public has perhaps been more incensed or outraged by films and periodicals in recent years than books. Films such as *Deep Throat* so offended the public morality that there were numerous legal efforts to ban the movie in many communities. Al Goldstein, the publisher of *Screw* and *Smut*, was tried on charges of mailing obscene material (although a mistrial was subsequently declared).[158] Similarly, Larry Flynt, the publisher of *Hustler,* was also tried and convicted for "organizing to commit the crime of selling obscene literature" in Cincinnati. He was later tried on similar charges in Georgia and subsequently shot by a would-be assassin. Flynt, however, had a Christian conversion, and announced his intention to make substantial changes in the content and format of his magazine.[159]

The pornography versus The First Amendment controversy has raged for years and involved broad segments of society ranging from physicians to newspaper columnists to criminologists. Even the American Bar Association has debated the issue at an annual convention.[160] Interestingly, some persons who merchandise or retail literature and/or material deemed pornographic have, in some instances, in recent years, launched a legal counterattack and gone to court to protect the individual's right to buy and sell any kind of literature that he wishes.[161]

Sex magazines, in general have supplanted the porno book of yesteryear. They are showier, more explicit, and require less attention or imagination of the reader. Such periodicals assuage anatomical curiosity and provide sexual inspiration, stimulation, and gratification, even if vicariously. Sexuality has traditionally been suppressed and repressed in our society and the pornographic "slicks" simply provide a mechanism for evading these societal constraints. Persons can readily indulge their sexual fantasies, regardless of how socially convoluted.[162]

The enormous experimental and research efforts to determine if erotica and pornography had a detrimental effect on individuals have been inconclusive and controversial. The President's Commission on Pornography reported that exposure to erotica induces no antisocial behavior. The President, many authorities, and some of the public rejected its findings, however.[163] Exposure to pornography and erotica, in some cases, does not seem to have any permanent or detrimental effect, yet experiments have suggested that persons exposed to sexual modes and activities previously unfamiliar or untried may possibly explore them or ultimately incorporate them into their own repertoire of carnal gratification techniques. Overall, it would appear most Americans have taken obscenity, erotica, and the inundation of sexual material of recent years in stride. In general, the contemporary interest, or even predilection of many persons, for sex magazines, X-rated movies, nudity and sexual suggestiveness in entertainment, and a new catholicy in sexual taste and preference is seen as more of an idiosyncratic interest rather than a perverted or depraved preoccupation. For some individuals, however, a preoccupation with obscenity and sexually explicit language may be considered to be a manifestation of sexual depravity, and symptomatic of mental pathology.

OBSCENE LANGUAGE AS MENTAL PATHOLOGY

In one dramatic account of such verbal pathology, in this instance, pre-juveniles, "The Baby Disturbers: Sexual Behavior in a Childhood Contraculture," the author details the verbal sexual misadventures of a group of preadolescent boys institutionalized in the children's ward of a large psychiatric hospital.[164] The boys were between 5 and 10 years old. These youngsters had been "socially aberrant" in their neighborhoods where they lived with their parents and their aberrant behavior continued in the hospital ward. The boys, convinced that they had been rejected by their parents and society, who relegated them to the "garbage dump" (their name for the hospital) because of their "badness," created their own contra-culture and elevated "sexual vulgarity, vituperation, and aggressiveness to the level of virtuous behavior." As each new boy came in, he was incorporated into a group and inculcated with its deviant norms. The boys' verbal repertoire consisted largely of sexual obscenities and other explicit sexual words and phrases, some traditional, and some of their own innovation. Much of their play was sex play and they frequently threatened the staff with sexual assault or mutilation. Ultimately the group of boys even adopted the name "the Baby Disturbers," and spent much of their time trying to terrorize the staff or in disrupting staff routine. In situations with the appropriate circumstances, the formation of a deviant contraculture can be precipitated, even among children. In the case of the Baby Disturbers, the essential contracultural theme was the direction of sexually deviant language and disruptive actions at the staff or the hospital which the boys viewed as representing the dominant culture that "controlled and humiliated them." Thus, the deviant behavior described, even though constituting private patterns of social norm violation, was in large measure, precipitated, sustained, reinforced, and perpetuated by group pressure and sentiment.

Dirty Words on the Wall

Some individuals are not content to utter erotic or obscene words but prefer instead, or in addition to, to write them in prominent, public places, such as on the walls of public buildings or public toilets. Graffiti, as such obscene public writing is known, is presumably as old as culture, inasmuch as archeological ruins of ancient cities have revealed traces of graffiti. Some scholars have been able to reconstruct various aspects of social life in different ancient cities such as Pompeii through a detailed study of graffiti.[165] According to some authors, "graffiti, as an aspect of culture, can be used as an unobtrusive measure to reveal patterns of customs and attitudes of a society."[166] Graffiti may reveal attitudes toward homosexuality or other sexual practices, modes, or techniques. It may also contain racial slurs, attacks, or derogatory remarks. Graffiti not infrequently, involves or incorporates anatomical drawings, often distorted, and usually of some aspect of the genitals, or portraying sexual intercourse. Graffiti, also, often involves social taboos such as portraying or mentioning defecation, or some other scatalogical activity.

One comparative study of graffiti that examined obscene writings in trade schools, junior and four-year colleges, and professional schools revealed a much higher frequency of inscriptions in toilet stalls—almost five to six times as many—in the restrooms of trade schools as opposed to the other types of institutions.[167] Also, the trade school students appear to produce a somewhat larger frequency of "drawings of female genitalia and of coitus."[168] Hostile comments were "considerably more frequent in the trade schools and junior colleges."[169] The trade school students would presumably be less articulate and verbal then students in the other institutions, and might well use graffiti as a vehicle of expression, particularly in manifesting their sexuality. Certainly, they might be anticipated to be less constrained in such activities as producing graffiti. In regard to the high frequency of hostile content in the graffiti, the authors of the study concluded that:

> . . . Those persons who displayed their hostility on the toilet walls of trade schools are talented in expression of hostility, and beside their efforts the weak and limited expressions of presumably brighter and more verbal students in colleges and professional schools appear pitiful.[170]

Graffiti may be an outlet for a person's thoughts or a manifestation of their sexuality. It may also be a plea for advice (or an attempt to give it)—especially matters pertaining to sex and courtship. Graffiti may be an instance of weakened inhibitions—such as being drunk, etc. One writer has pointed out that, " . . . in politically repressed countries, graffiti are often the only indication of the people's opinions."[171] In recent years, the original sexual or scatalogical limericks incorporated into graffiti have often given way to philosophical slogans, observations, and political expression—not infrequently of leftist propensity.[172]

One interesting explanation of graffiti is that males universally suffer from "pregnancy envy" and seek substitute gratifications some of which revolve symbolically around defecation and feces.[173] Thus, according to this theory, graffiti has an anal erotic basis, and, in effect, is a kind of verbal defecation and latrinalia is essentially symbolic feces.

Perhaps, more simply, graffiti may be viewed as an expression of hostile sexuality which manifests itself in the absence of external social control. The graffiti artist frequently leaves his work, as it were, on the walls of empty restrooms or halls of public buildings, or in the isolation of the toilet booth. In any event, the graffiti artist is alone and isolated or insulated from social control. The writing or markings are often hostile or anti-social and represent an assertion of self and presence and repressed, unbridled, unrestrained sexuality. It is raw sexual behavior that employs verbalism to communicate in a symbolic carnal fashion.

Some social scientists have pointed out that gang graffiti may even be used as a means of establishing territoriality and marking boundaries. The graffiti gets thicker the closer to the center of a juvenile gang's territory.[174] The graffiti is a sort of "no-trespassing" sign to outsiders. Also, in recent years, graffiti in some instances appears to be increasingly an attempt to deface public property rather than to make a profane statement. In Philadelphia, the annual cost of graffiti even in 1972 was $4 million, and the New York subway spends $500,000 per year to clean up after graffiti artists.[175]

"Dirty words" whether spoken, or written in books or on restroom walls are offensive in terms of our cultural value system and are accordingly, socially proscribed. The norms prohibiting writing obscenity in public places is violated in an endemic fashion, however. Secretly verbalizing hostile expressions and publicly proclaiming tabooed sexual words and thoughts apparently provides a means of experiencing certain vicarious carnal gratifications, and blatantly violating the social norms circumscribing sexual expression, but within a context of anonymity, and affords a sense of sexual self-assertion, not otherwise available.

COMMERCIAL CONFIGURATIONS OF VERBAL DEVIANCY

Not all verbal sexual deviancy can be categorized as entirely private patterns. In our society much of the verbal sexual deviancy extant occurs within the context of commercial configurations of economically exploited sexual language, the most prevalent type being pornography in its myriad forms.[176] Pornography is not new, of course, inasmuch as there have been efforts to subvert formal language into salacious content since the beginning of civilization. There are ribald and sexual stories, and double entendre salacious sayings in the oral repertoire of even preliterate peoples. Pornography was well developed as a literary form in ancient times. Throughout history, and throughout the world, societies everywhere have seen attempts to facilitate mental sexual imagery, provide an impetus to carnal stimulation, and afford erotic gratification, using written and oral accounts of sex, sexual anatomy, obscene language, and lewd and suggestive prose. In some periods of history, pornography has flourished to the point of representing almost the literary zenith of the era, and in fact, some of our literary "classics" are well written pornography. In yet other times, and in some places, however, pornography has, in effect, almost withered on the vine, save for a few writers determined to perpetuate the tradition of literary erotica, and perhaps some amateurish efforts of questionable quality. It is interesting to note that many renowned painters produced erotic works even if they withheld them from public view, and similarly, many of our most acclaimed writers likewise had occasion to address their literary talents to carnal topics in their prose. In some instances, these efforts were also done, essentially on a non-publicized basis, and were largely avocational rather than for economic gain or fame. Mark Twain, for example, best known for his rollicking fictional accounts of growing up in Missouri, and for his sparkling homespun humor, had occasion to author *1601: Conversation as It Was by the Social Fireside in the Time of the Tudors,* a fictional and scatologically preoccupied account of Queen Elizabeth and several distinguished literary friends along with some members of her court having a discussion after dinner.[177] The book centers around an attempt on the part of Queen Elizabeth to determine the person responsible for a "monstrous flatulence" which disrupted the social gathering. Ultimately, the topic of conversation moves on to a "discussion of extra-marital fornication within the Queen's court." Twain purposely attempted to cram the book with as many obscene words as possible. As he once wrote to a Cleveland librarian, "If there is a decent word findable in it, it is because I overlooked it."[178] For many years *1601* was privately printed and distributed. His fame as a pornographer, among private erotic circles, spread, and when he visited Europe years later, was privileged to be able to be admitted to the secret treasure vaults of the Berlin Royal Library and be able to leisurely inspect the pornographic holdings of the Kaiser.[179] Benjamin Franklin also indulged in pornography to the extent of a "letter to the Royal Academy of Brussels outlining his plan to convert the offensive odor of flatulence into sweet smelling aromas by the addition of chemical powders to food."[180]

Early Erotic Literature

Erotic literature and other art forms were, of course, quite prominent in the earlier great civilizations, and in some instances there was concern about its control. The Spartan population was "rallied to feasts and the like with erotic songs and jests," but Plato, in 378 B.C., is reported to have insisted that the Odyssey be expurgated for juvenile reading. The centuries-old Chinese erotic novel, *Chin P'ing Mei,* was forbidden to readers until 1912, under penalty of a 100-lash flogging. Even Ovid's immortal *The Art of Love* had its Roman objectors. The third part of the book directed at women, which provided elaborate instructions on how to best cater to a man's sexual appetites (a kind of Roman *Sensuous Woman,* as it were) was considered to be so offensive that Ovid was permanently expelled from Rome in the year 7 A.D. by the Emperor Augustus.[181] Among the concluding passages in the book, Ovid instructed women:

> . . . My dear ones, feel the pleasure in the very marrow of your bones; share it fairly with your lover, *say pleasant, naughty things the while* [italics ours].[182]

Victorian Pornography

In the days of Victoria, in England, in the nineteenth century, it may have appeared to the untutored that proprietous comportment, and rigid community standards of morality had the upper hand over carnality, and that pornography was a dead literary form. In reality, nothing could have been further from the truth. Out of that period, for example, was to come the heroic-sized classic *My Secret Life,* authored by Frank Harris. This monument to the persistence of pornography consisted of 4,200 pages of sexual and erotic minutiae. It was published privately in eleven volumes, over several years, around 1890, and clandestinely distributed. It represents a chronicle of 40 years of sexual detail, and, thus, stands as a kind of carnal history of the period. The author, himself, asserts at the outset his determination, "to write my private life freely as to fact, and in the spirit of the lustful acts done by me or witnessed; it is written therefore with absolute truth, and without any regards for what the world calls decency."[183]

With the twentieth century came not only, perhaps, a wider array of pornography, both of amateurish bent and largely devoid of literary merit and genuine artistic accomplishment, but pornography was also reaching an increasingly wider constituency. Where at one point, only the more affluent citizenry might bring home from their trips to Europe smuggled copies of the various works of Henry Miller or other erotic best sellers published by Olympia Press or other similar houses, increasingly legal permissiveness, the erosion of earlier community norms of decency and strict morality, and new publishing and distribution mechanisms have all tended to make for an enormous increase in the range and amount of salacious literature available to the general public.

PORNOGRAPHY AND THE LEGAL SOJOURN

Actually it was only early in the nineteenth century that pornography really began to arouse public concern in this country.[184] In 1815, six Philadelphians were convicted in court for exhibiting an indecent painting for profit. In 1842, a law was passed barring obscene pictures in the United States, and in 1865 similar items were barred from the mails (for fear that Union soldiers might receive such material and be demoralized). With the movement to the cities, however, the demand for pornography grew. It was literary masterpieces like *Ulysses* and *Lady Chatterley's Lover* that broke the legal ice that had frozen most pornography out of the American market. In 1933, *Ulysses* was declared nonpornographic in District Court, and in 1959, *Lady Chatterley's Lover* was allowed to circulate by court decision. Two years earlier, the landmark Roth decision, however, had drawn a distinction between sexual and obscene materials using the definition, "whether to the average person applying contemporary community standards, the dominant theme of the material taken as a whole appeals to prurient interests."[185]

With the legal gates down, the flood of pornography roared through the spillway and washed across the United States. The former clandestine classics were now readily available in the local book store of Mainstreet America. A veritable deluge of "soft" pornography appeared in the paperback book and magazine racks often produced not so much as literary efforts as pure economic exercises in pandering. Such books and magazine articles are often "mass produced" in a fashion, not unlike coffee pots or cheap clocks. One writer, for example, reported on his own sojourn as an assembly-line worker in a porno factory.[186] As a staff writer, he was expected to work from 9:30 A.M. to 5:30 P.M. and produce 40 pages of erotic material per day for a weekly salary of $120. The staff writers worked on novels with the subject matter category being assigned. The main categories of novel themes were S (straight sex), G-M (gay male), and G-F (gay female). There were secondary categories of such topics as pederastry and bestiality. The basic task was to translate sexual fantasy into sheer verbage, using such managerial instructions as, "Emphasis on the innocence of children, lechery of adults. Boys from six to thirteen; girls six to fifteen. Emphasize hairlessness, tiny privates, lack of tits, etc."[187]

HARD CORE PORNOGRAPHY, MEDICAL EROTICA AND SEX MANUALS

In addition to the artistic literary pornography, and the mass-produced soft-care pornography, there has been, of course, the so-called hardcore literature for those of less demanding literary taste, but more of a salaciously depraved reading habit. There have also been the so-called "sex manuals" that have traditionally and obstensibly been designed for persons seeking more insight, if not sophistication concerning sexual physiology, and a more harmonious marital sexual adjustment. Many such books, although originally written utilizing a professional or clinical tone, have obviously provided some degree of carnal titillation, if not vicarious sexual stimulation for many readers, male and female. The trend in the content of such books, however, has tended to become increasingly erotic and to provide advice aimed at persons with more catholic sexual taste. Van De Velde's classical *Ideal Marriage* first published in 1930, and a perennial bestseller for decades thereafter, was antiseptically clinical, and while relatively complete in its exposition on the physiology of sex, was hardly innovative, much less daring in its suggestions for erotic diversity.[188] In places, perhaps to soften the clinical regimentation of the book, the author even inserted several "intermezzos of twenty aphorisms"—romantic and profound sayings and passages from books and poems. Subsequent sex manuals were somewhat more erotic in content and imaginative in suggestion even if still authored by physicians or other professionals. By the 1970s, however, numerous volumes dedicated to sexual instruction were being authored by lay persons, who were more concerned with carnal variety, than rehashing basic lessons in gynecological anatomy. The super best-selling, *The Sensuous Woman* by "J.," for example, counseled women to "train like an athlete for the sake of love," by masturbating, and to sweeten up their oral sexual activities by applying whipped cream, with vanilla and powdered sugar (with perhaps shredded coconut or chocolate, as a "finishing touch"), to their partners' penises.[189] Those with a weight problem are advised to use "one of the artificial whipped creams now on the market." "J." was particularly emphatic about the erotic properties of verbal sex. She counsels, for example:

> One of the most erotic areas of a man is the *inside* of his head. His response to sexy pictures, pornographic literature or your voice on the telephone cooing provocative sexual suggestions is usually instantaneous and obvious.
> The smart woman never forgets the importance of arousing him mentally. Whispering to him *exactly* what you intend to do to him in bed will create pictures in his mind that are likely to excite him almost as much as the actuality.[190]

Alex Comfort's also best-selling, but perhaps more sophisticated, *Joy of Sex,* recommended "lighthearted bondage and spanking to rock lyrics."[191] Reuben's, *Everything You've Ever Wanted to Know About Sex But Were Afraid to Ask,* was encyclopedic in sexual esoteria, and equally open in its endorsement of carnal hedonism.[192]

PORNOGRAPHY IN THE POPULAR "SLICKS"

In addition to erotic books, recent years have seen a literal publishing explosion in the publication of erotic periodicals of all variety and format ranging from the dingy pulp men's "adventure" magazines with a few fictive accounts of sexual escapades or information such as cavorting with prostitutes in Tijuana, or the details of female masturbation, to the new crop of slick, "girlie" periodicals such as *Playmate, Penthouse, Gallery, Genesis, Oui,* and *Hustler,* that feature quality layouts, very professional photographic essays of total, and sometimes gynecologically complete, female nudity, and instructive essays on such topics as oral sex, and sado-masochism. The ubiquitous presence of such magazines in the corner drugstore and the neighborhood newsstand suggest a significant erosion of the norms, both legal and social that formerly proscribed public pornography, and perhaps a much enlarged public reservoir of prurient interest which motivates the purchase and consumption of periodicals obviously designed to stimulate, if not satisfy carnal appetites. The list of erotic magazines would not be complete without mentioning *Screw,* a tabloid of less slick format than the average "girlie" magazine, and featuring gross sexual humor, reviews of pornographic films and products, and ads from prostitutes and "willing" amateurs. Allied to the expansion of the pornographic literature industry, has been the growth of the ancillary products field which has included the production of almost 5 million dildos in the last decades, the enormous sales of all manner of vibrators and other sexual devices, and even more recently the crafting of leather sexual harnesses and "bondage" equipment.

A popular press with elements of erotica, even if subtle by today's standards, in its contents was even present in the Victorian Era. One writer, for example has observed:

> The mid-Victorian age witnessed the emergence of the popular press. Newspapers and magazines proliferated as literacy increased and publication taxes ended. . . .
> Periodicals said a great deal about the female sex, but implied even more about female sexuality. The majority categorized women as either angels or devils, a dichotomy popular in Western literature at least since Biblical days.[193]

No doubt, many readers, both male and female derived some modicum of carnal stimulation or gratification from even these relatively erotically sterile tid-bits of sexual allusions.

Sometimes erotic symbolism is utilized in a hidden or latent fashion in product advertising in a variety of popular periodicals as a means of subliminally promoting sales. Occasionally, such sexual symbolism or obscenities may appear accidentally in large circulation periodicals. In a recent issue of the Montgomery Ward Catalog, for example, a full-page, full-color photographic advertisement for a bed and spread, also showed a "common four-letter vulgarity for sexual intercourse" scrawled on the wall behind the bed. Inserted by a disgruntled employee, the obscene word appeared in eight million copies of the catalog, and no doubt, startled, if not offended, a number of readers across the country.[194]

SPOKEN PORNOGRAPHY

Commercial spoken pornography has been as prominent as written pornography. There were explicitly sexual plays and dramatic performances in Greek and Roman times, and Medieval troubadours included ribald and lewd songs in their repertoires for audiences who craved entertainment more carnal than heroic ballads. Although not commonly known, Gilbert and Sullivan had occasion to write an obscene opera called *The Sod's Opera* with characters such as a butler named Scrotum (Sir Arthur Sullivan, it will be remembered, also composed "Onward Christian Soldiers").[195] In recent years, the Broadway theater has been increasingly open in its portrayal of the full spectrum of sexual themes and activities with attendant verbal dialogue and/or songs. These have ranged from nudity, masturbation, and homosexuality in such plays as *Hair, Oh Calcutta!,* and *Geese,* to bestiality in *Futz.* Similarly, films, both underground and regular commercial features, have turned to salacious content and carnal themes as a means of increasing the box-office take. The sexual content of such films has ranged from relatively naive suggestive scenes (or lack of scene) in *The Outlaw* and suggestive lines in *The Moon is Blue,* to movies offering nudity, coitus, homosexuality, and sado-masochism. *The Story of O* and *The Story of Joanna* feature bondage and the sexual torture of females, and, of course, *Deep Throat* and *The Devil in Miss Jones* show explicit scenes of fellatio along with the verbal story line. One pornography film, *Sweet Movie,* features a striptease for children and scenes of a "band of rollicking adults who vomit, defecate, and urinate on one another to the strains of Beethoven's *Ninth Symphony.*"[196] Even radio and television now provide a medium for erotic communication. Al Goldstein, the publisher of *Screw,* now produces *Midnight Blue,* a "thrice-weekly hour-long softcore cable-TV program that now takes ads for massage parlors."[197] Pornographic television programming now include such catholic erotic offerings as male strippers, dramatizations of sadomasochism, visits to a tropical fish store where the salesladies are topless, and Al Goldstein (the publisher of *Screw*) interviewing Carol Connors (who appeared in "Deep Throat").[198]

Some writers have also underscored the existence of so-called "topless radio" shows where listeners are "invited to call in and discuss matters oriented to sex and sexual activity." Topics might include the "endless varieties of oral sex," and "the number and frequency of orgasms."[199] These programs were mostly aimed at, and solicited, the participation of women. Most have been forced off the air, however, by the FCC inasmuch as many listeners who did not seek to be sexually enlightened, much less stimulated, complained of having their audio privileges invaded without consent.

"BLUE" ENTERTAINMENT

Pornography is also often dispensed orally on a commercial basis via the media of "blue" nightclub comics, and so-called "party" records. These two instruments of verbal sexual communication have been relatively neglected by social scientists, although at least one sociologist[200] has recently provided an exposition on this type of verbal sexual activity. The "blue" comic is the heir to the medieval troubadour with his lewd songs and jests, the Mister Interlocutor of the nineteenth century minstrel shows, and the burlesque show comedian of the twentieth century. The blue comic is often featured entertainment at night clubs and cabarets and offers salacious humor and obscene language as his means of "entertaining" the audience. He becomes a kind of carnal cheerleader, as it were, whipping up the level of sexual stimulation in the audience and facilitating their vicarious carnal imagery and gratification. Blue comics may take on individualistic styles, perhaps relying on a scatological obscenity theme, or emphasizing homosexual activity or some other sexual entertainment such as exotic dancers or strippers, and often command extremely lucrative salaries. Some blue comics have had such distinctive styles and a social impact that they have become virtual cult heroes and individuals of natural controversy, and show business legend. Perhaps the most publicized and controversial of all was the legendary Lenny Bruce.[201] Other more recent heirs to Bruce's legacy of carnal following might include George Carlin, Cheech and Chong, or Richard Pryor.[202]

The occupational specialty of blue comic is a unique one—the societal steward of obscene or sexual humor who regurgitates it verbally for the sexual stimulation and carnal gratification of an audience who, at least on that occasion, chooses to tolerate the violation of language norms and becomes avid fans of verbal sexual deviancy. For those persons who need their memories refreshed and their prurient interests renewed or appeased, or who do not have direct access to the blue comic, the "party record" represents a means of being sexually titilated on a second-hand basis by the recorded voice of a blue comic, and thus, effect to retrieve their sexual language, at will, and be stimulated as their carnal appetites dictate.

SUMMARY

Language as a symbolic system of shared experience, permits us to vicariously engage in behavior in our mind, and to transmit our feelings and experiences to others. Sexual behavior and feelings are among those experiences that can be communicated verbally. Since the genesis of civilization, man has dealt with his carnal appetites and drives using verbal sexual mechanisms of rich diversity and elaborate content. These verbal sexual mechanisms have, in many instances, tended to violate existing social norms attempting to regulate sexual expression and channelize carnal impulse. Such private patterns of normative violations have, not infrequently, been treated as pathological, if not criminal, and have often elicited severe social and legal sanctions. Concomitantly with such labeling of private sexual deviancy has been the often more tolerated economic exploitation of verbal sexual expression, with various commercial configurations of verbal sexual deviancy, serving as mechanism of patterned evasions of the norms of sexual control.

Language norms may proscribe the use of various categories of words and phrases. They may include blasphemous words or words used inappropriately relative to religion, words pertaining to certain anatomical components or bodily functions, or words that have a sexual meaning or reference. Language norms may also attempt to control or sanction the use of certain tabooed words by particular categories of persons. Words used by adults may accordingly, be inappropriate for children to use. Women may be constrained not to use some phraseology permitted to males. Words used between married couples or lovers may be proscribed for public use. Thus, the inappropriateness of some language may be a function of the category of person using it. Similarly, there is a contextual element to language norms. Language permitted within the context of an adult party may be forbidden at work. Some words, used openly with some relatives or kinsmen, may be inappropriate with other kinsmen. Language appropriateness or inappropriateness is relative to time, place, and circumstance.

Sexually explicit sexual talk or even sexual obscenities may be component to lovemaking because such talk enhances sexual fantasy and sexual stimulation, and accordingly facilitates carnal gratification. Even such sex talk is not always a modal communication pattern between some spouses, however, and in some families, it may be particularly dramatic when these language norms are violated.

Not all sexually explicit words are necessarily obscene or completely objectionable. Such words, along with labels for some anatomical parts of the body or bodily function, may be used in a Latin or scientific form and, thus, be acceptable. There may also be various euphemistic forms of words for such things which are more acceptable in common or public use than the more tabooed Anglo-Saxon "four-letter" words. There are even certain literary phraseologies for sexual activities, anatomy, or bodily functions that may serve to convey the information in a non-offensive fashion.

Where language norms are violated, however, there may be relatively severe social sanctions. A child who uses dirty words may have his mouth washed out with soap. A person who uses obscene language in a public place may be ejected, arrested, and fined or jailed. Obscene language in literature may lead to the literature being banned, and the author and/or publisher being subject to legal sanctions.

Some individuals may violate the social norms and proscriptions concerning language and may employ obscene or other inappropriate language. They may do so for a number of reasons: because they are inarticulate with more appropriate vocabulary, because of the situational context such as during lovemaking, or as a mechanism for generating vicarious sexual imagery or aiding in obtaining carnal gratification. In some instances, however, there may be a pathological and/or compulsive element to the use of sexual obscenities and sexually explicit language. An illustration of such verbal sexual pathology is the obscene phone caller. There is a widespread problem of individuals making anonymous telephone calls mostly to women, and either breathing heavily into the receiver, using obscene language, or trying to elicit intimate sexual information from the person called. The callers are sometimes simply "thrill seekers," not infrequently, juvenile or adolescent males. In other cases, they are a kind of verbal voyeur who obtains vicarious sexual thrills and gratification from obtaining intimate information about the female's sexual habits or preferences. In yet other instances, however, the caller may derive vicarious carnal gratification from the shock of the woman when he makes obscene remarks to her over the phone. In offending propriety, the caller achieves a sense of sexual mastery from the salacious interaction. In general, obscene phone callers are lonely, frustrated, and feel sexually inadequate. They rarely are prone to violence or move on to more serious sexual offenses.

There are callers who do not use obscenity or try to elicit sexual information from the female. Instead, they try and engage the female in conversation, and then sexually stimulated by her voice, masturbate. This practice appears to be especially prevalent with openline crisis therapy agencies employing women counselors. The women cannot hang up or report the call because to do so would be antithetical to the agency's mission. On the other hand, they frequently feel angry and sexually exploited by being used by the caller in his vicarious dyactic activities. The callers sometimes even try and get the counselor to encourage him or participate more fully in his fantasy. In employing such verbal deviancy, the telephone masturbator is, in effect, victimizing the agency that is available to help him. Just as some persons are sexually stimulated by directing anonymous obscenities at others, some individuals are stimulated by having sexual obscenities directed at them. In this regard prostitutes and massage parlor masseuses frequently report that patrons request them to yell at them or verbally abuse them with sexual language.

Some verbal sexual deviancy and obscenity is tolerated, and especially in some situations, but there are social limits, and when these limits are exceeded the offender may well be sanctioned. Persons who swear in public may be arrested, and individuals who are habitual users of obscene language may be ostracized or avoided. Inappropriate or obscene language may precipitate fights, cause the politician to lose the confidence of constituents, or result in individuals being rebuffed in their interpersonal relationships.

Obscene or pornographic literature or films can be banned or their publisher or distributors can suffer legal sanctions. The banning of books whether relatively innocuous by today's standards or genuine hard core pornography, generally brings controversy and the issue of degenerate smut versus the freedom guaranteed by the First Amendment is usually raised, bringing a variety of authorities into the argument. In recent years, there has been an increasing trend for some persons who produce or sell pornography to launch a legal counterattack and go to court to protect the individual's right to buy and sell any kind of literature that he wishes. Sex magazines, having largely supplanted pornographic books, have tended to take the brunt of public criticism and attack for violating the norms of verbal deviancy, conformity, and propriety.

A number of authorities, including the President's Commission on Pornography, have indicated that exposure to pornography or erotica produces no anti-social behavior but the evidence is not compelling to many social scientists and some individuals do not accept such findings as valid.

For a detailed treatment on the relationship between pornography and behavior by two investigators that take some issue with the work of the President's Commission on Pornography, see H. J. Eysenck and D. K. B. Nias, *Sex, Violence and the Media* (New York: St. Martin's Press, 1978). Although interest in pornography does not necessarily indicate pathology or deviancy, there are instances of preoccupation with obscenity and sexually explicit language being viewed as personal pathology and treated as such.

In one study of a group of children hospitalized in a mental institution, their "socially aberrant" behavior centered around their excessive use of sexual vulgarity and obscenities, sexual play, and disruptive behavior. The boys, resentful about having been rejected by parents and society, created a deviant contraculture and used offensive sexual language and play to terrorize and disrupt the hospital staff. In this instance, the verbal deviancy was, in large measure, precipitated, sustained, reinforced, and perpetuated by group pressure and sentiment.

An interesting and endemic mode of verbal deviancy is graffiti or obscene or sexual writing on the walls of public buildings or in toilet stalls. Graffiti may reveal prevalent sexual or even political or philosophical attitudes. It may also be a plea for sexual advice, a manifestation of hostility, or an expression of sexuality. It may serve as a marker of gang territoriality or simply an act of defacement of public property. It is a kind of verbal defecation and a verbal attempt to communicate in a symbolic carnal fashion using raw sexual expression.

Pornography has, of course, historically been the principal form of commercialized configurations of verbal deviancy, and some erotic and proscribed masterpieces were known and read clandestinely even in ancient times. Just as pornography has a lengthy history, so too do the social and legal efforts to repress, proscribe, or control it. In recent years, however, our society has clearly moved away from an earlier, more strict observance of sexual conformity, and control in literature. More recently, medical erotica and sex manuals have tended to supplement, if not supplant, more traditional forms of sexual literature as a source of sexual titilation and carnal gratification. Spoken pornography in the form of obscene dialogue in X-rated movies, party records, and the night club repertoire of "blue comics," not to mention porno cable television programs that include obscene conversation and sexually explicit topics and scenes, have all become prominent modes of contemporary pornography and, thus, verbal deviancy. In spite of vigorous social efforts to proscribe and minimize verbal deviancy, violations of the norms have historically occurred and such behavior has continued to provide sexual stimulation and carnal gratification for many, even if socially forbidden and sanctioned.

Chapter 5

ANATOMICAL EXPOSURE AND CARNAL CONNOTATION

Sexual Deviancy in Symbolic Context

Among other qualities differentiating him from the lower animals, man is the only species that may derive mental gratification from observing others of his kind naked or in the act of sexual intercourse with another. The other animals do, however, rely on visual stimuli to some degree as an aid in sexual receptivity and thus mating. In this regard some researchers have observed that, ". . . throughout the mammalian kingdom, exposure of the female genitals seems to be a cue for coitus."[203] The bright plumage of some male birds, for example, is a factor in attracting and courting females. Humans, on the other hand, develop cultural attitudes in regard to the naked body and the degree and circumstances in which it may be exposed to others. Such attitudes may address themselves to such questions as modesty, appropriate modes of clothing the body, and conceptions of privacy. All such attitudes are subject to extreme variations among the various societies.

THE CULTURALLY RELATIVE CONTEXT OF NUDITY

In general, modesty values usually, but not necessarily universally, concern the covering of the genital area. Supplemental modesty values may dictate also partially or completely concealing the nates and the female (and sometimes the male) breasts. In some societies, other parts of the anatomy including the feet, the face, and even the arms or legs are covered in the interest of modesty. Occasionally, the genitals are not covered but other parts of the body are. Taureg men of the Sahara cover their faces, but in some parts of the Middle East, it is the women who are veiled. In Bali and in some parts of Oceania, the females expose their breasts.[204] In Japan and China traditionally, however, the females kept their bodies covered with the exception of their faces and hands. Devout Mormons wear Latter-Day Saints undergarments or underwear "without interruption." Even when taking a bath, they always keep one toe within at least a foot of their underwear so as not to violate their religious proscription.[205] All modesty values, however, regardless of the society, are usually subject to further variation based on such factors as age, sex, time, circumstance, and occasion. What may be modest for one age group may not be for another. Children may be dressed in the minimum of clothing, perhaps even left naked, but adults are usually culturally compelled to be dressed in conformity with some normative standard, except in special circumstances. In this regard our society, like most others, has an elaborate system of constraints, and proscriptions and prescriptions concerning how, when, where, and why the body must be clothed, the circumstances appropriate to various degrees of undress or nakedness, the person or persons who may be privy to one's nakedness, and the situations and conditions in which nakedness or partial nakedness is rendered an erotic stimulus for others.

NUDITY AND SEXUALITY

Although there are numerous cultural justifications concerning the norms of modesty, there is clearly a strong element of sexuality in nudity, and the very fact of the genitals being uncovered suggests symbolically that they are more accessible. Nudity, then, at a symbolic level represents the facilitation of, and receptivity to, potential sexual behavior, and, thus, there is more of a probability as well as possibility of sexual interaction. Weinberg in discussing modesty and sexual connotations, has commented:

> The manifest function of sexual modesty (i.e., those consequences evaluated by a common-sense rationality) is maintained by social control

over latent sexual interests. Common-sense conceptions of modesty also put most emphasis on the covering of the body when in the presence of the opposite sex for the performance of this function.[206]

Persons are carefully socialized concerning the norms of modesty and generally inculcate a strong sense of personal self and social consciousness concerning their anatomical privacy. Similarly, individuals are also socialized and culturally sanctioned in regard to the violation of the bodily intimacy of others. Thus, just as it is a serious violation to peep at others who are naked or involved in sexual activity, it is likewise usually a social offense to expose one's own nakedness to others. Freed points out that there is indication in the Biblical book of Genesis of a Judeo-Christian heritage of proscription against nudity and/or looking upon nudity.[207] In Genesis (9:21–23) mention is made of Noah's sons who encountering Noah naked in a drunken stupor who, ". . . walked backward carrying a garment with their faces turned away, and covered their father without looking at him."

Individuals go naked, or expose portions of their intimate anatomy in the presence of others and especially others of the opposite sex in violation of social proscription, for several reasons. They can even justify their actions with various rationale. People can exhibit their bare anatomy out of pride, for economic purposes, or to frighten, disgust, or even interest members of the opposite sex. Public nudity, partial or total, may be fashionable, an act of defiance, or a concession to obtaining effective medical care. Persons may exhibit themselves in order to attempt to sexually stimulate the observer or as a means of sexually arousing themselves. Nudity may be pursued in the interest of health and vitality, to be more comfortable, or constituent to entertaining. Depending on the social context, anatomical exposure may be conceptualized as artistic, erotic, healthful, or even "cute," or it may also be defined and labeled as pathological, perverted, and/or criminal.

Wearing clothes is not natural to *Homo sapiens,* and, therefore, individuals everywhere must be culturally constrained to wear any type of bodily apparel, and thus any conceptualization of modesty must be assiduously inculcated and persistently sanctioned. Many young children are prone to disrobe and parade naked if not monitored on a regular basis. Some parents will even let their young children go naked as a concession to heat (in the summer), to alleviate the discomforts of skin rashes and infections, to avoid having to wash clothes, or even because the children may not be completely toilet trained. Slightly older children may sometimes engage in sexual curiosity games such as "Doctor and Nurse" that involve exposing their genitalia to each other or encouraging young children to disrobe in order that they may inspect the younger children's intimate anatomy. The problem of children and exposed anatomy is not infrequently a matter of consternation in many neighborhoods where there is a concentration of young children, inasmuch as the parents are frequently getting reports about their own offspring's shocking the neighbor's kids by disrobing or attempting to inspect their friends' genitals or vice versa. This practice is sufficiently typical of childhood behavior in our society that it has been a topic of discussion in some manuals on childrearing including Dr. Spock's well-known handbook. Similarly, "playing doctor" is so prevalent a sexual game among many children that it even evokes nostalgic memories in some adults.

ADOLESCENT FADISH NUDITY AS DEVIANCY

When children grow to adolescence, they may outgrow disposing of their diaper to run free and cool, and they may give up playing "Doctor and Nurse" (at least for a time) but they do not necessarily give up nudity. Although teenagers, and especially males, may go nude in single-sex groups, such as in swimming in a local creek or pond, nevertheless, they are usually relatively circumspect about modesty norms. There are certain near-institutionalized instances of nudity in the name of thrills, peer group conformity, and defiance, however. A case in point is the traditional sport of "mooning," which has been relatively endemic to many teenage populations, at least since World War II, if not earlier. (In an episode of the popular TV series, "The Bob Newhart Show," an old friend from Bob's college days visits and reminisces about instances of mooning in which he and Bob had been involved.) "Mooning" refers to the practice of baring one's buttocks and prominently displaying the naked *derriere* out of an automobile or building window. The automobile provides the protection of mobility and escape, and in this variation, only a small number of individuals may be involved. Mooning from a building usually occurs in some institutionalized setting such as a college dormitory. Mooning activity here often involves larger numbers of persons and may offer the protection of numbers and anonymity. Mooning, presumably, has no real erotic value, at least at any conscious level of awareness, although it does obviously have a sexually symbolic connotation. It is in a sense a juvenile act of bravado and defiance. It is an adolescent prank but also a symbolic insult to conformity and standards of propriety. It is the young's assertion of insolence and daring and says to the witnesses, in effect, to "kiss their ass." It is usually a fad or craze like flagpole sitting, goldfish swallowing, phone booth stuffing, panty raids, or streaking. It is usually an exclusively male activity, but in recent years, some females have been involved in mooning. Although mooning can evoke sanctions if the perpetrators are apprehended, it is normally a collective activity with more of a novelty and diversion motivation than salacious and is, accordingly, seldom viewed as pathological or perversion.

In the early 1970s, another configuration of teenage nudity, "streaking," spread across the nation's college campuses in epidemic fashion.[208] In many ways, streaking can be viewed in a social context similar to that of mooning. Streaking is a youthful assault on adult standards of conformity and social values. It, like mooning, is an act of sexual defiance. As Toolan, Elkins, D'Encarnacao et al. have put it:

> While streaking is not in itself a sex act, it is at the very least a more-than-subtle assault upon social values. Its defiance serves as a clarion call for others to follow suit, to show "the squares" that their "old hat" conventions, like love, marriage, and the family, are antiquated.[209]

Initially, streaking was a relatively isolated phenomena, confined to a handful of more venturesome and daredevil young people who were, in effect, Columbuses, as it were, on exploration voyages of public nudity. Like so many other campus fads, however, it expanded both geographically and in terms of the number of students involved. During its heyday, people streaked in stores, during public ceremonies such as parades and high school commencement exercises as well as on television programs such as the Academy Awards ceremony. Streaking even became prevalent in some high schools. Although late for the craze, there was even a streaker at the Olympic Games in Montreal. There were streakers on skis observed in Oregon and even five students who parachute-streaked over the campus at the University of Georgia.[210] At one point, running nude through public areas, "had become a fad of epidemic proportions among students from California to Maryland."[211] Such was the extent of streaking that, "one Los Angeles radio station broadcast 'streaker alerts' to warn the populace that naked youths were on the loose."[212] Streaking began essentially as a student prank, but spread across the country to many colleges and universities, crystallizing into a student fad with relatively institutionalized parameters. Streaking was, perhaps, not only springtime fun and pranks, but also a manifestation of the "new morality," and as such was, "perceived by many to be a challenge to traditional values and laws."[213] It was, in effect, the college generation flaunting their new liberated outlook in the faces of the older generation of more conservative posture. According to Anderson's analysis, streaking emerged as a full blown national fad for several reasons:

> The factors leading to the crystallization of streaking at ASU, and we would hypothesize on other campuses too, were: the emergence of a milling process, the emergence of core activists from within existing campus organizations, the emergence of support for the fad on the campus, and a weak initial response by social groups.[214]

Streaking, according to Anderson, terminated in time because of, ". . . social control groups assuming a stronger stance and adverse situational conditions."[215]

Toward the end of the streaking era, some college campuses saw hundreds of streakers on a single day. The University of Georgia experienced an informal streaking day when thousands of spectators gathered to watch several hundred streakers of both sexes. A similar occurrence took place at the campus at Memphis State University where a total of more than 5,000 spectators viewed more than 200 streakers, both male and female including some married students. One team of researchers managed to interveiw some of the nude participants and their findings are interesting.[216] The streakers did not consider themselves exhibitionists. Many reported that they had experienced negative feelings before their streaking, but positive emotional states during and after the streaking. The great majority indicated that they would streak again if the conditions were right. In terms of motivation, two principal themes emerged—the largest percentage spoke of their streaking as "attention getting," but a substantial percentage said their action was a "rejection of authority." They seemed to find security in the fact that friends were near by, and many seemed to be "comforted by the blanket of darkness." Although the young people were guilty of participation in a socially deviant form of behavior—public nudity, nevertheless it was concep-

tualized by society as a relatively innocuous college "rites of spring."
As James M. Toolan has phrased it:

> Streaking, I believe, can be viewed as a spring ritual similar to panty
> raids. It is a spontaneous outpouring of youthful sexual energy, and
> certainly seems an innocent enough activity: one or more youngsters,
> naked, sprint quickly past a group of startled, curious observers and
> disappear . . .[217]

As an act of defiant non-conformity, there were incidents of
youthful public nudity before the streaking era. Throughout the
period of the hippies and the flower people, there were reports and
pictures of young people in towns like San Francisco who sometimes
strolled down the street nude or partially nude. At some of the
various rock festivals, several women would take off their bras and
blouses, and ultimately both male and female would in some instances completely disrobe. Even public sexual intercourse at such
gatherings was not unknown.[218] During World War II, *Life Magazine* carried a picture of a man in one of the Nazi occupied European
countries walking down the street in hat and shoes and nothing else
as a means of protesting the rationing imposed by the German forces
and the resultant shortages. As long as social norms dictate clothing
the body as an exercise in modesty, exposing all or that part of the
body normally covered in public will represent a defiant act of nonconformity and non-allegiance to the community standards of propriety or decency.

NUDITY IN THE QUEST FOR SUNSHINE

For some persons nudity may not be so much an act of defiance
as an act of conviction, although they may recognize that in doing
so they, too, are defined as deviant for violating the norms of bodily
modesty. Nudists, as an ideological posture, take the position that
there is nothing shameful about any part of the naked anatomy or
any of the bodily functions such as urination or defecation.[219] Nudists maintain that nudism and sexuality should be essentially disasso-
ciated. Since they would run the risk of arrest and punishment if they
attempted to implement their anatomical beliefs in public, they withdraw, from time to time, to secluded camps where they can enjoy the
privacy from public scrutiny that will permit them to relax and
socialize with others of the same anatomical persuasion, while every-

one is nude. By sequestering themselves away from prying eyes, and, in effect, protecting the public from their nudity, the nudists can also protect themselves from charges of exhibitionism, indecent exposure, or creating a public nuisance. As the nudists themselves see their scope and aim:

> If the individual, in a state of complete nudity, leads a natural hygienic life in the open, has immediate contact with sun, air, light, water, warmth and cold, and takes well-balanced exercises, he will derive great satisfaction, regain hardihood, develop physical fitness, a feeling of freedom, a distinct sense of the enlargement of his personality, and the maximum mental benefit.[220]

To insure that no public labeling of nudists as immoral in behavior be validated, nudist camps often enforce stringent rules prohibiting alcoholic beverages, overt sexual activities, and develop elaborate procedures for monitoring the admission of newcomers as a means of keeping out undesirables, such as curiosity seekers, too many singles, and persons whose actions "might conceivably discredit the ideology of the movement."[221] At an informal level, but no less vigorously sanctioned are social norms that discourage staring, sex talk or dirty jokes, unnatural attempts to cover any part of the anatomy, bodily contact, or any accentuation of the body. Photography is a taboo except for official photographers who take non-erotic pictures for nudist periodicals. The nudist may go without clothing, but not without their stringent norms of proprietous sexual comportment. Even an erection may prove embarrassing to a male nudist, inasmuch as it may suggest that he was sexually stimulated by looking at other nudists, an inappropriate response to the body. It is an official tenet of nudism that the naked body must be ridded of erotic connotation. In this connection they assert that:

> Complete nudity in association with the opposite sex will furnish adequate knowledge of the physical make-up of the other, will obviate the abnormally erotic effect of the concealment caused by clothing and will permit the full development of a sex life unhampered by false modesty and unassuaged curiosity. It will bring a mutual selection for mating and procreation based on an appreciative understanding of the complete personality of the mate.[222]

The nudists may, in preoccupation with a de-eroticized body, be overlooking the point that the erotic qualities of the nude or partially nude body, even if culturally contrived, are, nevertheless, important visual cues in sexual stimulation. Effective and pleasurable sexual interaction depends on physiological arousal and receptivity, and the quality of sexual gratification is enhanced by the mental machinations which attend the erotic context of human anatomy. In any event, the well-intended motives and rationale of nudists does not insulate them from public disapproval or being labeled as deviants for their patent transgressions of our cultural standards of bodily modesty.

EPIDERMAL EXPOSURE AS FASHION

Apparently, not all persons of nudist persuasion sequester themselves in camps. It would also appear that some individuals enjoy nudity but are constrained to de-eroticize it. For years in Europe, nude or at least topless (for females) swimming and sunbathing has been popular. In this connection the beaches of such resorts as St. Tropez in southern France are often the scene of many young nude or topless female bodies basking in the sun. For the less adventurous, the European bikini bathing "suit" accomplishes essentially the same goal as nudity. The young European males and tourists by the busload flock to the beaches to ogle the suntanned bodies. Although resisted in this country, nude bathing beaches have now become a reality. Black's Beach in San Diego has been sanctioned by city ordinance as a "swimsuit optional" beach.[223] On a nice weekend between 10,000 and 12,000 persons of all ages will frequent the 900 foot stretch of sand. Eight out of ten who go there are completely bare, although there are some women who go topless with a string bikini on the bottom. Black's Beach also attracts its share of observers, some with cameras and even telephoto lenses, although it is said to be risky to actually go on the beach itself to take pictures. The regulars at the beach refer to those who come to gawk as "dirty-minded voyeurs." Tourists naturally come from all over to observe, but the San Diego City Convention and Visitors Bureau pretends that the beach does not exist. Several agencies have started trying to contact nudists throughout the country and lure them to Black's Beach for a vacation, and many sun-worshippers do come from distant places. Although many of the nude bathers are undoubtedly genuine ideological nudists, some of the other persons on the beach are going nude for a lark or to exhibit their anatomical pulchritude. It was reported, for example, that one young woman strolled about nude with the phrase, "Eden—Behave or Lose It" painted in lipstick on her back suggesting a degree of levity not normally encountered in real nudists. Although nudity is legal at Black's Beach, there are signs at the edge of the beach requiring swim suits or other clothing beyond that point. Undoubtedly, many other "swimsuit optional" beaches will be opened around the country, and there will probably be increased public toleration of nudity in the future, even if only situational and confined to limited areas.

Some nudity or partial nudity may result from pride or fashion. The late Hollywood movie star, Tyrone Power, and his wife, Linda Cristiansen, were reported to have had busts of themselves sculpted which depicted them nude from the waist up. The busts were supposed to have been prominently displayed in the living room of their home. Allegedly he was as proud of his manly physique as she was of her well-endowed breasts. Presumably, the persons most attracted to the revealing fashions of recent years were those individuals who had something to show or at least thought they had something to show. It is not likely that many flat chested women would be enamored of Rudy Gernreich's topless bathing suits, or dresses with plunging necklines. Although some persons obviously have exaggerated conceptualizations of their anatomy, many of the females in bikini bathing suits, mini-skirts, and peek-a-boo dresses are persons with anatomical configurations appropriate for display. In this regard, it is interesting to note that as in numerous periods throughout history, some degree of nudity, and especially in well-endowed females, under the influence of dress (or undress) fashion, has been tolerated and quite often salaciously enjoyed by the public constrained to observe. Males were not without manifestation of anatomical display. The codpiece of several centuries ago was designed to call attention to the male genitals that were clothed but still prominent in their exaggerated presence.

GENITAL EXHIBITIONISM AS DEVIANT BEHAVIOR

Nudity or exposure of intimate portions of the anatomy may be socially tolerated to a degree in some circumstances. Mooning and streaking may be viewed as adolescent pranks and teenage fads, and nudism may be conceptualized as simply an eccentric ideology espoused by generally harmless "kooks." Public swimming and sunbathing *sans* suit or topless may be seen as a daring manifestation of sexual liberation, and the behavioral province of the *avant garde* but there is seldom more reaction than mild public disaffection and, perhaps, more stringent enforcement of modesty laws. There are other contexts in which individuals expose their bodies or their sexual organs, however, which are not greeted with the same degree of public toleration. Where a male deliberately exposes his genitals to others, and especially females, his action is generally viewed as abnormal, perverted, and criminal. Exhibitionists have long been the subject of clinical discussion since Lasègne first coined the term in his classic article.[224] Some authorities like N. K. Rickles have attempted to articulate three main categories of exhibitionists:[225]

A. Depraved exhibitionists, for whom exposing their genitals is a constituent part of a larger syndrome of unconventional behavior aimed at complete sexual gratification.
B. Exhibitionists who suffer from organic brain disease, such as feeble-mindedness, epilepsy, and schizophrenics, who have become careless, lost the sense of social amenities and the ability to tell right from wrong.
C. The compulsive psychoneurotic exhibitionist. It is this latter category of exhibitionist to which most of the clinical and criminological literature has been written.

Female Exhibitionism

Exhibitionism is almost exclusively a male offense. Females would appear not to expose themselves in a compulsive manner. Prostitutes, of course, may expose themselves to males in a deliberate attempt to arouse the man and obtain a customer. Some women, particularly emotionally disturbed or intoxicated females have been known to disrobe in public. The drunken female party goer who strips naked and jumps into the host's goldfish pond or swimming pool is sufficiently frequent that many persons have at least heard of or seen such an occurrence. There are even cases of women disrobing on airplanes. In one anthology of erotic situations which airline stewardesses have reported, one told of a middle-aged woman who, while drinking her fifth martini at the cocktail lounge of a jet passengerliner, calmly removed her blouse and skirt and leaned against the bar, "not a bad figure for an old bag, eh, boys!"[226] Such instances of anatomical exposure appear to be primarily where the individual is drunk and perhaps is only barely aware of what they are doing. Cases of compulsive female exhibitionism, however, are essentially clinically unknown.

Male Exhibitionism

As pointed out in an earlier chapter, there is something of a double standard operating in regard to voyeurism and exhibitionism, with males being subject to more stringent social control than females.[227] If a male surreptitiously observes a nude female, he may be accused of criminal voyeurism, and the female is considered as the victim of the offense. On the other hand, if a female even accidentally observes a male while nude, she may still be considered the victim, and the male may even be conceptualized as a exhibitionist exposing himself. Among adolescent males, voyeurism is apparently more frequent than exhibitionism, but instances of exposure are not unknown. Inasmuch as some young males are apprehended or reported while streaking or mooning, not all cases of exposure must be viewed as exhibitionism. Some therapists suggest that with adolescent males where there is a pattern of deliberate exposure of their genitals to females, that the males have "serious concerns about the security of their sex roles." The young men may not have established a satisfactory relationship with females, and may instead be frightened of women or even angry toward them. The episodes of exposure may be an attempt to "interest, frighten, or disgust them." Isolated cases of exhibitionism may be related to unusual stress but a repetitive pattern of exposure suggests a more compulsive motivation.[228]

Exhibitionism, and especially among young men, although deviant and a criminal offense does not always suggest pathology, but may only be a manifestation of cultural pattern. According to Melitta Schmideberg, for example:

> Exhibitionism is not necessarily an indication of mental abnormality. In certain slum-neighborhoods this is an accepted form of courting, and only in respectable middle class areas are passers-by likely to call the police.[229]

Many otherwise normal males, young and old, may succumb to stress, or the temptation to be promiscuous or erotic with the opposite sex and impulsively expose their genitals. For some depressed persons, the daring act of exhibiting themself may give them "a sense of exhilaration like taking a drink."[230] For yet other individuals, and especially younger males, exposing themselves may simply be an act of poor judgment, or lack of appropriate internalized control when coupled with the enthusiasm of adolescent sexuality. For some exhibitionists, the act of exposure may be sudden and impulsive, with little or no previous mental predisposition to commit such an act. In other persons, exposure may accompany stress, depression, or trauma. In the typical compulsive exhibitionists, there is often a history of repeated offenses, although not necessarily involving apprehension. Even though there may be many episodes of exposure without arrest, some authorities speak of the "need of the exhibitionist to be apprehended."[231] Arrest, so James Mathis asserts, gives the offender "excitement and a feeling of manliness for posing such a 'threat'." Arrest, he says also, "tends to alleviate his sense of shame and guilt, similar to the atonement acts of the compulsive neurotic." Some exhibitionists may expose themselves with greater frequency over time and with increasing openness, as if inviting arrest.[232]

Many exhibitionists tend to exhibit a sense of "detachment" about their act.[233] In such instances, they may deny that they were the offender, or tell the police that their actions were simply due to an urgent need to urinate. Others speak of their condition during the act as "dreamlike" that prompts some professionals to raise the possibility of "amnesia" and the attendant question of "irresistible impulse."[234]

Exhibitionists seldom attempt bodily contact with their "victims," much less more violent sexual offenses. Some men exhibit only to certain categories of females, i.e., adolescents.[235] Some masturbate after they expose themselves, while others do not. Usually, the "victims" are strangers.[236] Where men exhibit only in front of very young girls, it has been suggested that the offender symbolically "soils" a virgin, as it were, by his act. In some instances, the victims may even have to wear certain kinds of clothing.[237] If a female does respond to the exhibitionist, he will generally become panicky and run away (there are instances of women accepting the exposure as an invitation to sexual intercourse and inviting the man to her apartment. The exhibitionist almost invariably leaves without speaking).[238] More men are arrested for the crime of exhibiting their genitals to females than any other sexual offense.[239] Many exhibitionists apparently give up their exposure behavior as they mature and before they are apprehended. Of those who are apprehended, a majority do not repeat the offense.[240] Interestingly, according to

Blank, "white exhibitionists are encountered more frequently than Negroes and Roman Catholics more than other religious groups." This would suggest that one factor contributing to exhibitionist behavior is "a more repressive sexual upbringing."[241]

For many exhibitionists, and especially younger males, according to Irving Barnett, the act is a kind of communication. In describing one of his patients he says that:

> His acts of exposure can be seen as a desperate attempt to assert his masculinity and to communicate with girls.[242]

Probably no sexual offense is more clouded by myth and exaggeration than is exhibitionism.[243] The exhibitionist, for example, is often thought to be a dangerous, or potentially dangerous, criminal. Such individuals in fact, however, are more passive than normal, and as Mathis puts it, "Exhibiting his penis to a strange female is about as feebly aggressive as he will become!" It is commonly believed that an act of exposure is inviting sexual intercourse. Actually, the behavior of exhibitionists in effect tends to disavow sexual intercourse. Some view the exhibitionist as a type of homosexual, but, in fact, there is "no overt association between the two conditions." Contrary to popular belief, the exhibitor is often not a deliberate offender, but is not under conscious control at the time of the exposure. It is also generally believed that the exhibitionist is an oversexed individual. In actuality, such persons are usually undersexed and enjoy a less than satisfactory sexual adjustment with their spouses. In view of the severity with which the offense is treated, it is relatively easy to demonstrate the popular belief that exhibitionists will progress to more serious sexual activities such as rape, etc. Experience has shown, however, that it is extremely rare for persons who expose themselves to subsequently commit more serious sexual crimes. Additionally, as an individual ages there is the strong likelihood that there will be a "spontaneous reduction in the impulse to exhibit."

Even though most of the myths concerning exhibitionism have been professionally refuted, offenders, and particularly repeat offenders, are often treated severely by law enforcement agencies and the courts. The convicted offender may face loss of job, labeling as a pervert, the break-up of his marriage, and social ostracism, in addition to legal punishment. The recidivism rate for offenders is close to 10% where there is no previous record of arrest. Such persons are usually felt to be good probation risks.[244] Fortunately, many courts are using probation in such cases, to good effect, although often the stipulation for therapy is constituent to the probated sentence. Group therapy seems to have been a particularly effective approach inasmuch as "external pressure is needed to prevent the exhibitionist from using his pathological denial system to escape treatment prematurely."[245] Other successful therapy techniques have included such approaches as having the offender (client) undress and appear naked before a mixed sex psychiatric team while his "exhibiting behavior is discussed and related to his current feelings." The psychiatrists attempt to show no anxiety or apprehension while the subject's anxiety is "maintained at a high level by the intimacy of the questioning and by the proximity of the audience."[246]

Exhibitionism and Age

Exhibitionistic acts appear to occur particularly at two peak periods in the life cycle. The onset of exposure symptoms often occur in midpuberty. This is the period, according to one social scientist, when the individual seeks to "establish an identity and to free himself from a mother who has endangered his masculinity." The second peak period of exhibitionistic tendencies is often during the time of courtship and early stages of marriage. The male may experience frustration and be threatened by the fact of his attraction and ties to a female.[247] The offense then occurs at periods of stress and ambivalence, when the individual has concerns about his masculinity. Even when exhibitionism occurs later in life, it is not infrequently associated with identity crises, such as middle age or when faced with marital disruption. One author, for example, reported a "man that exhibited after his wife told him that she enjoyed sexual intercourse more with a neighbor than with him!"[248] The exposure of genitals is a mechanism for reassurance of masculinity. As one therapist has phrased it:

> The exhibitionist's compulsion that his penis be seen indicates a reliance on the visual confirmation of another person and, by the same token, a lack of confidence in his own power to perceive his bodily configuration. The difficulty in perceiving himself arises from his doubts about his tentative masculine identification which receives powerful reinforcement by displaying his penis to another person.[249]

Aside from neurotic problems of sexual identity crisis, there is also the consideration of sexual insight or sophistication, which may be lacking in some males, especially those of lower or lower-middle socioeconomic background. At one group therapy session of exhibitionists, the therapist reported that:

> None of the men know how most men dealt with sexual tensions, other than by immediate gratification.[250]

One man in the session indicated that, as an adolescent, he had been unable to control erections at school and dances. He had not been told about taking cold showers or concentrating on other things. Exhibitionists, apparently, can be "treated" on a probationary basis sometimes with psychotherapy and often with continued group therapy, provided they are constrained to continue with the therapy.[251] Fortunately, probation seems to be the modal punishment for most exhibitionist offenders.

As McWhorter has observed, there is a kind of comic (and perhaps tragic) stereotype of the exhibitionist as a ". . . dirty, leering older man, dressed in sneakers and raincoat," terrorizing women with their genital display.[252] Such a stereotype is perpetuated in cartoons, such as often appear in *Playboy* magazine, or in character portrayals like the example on the popular sitcom *Mary Hartman, Mary Hartman,* where the heroine, Mary, has an octogenerian grandfather known to the local police as "The Fernwood Flasher." As McWhorter has pointed out, such a stereotype is largely inaccurate, the offender is seldom dangerous, and the traditional sanctions for the "crime" are inappropriate.

Presumably, the intent of laws prohibiting indecent exposure or exhibitionism was to protect the public, and especially females, from the culturally defined carnal offensiveness of naked anatomy and genital organs, as well as to maintain an appropriate level of behavioral decorum detached from sexual connotation. Women have been assumed to be especially sensitive and subject to psychological trauma at the sight of male genitalia. In this regard, however, one study suggested that female victims of exhibitionism, "felt in retrospect that they had not been hurt by the exposer." Interviews with women who had encountered an exhibitionist revealed that, "the event did not so much harm them as surprise them." They tended to find the event, "rather weird and even inconvenient," rather than "dangerous." The victims had apparently used a variety of strategies in defining and coping with the encounters and, thus, in effect, neutralizing the event.[253] The momentum of the female liberation movement and unisex cultural tendencies may well serve to precipitate a larger incidence of male sexual identity anxiety in the future, which may in turn engender an increased frequency of exhibitionism. Given the sexual sophistication of today's women and the erosion of cultural insulation for them, in terms of matters sexual or otherwise, female observers may come to be relatively inured to the sight of male genitalia in public or otherwise and their reaction to such phenomena, blasé, if not humorous, rather than shock. Indeed, in some instances, they respond with enthusiasm and gusto. The owner of a nightclub that featured male strippers and had largely a female clientele, reported that the patrons, in addition to being amused and entertained, also become excited and physically vigorous in their very open response to the sight of gyrating, naked, beefcake. As she described the reaction:

> Women get turned on more than men do. They reach right out and grab.[254]

In one such establishment, an excited patron ripped the bikini off the male stripper.

SEXUAL SYMBOLISM IN THE MARKETPLACE

Some nudity is motivated by economic factors and effected with the intent of entertainment. Since before the turn of the century, and even earlier, many periodicals and newspapers have carried photographs of attractive females, often scantily clad or in tight fitting or otherwise sexually suggestive clothing. In an earlier, more circumspect day, such females would have been depicted in "tights," but more recently they might be shown in a string bikini in the newspapers and perhaps with nothing on in some periodicals, including even the more staid and solid family-type periodicals. American advertising has, for many years, employed sex as a mechanism for merchandising. In some instances, the sex may be largely symbolic in the form of suggestive slogans, geometric forms with Freudian sexual connotation, visual associations, and even animated motion. One television ad for an agitator washer used an animated version of its washer dressed in a tie like a man. Psychoanalytic studies had shown that some women, at least subconsciously, associated the agitator action of the washer with the thrusting of a penis and even liked to lean against the washer while it was on because of its vibrations. Using this unconscious association, the manufacturing company attempted to make its washer appear masculine in the animated ad, and, thus, maximize its appeal for the female purchaser.[255] In most instances, however, sex in ads appears in the form of nude or skimpily dressed, well endowed females. "Cheesecake" and calendar art have been successfully used to sell every conceivable type of merchandise from motorboats and cigarettes, to alcoholic beverages. Models for ads featuring semi-nude or suggestively clothed females often command very lucrative fees. On the other hand, many an aspiring model or actress may have had to pose in the nude for a very modest fee for calendar art, as a means of economic survival. The now-famous nude calendar photos of Marilyn Monroe, for which she posed in the days before she became successful, is a case in point.

TWO DIMENSIONAL NUDITY IN PERIODICALS

Parallel with the ad featuring the girl in the revealing bathing suit or in the nude has also been the "pinup" picture in the periodical. Stressing bare anatomy or form-revealing clothing, such pictures clearly have a salacious design and are intended to promote and facilitate vicarious sexual imagery and stimulation, if not gratification. As pointed out in Chapter 3, there has been a decided trend in pinup and cheesecake from the mere suggestive poses and only slightly revealing costumes featured in the *Police Gazette* of yesteryear, to the startlingly anatomically revealing photographs of today's periodicals for men. As pointed out in that section, the limits of salaciousness have moved rapidly to include curves, cleavage, nipples, pubic hair, and, most recently, detailed exposure of the female genitalia, both inside and out. Female nude pictures in some popular periodicals would seem to be more closely akin to illustrations in a gynecological textbook than traditional cheesecake. Some periodicals aimed at the amateur photographer may have occasionally slipped in a demure and artistic nude photo and *Esquire* may have had its pulchritudinous Varga girl paintings, but *Playboy* really brought nude photography into the American home via its centerfold "Playmate of the Month." But if more "tastefully" done nude photos in *Playboy* tended to offend the basic sense of anatomical propriety of many Americans, they had only to await the coming of competitors like *Oui, Gallery, Penthouse, Genesis, Hustler,* and others of the *genre,* with their photo essays on nudity and sexually suggestive behavior, to have their traditional conceptualizations of appropriate standards of modesty and epidermal propriety completely shattered. In spite of countless court cases and strenuous efforts, both formal and informal, in many localities, the slick "girlie" magazines featuring total nudity and completely revealing examinations of female genital anatomy, are openly available in most cities and many small towns. Although some of the more "conservative" periodicals like *Playboy* may even be available on magazine shelves in grocery stores, in some areas a would-be purchaser of it or a similar magazine might have to "ask at the counter" for it. In the larger cities, genuine hard core visual pornography is readily available in "adult" book stores. The nudity trend in periodical photos has perhaps gone far toward assuaging traditional male curiosity concerning the anatomical intricacies of female genitalia, but at the same time, it has afforded part-time employment to women who have few talents or marketable assets except their breasts, plump buttocks, and a willingness to expose their entire epidermis for a price. It is difficult to conceive of what direction such periodical photography will take in the future, but further exploitation of carnal tastes would seem inevitable. In this connection, it is interesting to note the appearance of *Playgirl* with its centerfold "Playboy of the Month" nude photo and the increasing appearance of nude males in some periodicals, perhaps catering to readers of a homosexual persuasion.

Nudity was not only a feature of men's "girlie" magazines. In the 1950s and 1960s some fashion magazines, and even popular consumer and family-type periodicals, also carried advertisements which depicted nude and semi-nude female models. Often, they had nude photographs in connection with their articles. By the 1970s, nudity in periodicals (both male and female) was endemic to many. Partial nudity had not infrequently been replaced with full frontal exposure and sexually suggestive poses.

Strippers and exotic dancers were, in a sense, in competition with two-dimensional nudity in magazines. Consequently, the product had to be improved to meet the competition. In an effort to enhance the erotic qualities of a striptease act, some female performers dispensed with their skimpy halter tops or "pasties" and danced "topless." The innovation was well-received by patrons, and the idea spread to other places of entertainment.

As researchers like Skipper and McCaghy have pointed out, strippers tended to have reached physical maturity early, and in comparison with most women, not infrequently are endowed with larger breasts.[256] Such physical assets serve as an "attention-getter" in their act, and some strippers, who are particularly large-breasted, have advertised the fact or built their act around their large breasts. As one stripper phrased it, "After all, a pair of 48s can make a girl feel like a real person. Everyone pays attention."[257] One such stripper is Morganna, who is alleged to have a 60-inch bustline. To generate publicity for her act, she often runs onto baseball fields at well-attended, big league games and surprises players by hugging and kissing them.[258]

San Francisco became the capital, as it were, of topless acts, and with the attention being focused on the naked breasts, some dancers and strippers sought means of augmenting their bust dimensions (which in many instances already exceeded those of the average female). These means include silicone implants, injections, and plastic surgery. Perhaps the stripper who attempted to capitalize on silicone-augmented breast size more than any other performer, was Carol Doda. She started her career with a relatively modest bust line but subsequently had a series of silicone shots, and in time, achieved near bizarre dimensions. She remained a major tourist attraction as a stripper (and anatomical curiousity) in San Francisco for a number of years.

Quickly, toplessness spread to other places of public accommodation such as bars and restaurants, and in the gambling cities like Reno and Las Vegas, there were even topless female blackjack and faro dealers. The topless establishments experienced dramatic increases in the volume of business, and, in turn, attractive economic inducements could be offered to female employees to expose their breasts. For many people, toplessness in business establishments was an outrage to public decency, but in some areas, the anatomical business fad resisted legal and social efforts to suppress it.[259] The customers were attracted out of curiosity and because the close observation of bare female breasts afforded a unique opportunity for vicarious sexual stimulation. The topless barmaids, of course, realized that their exposure was counter to traditional norms of modesty. As one topless barmaid interviewed by a researcher expressed it:

> They [the customers] talk about your body a lot, which I don't mind. You know, somebody comes over and stares. I have to laugh. When

you're taught all your life, you know, that you don't go around undressed, and then all these girls are running around nude, you can
expect them to stare. Your body is an art, and you're making an honest
living, but just the same, it's something that you've been taught
against.[260]

ECDYSIASTIC EROTICISM AS SIMULATED OR SYMBOLIC SEX

Perhaps no violation of the traditional social norms of modesty
is more long standing than the exotic dancer and especially the
stripper. Since the time of Salome there have been female dancers
who performed before men to provide sexual stimulation and vicarious carnal gratification. In spite of the traditional American values
concerning the privateness and sacredness of the human body, nude
exotic dancers and strip-tease "artists" have evaded the norms of
modesty and the community standards of anatomical propriety with
their epidermal exposure and ecdysiastic eroticism. The strip-tease
dance is America's contribution to the erotic dance. Strip-tease is the
gradual disrobement of the performer down to the minimal covering
of the genital area while keeping time to some musical accompaniment. It provides entertainment but also affords sexual stimulation.
An American innovation, it has found an enthusiastic reception in
many other parts of the world.

Stripping is a well-structured and institutionalized entertainment vocation that offers occupational specialization and employment for 7,000 females in the United States.[261] Its work dynamics
are not unlike other vocations in that it possesses conventional occupational processes such as recruitment, socialization, and control.
Stripping, however, must be considered a deviant occupation. This
is due to legal considerations in some instances, and in practically all
instances, stripping is in violation of community standards of proprietous anatomical comportment and "good taste." Stripping is
particularly popular in many resorts areas, but is found in most large
cities in America. It is outlawed in many parts of the country or at
least certain limits on anatomical exposure may be legally enforced.
Even where it is legal, if the performer becomes too suggestive or
obscene, or if she removes more clothing than the statute specifies,
she may be in violation of the law. Resort tourist audiences and big
city audiences are prone to want a sexually provocative act, however,
and because such audiences make a significant contribution to the
local economy, law enforcement officials may be flexible in interpret-

ing the law and/or be lax in enforcing it. Thus, the law may call for relatively circumspect performances, but the local police may tolerate obscene performances, and particularly lewd behavior such as "flashing" (lowering a G-string from time to time) if this is popular with the tourists and conventioners who spend considerable money in the community.

Although stripping has historically been a female vocation exclusively, the recent phenomenon of male strippers has added a new dimension to commercialized symbolic sex. Originally featured as a kind of novelty several years ago, male strippers have become a popular form of entertainment in some disco clubs and night spots around the United States.[262] The audiences are almost always female, often by design of the club owners. Some of the women came out of curiosity or to "gape and giggle." In other cases, their presence may represent more of "a kind of flout to their husbands and boyfriends."[263] Whatever the reason, the patrons would appear to enjoy themselves and often get caught up in the atmosphere of activity to the extent of stuffing money into the stripper's G-string as he dances and gyrates through the audience.[264] One news story about male strippers described a group of nurses, convention of female bus drivers, and parties of "bachelorettes" among the patrons of such shows. A matronly patron observed, "It sure beats going bowling."[265] As long as the male performers do not disrobe beyond a bikini brief or G-string, they seldom violate any law or statute, but community standards of proprietous behavior may sometimes be offended. One U.S. Navy petty officer, who was moonlighting as a male stripper in a nightspot that catered to women, was discovered by his superiors and punished. He was offered three choices—a disciplinary hearing, court-martial, or a discharge for disgracing the uniform. The petty officer elected the discharge.[266] A number of male performers, like the petty officer, are stripping as a "moonlighting" job. They are apparently motivated both by economic and psychological considerations. Some male strippers make $600 a week including the tips that women stuff in their G-strings. The men also enjoy the attention they get. As one male stripper put it, "It's an ego trip for everyone."[267]

Stripping and Occupation Origin and Identity

Strippers are not unmindful of their "sexual deviant" stigma because they expose their anatomy for economic gain. Various writers have reported that strippers often enjoy a negative image with some members of the public. Skipper and McCaghy, for example, found that college students held a negative image of strippers and tended to think of them as "immoral" or "prostitutes."[268] The students also spoke of strippers as "oversexed" and "hard women." Salutin, another researcher, commented, "Strippers are viewed as 'bad' then because they strip away all social decorum with their clothes; they taunt the public with their own mores by teasing them and turning them on."[269] The stripper is, in effect, exploiting her body and her sexuality and is, accordingly, a prostitute of sorts. Inasmuch as strippers sell sexuality and, thus, cater to a clientele seeking sexual stimulation (even vicarious), theirs is thought to be a basically depraved occupation serving a depraved clientele. Some patrons are simply indulging their curiosity, others are "out on the town," some are seeking erotic entertainment, but some, because of socio-economic background, or emotional disorder, may have difficulty in controlling or suppressing the sexual stimulation they derive from the salacious performance. They may yell and shout obscenities, and according to some writers, may even publicly masturbate. One writer, Terry D'Andre, says that such patrons are labeled as "degenerates" and referred to as "the gentlemen of the press."[270] Overly libidinous fans may proposition, paw, assault, or even bite strippers. (In Chapter 3, the account of an overly stimulated patron leaping up on stage and biting a stripper on the vagina, which required several stitches was reported.) Strippers only compound their anatomical deviancy by the fact that they work in the same milieu, and often associate with other social deviants—B-girls, addicts, hustlers, alcoholics, and the other regular habitués of bars and strip joints.

Strippers, along with go-go girls, not infrequently come from unhappy, broken or unstable homes.[271] Often, they matured young and were sexually precocious at an early age. In many instances, they entered the occupation in time of crisis or stress, particularly financial crisis, and the lucrative economic remuneration for publicly displaying their bodies motivates them to stay in the occupation. They rationalize that what they do is no different from what all women do. All women, as they see it, even wives, are really exhibitionists and prostitutes, but just charge a different kind of price, such as a dinner or marriage. They even redefine stripping as an "art form" and, therefore, socially redeeming. Stripping becomes show business and, thus, glamorous, exciting, and provides them with personal recognition and a sense of worth, even if they must endure some of the unsavory patrons and the label "sexual deviant." As Salutin put it, "Strippers like stripping because it makes them feel important, especially when the audience claps and cheers. They feel exhilarated. They also like the money."[272]

THE STRIPPER AND PATRON AS CARNAL DYAD

The stripper, as a performer, offers a service to her clientele— in this instance, her audience. Her service, however, entails the economic exploitation of deviant nudity. By exposing her nude anatomy, she provides erotic entertainment and vicarious sexual gratification. The audience comes to the establishment to observe the sexually suggestive act of the stripper, and presumably is appreciative for the opportunity for vicarious carnal gratification. The relationship between stripper and audience is sometimes a strained one, however. A recent study explored the social organization of the entertainment establishment offering stripping as the featured attraction, the normative sub-culture of stripping, and the patterns of interaction between performers and customers.[273] The authors of the study concluded that the pervasive motif within the strip club is the "counterfeiting of intimacy." Both performer and customer, however, recognize this "inauthentic relationship," and there are resulting feelings of alienation, and sometimes hostility and violence. The strip club provides artificial intimacy at a cost. It also represents the commercialization of carnality and the providing of salacious stimulation in the form of nudity and sexually suggestive behavior to persons who seek visual sex as substitute and supplement to genuine sex—for a price.

Sex can assume many symbolic configurations. In this society even the exposed genitals, or other parts of the anatomy, and bodily gestures and contortions that simulate or approximate coitus and other sexual interaction, all tend to have a salacious import and sexually stimulating effect on the observers. In view of such behavior, possibly precipitating sexual activity itself, an elaborate normative system operates to carefully define the limits of nudity and prescribe appropriate rules of modesty and anatomical comportment. Violation of such norms and especially those which prohibit the exposure of genitalia may evoke severe social and legal sanctions. In the face of such contraints, however, many individuals do violate the norms with private patterns of deviantly-labeled behavior. At the same time, however, certain commercial configurations of norm violations concerning nudity and the simulation of sexual activity provide a deviant outlet for those persons seeking to appease their anatomical curiosity and assuage their carnal appetites with symbolic sex.

Interestingly, stripping is said to be losing its attraction for many patrons. Apparently, more vivid forms of sexual symbolism that presumeably provide a more enhanced carnal gratification have taken its place. A decade back, Blaze Starr, the famous stripper said:

> Strip Houses are suffering everywhere—on Bourbon Street in New Orleans, in New York and San Francisco. The courts permit bottomless and topless waitresses. Nudity is everywhere.[274]

According to Ms. Starr, stripping provided "a suggestion of sex" but with "a little subtlety." In the sex movies being shown, however, one could "see the whole thing in the raw." She saw burlesque as ". . . one of America's most cherished art forms," essentially being killed by pornography and sex movies. As she succinctly put it, "If they get much filthier, I'll be out of business . . ."

THE VAGARIES OF SYMBOLIC SEX

Throughout history, sex has manifested itself in an extremely wide range or symbolic representations but recent years in the United States have seen a particularly catholic range of symbolic sexual forms. In Illinois, for example, it was reported by the minister of a United Methodist Church that a counseling program conducted by his church included nude therapy sessions. It appears that between 20 and 25 men and women participated in various "experiments" in both the church and at a weekend retreat at a motel in a near-by town. The "experiments" included nudity, "physical contact" (sexual intercourse was supposedly not involved), and therapy sessions "in which men, women and children breast fed on women who had stripped to the waist." The nude therapy activities came to public attention during two child custody cases in which the husbands claimed the wives were unfit mothers because they had been involved in the sessions. Participation in these therapy sessions undoubtedly had certain sexual symbolism value and must have afforded some degree of sexual stimulation, if not gratification.[275]

In New York, two women opened an establishment called The

Erotic Baker, Inc., which featured risqué pasteries and erotically shaped cakes and breads such as ". . . gingerbread men—and women —considerably more explicit than the ones grandma used to bake." Some of their specialties included ". . . rump cakes, crimson lips, bun loaves, his or her breads, candy cremes, hearts and an assortment of kisses," not to mention "licorice whips."[276]

In a similar vein, a baker in Dallas, Texas produces "porn-cakes." He has an album picturing 63 "X-Rated" male and female designs for decorating a cake. Most of the designs feature nude figures with minute anatomical details. The customer can pick any of the designs and the baker will create a cake and decorate it, accordingly. The baker indicates that most of his orders for the "porncakes" are from women who order them for men's birthday parties.[277]

In the recent gasoline shortage when drivers sometimes had to wait hours in lines of automobiles sometimes several miles long, some drivers were being entertained while they waited by a curvacious belly dancer who minimized the impatience of the drivers with her carnal gyrations and bumps.[278]

A most singular form of deviant sexual symbolism surfaced recently in the form of "X-Rated" puppets. In the Norfolk, Virginia area, an enterprising puppeteer developed a puppet stage show entitled, "Pinocchio's Hot Night Out," starring a promiscuous Pinocchio. After performances in a local theater to near sellout crowds, the puppeteer took his show to several taverns in the local area. The Virginia Alcoholic Beverage Control Board took exception to the sexual performance and threatened to take away the liquor licenses of tavern owners who allowed the puppet show performed in their establishment. The ABC Board contended that, "prohibition of 'lewd conduct' where alcohol is served applies to wooden people as well as those made of flesh and blood." The tavern owners cancelled the puppet show and the puppeteer, his reputation enhanced by the publicity, hoped to move on to Las Vegas and a more receptive socio-legal milieu.[279]

Perhaps, however, the newest vehicle for symbolic sex is television. In spite of some public opposition, there are now cable TV channels presenting such varied sexual offerings as male and female strippers, fellatio performances, visits to a tropical fish store that has topless salesladies, and dramatic demonstrations of sado masochism.[280] Given the American penchant for television viewing, the "lewd tube," as porno television has been called, may well become the prime purveyor of sexual stimulation and carnal gratification via televised symbolic sex.

SUMMARY

Humans, among the animal kingdom, are the only species that can mentally derive carnal gratification from observing other humans nude or involved in sexually suggestive activities. Such sexual stimulation or gratification may well be a function of social context and cultural interpretation, however, inasmuch as values concerning nudity, modesty, the invasion of anatomical privacy, and the taboo areas of the body vary widely from culture to culture, and are subject to differing interpretative postures and context. Individuals are socialized concerning the norms and values of modesty, and anatomical exposure, as well as the invasion of privacy and come to inculcate a strong sense of personal self and social consciousness concerning exposing the proscribed portions of their own anatomy or the violation of the bodily intimacy of others.

Persons do, however, violate such social proscriptions and expose portions of their own intimate anatomy for a variety of personal and social reasons, as well as invade the anatomical privacy of others in a deviant fashion. Depending on situation and circumstances, anatomic exposure may be conceptualized as artistic, erotic, healthful, or even "cute," or it may also be defined and labeled as pathological, perverted, and/or criminal.

Exposing one's own genitals or exploring those of another may even be component to the play of children as a means of assuaging their sexual curiosity. Going naked in public such as with streaking may be part of a prankish adolescent fad or an act of defiance in the face of a more conservative adult ideology and value system. Some individuals go nude in the company of others in the quest of sunshine, health, and sexual detachment. They must often seek to accomplish these goals by sequestering themselves in camps or colonies as a means of obtaining privacy and non-interference for their anatomical persuasion as well as protect the public from their nudity. Increasingly, such nudity practices can be effected in a more public context such as the nude beach.

Although streaking and nudism may be tolerated under certain conditions as simply idiosyncratic behavior, compulsive exposure of the genital anatomy is considered pathological and deviant.

Generally speaking, there are no female exhibitionists, save perhaps an occasionally mentally disturbed person. Compulsive nudity in a female is apparently more an instance of drunkenness or situational disequilibrium.

Male exhibitionism, although stereotypically a behavior of the aged, is actually more characteristically associated with mid-puberty and middle age and the crises attendant to these age periods. Exhibitionism is not infrequently a function of stress and identity crisis. There is seldom, if ever, any tendency to sexual violence, and the exhibitionist is essentially an insecure person attempting to reassure or reinforce his image of masculinity. In spite of the generally innocuous propensity of most exhibitionists they are generally treated in a relatively severe fashion. Given the sexual disequilibrium of recent years, it may well be that exhibitionism may not create the psychological distress among victims that it once did.

Sexual symbolism also appears in the form of nudity, sexual suggestiveness, and subliminal sexual forms in various kinds of advertising in the mass media. Additionally the sexually suggestive periodicals with their "gatefold" photographs of nude females (or males) is patently an attempt to offer two-dimensional symbolic sex to the readers. For millions of Americans, carnal gratification arrives in the form of viewing a one-third life size centerfold image of a *Playboy* Bunny "with a staple in her navel."

The forms of symbolic sex assumes many configurations including topless employees in commercial establishments, belly dancing, and that most American of carnal configurations—stripping. Stripping may be viewed as depraved from some community perspectives and as an art form from the standpoint of the participants. Stripping assuages curiosity, fulfills libidinous appetites vicariously and symbolically, and affords ego trips and social mobility to the performers. Stripping, however, is losing carnal ground to pornography and sexually explicit movies.

Even today symbolic sex is assuming unusual and bizarre forms such as erotic pastries, nude church therapy, and lewd television performances on cable television. Sexual stimulation and carnal gratification does not have to be the result of physical encounters—it may just as often result from exposure to or involvement in a context of symbolic sexuality.

Chapter 6

MASTURBATION AND MECHANICAL COITUS

Sexual Deviancy in "Imitative" Context

Masturbation is the stimulation of the genitalia to orgasm without heterosexual interaction. Inasmuch as this form of sexual activity is often viewed as departing from the "normal" or "natural," and, thus, prescribed mode of heterosexual orgasm involving intergenital stimulation, it is often considered as deviant sexual behavior, normatively speaking. In seeking to obtain orgasm by simulating the sensation attendant to intergenital coitus, masturbation becomes, in effect, a kind of "imitation" sexual intercourse. Stricter interpretations of masturbation may employ it only as a label for autoerotic, or self-obtained sexual gratification, but it may also be used to describe other configurations of genital stimulation by another person, other than by penis-vaginal intercourse, the most common mode being the manual manipulation of one's genital organs or area, by another individual, and especially manipulation to orgasm.

MASTURBATION IN CROSS-CULTURAL PERSPECTIVE

Self-genital stimulation of some degree and vigor is almost universally observed among infants and children. In some societies, especially primitive and folk groups, parents or relatives may manipulate a child's sexual organs as a means of pacifying him/her. William Stephens, in his exhaustive cross-cultural survey of marital and familial behavior, specifically mentions the Hopi, Alor, Navaho, and the Kaingang as societal groups who routinely engage in such a practice.[281] Masturbation can even be encouraged past puberty in some societies, but in general by the time of adolescence there are strong proscriptions against sexual self-stimulation, and often concerted efforts to channelize the sexual drive into more adult heterosexual modes, either through early marriage, or permissive premarital sexual intercourse. In some of these societies, there may be compelling reasons for delaying the marriage of young people, and especially young men. In some cases, for example, there may be a need for the young men to serve as warriors before taking on the responsibilities of husband, father, and farmer or livestock husbandryman. Such a necessity for military service is not without sexual problems for both young men, and societal group, and often engenders appropriate sexual coping mechanisms. The males must be "weaned" away from juvenile sexual self-stimulation practices since such activity might erode or dilute the new adult male role that they have been assigned. Complete sexual license with the unmarried females, however, cannot be permitted because of children that might be born to such casual sexual liaisons, and other problems such as emotional entanglements at a time when the men's attention should be solely devoted to the affairs of livestock and war. Some primitive and folk societies resolve the problem by institutionalizing some limited or occasional sexual license. Others, such as the Massai of Africa, as a cultural custom, see fit to mutilate the sexual organs of the young men when they are circumcised during their early teens. This serves the function of preventing masturbation and sexual intercourse during a prolonged period of healing—sometimes up to several years—while they are training to be members of the *Ol Morane,* the military-like corps of livestock guards and warriors.[282] The Zulu, however, in their heyday in the late 19th century employed the mechanism of heterosexual masturbation as a means of addressing the problem. Encouraged in sexual play with females before puberty, the Zulu male after maturity was subject to rigidly enforced celibacy. His primary task was the herding, and guarding, of cattle, and drilling or waging war as a member of one of the warrior *impis* (military units). Only after marriage later in life could the warrior enjoy heterosexual intercourse. The tribal sanctions for heterosexual relations during the celibate period were severe—the genitals sawn off with an iron knife by the witch-doctor, for consensual intercourse, and a sharpened stake hammered up the rectum as penalty for rape. As a sexual outlet for the young warriors, however, the king would occasionally order a ceremonial day of *ukHlobonga*, of masturbation performed on the men by the unmarried women.[283] Although in Western societies there are no comparable ceremonial occasions for masturbation, the same problem of sexual outlet for the young between the period of puberty and marriage exists. This is discussed in detail in another chapter.

In such primitive and peasant societies, however, masturbation along with other kinds of childhood sexual experimentation, is viewed, and utilized, within a functional and developmental context. Sexual awareness and maturity must be nourished and shaped to prepare the young person for the psychological and social responsibilities of adulthood, marriage, and parenthood relatively early in life. In this way, the individual can, upon attaining adulthood, be more quickly and effectively integrated into the total ongoing productive process of the tribe, village or society. Masturbation is tolerated because it is necessary that the individual be psychologically secure in his or her sexuality and comfortable with their own self-conceptualization. In societies with a marginal economic base, however, childhood and adolescence are necessarily brief, and the shift to adult status, abrupt. After puberty, the adolescent is weaned away from masturbatory self-indulgence and oriented toward the obtainment of sexual gratification within marriage and the deeper and more profound satisfactions of social, as well as carnal, fulfillment. Masturbation is, thus, tolerated and used in such societies as a socialization mechanism for adult sexuality which, in turn, is viewed as a social behavioral mode essential to the integration of the family group, and concomitantly, the larger society. Masturbation, as with other forms of sexual expression, would appear to be well integrated in, and functional to, the larger pattern of social cohesion in such primitive and peasant societies.

MASTURBATION IN WESTERN SOCIETY

Societal attitudes toward masturbation can be indicative of more basic cultural conceptualizations of self-group, and sexual interaction. Variations in such attitudes can, accordingly, represent fundamental divergences in these cultural conceptualizations. In industrial societies such as our own, for example, a somewhat different interpretive view of masturbation and attendant social values concerning the practice are taken. Traditionally in our society, masturbation was conceptualized as an inappropriate, undesirable, and, thus, unacceptable form of carnal gratification; this ideological posture was undergirded and bolstered by both religious and medical rationales. Masturbation, like all forms of hedonistic self-indulgence, would be antithetical to the physical resolve, discipline, and sensory asceticism appropriate and requisite to the demands of a developing Protestant, capitalistic, industrial economy and society. All forms of sensate self-indulgence were to be discouraged in the individual. The collective aims of society could best be accomplished through the social imposition of self-control and self-sacrifice. The individual, in effect, was expected to submerge his own sexuality and sensual fulfillment in attainment of larger religious and social goals. By subverting his need for carnal gratification to the needs of productive society, the individual still made a contributive, and, thus, integrative, input to the cohesion of the larger social entity.

Masturbation carried the onus of religious stigma, inasmuch as it represented a subversion of the sexual urge that would presumably motivate and thus, lead one into socially countenanced heterosexual interaction such as in marriage, as well as manifesting an unproductive concern with self-indulgence. The traditional concern in our society (as in England) with health and well-being is essentially the Cartesian perspective of an industrialized society viewing the body as a machine that must be well maintained to be efficient. If masturbation represented the "misuse" of the body, and, thus, constituted a health problem, it therefore follows that it is bad and is to be socially proscribed and sanctioned. Masturbation, then, in the view of industrialized society, was traditionally seen as dysfunctional to the goals, and, thus, well being of society and, like various other forms of carnal expression and gratification, rationalized as morally and medically suspect and accordingly, condemned.

In Western societies, masturbation has traditionally been proscribed and discouraged because of strong moral and medical values, as opposed to only the concern with the breaking of juvenile patterns, found in non-industrial societies. The moral objections to masturbation grew out of the general early Christian ideological posture (and particularly the teachings of Saint Augustine) that sex was a necessary evil, that accordingly was only justified as a means of procreation.[284] Even later when the Augustinian view was tempered by other theological writings, any sexual gratification outside of marriage was still considered sinful. Masturbation has traditionally enjoyed both biblical label and injunction as the "Sin of Onan," even though this was a misinterpretation of Holy Scripture.[285] Beyond specific religious proscription, masturbation has been viewed as morally bad because it involved a surrender to lust and carnality, because it is narcissistic and selfish, and, thus, unaccompanied by love, affection, or tenderness toward others, and because it is an unessential and socially nonfunctional preoccupation with self-indulgence and hedonism.

Masturbation as Medical Malady

Although masturbation received little medical attention prior to the 1700s, in the latter part of the 18th century, the medical writer Tessot in his influential book, *L'onanisme: Dissertation sur les Maladies Produites par la Masturbation,* frightened both public and medical profession, when he asserted that "masturbation leads to inevitable ruin."[286] Over the next 150 years, most of the medical profession joined in a general condemnation of masturbation, and issued dire prognoses about its effects. Masturbation, so it was believed, could and probably would lead to an early death, and also, "spinal tuberculosis, general paresis, generation of malformed children, eventual impotence (if a man) or sterility (if a woman) and epilepsy ultimately leading to insanity were inescapable."[287] Numerous medical treatises were written during the 1800s that both identified masturbation as a causal agent in a wide variety of neurological and neuro-psychiatric diseases as well as suggested remedies and preventative measures. There was particular concern with masturbation among children and young people, and among institutionalized patients and inmates. To aid parents in coping with the maligned practice among children, so-called "masturbation clinics" were conducted and devices such as aluminum mitts and chastity belts were prescribed to parents for their children while they slept.[288] The remedies mentioned in the medical books of the day range from the ludicrous to the barbarous. Schwarz, for example, writes that in 1827, Dr. Heinrich Robbi, a German physician, published a book on masturbation in which he charged that the practice derived from "French influences," but suggested that "German nationalism," might be an effective antidote.[289] Other books such as Johann Flecks,

Erroneous Turns of the Sex Drive, published in 1829 suggested a corset-like leather harness with a rigid tube to encase the penis, as a means of preventing masturbation. Other medical inventors produced similar devices of leather and steel which, when worn, prevented the individual from having access to his sexual organs. In time, other physicians such as Dr. John Moodie of Scotland developed a similar harness for young women not unlike the medieval chastity belts in design.[290] By Victorian times and into the early part of the 20th century, the medical profession began talking about a disease they labeled "spermatorrhea," "involuntary seminal emissions" or "sexual neurasthenia." The "disease" they had literally invented was nothing more than nocturnal emissions, more commonly known as "wet dreams" today. Victorian morality and female propriety no doubt moderated the frequency of marital intercourse, and masturbation was viewed as a disease. The nocturnal emissions that subsequently resulted were often viewed as evidence of involuntary masturbation during sleep. Various appropriate devices to alleviate this problem soon appeared, including machines that alarmed or gave an electric shock to the individual when his penis would expand during a nocturnal erection.[291] Also popular were "spermatorrhea bandages" that simply strapped the penis to the body, and, thus, prevented erections, as well as "spermatorrhea rings" that encircled the penis and sometimes had spikes that painfully pricked the penis if an erection occurred. Various cages to enclose the genitals were also suggested. If one wonders about the motivation for submission to such medical torture, it should be recalled that the prescribed treatment for excessive masturbation, in this period, was "cautery of the prostate gland and cutting of the nerves leading to the penis in males, or removal of the clitoris or the ovaries in females."[292] Impotence or sterility was the result. Preventative measures were, accordingly, seen as the lesser of evils. Although many such devices were developed in England or on the Continent, American inventors were not without resources. During the period between 1856 and 1932, patents on 33 sexual restraint devices such as "masturbation-locks," etc., were issued by the U.S. Patent Office.[293] Many of the anti-masturbation devices of this period were designed for men, but some were also invented with females in mind. In 1908, a sanatorium nurse named Perkins invented an elaborate harness-like device which she called "sexual armor." Over time, other inventors improved on her design, adding such additional features as shoulder braces containing chains and handcuffs. Schwarz notes that even after World War I, some medical supply houses still listed some models of sexual restraint devices in their catalogs. In time, however, the voice of medical reason prevailed, and physicians such as Max Hodann, authored writings viewing masturbation in a non-pathological light. His book, *Masturbation—Neither Vice nor Disease* in 1929, began to turn the medical tide.[294] Interestingly, even in contemporary textbooks on urology, some physical problems are still attributed to "excessive self-indulgence" (presumably extreme cases). Perhaps, even more interesting is the fact that in a recent study of the sexual attitudes and knowledge of high school, college, and medical students, 16% of the medical students and residents "indicate a belief in an etiological connection between masturbation and mental illness."[295] Third year medical students were less likely to hold such a view than second year students, but surprisingly, "residents show an increased tendency to view masturbation and emotional illness as linked."

MASTURBATION AND MENTAL ILLNESS

During much of the period when masturbation was viewed so dismally, medically speaking, and especially during the late 19th century and early 20th century, masturbation also came under the scrutiny of psychiatry and the emerging school of psychoanalysis. Early in the 19th century, the label "masturbatory insanity" was being applied to some cases of mental disturbance, and particularly those patients in some mental hospitals who were observed masturbating on occasion.[296] Freud wrote of masturbation occurring even in early infancy, and continuing through the "Oedipal" state and into puberty as part of normal psycho-sexual development. Masturbation could become part of a neurotic syndrome, however, particularly if compulsive and if continued on past adolescence. Heterosexual activity was conceptualized as healthy and appropriate for adults who had experienced normal personality development and had outgrown the self-centeredness of adolescence and who could share and communicate. Continued masturbation into adulthood, therefore, according to psychoanalysis, would suggest a fixation at an infantile or at least a non-adult level of psycho-social sexual development and might, therefore, suggest the inability to achieve an adult heterosexual relationship. It could even lead to impotence. The psychoanalysts have filled hundreds of volumes, in the intricate dialect of their disciplines, with the various problems of neurosis, phobias, psychoses, etc., some associated with masturbation.

Throughout most of the 19th century and the early part of the 20th century the preoccupation in the medical and psychiatric field with masturbation as a causal factor in mental illness was almost an obsession.[297] This was more the case with English, French, and American medical authorities than with those in Germany, however. There were some who even asserted that children inherited a tendency to masturbate. Joseph Howe, for example, asserted that, "the child of masturbating parents enters the world with vitality so impaired that there is a constant invitation to the attack of every affection."[298] Some persons were actually confined to mental institutions because of masturbatory practices and others were threatened with incarceration. There was a blurring of the line between mental illness, immorality, and social nonconformity. Laziness, ennui, disobedience, or insubordination to parents were all seen as possible indicators of masturbatory practices with the attendant "moral insanity." Edward Spitzka, a somaticist alienist, and leading advocate of such a theoretical posture, believed that, "an unwillingness to work at an appointed task was a symptom of masturbatory insanity in adolescence."[299] It was believed that masturbation tended to weaken the individual and racial stock because it was unnatural and caused greater excitement to the nervous system than "natural" coitus. Additionally, it was believed that masturbation resulted in the excessive loss of a chemical called "spermin" that was produced by the testes, prostate, thymus, and blood, and which when retained in the body, "acted as a catalyst to break down nitrogenous waste products in the nervous system.[300] The excessive loss of "spermin" could result in "autointoxication and nerve damage." This, in turn, would cause the "aberrant mental behavior of masturbators." Masturbation was, of course, also perceived as erosive of the human will, the social fabric of morality, chasity, the strength and respectability of marriage and the family, and symbolic of disrespect to authority.

After the medical, psychiatric, and moral onus on masturbation had been eroded by the enlightenment of the first few decades of the 20th century, there still remained a considerable residue of concern about the "problem" of masturbation in boys. Parents might view even clandestine masturbation as unwholesome, if not unhealthy, and would provide both admonishment and sanction against the practice. In stubborn cases, where medical advice was sought, the family physician might recommend circumcision to relieve irritation, and, thus, temptation where the boy still enjoyed the physical integrity of foreskin. The Boy Scout manual, as a guide to the development of character in young men, included an enigmatic section on "Conservation" which, to the insightful, could be appropriately decoded as advice against self-abuse.

MASTURBATION AND SEXUAL DYSFUNCTION

Perhaps the most outspoken condemnation of masturbation along with other sexual advice and insights was to be found in Jefferis and Nichol's classic book, *Light on Dark Corners,* first published in 1894, kept in print for several decades, and recently reprinted, where the authors reassure the readers that contrary to popular belief, it is not possible to tell a masturbator by looking in his face. Having implicitly implanted the suspicion, however, that perhaps it is possible, they then go on to detail the effects of "excessive self-abuse" including impotence, sterility, neurasthenia, and a general nervous letdown. Most chilling was their prediction that,

> Early masturbation, if carried to excess, causes indifference to the normal sexual relationship. This is due to the fact that after years of mechanical excitations, the organs become so toughened that the substitution of the natural method fails to produce the desired result.[301]

Interestingly enough, the medical stigma of masturbation has lingered on in part, in that it has been believed to some degree by laymen, if not medical authorities, that premature ejaculation in the male may be the result of a heavy regimen of masturbation when younger. Masturbation it is said, in effect, acts as a dysfunctional conditioning mechanism. Such a causal relationship has been asserted both in factual and fictional writings. As an illustration of the persistent belief in the causal linkage between masturbation and premature ejaculation in modern fiction, consider an episode in a novel of the Korean War period. The author describes a conversation between the young wife of an Air Force pilot who was away on a mission, and another officer pilot who was a good friend of her husband. Essie the wife reveals:

> "I've never had any satisfaction with Pete [her husband]. Do you know what I mean, Dick?" She was still staring at the table, and she was a little pale, he thought.

"Well—that could be in your own mind, too."

"He's—he's on and off. Like a jackrabbit."

"Essie! Damn it, I don't want to preach, but this stuff ought to stay inside the family. I mean, what the hell, we're civilized people, I suppose, but we're not *that* damned civilized."

"Yes we are. Or we ought to be. I read about Pete's trouble in a book on psychology. Premature ejaculation comes from mother attachment and excessive masturbation in youth."

"Oh, Essie, for Christ's sake—."[302]

Recently, however, the work of Masters and Johnson has demonstrated the invalidity of such an assumption. They state, for example, that:

> Despite strong cultural beliefs to the contrary, masturbatory practices, regardless of frequency or technique employed, have not been identified historically as an etiological factor in the syndrome of premature ejaculation.[303]

MASTURBATION AND MATURATION

Masturbation would appear to be an endemic, if not normal practice among most boys, although it apparently is not without some mental distress or anguish. No one has, perhaps, provided more vivid or humorous literary insights into the self-perceptions of a boy masturbator than has Philip Roth in his bestselling *Portnoy's Complaint,*[304] and in his lesser known essay, "Whacking Off."[305] In his writings, Roth describes a pattern of adolescent discovery of self-induced orgasm, compulsive masturbation, and inventive fantasy as the protagonist seeks sexual release in all manner of orifices from cored apples, to milk bottles, and fresh liver.

Nor does masturbation cease at time of adulthood. Kinsey's research revealed that 90% of males surveyed masturbated as often as 2 or 3 times per week. Even after marriage, masturbation may continue, although with decreased frequency. Interestingly, Kinsey also reported that masturbation was more widely practiced and for a longer period of life by males of higher socio-economic background and better education.[306] Masturbation is reportedly most satisfactory as a sexual outlet when accompanied by sexual fantasy. The better educated and higher social level males are apparently better capable of a rich sexual fantasy life. Such activity may, of course, be associated with temporary deprivation of heterosexual outlet, such as in the absence of wife, during the wife's pregnancy, illness, or her menstrual period. It can occur at other times, however, and may or may not represent a problem in the marriage. Gadpaille, for example, has written regarding various psychiatric and marital disturbances of which masturbation may be symptomatic.[307] He suggests that in the area of marital disturbances, masturbation by the husband may represent a response to a spouse's inhibitions, frigidity, rigidity, or lesser sexual interest. It may also represent a husband's inability to deal with premature ejaculation or perhaps suggests a deep seated hostility or power struggle resulting in the withholding of sex as a weapon.

By the middle of the 20th century, male masturbation was being viewed in a less negative fashion. Some medical-sexual authorities such as Dr. Abraham Stone were conceding that the dangers of masturbation had been "grossly exaggerated," and that "as a rule," the practice would not prevent good sexual adjustments in marriage. He did suggest, however, that persons with a history of regular masturbation might "find it difficult to readjust their sex habits and to derive complete satisfaction from the sex union in marriage."[308] By the late 1960s, Dr. Wardell Pomeroy, of the Kinsey Institute, authored a book of sex advice to young males in which he advised them to masturbate as frequently as they wished. He did, however, suggest to them that they might attempt to masturbate as slowly as possible in way of training for the time when they would be lovers and husbands.[309] Component to the recent sex education program of many schools around the country are units on masturbation that both explain and encourage the practice. One writer, for example, tells of a sex education curriculum guide for the seventh and eighth grades in the city where she lives that includes developing "an understanding of masturbation," viewing films on masturbation, and learning "the four philosophies of masturbation—traditional, religious, neutral, [and] radical."[310] The writer goes on to report a Planned Parenthood pamphlet, *The Perils of Puberty,* intended for high school use that advises:

> . . . Sex is too important to glop up with sentiment. If you feel sexy, for heaven's sake admit it to yourself. If the feeling and the tension bother you, you can masturbate. Masturbation cannot hurt you and it will make you feel more relaxed.[311]

The Sorensen Report, published in 1973, provides some systematic perspectives of sexual activity among teen-agers in contemporary times.[312] The findings of this study in regard to masturbation suggest that 58% of the boys interviewed reported they had masturbated one or more times. Chilman surveyed the various research literature on adolescent masturbation and concluded:

> ". . . that about half of today's teenage boys and almost one-third of the girls masturbate by the age of 15. This figure probably rises to about 85 percent for males and 60 percent for females by the age of 20.[313]

Young boys and girls report masturbating at an earlier age than with older adolescents. Boys masturbate with greater frequency than girls, and a greater percentage of boys than girls say they enjoy masturbation a great deal or somewhat. Of those adolescents who masturbated, 80 percent believed they masturbated about as much as other boys or girls their own age. Slightly more than one-half or 51 percent of all masturbating adolescents, rarely or never express feelings of anxiety or guilt about their activity. Perhaps, most indicative of recent times, is the finding that of those adolescents currently masturbating, 27 percent of them using marijuana, as compared to 8 percent not using it, report a great deal of enjoyment.[314] Overall, it would appear that adolescents, and boys especially are masturbating at a younger age than in the past, are not in general, experiencing anxiety about the practice, masturbate more frequently than females, and are more prone to enjoy it. Chilman does indicate, however, that:

> . . . There appears to be a reduction in fear and guilt about masturbation among contemporary adolescents, though considerable embarrassment about the practice remains.[315]

There have been relatively few extensive studies of adult sexual behavior since Kinsey, but one conducted by Morton Hunt in the early 1970s suggested a slightly greater percentage of males in the recent study as compared to those in Kinsey's study of two decades ago (94 percent to 92 percent) had masturbated to orgasm. In terms of the age when masturbation began, however, a fairly significant change appeared from the time of the Kinsey data to the time of the Hunt data. Kinsey found that only 45 percent of all males had masturbated by the age of 13, but Hunt's data revealed that recently 63 percent of his reporting males had masturbated by age 13.[316]

Hunt also found that there is an increase in the frequency with which adolescents and young adults masturbate, as compared to Kinsey's respondents. Hunt reported a far greater tendency for young single men to continue masturbating into early adulthood and beyond. Of Kinsey's group, more than one-fifth had stopped being "active" masturbators by age 30. Only one-tenth of Hunt's males had stopped by this age. Hunt's masturbators past 30 were doing so almost twice as frequently as were those reported by Kinsey (60 to 30 times per year).[317]

MASTURBATION IN MARRIAGE

Even among married males, the percentage of masturbators and the frequency of their masturbation had both risen between the Kinsey and the Hunt surveys. Kinsey reported that more than 40% of husbands in their late 20s and early 30s still masturbated with a median frequency of 6 times per year. Hunt found that 72% of the husbands masturbated with a median frequency of 24 times per year.[318]

The general increase in masturbation reported by Hunt does not seem to be related to any reduction in genital coitus but simply an enlargement of opportunity for expression of sexual gratification. As Hunt phrases it:

Any increase in masturbation is therefore not a case of *faute de mieux* but a natural and normal result of the lessening of psychosocial restraints against most forms of sexual expression.[319]

Whereas during the Victorian era, "society would not admit that adult men masturbated,"[320] by the time of the sexually liberated 1970s, some authors, such as M, who produced *The Sensuous Man,* was quite vocal in his praise and encouragement of masturbation as a pleasurable and satisfying pastime and means of obtaining relief from tension. The question of masturbation after marriage, however, continues to trouble many persons even today. Medical authorities and psychiatrists, however, are generally reassuring, and contend that "masturbation is an acceptable variation within marriage today." They often especially commend it during periods when spouses are separated or ill. These authorities even suggest "learning" how their spouses masturbate by watching them. Such experiences, they say, "can be both exciting as well as useful in enhancing their knowledge of each other's sexuality."[321] Some physicians do admit the possibility of masturbation after marriage as manifesting some organic pathological condition or psychiatric disturbance. In the absence of such disorders, however, they suggest that marital masturbation may be more symptomatic of marital disturbance, especially when it serves as a substitute for intercourse. Such an action could serve as a weapon according to one author, inasmuch as, "sexual withholding and its flaunting by preferring masturbation is an extremely hostile act."[322] It could also arise out of sexual dysfunction. As the same author suggests:

> The retreat to masturbation may be secondary to other, preexisting sexual problems. Premature ejaculation and male impotence may force the wife to compensate her frustration by masturbating. The same conditions may undermine a man's sexual confidence to such an extent that he will ultimately limit himself to masturbation rather than risk continued failure. Female anorgasmia both frustrates a husband and undermines his sense of sexual adequacy.[323]

Such substitute reliance on masturbation, even in the instance of sexual dysfunction is not without problems, however. Masters and Johnson, for example, report the case of a married woman who encouraged her husband to seek sexual therapy because of his history of premature ejaculation. Because of the wife's "consistently high levels of sexual frustration," resulting from her husband's sexual dysfunctioning, she moved into a separate bedroom in order "to establish the privacy necessary to accomplish her own tension release satisfactorily" through masturbation. The husband, denied sexual release with his wife, sought sex outside of marriage, and became involved in several affairs, including one with his wife's recently widowed friend. The wife discovered her husband's affair, and her subsequent "anger, resentment, and wounded pride," effectively disrupted their marriage.[324]

From various clinical reports, and letters to the editor in different sex-related periodicals, it would appear that both wives and husbands in many marriages practice masturbation occasionally, if not frequently. They sometimes do it with their spouse's knowledge and consent, and on some occasions even observe their spouse's self-stimulation activities. In some cases, the masturbation may replace coital intercourse for one reason or another, while in other situations it may be supplemental to a normal regimen of coitus and

simply serve as an additional outlet for sexual gratification and carnal pleasure. One study of masturbation practices among 38 married
couples in Denmark revealed a relatively institutionalized pattern
among some of the couples.[325] The couples had been married for a
mean average of 10 years, and the majority of the subjects indicated
that they loved their spouse, were content with their marriage, and
had never seriously regretted the union. More than half the men still
masturbated as did more than one-third of the women. Where both
spouses masturbate, the husband tended to masturbate more frequently than his wife. Among the couples where both individuals
masturbate, in the majority of cases both the husband and wife keep
the practice secret from the spouse. A significant percentage of the
men who masturbated did so "as a matter of routine before brushing
their teeth and washing their hands." It was concluded that the men
masturbate as a supplement to their regular life, while the women
appear to masturbate as a substitute for intercourse. In this study,
the men, in general, tend to be "more positively inclined toward
masturbation than are women."

FEMALE MASTURBATION

Although historically the same moral and medical objections
were directed at the practice of female masturbation as with male
autoerotic activity, the medical and social diatribes against it do not
appear to have been either as vitriolic or vocal. One writer on the
topic, for example, has commented that "early medical writings on
female masturbation are uncommon and nonspecific . . ."[326] He goes
on to point out, however, that later (in the 19th century) various
female medical maladies were attributed to masturbation. As pointed
out earlier, masturbation in either men or women was seen to be
related, if not possibly causally related to impotence (if a man)
sterility, epilepsy, insanity, spinal tuberculosis, and a host of other
physiological, and particularly neurological, disorders. In this connection, women, like men, who were "afflicted" with the masturbation habit were viewed by physicians as being, in large measure,
incurable by other than the most drastic measures such as removal
of the clitoris or ovaries. Also as previously discussed, female patients, like males, were sometimes subjected to wearing various re-
straining devices and contraptions similar to chastity belts and
"sexual armours." By the turn of the 20th century, some medical

authorities were even beginning to suspect (and publicly suggest) that female masturbation might not necessarily be medically harmful, although lacking in social acceptance.

Perhaps, in recent decades, a factor in increasing medical acceptance of female masturbation, was the fact that masturbatory practices appeared to be related to the ability to achieve orgasm after marriage. Kinsey, in his research, for example, found that approximately one-third (between 31 percent and 37 percent) of females who had never masturbated before marriage, or whose masturbation had not led to orgasm, failed to achieve orgasm in the first year of marriage. Almost as many did not reach orgasm in the first 5 years of marriage. Among those females who had masturbated to orgasm, "only 13 percent to 16 percent were totally unresponsive in the first year of marriage."[327] Kinsey had found that 62 percent of the females surveyed had ever masturbated, and 58 percent to orgasm. Hunt's more recent survey of sexual practices indicated that 63 percent of his females had ever masturbated.[328] Females are apparently masturbating earlier in life, however. Only 15 percent of Kinsey's females had masturbated to orgasm by the time they were 13, while Hunt found that 33 percent of the females had done so. Likewise, Hunt found that more married females had masturbated. Kinsey had reported that 44 percent of the married females in his survey had experienced masturbation at some time or another, while Hunt reported 61 percent of his married females did so.[329] In the *Redbook* study of the sexual behavior of females in the United States, it was reported that 7 out of 10 women who responded to the questionnaire indicated that they masturbate occasionally, and 2 out of 10 said that they do so often. The survey differentiated the women into categories based on reported sexual satisfaction in marriage, and among those women who indicated a poor marriage, 8 out of 10 said they masturbate, and 3 out of 10 reported they did so often. Various reasons for masturbation were offered by the survey respondents. Some gave "husband has been absent" as a reason, and some mentioned "coitus has not been satisfying." Others apparently relied on masturbation as supplemental sexual gratification, and spoke of, "enjoying apart from intercourse," and "used as a means of relaxing tension." In some instances, however, female masturbation figured as an instrument of marital hostility. One wife, for example, explained that, "I masturbate only when I quarrel with my husband, and I don't know why exactly—maybe it's to get back at him. Only he doesn't know it." For the women in the study, however, masturbation appears to offer only "limited satisfaction." The study results showed that only one-half of the women who had ever masturbated since marriage described it as always satisfying. For the other women who had masturbated, 3 out of 5 indicated that it is sometimes satisfying. For the remaining 2 out of 5, masturbation is reported as not satisfying at all.[330]

Females who masturbate after marriage often continue the practice into their later years, (the 50s, the 60s, and even the 70s) perhaps even increasing the frequency after menopause, or after their husbands die or become unable to engage in sex on a regular basis. Authorities such as Masters and Johnson view this "relative increase in frequency of masturbatory rate . . .[as] understandable." They suggest that:

> Psychosocial freedom to enjoy masturbatory relief of unresolved sexual tensions has more and more become an acceptable behavior pattern for those women so handicapped by limited partner availability in this age group.[331]

In a survey of 100 undergraduate women at the State University of New York at Stony Brook, 49 of the subjects had masturbated to orgasm, and 25 more masturbated without orgasm (interestingly, 71 of the women had experienced sexual intercourse at least once, 70 had received oral-genital stimulation, and 85 had received manual-genital stimulation).[332] In general, masturbation had begun as an accidental discovery for these females. Although a majority indicated that they continue to masturbate because of pleasurable sensations or to effect physical release of sexual tension, a substantial majority spoke of a release from diffuse or general tension such as getting to sleep, relieving boredom or loneliness, and relieving menstrual cramps. There appeared to be only a tenuous relationship between masturbation and sexual intercourse.

Other clinical studies seem to support the finding of the relatively prevalent practice of female masturbation. One physician reported his own research with 1,000 females and wrote that approximately 80 percent of the single females he studied said they masturbated (as opposed to Kinsey's finding of 60%).[333] He also reported that the majority of his single females who did masturbate, did so once or twice per week on the average. He offered the figure of approximately 60% of the married women "with sexually active husbands," said that they masturbate on occasion. The frequency of masturbation increases if the husband becomes impotent. Like many other physicians, he believed that masturbation was an aid to women who have difficulty in achieving coital orgasm, and also in preparing unmarried women to more quickly be able to experience climax in coitus after marriage. In this connection, he frequently prescribed masturbation. As he explained:

> It is my opinion that it is a healthy practice for young women to masturbate prior to marriage and I so advise those who do not. About 50% have taken this advice and have had early satisfactory adjustment to sexual intercourse.[334]

This physician also encouraged married women with orgasm problems to use masturbation as a means of overcoming their difficulty. He told of a 39-year-old married patient who sought help because of inability to experience orgasm except on extremely rare occasions. He suggested masturbation, but she was still not successful. At this point, he advised her "to purchase a Wahl home vibrator to aid her to learn to climax." This device apparently helped her to climax and she was then able to rely on manual masturbation. The doctor reported that within a very short time she was experiencing orgasm in coitus "most of the time." (p.184)

MECHANICAL MASTURBATION AND THE ELECTRIC ORGASM

The mechanical vibrator is apparently becoming a widespread device used by women as an aid to masturbation. Women's magazines, and household gift catalogs of recent years, very frequently have advertisements offering both electric and battery powered models of vibrators to women obstensibly for the relief of tired and tense muscles. There is little doubt from the wording of the ads and the type of vibrators that they are being offered as masturbation aids, and undoubtedly are being purchased as such. Some of the battery powered models recently advertised in leading women's magazines, are elongated wand models that generally resemble a penis and come in various sizes. The phallic shaped battery powered vibrators have recently been largely superceded by electric, "state of the art" vibrators that resemble a hand-mixer, and which are said to be more efficient and more effective. Some women writers have asserted that the change in the shape of vibrators is more related to the new female ideology concerning the clitoral orgasm. As Coyner phrases it:

... Since the clitoris is the center of woman's sexuality, and a vagina may need a penis (or a penis-substitute) but a clitoris surely doesn't, why does a woman need a man? Certainly not just for sex. Hence the recent changes in the size and shape of vibrators used for sex. Old vibrators were trembling penis-substitutes. Some new vibrators are designed specifically to stimulate the clitoris.[335]

(In some of the men's sex oriented periodicals, ads for vibrators are explicit and usually offer a wide variety of vibrator devices designed to either aid in masturbation, or to facilitate coital sex.) Many of the popular marriage and sex manuals such as *The Sensuous Woman,* recommend vibrators to women as masturbation aids, and to couples as a device for foreplay and enhancing their coital sexual gratification. Physicians and psychiatrists are often prescribing vibrators today. Letters to the editors of different sexually-oriented periodicals from women often mention the use of vibrators by both single and married females. Similarly, surveys of sexual behavior conducted in recent years have reported the use of vibrators by females, both for masturbation purposes, as well as for the enhancement of coital sexual gratification. The *Redbook* survey indicated that one woman out of five had experimented with "vibrators, phallic objects, oils and feathers," and other devices as supplemental means of "stimulation during love-making." The study said that the women respondents "with rare exceptions, report them to be pleasurable."[336] Hunt in his recent sexual practices research, included several accounts of females using vibrators for masturbation. One of the women he interviewed was a mother of two teenage girls aged 13 and 14 who used vibrators. The mother revealed that:

They both have massage vibrators, and they use them to masturbate with. Pretty often, too—Susie, for one, was doing it absolutely every night, at bedtime, last year.[337]

He also spoke of adult women who routinely used vibrators to help them masturbate in the absence of coital outlets. It would appear that some women have developed something of a masturbatory dependency on their vibrators. As one 34 year old related:

I don't *need* it these days—my sex life is usually pretty busy—but I always take my vibrator with me when I travel, because you never know. Like I went to Acapulco a few months ago, and it was beautiful there, but at first I hadn't met any men. And everything just made me feel in the mood to enjoy myself, but I had forgotten to pack my vibrator at home—which was too bad, because it would have been groovy to have it there, right then.[338]

The mechanical efficiency of the vibrator as a device to facilitate masturbation may well be dysfunctional for some women and is recognized as such. One of Hunt's subjects, for example, explained that:

> If I want to [masturbate] for whatever reason, there's no reason on earth why I shouldn't, so I do. I *like* it, if I'm in the mood for it. But I don't get into that heavy bit with lotions and vibrators and all that. I really like sex with a man, and if you get used to a vibrator you're going to be disappointed in any man. The way I do it is good enough.[339]

In the well-publicized *Hite Report,* the author reported on the sexual behavior of 3,000 women in the country.[340] The sampling procedures involved in the study are questionable, and the findings may well represent the biased responses of a group of females more sexually sophisticated than the average. Nevertheless, the results are insightful. The author reported that 82 percent of her respondents said that they masturbated and 95 percent of those indicated that they could "orgasm easily and regularly, whenever they wanted."[341] Most of the women in the study believed that masturbation was important as a substitute for sex with a partner, although others spoke of masturbation as a "learning experience," a "means of independence and self-reliance," as a means of having "better sex with another person," and as "pure pleasure, important in its own right." Tabulation on the percentage of women who employ vibrators to facilitate masturbation was not provided but judging from the comments of respondents which were included in the text of the report, it would appear that a significant number of those questioned did, in fact, employ a vibrator to facilitate or enhance masturbatory orgasm. In addition to vibrators, the respondents also spoke of routinely using other mechanical and non-mechanical aids to masturbate including various lubricants, shower hoses and water jets, and various phallic-shaped objects such as hair brush handles, candles, or bottles. One of the subjects questioned, perhaps of more innovative bent than most, reported that she masturbated with an electric toothbrush. For many of the women, masturbation appeared to be a relatively routine practice, often more planned than spontaneous. Interestingly, perhaps because of early guilt and negative connotations associated with masturbation, a number of respondents indicated that they enjoyed masturbation physically but not psychologically. Nevertheless, some women said that over a period of time they had come to find masturbation more physiologically satisfying, suggesting some degree of dependence and an implicit rationalization for that dependence.

Some recent publications have been quite explicit in demonstrating how to maximize masturbatory sensate pleasure. *Good Vibrations: The Vibrator Owner's Manual of Relaxation, Therapy, and Sensual Pleasure,*[342] for example, contains both diagrams and detailed instructions for women for the use of the electrical vibrator to effect masturbation. Perhaps the most vocal advocate of female masturbation, however, has been Betty Dodson who published her impassioned exposition on the benefits of female autoerotic activity under the title, *Liberating Masturbation.*[343] This book underscores a theme espoused by the women's liberation movement of recent years. Among the ideological tenets of the movement was the concept of female vaginal orgasm as male perpetuated myth.[344] The basic assumption was that clitoral orgasm was the only true orgasm and that sexual fulfillment was not only possible, but perhaps even preferable, without the presence of the male penis, or even the male for that matter. The Dodson thesis simply extends this logic. Liberation requires sexual independence from males, and thus, masturbation. As Dodson has phrased it, "I became more and more convinced that sexual liberation was crucial to women's liberation and that masturbation, in turn, was critical to sexual liberation."[345] She went on to assert that masturbation makes women independent, and stated that, "With self-sexuality, or masturbation, you create your own sexual base. By giving yourself your own orgasms, you're no longer dependent upon any other form of sexuality to give you pleasure."[346] Dodson does not provide such advice for the simple purpose of females avoiding the physiological frustration attendant to sexual deprivation. Rather, she suggests, at least implicitly, a more complete detachment from dyactic involvement, both physically and socially. In this connection, she recommends to her readers that they start "having an intense love affair" with themselves, and goes on to detail the specifics of creating the setting for having "dates" with oneself.[347] Thus, masturbation within this context indicates a trend toward a completely autoerotic sexual experience. Nevertheless, many feminist writers have predicted that female centered sexual gratification, and especially masturbation, will become the preferred mode of carnal fulfillment. Coyner, for example, speaks of "more emphasis on oral sex, manual sex, and electrical sex (with vibrators) than ever before."[348] After all, as she puts it:

... Why continue having sex with men if it's no fun, if it's a constant
struggle, if one feels left out or not taken seriously?[349]

Other experts tend to see the vibrator less within a context of
sexual liberation and more as a mechanized means of enhancing the
sexual experience. One writer has called the vibrator, "the last sexual
frontier for many people," and has mentioned reports of a woman
being able to enjoy as many as "50 consecutive orgasms using the
machine" in the course of an hour.[350] It has been asserted that the
occasional use of a vibrator by a couple can afford them, "a different
breadth of experience." Even though medical experts and sexual
therapists are contending that the use of a vibrator is not "kinky"
or "perverted," there are still those who warn that it could "get in
the way of a man-woman relationship," and as Margaret Mead
points out:

> Americans seem to prefer having machines to do everything. We have
> invented mechanical gadgets to substitute for what is natural. Ma-
> chines alienate people from their bodies and from their emotions.[351]

And as an additional caveat, Virginia Johnson writes that:

> ... overindulgence with a vibrator like overindulgence in food, can so
> easily become a way of masking real needs and genuine feelings.[352]

MALE MECHANICAL MASTURBATORY DEVICES

The vibrator and sex device ads which appear in various
"men's," and sex-oriented periodicals often include vibrators for
men that consist of a battery operated vibrating ring which encircles
the penis as well as more conventional wand-shaped vibrators for
women. Various magazines carry ads which offer conventional vibrators with an array of "his" and "hers" attachments. In a recent issue
of one of the more explicitly sex-oriented magazines, an ad offered
an "artificial female organ," which was claimed to "help anxiety,
tension, and other problems related to sex." The same periodical also
carried an advertisement extolling the carnal virtues of a masturbation device not unlike a milking machine, which the ad claimed
offered "erotic sensations so natural, it would fool Mother Nature!"
The machine, it said featured a "massaging membrane that travels
up and down." Then, in alluding to the vicarious nature of the carnal

gratification which the device facilitates, the ad went on to suggest that it "leaves you *free* [italics theirs] to make fantasies 'come true'." The sex periodical *Screw* carried an ad offering a motorized device patently designed for male masturbation, called a "Suckalator," which featured an orifice shaped like a mouth complete with female lips. Perhaps most interesting of all masturbation devices, however, are the life-sized female "love" dolls made of inflatable vinyl, or in some instances foam rubber. The dolls are complete with pubic hair, and all external anatomical features, including exaggerated breasts, and are often designed to resemble attractive, teenage women. Some of the more deluxe models may even feature more realistic anatomical simulation including such accessories as "electronic" vaginas, mouths with "deep throats" powered by "air suction," and "electronic hands" with fingers that "bend into any position, just like a human hand." The electronic hand, it is said, "vibrates, pulsates, and gently massages." Some such dolls even come in "Scandinavian" and "Greek" models (the "Greek" models are listed as having "extra large busts" and "added Greek features." These doll devices may cost upwards of $100 and are clearly intended to serve as sex outlets for persons who may lack heterosexual opportunities. They are contraptions that serve to accomplish mechanical masturbation, but they apparently also serve to aid in generating sexual fantasy, presumably for those persons with limited capacity for imaginative imagery. The use of such dolls for carnal gratification would seem to suggest an element of necrophilia, and inasmuch as the individual sexual fantasy effort and masturbatory activities, must be even supplemented by machine, the pattern of sexual interaction with an artificial sexual surrogate partner would clearly seem to fall in the socially pathological category. It should be recalled, however, that vibratory devices for sexual purposes are by no means new. The 1902, Sears, Roebuck, and Co. catalog lists several pages of "electric belts." These devices carried "the soothing current direct to the sensitive sexual organism." The belts were advertised as having "strengthening curative properties" for such disorders as "seminal or vital weakness," "impotence," and "emissions, drains, losses." With the addition of a stomach attachment, the belts were said to be also useful in treating indigestion, constipation, and cancer of the stomach.

The appearance of mechanical devices to facilitate masturbation, either male or female, has not universally been greeted as technological progress or socially desirable. In some states, such devices have been labeled as obscene and offensive. In 1980, for example, a bill was introduced in the Arizona legislature that sought to define as obscene, and, thus, outlaw its sale, "any item designed or marketed as useful primarily for stimulation of human genital organs." The legislation did not pass but would likely have stood the constitutional test if it had. Similar legislation in Georgia, which has been enacted into law, does make dildoes and artificial vaginas obscene, and, thus, illegal. A conviction under this law (Sevell v. State) was, in fact, ultimately upheld as constitutional by the United States Supreme Court.[353] Similar legislation may yet be introduced in other states.

MUTUAL MASTURBATION IN COURTSHIP

In addition to auto-eroticism, manual manipulation of one's genital organs to orgasm, by a person of the opposite sex is an extremely prevalent sexual outlet for many persons. It is both recommended to and practiced by married couples when regular coital sex is not feasible or desired—perhaps during certain stages of pregnancy, during the illness of one of the spouses, or during the wife's menstrual period, for example. It is a widespread practice among adolescents and young single adults, especially those persons of middle or upper-middle class background. For such persons, "petting to climax" may well be a constituent stage in courtship and sexual experimentation. Kinsey found that males, especially the better educated ones "tended to adopt petting as a way of life over a period of some years." The same was essentially true of females, especially those born after 1920. He reported that in the younger generation of females, 94 percent of those who were still single at 20 had petted, and a quarter of those had petted to orgasm. The percentage of those who petted to orgasm grew larger the longer they remained unmarried. A total of 40 percent had done so by age 25.[354] Kinsey also found that 89 percent of his males had petted by age 25, with about one-quarter having petted to orgasm by 25. Hunt, in his later survey, however, reported that 95 percent of the males had petted by the age of 25, and two-thirds of the under 25 males had petted to orgasm by various techniques "in just the 12 months prior to completing their questionnaire." Of his females, Hunt reported that of the 18-to 24- year old females, "substantially more than one-half had petted to orgasm" in just the past year.[355] Hunt also concluded that young people "move on far sooner to regular premarital intercourse." Thus,

it is a sexual compromise for a shorter period of time during courtship than in the past.[356] Persons with less education or from lower
socio-economic backgrounds have traditionally been more prone to
engage in actual intercourse relatively early and, to be less inclined
to be involved in substitute activities such as heavy petting and being
masturbated to orgasm by their dates of the opposite sex. For the
middle class adolescents and young adults, however, manual manipulation of one's genital organs to climax by a person of the opposite
sex, has long been a traditional form of sexual gratification, that
served as effective carnal outlets while preserving technical virginity.
It also acted as an intermediate stage in sexual interaction during
courtship. In connection with this concept, Chilman has observed
that:

> It is frequently observed that premarital petting, especially heavy pet-
> ting to orgasm, has been a device used to maintain the "technical
> virginity" of females. Although this is undoubtedly true, the gradual
> growth of sexual intimacies may be helpful to young people as an aid
> to their evolution into sexually mature adults.[357]

Chilman indicates that heavy premarital petting "increased
somewhat between the early 1920s and the early 1970s, especially for
females and younger adolescents." Although she believes that data
on this phenomena are "sketchy and unsatisfactory," she concludes
that, "apparently petting to orgasm has occurred for over half of
both the male and female adolescent participants for at least the last
half century." Robert Ruark has perhaps preserved the institutionalized mode of such interaction in his fictional description of a young
courting couple several decades ago. He writes:

> Alec did not, in fact, importune. Some memory of his collegiate con-
> junction with Fran Mayfield checked him from an actual consumma-
> tion with Amelia, though the necking had increased swiftly to petting
> and the petting frantically to everything short of penetration. Amelia
> was more than willing, when the musky moments became almost un-
> bearable, and Alec was deliciously shocked at the knowing sinuous
> clutch of fingers which brought him relief into a hurriedly produced
> handkerchief . . .[358]

PUBLIC MASTURBATION

In spite of the erosion of moral and medical constraints concerning masturbation, and the significant increase in social permissive-

ness toward the practice, there does still remain, however, certain contexts in which masturbation is still viewed as inappropriate, or socially deviant. Public masturbation is rigorously proscribed and legally sanctioned. Furthermore, the interpretation of the concept of public is given wide legal latitude. Persons who publically exhibit their genitals, not infrequently may also attempt masturbation. If apprehended, they may face severe legal punishment, and in all likelihood, suffer the further stigmatization of being labeled as mentally disturbed or sexually perverted. In recent years, public masturbation has occurred within the context of entertainment in some instances. The play, *Oh Calcutta!,* which contained scenes involving nudity and various kinds of sexual activity, also had one scene called "Four-in-Hand," which portrayed four members of the cast masturbating. The play encountered legal resistance in some areas, but did manage to stay open in most locations, often to record audiences, suggesting a much liberalized social perspective on sexual explicitness in public entertainment. A few rock musicians attempted masturbation on stage as part of their act, and in at least one occasion, one such performer was arrested for his lewd activities. Law enforcement officials frequently "raid" couples in parked automobiles in "lovers' lane" situations and often catch the adolescents or young people involved in intimate courting activities which may involve various stages of undress for one or both of the couple, and/or manipulation of each other's genital organs. The law enforcement agents, may in such cases, arrest the couple for "indecent exposure," "creating a public nuisance," or even more serious offenses.

MASTURBATION AND TELEPHONE FANTASY

Instances of individuals masturbating in the "telephone presence" of another person has been reported, and such sexual activity is viewed as inappropriate, and offensive, if not socially pathological.[359] In this instance, masturbating while talking with a stranger on the telephone represents a kind of "public" situation that is unacceptable to the standards of public propriety and decent behavior. The offender, taking advantage of the existence of telephone counseling services, often staffed by female personnel, manages to use the telephone conversation with the unknown female as the basis for sexual fantasy and vicarious carnal stimulation. The male caller can embellish the sexual drama of his own imaginative ability and masturbate as a constituent part of the fantasy. The degree to which the offender vicariously involves the female counselor can be, perhaps, perceived by a remark reported in one such case. A female counselor related:

> A man masturbating while saying: "Talk to me. Don't leave me." I was not able to locate the file but felt he had called before. As he became more excited he became more verbal with remarks like, *"Open your legs"* [italics mine].[360]

The telephone masturbator manages to reinforce his sexual fantasy, and thus, enhances his carnal gratification with the verbal involvement of the female telephone counselor. Because of the fact that the telephone counseling services exist to help individuals, the women are reluctant to hang up and yet they resent being used as a participant in the offender's carnal fantasy. They cannot attempt to trace the call and have the caller arrested inasmuch as this would be antithetical to the purposes of the counseling service and would cause other clientele to avoid use of the service. Although the counselors may, at least, attempt to minimize their cooperation with the caller and, thus, their participation in his sexual fantasy, they are constrained to tolerate the telephone masturbator and this inevitable pattern of sexual deviancy. To willingly and enthusiastically interact over the phone in response to his cues and directions would, in effect, make her a co-deviant in this private, but "public" pathological pattern.

The telephone masturbator does not represent the only private pattern of imitative sexual gratification that is socially conceptualized as pathological. The various mechanical devices designed for male masturbation may also well be viewed in a similar manner. Although medical and psychiatric authorities can approve and recommend vibrators to aid some women in masturbation, and, thus, subsequently in achieving orgasm in coitus, there have been few if any instances, of similar advice and prescription for males. Such devices do exist, however, and while some of them no doubt aid the individual in achieving and maintaining erection, and, thus, facilitating effective coitus, especially in some men who experience difficulty or occasional impotence, many such mechanisms are intended to supply sexual stimulation as an end in itself. In effect, they furnish a kind of enhanced masturbatory experience for those individuals who cannot or do not avail themselves of more conventional heterosexual outlets.

Massage Parlors and Commercial Masturbation

Masturbation has also assumed commercial configurations in recent years. In this period, literally thousands of so-called massage parlors have sprung up around the country. Some of these establishments offer nothing but amateur-quality massages and spurious sexual services; others are little more than thinly disguised brothels, which specialize, sexually speaking, in offering masturbatory services constituent to the massage.[361] By refraining from other than giving "locals" (i.e., manual manipulation of the client's penis), the parlors can often avoid legal prosecution for prostitution. Accordingly, they can locate themselves in areas quite visible and accessible to their potential clientele—often adult and middle-aged, middle class males who may be looking for new variation in sexual gratification, or because of the routine of their work may be temporarily separated from their spouse. The public, however, sometimes assumes patrons of massage parlors have problems of sexual dysfunction, are sexually perverted, or have neurotic difficulties. In some instances, judges have sentenced patrons of massage parlors who have been arrested in police raids to required psychiatric counseling. Studies of parlor patrons suggest that they are socially conventional and psychologically well-adjusted (with some exceptions, of course). One such study revealed that the average patron is a white, married male, from out of town, who is 35 years old and who is employed in a "lower-or middle-class job." He "goes to church on Sundays," and has had some college experience. Additionally:

> He is likely to be verbally and sexually assertive, reports having had a variety of sexual experiences in the past, has come to the parlor because of lack of sexual partner at this particular time or because of curiosity, will come to orgasm during the local or genital massage, and will find it sexually satisfying. He is likely to have high self-esteem, to consider himself personally and sexually adjusted, to consider his value system as liberal and to be somewhat sympathetic to the goals of the women's rights movement.[362]

The parlors may well offer a wide range of erotic embellishments for their massage and sexual services including vibrator massage, mirrored rooms, massage on water beds, and even "his-and-hers" massages where the patron can also massage the masseus. The masseus may be scantily clad, or in some instances, for a fee can be obtained topless, bottomless, or even completely naked.

Even dual bathing experience may be available. Although offering only penis manipulation to orgasm rather than the complete range of sexual gratifications found in most brothels, the parlors may often be preferred. They allow the patrons to avoid the venereal disease danger of brothels, and since they are often tolerated by law enforcement officials, they also allow them to avoid the legal danger. Since they are visible rather than clandestine, there is less social stigma attached to patronizing them, and since the clients do not actually engage in sexual intercourse the individuals who go there do not have to bear the guilt associated with infidelity and, thus, adultery. Their cost restricts their services to men of successful financial means and, thus, the use of their services is viewed by some men (and some elements of the public) as one of the hedonistic rewards of hard work, success, and affluence. Little effort is required of the patron and the parlors attempt to maximize all elements of the situation so as to enhance erotic imagery, sexual fantasy, and carnal gratification. In the service oriented society of today, the customer simply lies there, wrapped in erotic reverie and totally indulges his narcissistic hedonism while seemingly sensual females minister anatomically to his sexual appetites.

The purveyors of such sensate narcissistic ministrations are not without dissaffection for their responsibilities, however. As one recent exposition on massage parlors points out, the masseuses often enter the occupation in the belief that they will be genuine purveyors of health services, but very soon face the exigent necessity of also providing masturbatory services.[363] They become entrapped, so to speak, by the lucrative financial remuneration that the vocation offers and are disinclined to abandon it. They, unfortunately, are faced with the realization that their clientele and the general public consider them, and so label them, as prostitutes. Some, however, manage to cope with their deviant responsibilities and label, by elaborate systems of rationalization including the device of anatomical compartmentalization which lets them cope with their dilemma and wear the more comfortable label of "Hand Whore." In another study, a masseuse rationalized that:

> I've just done hand jobs since the first day on the job. After all, I go to church and believe in God. There's really nothing wrong with locals, the penis is just another part of the male body and needs to be massaged, too.[364]

Unlike many prostitutes, massage parlor masseuses are more likely to be from a middle class background, and have some college education.[365] Masseuses do have concerns about their self and social image, and in addition to the anatomical compartmental rationalization, they tend to use the volitional nature of rendering sexual services to patrons as an additional means of rationalizing the sexual activities attendant to their vocational role. As one masseuse put it, "I'm not a common prostitute, I only do those customers that I especially like."[366] In any event, massage parlor masseus has emerged as a singular occupational specialty—a vocation devoted to the personal delivery of mastubatory carnal gratification, offering attractive financial rewards for those persons of limited technical skills, but a willingness, in a limited anatomical fashion, to assist a clientele achieve orgasmic satisfaction.

SUMMARY

Social changes over time have accomplished to bring about significant alterations in basic value orientations concerning sexual expression and behavior. The shift in social attitudes and posture in regard to masturbation in our society in recent years has been, perhaps, more extreme than in the instance of other forms of carnal gratification. With the erosion of medical and moral rationale for the social proscription and suppression of masturbation, the practice has moved with surprising rapidity from the category of behavioral pathology to that of sexual exercise and hedonistic treat. Female masturbation may well have made the greatest transition in this regard. Although medical and moral constraints against female masturbation traditionally did not appear to be more severe than those prohibiting male masturbation, they apparently were more effective. Perhaps the earlier social model of the virtuous, nonsenuous, female was sufficiently asexual in its portrayal of feminity, that carnal self-indulgence was simply precluded as a natural behavioral mode. In any event, the socialization of females, directly or indirectly, tended to strongly inculcate the cultural negativism toward masturbation. Anatomical and physiological considerations may have made males more susceptible to genital excitation, and opportunity structure may also have been more favorable for males to indulge in masturbation than in the case of females.

As sexual surveys in earlier years have shown, females were much less likely than males to have masturbated to orgasm, especially before marriage, and were also less likely to have masturbated at an early age. Some females were found to be essentially unaware or partially ignorant of the existence of female masturbation. Studies such as Kinsey's, however, had shown a positive relationship between female masturbation before marriage and the ability or probability to achieve coital orgasm after marriage. This insight, along with other illuminating information concerning sexual practices, was broadly disseminated in our society, and undoubtedly many persons, male and female, derived both edification and inspiration from the sex studies. Some researchers and especially Lo Piccolo and Lobitz[367] were instrumental in developing therapy programs for non-orgasmic women that involved having the women receive instruction in masturbation techniques and do "homework." When the women had learned to respond to self-stimulation, they could more readily learn to achieve orgasm with a partner. Sexual incompatibility due to the non-orgasmic wife was presumably much more widespread several decades ago than today, and many females fearful of such a dilemma in marriage, often experiment with masturbation as a way of preparing for sexual adjustment in marriage. Similarly, many married females with problems of sexual adjustment may have taken up masturbation as a means of dealing with sexual frustration after they read the finding of the sex surveys. Certainly, many physicians, marriage counselors, and psychiatrists took their cue from the sex surveys and increasingly began to recommend masturbation to their female patients as an aid to their sexual equilibrium, both before and after marriage. Thus, masturbation for females began to move from being a medical problem to being a medical therapy. In this connection, in recent years the proscription of masturbation to females by physicians has become a relatively common medical palative, and knowledge of this has prompted many women of all ages to take it up for therapeutic reasons. When the medical prescription to masturbate as a means of facilitating orgasm in intercourse became fashionable, there was a veritable flood of "how-to-do-it" books that featured instruction in orgasm.[368] Something of the taboo against female masturbation still lingered, however, and physicians found some of their patients still reticent in regard to taking up such blatant carnality as a medical regimen.

In the late '60s and '70s came more sex surveys, a veritable flood of sex books and movies, and a further erosion of religious and social norms governing sexual comportment. The result was a kind of "sexual enlightenment" based on the new sexual liberalism and sexual sophistication. The propaganda effect of the sexual literature of recent years has been formidable in its impact on traditional sexual values and norms. The encouragement of masturbation, and female masturbation especially, has been a prominent theme in much of this literature with an emphasis on masturbation as a kind of preparation for more effective coital intercourse and for sheer carnal pleasure. *The Sensuous Woman* by "J," for example, contends that "you must train like an athlete for the act of love."[369] Other sexual advice books have been more emphatic in encouraging masturbation for the sensory gratification it affords. Attendant to this theme, various mechanical devices such as electrical vibrators are being recommended by both medical authorities and advocates of the pleasurable pastime orientation. The use of masturbation as a principal mechansim of carnal gratification, and especially the use of an electric vibrator as a mechanical means of increasing and enhancing the sexual stimulation and orgasm also has sexually political implications. Masturbation is seen by some feminist advocates as "sexually liberating." As one writer phrases it, "Nevertheless, the most exciting feminist emphasis on sexual self-knowledge leads away from men and specifically to masturbation."[370] She goes on to say that women want to teach other:

> . . . women [to] encourage each other to regard masturbation not just as a second-rate sexual outlet, but as a first-rate way to cherish and love one's own body. Masturbation is an important step in ceasing to be somebody else's sex object, and becoming a sexual being. Giving one's own body pleasure is advocated in the same context as keeping it healthy.[371]

This emphasis on masturbation, especially as facilitated by a mechanical device, as a major mode of sexual satisfaction is not without social controversy. Some feminist writers have encouraged masturbation as a means of making women sexually self-sufficient. Others have encouraged masturbation for other purposes contending that it can simply be an additional means of sexual gratification within an expanded love-making repertory. Without question, however, masturbation does promote a kind of sexual self-sufficiency, at least on a physical plane in either males or females. Sexual self-sufficiency, in turn, could tend to erode or diminish the motivation for intimate and emotional involvements with persons of the opposite sex. If social and sexual participation in marriage and family is perceived as oppressive, sexual self-sufficiency even if accomplished through masturbation, could appear as a viable mechanism for perhaps relieving oneself of the emotional hazards constituent to romantic involvements. If courtship, marriage, and family are seen as stultifying to self-realization and ambition, singlehood sexual self-sufficiency may seem to be an estimatable alternative life style.

From one standpoint, sexual self-sufficiency achieved through masturbation and abetted by an electrical vibrator might represent a psychiatrically sound step toward self-awareness and social independence. From another perspective, however, it could suggest a behavioral mode with pathological implications. Socio-anthropologically speaking, the purposes of the larger social enterprise to meet, mate, and produce progeny would be subverted, and accordingly, sexual self-sufficiency would be dysfunctional. At a personal level the volitional persuasion to avoid emotional involvement with individuals of the opposite sex, if carried to its extreme, could have everyone withdrawing from social intercourse and enjoying a near totally narcissistic, and almost schizoid, existence through their sexual, and otherwise self-sufficiency.

In a worst case senario, the individual would subsequently live a socially alienated, mechanical, and probably lonely, existence deriving carnal gratification and succor from an electrical vibrator or artificial vagina. In a kind of human ant colony setting, *Brave New World* style, sexual self-sufficiency would be to become, in effect, merely an animated, but socially muted, element in the technological culture of our future existence.

Males, traditionally less effectively constrained by social proscriptions attempting to suppress masturbation, have also been affected by changing sexual values. Males, like females, are experimenting with masturbation at an earlier age and are continuing the practice to an older age than in the past. Some studies suggest that where, traditionally, masturbation (at least at any significant level of frequency) essentially ceased at marriage, today there is evidence that many males continue to practice masturbation throughout the life cycle, even if married. As with females, this trend suggests that there is a tendency to want to maximize the carnal gratification experience, and that masturbation serves as supplement to, as well as substitute for, heterosexual coitus.

The massage parlor phenomen is particularly interesting in view of the supposed greatly increased availability of heterosexual outlets resulting from the erosion of traditional sexual morality, as well as the supposedly much liberalized toleration and practice of sexual variation within marriage. Inasmuch as the patrons of massage parlors are predominantly middle age males, the popularity of the parlors perhaps indicates a desire for expanded carnal horizons among a segment of the population that apparently experiences some degree of erotic deprivation. The massage parlor affords masturbatory gratification, but within a dramaturgical setting that maximizes the opportunity for vicarious, as well as physical, carnal fulfillment. The massage parlor offers the opportunity for actualizing sexual fantasies and provides an unusual narcissistic sexual experience—hired hand-maidens, as it were, dutifully perform their masturbatory ministrations on the client while he passively enjoys orgasm as part of a larger pattern of carnal gratification. It is significant to note that the social dimensions of commercial masturbation stand in contrast to the Dodson thesis that suggests masturbation can afford sexual independency from dyactic involvement. The element of vicarious gratification facilitated by the dramaturgical components available in the massage parlor experience, plus the facts of masturbation administered by a female masseuse, indicates a continued desire for *sexual gratification within the context of an interpersonal relationship,* even if subject to commercial impersonality and the erotic milieu is contrived and unnatural.

In the final analysis, masturbation will probably attend and precipitate an earlier sexual awareness and sexual precociousness among young people. Masturbation will become an even more widespread alternate mode of sexual expression. As individuals attempt to maximize the intensity of their sexual experiences, masturbation, perhaps with the aid of even more sophisticated technology than today's vibrators, will become a major mechanism of supplemental sexual fulfillment. For some seeking sexual and emotional independence, an elaborate regimen of masturbation may become the principal mechanism of carnal gratification.

Although masturbation in the future, unencumbered by social proscription, will undoubtedly serve a variety of medically and psychologically therapeutic functions, and may help to intensify and broaden the total sexual experience, it may not be without some residual social dysfunctions. Some persons, for whatever the rationale, may seek increased sexual sufficiency through masturbation and withdraw more into a behavioral mode of narcissistic "independency." Such a tendency could weaken the motivation for sexual interaction with others and sexual bonding. Given the sexual basis of solidarity inherent in some groupings, this tendency could, conceivably, in some instances, serve to erode social cohesion.

In spite of the mechanical and convenient efficacy of masturbation in affording pleasurable sensations and effecting the physical relief of sexual tensions, the practice, with its socially solitary context, like other forms of socially solitary behavior, is not without an element of emotional sterility. Such a routinized mode of obtaining sexual gratification, and the continued absence of significant others and a meaningful social context for sexual interaction, could render the habitual practitioners of masturbation inured to their autoerotic behavior and leave them insensitive to the sensory and emotional subleties and vagaries of conventional heterosexual gratifications.

Chapter 7

HOMOSEXUALITY, BISEXUALITY, AND TRANSSEXUALITY

Sexual Deviancy in Counterfeit Context

Perhaps no mode of human sexual expression or carnal gratification is more subject to social controversy, or has tended to elicit more emotional negative sanctions on occasion, than has homosexuality. Inasmuch as our own society, like most others, has tended to adopt and maintain a rigid ethnocentric posture in regard to culturally-approved patterns of sexual behavior, any sexual behavior significantly at variance from the prescribed heterosexual and genital mode is deemed deviant. Within this normative context, heterosexual coitus is viewed as "real" or "genuine" sex, and as such is approved under certain specified conditions and circumstances. Homosexual behavior, on the other hand, because it affords carnal fulfillment outside of the conventional mode and attempts to substitute the gender of the participants and the techniques of sexual gratification, is conceptualized by many as inauthentic or "counterfeit" sex, and as such is proscribed, and is frequently severely sanctioned.

Homosexuality can perhaps be appropriately categorized within a counterfeit context for two reasons. First, homosexual behavior deviates from the normatively prescribed heterosexual pattern, and because of its inauthenticity, is, thus, "counterfeit" sex. Because it is socially condemned, and often severely sanctioned, persons of homosexual persuasion not infrequently are compelled to disguise

the fact and to engage in role falsification as a mechanism of concealment. The homosexual must often resort to heterosexual role falsification, and, accordingly, must engage in a kind of "counterfeit"
lifestyle including his sexual expression and gratification. Heterosexual role falsification may well make for a tragic family situation, and
indeed, there may well be tens of thousands of marriages where one
or the other partner is a homosexual counterfeiting a heterosexual
identity and pattern of sexual behavior. The values of our society are
such that homosexuals may feel compelled to deny their sexual
proclivities, even perhaps to themselves. Often, to give credence to
their assumed heterosexual image, and, thus, to legitimate their more
socially approved sexual identity, they may even marry, regardless
of how ill advised such a venture may be. Many homosexuals are
successfully able to mask their true sexual inclinations from the
community, and even from their spouses. Such marriages may even
include children and may appear to be largely successful. These
marriages, are, however, frequently painful for the homosexual, and
the sexual adjustment of the couple may often be less than satisfactory. Since they are often not sexually fulfilled in marriage, these
homosexuals may seek sexual contacts outside of marriage sometimes resorting to casual and furtive sexual activities with other
homosexuals, in public places. Such behavior is socially perilous
inasmuch as there is the ever-present danger of arrest, and attendant
exposure and public scandal. Such an eventuality could have disas-
trous effects in terms of the erosion of marital and family relationships. In the event of public disclosure, not only the homosexual, but
in some instances, even the spouse, may suffer social reprisals as well
as personal humiliation. In some instances, the spouse, or other
member of the family may know of the homosexual's social facade,
but go along with the sexual counterfeiting in order to protect children or other family members, and to preserve the marriage, even if
sexual interaction within the marriage is non-existent.

HOMOSEXUALITY AND CULTURAL STIGMA

There is considerable professional disagreement as to exactly
what is homosexuality. There are those who historically, and even
today, maintain that homosexuality is a disease, a mental aberration,
and, thus, a psychiatric problem. Some blame the condition of "glan-

dular imbalance"; others, speak of inappropriate socialization, and yet other authorities view homosexuality as partially the result of some set of traumatic personal experiences. There are many who take issue with the disease conceptualization, however. Dr. Richard A. Gardner, a New York psychiatrist and author, has observed, for example, that "anyone who claims to be certain homosexuality is a psychiatric disorder is 'being grandiose'," even though he, himself, personally views it as a "psychiatric disorder, a disturbance."[372] The ideological legacy of the psychoanalytic school of psychiatry is essenitally a conceptualization of homosexuality as a "neurotic" or "perverted" mode of sexual behavior. One critic has suggested that, "Freud was more influenced by prevailing Judeo-Christian attitudes than he thought."[373] As this author views psychoanalytical thought, it is biased in the sense of seeing sex for procreation, and the desire for children, as natural. Other sexual persuasions and ideologies are accordingly unnatural. As he phrases it:

> Psychoanalysis holds that sexuality has inherent aims, and not merely learned ones. It assumes that the one natural course awaiting all of us is heterosexuality and fulfillment through becoming a parent.[374]

It has been argued that psychoanalysis has a strong religious bias, and that this is particularly manifest in their labeling of homosexuality as "perverted." Dr. Thomas Szasz, who authored *The Manufacture of Madness,* asserted that the psychiatric perspective on homosexuality is, "a thinly disguised replica of the religious perspective which it displaced." Szasz contended that psychoanalysts were like preachers. In regard to the advice, to live contentedly, which Karl Menninger gave to a homosexual man, Szasz commented that it "bears out the suspicion that his medical role is but a cloak for that of the moralist and social engineer."[375]

The historical Judeo-Christian posture toward homosexual activity was, in large measure, one of "uncompromising condemnation."[376] Sodomy or homosexual intercourse was considered to be the "vicium contra naturam" or vice against nature.[377] Such sexual behavior evoked "profound fear and loathing" in the popular mind and, as "unnatural" sexual gratification, it was viewed as "one of the most execrable forms of religious deviation."[378]

The sanctions for homosexuality were extremely severe in some countries. In England, for example, "during the first 35 years of the nineteenth century more than 50 men were hanged for sodomy. . . ."[379] The hostile public reaction to homosexuality in that period apparently stemmed from several sources, including the Evangelical Revival of the times, the Victorian rigid sexual ethic, and the "social and political tensions of the day [which] helped nourish hostility toward outgroups."[380] It also may well have resulted from "the hardening of sexual stereotypes" which was occurring in that period. In order to keep women confined to a "narrow range of social roles," there could be only intolerance of "sexual ambivalence." In short, in order to keep women "feminine," homosexuality had to be condemned and sanctioned.[381] It has even been argued that the "organizational process of bureaucratization" was a historical factor in "generating and sustaining hostility toward male homosexuality," inasmuch as homosexual attachments might dilute loyalty to superiors and erode discipline.[382]

THE CULTURAL ORIGINS OF HOMOSEXUAL BIAS

Actually, there are several dimensions of homosexuality that would easily attract disfavor and sanction within the Judeo-Christian ideological framework which undergirds much of the social and legal normative system of Western culture. The first is the obvious disapproval of romance and/or permanent sexual bonding between two persons of the same sex. Such a union runs counter to historical precedence, and, more importantly, is contraindicated in terms of the functional importance of mixed sex bonding. Male and female have physical characteristics that are complementary in terms of social organization. Man, theoretically the physically stronger, in primitive or folk society becomes the hunter, the herder, or cultivator. The female, because of her physical capabilities, including the capacity for conceiving and bearing children, more frequently becomes the food gatherer and steward of home and hearth. The social structure of many societies is based, at the most fundamental level, on the sexual division of labor, and the mutually supportive and complementary sex roles that attend it. The homosexual, by becoming involved in a sexual union with a person of the same sex, in effect, attempts to subvert cultural history and the cultural functionality of the opposite sexes. It is interesting to note that in some fictional accounts of homosexuality such as the movie *Staircase,* the homosexual couple fakes a conventional marriage, with one member of the dyad taking on a sex role opposite that of the other. Such a pattern is actually quite frequent in real homosexual unions, with one person playing the dominant "male" role, and the other playing the subordinate "feminine" role. Even in some real, and fictional situations of non-homosexual single sex dyads living together, such as the two men in the *Odd Couple,* frequently the two individuals tend to take on mixed-sex social roles at least in the home, for the sake of cultural functionality. Such couples, obviously, resembles a heterosexual a couple in cultural function.

The homosexual couple, as mentioned above, is socially labeled "deviant" by virtue of sexual bonding between two persons of the same sex. Beyond the single-sex dyad arrangement, however, the couple is also in violation of social custom and norm inasmuch as they cannot have offspring and, accordingly, violate religious and cultural mandates to perpetuate the species, and, thus, the social entity. By entering into such a sexual bonding where reproduction is not possible, they have rejected the cultural injunction to multiply and are considered deviant because the only end to their sexual interaction is carnal gratification, which is theoretically, only residual to procreation. In this latter sense, the homosexual couple is in the same "deviancy boat," as it were, as the Catholic couple, morally constrained not to use birth control methods but who employ contraceptive techniques and enjoy a normal, if not enthusiastic, regimen of sexually-gratifying coitus. Like the homosexual pair, the Catholic couple subverts the moral prescription for parenthood but accomplishes to enjoy sexual gratification by design, which is not component to procreation. Also, the homosexual couple is not unlike the childless couple who adamantly refuse to have children, in a society where large families are valued, and where children in general are considered to be essential assets to the society.

The actual techniques of homosexual sexual gratification violate religious proscription and cultural mandate in Western culture, and are, thus, deviant and offensive to the public. Oral sex and anal intercourse, are socially and legally sanctioned in our society in most states, regardless of consent and the sex of the participant. Thus, whether the couple is a homosexual dyad or a married heterosexual couple, the law views oral sex and anal intercourse as punishable "unnatural sex acts;" the fact that there is widespread adoption of such modes of carnal gratifications among married couples, notwithstanding. The Judeo-Christian perspective of such activities can be easily summarized in that the name sodomy derives from the biblical city Sodom, which along with Gomorrah, epitomize sin and carnality. There are numerous instances of convictions for sodomy both here in the United States and abroad. Interestingly, an English homosexual reform law passed in 1967 permits consenting males over 21 years of age to be legally penetrated. A married couple who employed the same mode of carnal gratification, even if consent was present, might be "liable to life imprisonment."[383] In the United States, most states still retain an anti-sodomy statute that could convict even married couples of consensual sodomy. Even though sexual attitudes are considerably more enlightened than in times past, "unnatural sexual practices" still often elicit very emotional negative public reactions. Thus, the very technique of sexual gratification itself, is socially condemned, apart from the single sex dyatic interaction. A homosexual relationship, even if platonic would be socially disapproved. Where oral and anal sexual practices are constituent to the relationship, there is a doubly strong condemnation. To resort to other than the "natural" and conventional mode of carnal gratification is to be depraved and corrupted.

CULTURAL LABELING AND SOCIAL SANCTION

Finally, homosexuality and homosexuals are socially disapproved because they are "different." Members of our society have a long standing tendency of suspicion and hostility to those who practice a variant life style, or contrasting patterns of behavior. Such pariahs have included members of ethnic minorities, "unorthodox" religious groups, and even "hippies," as well as sexual "perverts." Homosexuals, as sexual "perverts," are not only different in the sense of sexual variation. They are considered morally degenerate to the point where they may constitute a latent, if not manifest danger to the public, in the sense that they might commit sex crimes such as molesting children, etc. Homophobia in our society is pervasive and often intense.[384] A Harris public opinion poll conducted in 1969, for example, reported that 63 percent of the nation consider homosexuals "harmful to American life."[385] There have been innumerable instances of persons who were accused of or revealed as a homosexual who were fired from their job, publicly disgraced, or even punished legally. Some of the more newsworthy incidents of such punitive public reaction have been the incidents of presidential assistant Walter W. Jenkins, who left the government after being discovered in a homosexual act, and Sergeant Leonard Matlovich who after publicizing the fact that he was homosexual, was subjected to a "fact-finding hearing," and subsequently discharged from the Air Force. Homosexuals have been fired from school teaching jobs, and forced out of political office. They have been dropped from clubs and organizations, and publicly ridiculed and insulted. At an informal level, many homosexuals are subjected to beatings and robbings by individuals who may make a kind of game of "rolling queers." In some instances, such persons may even solicit fellatio from, or at least submit to it if approached by a homosexual, and then later attack their fellator. Such a practice is not uncommon with some groups of young males. They often feel safe even when victimizing a homosexual, in the belief that homosexuals are vulnerable because "they can't report their victimization."[386] In some instances, heterosexual boys may essentially institutionalize the practice of letting themselves be fellated by homosexuals, in that they may consent to it on a regular basis for a fee, or perhaps if the homosexual buys drinks for the boys or otherwise treats them to something.[387] Some gangs may have their own private "queer," and seek him out whenever they need money. The practice of locating homosexuals who will pay for the privilege of fellatio is known as "queer hustling," or "queer baiting." Such a relationship may be an on-going one, or on the other hand, the gang may assault the homosexual after the first sexual encounter. In the words of one heterosexual male who had a history of "rolling queers":

> It's OK [being fellated]. I don't mind it. It feel OK. . . . They usually just blow and that's all. . . . Oh, sure, but we really fix 'em. I just hit 'em on the head or roll 'em . . . throw 'em out of the car. . . . Once a gay tried that and we rolled him and threw him out of the car. Then we took the car and stripped it. . . .[388]

The practice of victimizing homosexuals by essentially seducing them, and then assaulting and/or robbing them is not only endemic to our society. Apparently the practice is also widespread in Australia, and some other Western societies. In Australia a few years ago, a cabinet minister told the Parliament that "beating up homosexuals was virtually a recognized civilian team sport here."[389] Australia has traditionally held a quite sexually conservative view of homosexuality and in some parts of the country, the legal sanction for persons convicted of homosexuality may be quite severe—up to 21 years in jail in Victoria, for example. In recent years, however, there have been moves there to reform the laws criminalizing and severely punishing homosexuals. The increased legal toleration of homosexuals, notwithstanding, there is evidence that there is a residue of stigmatization directed at even ex-homosexuals. In spite of the belief that homosexuality is "curable," some heterosexual individuals tend to perceive homosexuals as dangerous and threatening and this tendency persists even in regard to ex-homosexuals and the attendant social discreditation toward this group.[390]

CULTURAL CONTEXT AND THE TOLERATION OF HOMOSEXUALITY

In our own society, homosexuality seems to be more prevalent in some settings, and perhaps less tolerated, and more severely sanctioned in some contexts. Homosexuality seems to be closely associated with, and may even arise out of some occupational settings that afford opportunities, tolerance, and seclusion for the exercise of various forms of deviant proclivities including socially deviant sexual practices. Homosexuality would, for example, appear to be more visible, if not prevalent in the creative community, than of other vocational fields. Numerous American poets, playwrights, novelists, musical performers, as well as many actors and actresses are professed homosexuals. There is, in fact, a historical precedent from "Sappho to Colette to Oscar Wilde and James Baldwin,"[391] for this. Drama critic Clive Barnes has observed that, "creativity might be a sort of psychic disturbance itself, mightn't it? Artists are not particularly happy people anyway."[392] Creative occupations such as show business, design, or literary activities might seem to attract, encourage, and support persons with a decided experimental bent in their sexual inclinations. Sex and even sexual "perversion" may become something of a "tool" or mechanism of social and career mobility in some of the creative occupations. Many a starlet and aspiring actor have found that the career ladder may often be climbed faster via the "casting couch." Presumably, the industry exploiters, those who affect the "sexual ripoff" of the aspirants, are not infrequently members of the same sex as their victims.

OCCUPATIONAL DISSAFFECTION AND HOMOSEXUAL PREDILECTION

Homosexuality, of lesbian variety is apparently not uncommon in certain female occupations such as prostitution and stripping. In fact, it has been asserted that lesbian activity among the members of these occupations may to some degree be a reaction to the basically degrading and unsatisfying relationships with their clientele. In regard to strippers, for example, McCaghy and Skipper have observed that:

> Due to lighting conditions the stripper is unable to see beyond the second row of seats, but from these front rows she is often gratuitously treated to performances rivaling her own act: exhibitionism and masturbation. There is no question that strippers are very conscious of this phenomenon for they characterize a large proportion of their audience as "degenerates."[393]

Strippers find that even when they encounter men socially, they are frequently sexually propositioned, and usually with little finesse. They are often treated as prostitutes by men, and, sometimes, even in their romances with men find that they are being exploited. Thus, they frequently develop a disillusioned and disaffective view of their clientele and males in general. Strippers also become social isolates because of their hours and the places where they work, not to mention the social stigma attached to stripping. Furthermore, they operate with a female peer group, some of whom are lesbians, and, thus, they encounter cultural permissiveness toward and support, if not pressure for lesbian practices. Strippers have sexual drives, but when faced with the prospect of exhausting and exploitative sexual liaisons with men, some strippers will instead seek the embraces of sympathetic females with whom, in the words of one stripper, "You can lay down on the floor, relax, watch TV, and let her do it."[394] It has been argued that many strippers are essentially bisexual in persuasion rather than homosexual. In this regard, much of the literature suggests that lesbian tendencies in a woman are relatively well fixed by the time of adulthood. Thus, according to this line of reasoning, lesbians would either have to be attracted to the occupation of stripping, which does not seem to be the case, or else strippers who turn to sexual interaction with other females are not necessarily lesbian, which of course, would appear to be semantic hair-splitting. McCaghy and Skipper, on the other hand, argue that on the basis of their findings, lesbianism can perhaps be viewed as arising out of facilitative and encouragement mechanisms inherent in occupational structure. They conclude that the "structural characteristics of the occupation contribute to the incidence of homosexual behavior."[395] Although more than two-thirds of the individuals they studied were married, they still asserted that homosexuality, "is an important facet of the occupation."

Similarly, prostitutes also experience a degrading and unsatisfying relationship with their clientele, and this may be a factor in their own involvement in lesbian interaction. Winick and Kinsie have suggested, for example:

> Prostitutes may develop lesbian relationships because they distrust men and find it easier to develop affection for women. Lesbianism may be appealing to prostitutes who get tired of a continual round of men and turn to their colleagues for relaxation and a sentimental relationship after work. A woman with a strong personality and another who is submissive may develop a relationship based on their complementary needs. Men are ultimately paying the bills for such liaisons, adding a dimension that heightens the pleasure afforded by the relationship itself.[396]

THE MILITARY SETTING AND HOMOSEXUALITY

Other settings may also contribute to, or facilitate homosexuality. The military, and more particularly the Navy may well be such a setting, at least in times past. Winston Churchill, just before World War I, once commented that the traditions of the Royal Navy were, "Rum, sodomy and the lash." The isolation of military personnel, and especially those on naval ships, from society, often tended to cut them off from normal heterosexual outlets and subsequently some individuals sought homosexual outlets to obtain carnal gratification. Some such arrangements as the "cabin boys" on many ships were institutionalized. The absence of females and the concentration of all male crews in relatively close quarters all facilitated homosexual variants of sexual gratifications. Legend has it that men who were isolated on ships, and bounced by the waves were sexually aroused. Accordingly, it has been long-standing naval custom never to assign men to work alone in pairs where it could be avoided.[397] Interestingly, however, it has often been within the military or naval context, that the most severe sanctions for homosexual acts have been administered. In the British Royal Navy, for example, prior to 1861, sodomy was punishable by death. In fact, on February 1, 1816, on the orders of Edward Rodney, Captain of HMS Africaine, four members of the ship's crew were hanged for buggery. The same day, two other crewmen were punished for "uncleanliness," a euphemistic term for all sexually deviant behavior. One of the men received 200 lashes while the other received only 170 out of the 300 lashes to which he was sentenced, because the ship's surgeon warned that his life would be endangered if he received all 300.[398] In more recent times in the British navy and the U.S. military, the punishment is not so severe, although homosexuality is still a court-martial offense. The U.S. military particularly is unusually vigorous in attempting to identify homosexual offenders, and in invoking statutory sanctions. Williams and Weinberg, who have made a detailed study of homosexuality in the U.S. military have spoken of "the zealousness with which the military seeks out and prosecutes homosexuals."[399] This is done, they say, "based upon the magnitude of their perceived threat to good order." The Army itself states that:

> The Army considers homosexuals to be unfit for military service because their presence impairs the morale and discipline of the Army and that homosexuality is a manifestation of a severe personality defect which appreciably limits the ability of such individuals to function in society.[400]

Furthermore, the military usually makes no distinction between a confirmed homosexual and an individual who commits a single homosexual act. Even persons who have "strong tendencies toward homosexuality," which may even mean persons who associate with homosexuals, may also be liable for discharge. When a serviceman is suspected of homosexuality, or caught in the act, according to Williams and Weinberg, he is "processed to confess and thus avoid a hearing."[401] This causes minimal problems for the organization. The serviceman charged with homosexuality, may be incarcerated in jail, or in the hospital, and may be segregated from other inmates. In the Army, if he is to receive an undesirable discharge, the individual will be reduced to the lowest rank. They usually lose accumulated leave pay, will lose veterans benefits, and are told that they can expect "to encounter substantial prejudice," after discharge. Such treatment is facilitated by the fact that the serviceman is usually encouraged to incriminate himself, and thus actually participates in his own discharge process.

Homosexuality in the military during contemporary times, is apparently not just a problem for the U.S. Armed Forces. Recently it was reported that a homosexual vice scandal was discovered in the Queen's Household Cavalry, an elite English military unit. As many as 100 soldiers were said to be involved in homosexual activities.

Some of the soldiers were apparently earning extra money as male prostitutes, and for posing in "suggestive fashions" for different "gay" magazines.[402]

In times past, homosexuals were often convicted and either jailed, or separated from the service, usually with a less than honorable discharge, and the process was accomplished almost secretly, and usually without public fanfare. In recent years, however, some homosexual servicemen (and women) have resisted punishment or separation after discovery, and some have even deliberately revealed their sexual persuasion, and invited confrontation. Many of these cases have attracted national news coverage. Some of the recent incidents have involved Air Force T/Sgt. Leonard P. Matlovich who became something of a *cause célèbre,* when he announced his homosexuality in a letter to his base commander.[403] Other recent homosexual servicepeople who have fought to stay in the service include Wac Pfc. Barbara Randolph, and her lover, Pvt. Debbie Watson, as well as Air Force Staff Sgt. Rudolf S. (Skip) Keith, Jr.[404] The Defense Department and various governmental agencies have also been strict and vigorous in ferreting out homosexuals and discharging them, particularly those with security clearances, often on the rationale that they might be a "security threat." They have directed their attention not only to persons working in the governmental agencies, but also to persons with security clearances who work for private industries with governmental contracts. Various homosexual lobby groups, and the American Civil Liberties Union, however, have interceded on occasion and the Defense Department, and some other agencies have relaxed their position, especially on the matter of persons in private industry with security clearances.[405]

SEXUAL DEPRIVATION AND HOMOSEXUALITY

One social setting where homosexuality appears to be especially endemic, is the correctional institution. Research has overwhelmingly pointed to the extremely high incidence of homosexual activity in prisons and reformatories. It would initially appear that the sexual segregation characteristic of most prisons, which results in all male or all female population in the institution or at least within particular units or camps of the prison, denies inmates heterosexual carnal outlets and, thus, precipitates homosexual activity. Some new, experimental prisons are sexually integrated in the sense that male and female inmates may socially mingle on occasion, but of course, intimate behavior is prohibited. Certainly, some research indicates that homosexual behavior on the part of most inmates, may be first initiated after confinement, and is largely limited to the institutional setting.[406] In one such study of post-prison sexual behavior, the researcher interviewed nine former prison inmates who had first been involved in homosexual behavior while in prison, either as an "aggressor" or as a victim. The "aggressors," all claimed that they were "living exclusively heterosexual" or "normal" lives. The victims, who had been coerced into homosexual behavior in prison, gravitated into a homosexual lifestyle after prison.[407] In spite of the generally widespread belief that heterosexual deprivation is a major factor in prison homosexuality, few correctional institutions have undertaken presumeably remedial efforts. In this regard, the Mississippi State Penitentiary at Parchman for many years has had a conjugal visitation program. Once a week, on Sunday afternoon, wives and family members may visit the inmate at his camp, and even come inside the camp fence. Inside the grounds, the inmate and his wife may go to one of several small houses, called "red houses" inside the camp fence, and engage in coitus. A study of this practice at Parchman, asked camp sergeants about the influence of such heterosexual privileges on homosexuality among the inmates.[408] The majority of the sergeants expressed the opinion that conjugal visitation did reduce the incidence of homosexuality. They attributed the greatest benefit of the program, however, to keeping marriages from breaking up. The inmates were also queried about the practice. The majority of them also attributed the greatest benefit to keeping marriages from breaking up. A substantial minority, however, spoke of conjugal visitation as reducing homosexuality. Parchman also has a program whereby selected inmates, after three years of confinement with good behavior, are given 10 day "Holiday Suspension" home leaves once a year. This leave, of course, permits them to visit their family and enjoy a normalized sex life for a short period. Although personal interviews with guards and inmates at Parchman suggest that the conjugal visitation program and the home leaves at that institution do have some influence in reducing the incidence of homosexuality, there is little, if any, empirical evidence to support this assertion. On the other hand, it has been argued before that prison homosexuality is not so much based on sexual deprivation as on other factors.[409] Prison populations, in general, are made up of people with lower- and lower-middle socio-economic backgrounds as opposed to middle and upper-middle ones. Kinsey and other researchers pointed out that such men are less capable of sexual fantasy and mental imagery. In short, the less educated lower class individual is less likely to be bothered by sexual deprivation inasmuch as he is less likely to fantasize about it. In a sense, sex for such individuals is "out of sight, out of mind." Some social scientists have pointed out that incarceration not infrequently brings about the, "extinction of basic biological sexual processes." They have also indicated that, "Men in severely stressful concentration or forced labor camps reported greatly diminished or entirely absent sex urges."[410] It would seem, therefore, that sexual deprivation *per se* is not necessarily the only factor in prison homosexuality. Other more significant factors might be the need for the establishment of primary relationships of the kind characteristic of married heterosexual interaction, and attempts at social dominance. Various researchers have pointed out that prison inmates are deprived of meaningful affective relationships, as well as sex.[411] Outside of prison, they would have had the opportunity for such relationships. The homosexual relationship affords the primary ties they require. In this sense, the homosexual behavior of prisoners represents an adaptive mode to both the need for outlet for carnal gratification when deprived of heterosexual opportunity, and perhaps more importantly, the need for emotionally meaningful, and ego-supportive primary relationships with others. In some instances inmates of correctional institutions go to elaborate lengths to simulate the structure of certain institutionalized primary groups such as the family. One researcher who studied female training schools encountered "make-believe" families composed of girls who played the role of "femme" or wife and "stud" or husband. In addition, there were frequently other girls who played ancillary family roles such as sister or mother. Sometimes "marriages" were acted out and formalized by "marriage certificates," and attended by other inmates playing the roles of "judges," "witnesses," or "ministers." The same researchers also studied similar contrived primary groups in co-ed institutions where the male inmates participated in the "make-believe" families in the roles of brothers, sons, and fathers. Homosexual behavior was often only correlated with the roles of "husband" and "wife." Such pseudo-family groups clearly served functions beyond mere sexual gratification.[412] Homosexuality is but one of a number of modal sexual adaptations prison inmates make to their situation. Some sociologists have written about such sexual adaptations.[413] Such adaptive modes include total abstinence, reliance on masturbation only, and periodic heterosexual gratification (this is generally speaking, only the prerogative of prison inmates in some foreign countries and in Mississippi where conjugal visitation and home leaves are permitted). Beyond these sexual modes are the different homosexual adaptive postures. *Sexual Exploitation in the Total Institution.* Some inmates came into prison as known experienced homosexuals, and often through dress or mannerisms openly advertise this fact, while others who are previous homosexuals manage to largely conceal the fact, except from those with whom they have sexual relations. These individuals are known as "submerged homosexuals." Some inmates may have had limited homosexual contact before coming to prison, but were not part of the homosexual sub-culture, and did not consider themselves to be homosexuals. Such inmates are often inducted into prison homosexuality as "kids" or the lovers of older homosexuals. Often, there are older homosexuals who may have been forcefully drawn into homosexual activity earlier in life, in a prison setting, as a "kid," and now play the role of "Daddy" or dominant person in a homosexual relationship. There are some inmates who initially assume the role of "Daddy" and collect "kids." They may not necessarily think of themselves as homosexual or be considered as homosexual by other inmates, even if they have fellatio performed on them by others. The young who are either forced or voluntarily assume the subordinate homosexual role may be known as "kids," "sweetboys," "punks," "ladies," or "gal-boys." Such individuals may be "turned out" into homosexuality by promises of favors or money. In some instances, they may voluntarily engage in homosexual activity with one inmate in order to obtain protection from others. A favorite "con" to effect the sexual cooperation of the young inmate involves two older inmates and an elaborate dramaturgical presentation. One older inmate accosts the young man and threatens him sexually. The other inmate, in collaboration with the first, intercedes and "rescues" the young man, who, then, is sexually propositioned by his rescuer. The younger inmate finds himself in a dilemma and usually becomes the lover of the inmate who rescued him.[414] In yet other instances, they may be physically forced into homosexual activity. They may be the victims of beatings or may even by physically restrained and gang raped.[415] In one widely cited article that detailed a horrifying account of homosexual rape in the detention centers and sheriff's vans in a large Eastern city, it was reported that approximately 2,000 such rapes occurred over a two-year period.[416] In many prisons, homosexual coercion and rape is endemic and every young inmate entering the institution faces the possibility of assault, or being brutally coerced into "voluntary" homosexual behavior. The young inmates are viewed as sexually desirable by the older individuals. As one long-term con put it:

> He comes in there, he's small, he's frail, he's cute, and after you're in prison awhile you know boys start looking much cuter.[417]

Although many inmates do resist the homosexual opportunities in prison, many others ultimately do find a "lady" for themselves within the institution. For the younger, and especially the more attractive and feminine looking, younger inmate, homosexuality may not be a question of choice, as much as that of survival. In regard to coerced homosexuality, female correctional institutions are perhaps equally as bad as male prisons. A female college student who was arrested in a peace demonstration in 1965, and subsequently forced to spend five days in the Women's House of Detention, in Greenwich Village, related that:

> The homosexuality was rampant and pretty hard to take. It was orgies all the time and the sex play was constant. There were hands all over me all the time.[418]

It is said that female prisoners are especially susceptible to the need for friendship, help, and attention during the early days of incarceration when they are perhaps, most frightened and disoriented. A significant percentage of females in some correctional institutes have children from whom they were separated when they were imprisoned. The loss of their children tends to make them feel alienated, and their anomie is compounded by the "absence of men as sponsors, guardians, bosses, patrons, and customers."[419] Thus, female inmates may be lured into homosexual relationships with more experienced women, who initially offer friendship and help, and later make sexual advances. In many instances by that time the relationship between the two had reached the point where the homosexuality was emotionally acceptable. Even correctional institutions for juveniles and children are not immune to homosexuality. On a tour of a children's reformatory in a southern state, this author had occasion to note while in a girls dormitory that all of the bedrooms had their doors removed. When he inquired about this, the dormitory matron explained that homosexuality was so rampant, even among the 9- to 14-year-old girls, that the doors were removed from the bedrooms so that the younger children could be heard, if they were to call for help if sexually molested by their roommate. In an article described in an earlier chapter, "The Baby Disturbers: Sexual Behavior in a Childhood Contraculture," the sexual activities of a group of disturbed boys in a mental hospital are described, and some of their sexual behavior was homosexual.

In male prisons, young inmates may be "turned out" as homosexuals by older inmates, and then "sold" to other inmates. Entire social dominance systems may emerge out of the sexual exploitation of younger "kids," or "punks," by sexually aggressive "jockers" or "wolves," who use strength, violence, and brutality to assault, rape, or coerce the younger men into performing homosexual acts. Such older inmates can rationalize their coercive behavior, and even homosexual rapes as simply being "tough and manly." As some inmates put it, "You have to take sex where you can get it."[420] Homosexual romances often blossom in prison, and on occasion "wedding" ceremonies are performed by an inmate to join a male couple in "marriage." Sexual rivalries also spring up, sometimes resulting in fights and even murders. Sexual abnormality becomes a way of life in the prison setting.[421] Even though homosexuality becomes accepted as a mode of adaptation in prison, inmates when released may hold considerable contempt for homosexuals in the outside world, and especially for "kid" or "punk" inmates after they leave prison, regardless of the fact that they may have been brutally coerced into performing homosexual acts while in prison. In this regard many prisoners, and particularly after release, reflect the societal condemnation of homosexuals as "perverts."

EMERGING HOMOSEXUALITY AND THE PUBLIC POSTURE

Recent years have seen significant changes in the public posture toward homosexuality, and in fact, in the assertive posture of homosexuals themselves toward a traditionally hostile society. Among other manifestations of such social change are the emergence of homosexual newspapers such as *Gay Life* in Chicago and homosexual periodicals with a national circulation such as *Blueboy*. There have been riots and protest marches by homosexuals and a number of cities and counties including Detroit and Washington, D.C. have enacted ordinances prohibiting discrimination against homosexuals in jobs and housing. Gays are actively being recruited for the police department in some towns and increasingly, homosexual candidates for political office are admitting their sexual persuasion during the campaign—and sometimes winning.[422] The number of homosexuals is not inconsequential. There are at least 2.6 million men and 1.4 million women that are exclusively homosexual. Furthermore, Kinsey had reported that 10 percent of American men "have long periods of more or less exclusive homosexuality."[423] Inasmuch as many individuals, although they may indulge in homosexual behavior, do not necessarily consider themselves to be homosexual, the actual number of persons who may be classified as homosexual may be greater than Kinsey speculated. In fact, there are many persons, who may be hidden homosexuals, or who have homosexual proclivities, but suppress them because of fear of social sanction. It is quite difficult to determine the outer parameters of homosexuality in the United States. Homosexuality is becoming more visible and more assertive, however. Numerous persons, including servicepersons, entertainers, politicians and government officials, have come out in the open and publicly admitted their homosexual persuasion, and in some instances, indicated their intention to become militant in the defense of their sexual freedom. Such a person was Dr. Howard J. Brown, the first Health Services Administrator under Mayor Lindsay in New York City.[424] For the first time, candidates for public office are being elected in spite of the fact that they are admitted homosexuals. Elaine Noble, for example, won a seat in the Massachusetts state legislature, even after admitting that she was a lesbian.[425] Homosexuals have begun fighting back physically. Long accustomed to being attacked, robbed, and beaten, often by gangs of young hoodlums out for some fun, some homosexuals have staged counterattacks. In San Francisco, a group of "gay vigilantes," known as the "Lavender Panthers," led by a homosexual Pentecostal Evangelist minister named Ray Broshears, was formed to patrol the streets, protect homosexuals from attack, and, if necessary, to fight back. The purpose of the Lavender Panthers, according to Reverend Ray was "to strike terror in the hearts of 'all those young punks who have been beating up my faggots'."[426] Although such vigilante activity has not made local law enforcement officials entirely happy, or even some other homosexuals in the area who do not like the public image such activities portray, the Reverend Ray thinks it is necessary. As he sees it, "Middle America has always had a little tinge of homophobia. . . . But I've had it up to here. All this queer bashing has simply got to stop."[427]

Homosexuals have been successful in some instances in combatting job discrimination. One individual, for example, was subjected to a hearing when he applied to take the state Bar Examination after law school because it was alleged that he had not used his correct name in obtaining a marriage license for a homosexual marriage. After the hearing, the Minnesota State Board of Law Examiners did subsequently permit the young man to take the Bar Exam.[428] Several years ago in New York City, Mayor Lindsay ordered the Department of Personnel, and the Civil Service Commission, "to issue a directive protecting homosexuals against discrimination in city government hiring and promotion practices." The directive, however, created consternation among many homosexuals, because of the fact that it only instructed agency heads to disregard "private sexual orientations" of applicants, that suggested that homosexuals would still be expected to maintain a low sexual profile.[429]

HOMOSEXUAL MILITANCY AND THE CULTURAL COUNTERATTACK

Homosexuals, along with other minorities, have become increasingly militant in asserting and protecting their rights. This militancy has included the establishment of a number of homophile organizations, such as the Mattachine Society, the Gay Activists Alliance of New York, and the Daughters of Bilitis. Other activities have included such efforts as lobbying, picketing businesses, the White House, and the Pentagon, and protest marches, as well as taking cases to court, and even violence such as the 1969 Stonewall riots on Christopher Street in New York's Greenwich Village, when gays fought back against police raids of a local gay bar. Homosexuals have long complained not only of police harrassment, but also discrimination in legal matters and in the courts. Recently, even judicial and social work attitudes are changing. In New York, in a new experiment, boys who describe themselves as homosexuals, and who are unwanted by parents or cannot adjust to youth homes, are being placed under the care of adult male homosexuals. This gives a significant degree of legitimacy to homosexuality as simply an alternate sexual mode and lifestyle. It has been hailed by the National Gay Task Force as "a spectacular advance in understanding homosexuality as a sexual preference rather than as a disease."[430] In 1970, Gay

Pride Week was celebrated in New York, Chicago, and Los Angeles to commemorate the anniversary of the homosexual demonstrations in New York in 1969. Several states, notably Illinois and Connecticut, have passed laws decriminalizing private homosexual acts between consenting adults. Where at one time, many ministers would turn away the homosexual seeking help and spiritual solace, and there was no place for the "immoral" homosexual in most religious faiths, today the gay church is thriving in some parts of the country. Begun in 1968 with a few persons meeting privately in Los Angeles, today the Metropolitan Community Churches, founded by the Rev. Troy Perry, have thousands of followers and dozens of congregations.[431] Other religious organizations for homosexuals have been organized in different areas of the country with equal success. Even the more conventional denominations have, in many instances, moderated their posture of condemnation of homosexuals, and have been more sympathetic to the psychological distress of homosexuals.

Homosexual couples have begun living together openly, and in some instances, attempted to break down the legal barriers to homosexual marriages.[432] Gay Liberation groups have sprung up on numerous college campuses sponsoring speeches, conferences, and social activities such as parties and dances.

In some cases, they have even promoted the teaching of homosexual studies.[433] Homosexual periodicals are more openly sold on newstands than in the past, homosexuality appears as a theme on some television shows, movies and plays, and for the first time, some of the main characters on several television shows are cast as homosexuals. Perhaps most significantly, homosexuality is being reconceptualized by the medical and psychiatric community. In 1969, for example, the Federal Government's National Institute of Mental Health issued a report which read in part:

> The extreme approbrium that our society has attached to homosexual behavior has done more social harm than good, and goes beyond what is necessary for the maintenance of public order and human decency. Homosexuality represents a major problem for our society largely because of the amount of injustice and suffering entailed in it, not only for the homosexual but also for those concerned about him.[434]

In 1974, the American Psychiatric Association moved to classify homosexuality as other than a mental illness, and many psychiatric practitioners are attempting more to help their homosexual patients come to grips with the social ramifications of their sexual persuasions, than with ridding themselves of the condition. This reclassification, and the other activities attempting to destigmatize homosexual behavior, has not been without legal and social controversy and is far from resolved as a public issue.[435]

Sexual Nonconformity and Behavior Modification. Some therapists, however, are still concerned with "reconditioning" homosexuals into a heterosexual mode of carnal gratification.[436] Using a variety of psychiatric techniques including psychotherapy, group therapy, behavior therapy, and different combinations of these, homosexuals are being motivated and aided in changing their sexual orientation. Such therapeutic efforts are apparently proving successful in many cases. Other kinds of therapy have also been used including "aversion therapy," where homosexual patients are shown pictures of naked men and given mild electric shocks. Some sex offenders including homosexuals have been faced with the prospect of submitting to aversion therapy as a condition of parole from incarceration. Understandably, such procedures have been offensive to some civil libertarians and to many homosexual groups and have generated controversy among some professionals concerning the ethics of therapy that involuntarily modifies behavior that is not viewed as pathological or even necessarily a problem.[437] In this connection, aversion therapy as applied to a variety of sexually sanctioned behavior is encountering public controversy and ambivalence, if not opposition from some quarters.

In spite of a much moderated negative societal reaction to homosexuality, the process of openly admitting such a sexual persuasion and coping with public response and sanctions is still a painful and traumatic personal process, and social discrimination is still pervasive and sometimes brutal, as evidenced by the revelations of various homosexuals.[438] The fact of the public's new sophistication in terms of sexual ecumenicalism, has not lessened the personal burden, social stigmatization, and self-condemnation of many homosexuals. As one commentator on homosexuality put it:

> If I had the power to do so, I would wish homosexuality off the face of this earth. I would do so because I think that it brings infinitely more pain than pleasure to those who are forced to live with it; because I think there is no resolution for this pain in our lifetime, only, for the overwhelming majority of homosexuals, more pain and various degrees of exacerbating adjustments; and because, wholly selfishly I find myself completely incapable of coming to terms with it.[439]

In the final analysis, the homosexual has become less the pariah than he has been in the past, and with the momentum of our current social concern with equality and freedom for the fullest possible exercise of subcultural plurality and individual life style, the homosexual may well be able to anticipate even more toleration, if not acceptance, in the future. Homosexual militancy may assure his participation in the main stream of social life, and legislation may protect his rights, but the fact of homosexuality will probably never be entirely forgotten or socially discounted. The homosexual shares with the other, heterosexual members of society, the invidious knowledge that he is sexually different, and, accordingly, deficient from the socially ideal and expected.

BISEXUALITY AS CARNAL PROCLIVITY

Carnal gratification is not necessarily a question of either heterosexual or homosexual mode. For some persons, bisexuality is an equally appropriate posture in terms of sexual activity. Kinsey, for example, reported that 37% of all American males and 20% of all American females "had some actual homosexual experience in the course of their lives." Additionally, there were significant percentages of both males and females, "who had responded erotically to persons of the same sex even though overt physical acts had not taken place."[440] This estimate may well be overestimated, but more recent studies such as that of Hunt's suggest that between 20% and 25% of males have had at least one homosexual experience during their lifetime, and between 10% and 20% of females.[441] Although even these figures may not be completely accurate, the fact of the matter is that significant numbers of heterosexual males and females have on occasion experienced homosexual sexual gratification, and some do so on a more or less continuing periodic basis. Similarly, homosexuals may frequently indulge in heterosexual activities, perhaps as part of a "cover-up" for their real sexual identity, such as when they are married to a heterosexual female. Such persons, then, are bisexual in behavior if not in persuasion. Other individuals, however, claim to be bisexual in orientation, although the estimated number of such persons is no more than between 3 and 4% of the population.[442]

Some writers, however, have given much higher estimates to bisexuality. One recent book on the subject asserted that there were "some forty million Americans [that] can be classified as bisexual on Kinsey's scale of sexual preference."[443] Bisexuality clearly presents some problems in classification and definition.[444] It also presents some difficulties in self-identification.[445] Some of the studies of men who seek casual sex and orgasm without emotional involvement, in "tearooms" or with "pickups" at truck stops confirm that many such men think of themselves as heterosexuals who are simply being serviced, as it were, by homosexuals who provide them with sexual gratification.[446] In other situations, homosexuals who engage in sexual activities with persons of the opposite sex may experience ambivalence in regard to the bisexual label.[447] The military, however, has had no such ambivalence and has moved to dismiss avowed bisexuals from the service because of homosexual behavior.[448]

Bisexuality is a more prevalent mode of sexual outlet in some parts of the world than in American society. It is reputed to be particularly associated with some Arabic societies. Recently in this country, bisexuality has become somewhat more prominent and is even being publicly espoused in some quarters. Various fashion and *avant-garde* periodicals are advocating, or at least depicting, bisexual relationships. A number of entertainers and celebrities have admitted that they are bisexual in persuasion, as have some leaders of the women's liberation movement. There has even been something of a bisexual movement on some college campuses. As one Vassar sophomore, an avid feminist, who engaged in several years of lesbian relationships, commented, "Coming out into the straight world blew my mind. But everybody does bisexuality now. It's really big."[449] The new tendency to bisexual gratification apparently gew out of several trends including the unisex movement, women's liberation, and a kind of hedonistic revolt against traditional puritanical conformity. Professional reaction to the new bisexuality is mixed. One practicing New York psychiatrist has been reported as commenting, "Bisexuality is a disaster for culture and society. . . . They're selling a phony sexual utopia in which the kingdom of the orgasm will supposedly replace the house of the ego."[450] Some other authorities take umbrage at such a position. One president of the American Psychiatric Association, for example, retorted that,

> It is getting to the point where heterosexuality can be viewed as a hangup. The new bisexual consciousness, besides being viewed as a rebellion against puritanism, may also be conveying a feeling of universality among men and women.[451]

Gender Dilemma and Transsexual Behavior

Homosexuality is not the only variant of sexual behavior that may occur within a "counterfeit" context. Transsexuality also "represents the counterfeiting" of more conventional sex. Significant numbers of individuals are dissaffected by the fact of the gender of their sex, and for various reasons, psychological, social, and physical, think of themselves as more appropriately members of the opposite sex.[452] In effect, they become males locked inside female bodies or vice-versa. Traditionally there was no absolute remedy for such a gender dilemma. Some such persons with a milder disaffection for their own sex feel compelled to "cross dress," and wear the apparel of the opposite sex. Such a propensity may go no further than occasionally wearing the undergarments of the opposite sex. Some married men, for example, feel more erotically aroused with their wife, when they are wearing some item of their wife's clothing, and are better able to experience orgasm in such a situation. Other individuals are inclined to indulge in a more elaborate charade, perhaps dressing completely like a person of the opposite sex, even to the extent of trying to fool persons of the opposite sex. Their behavior is a reaction to "gender discomfort." Transvestites ostensibly wish to retain their own sex, but simply enjoy counterfeited excursions into the realm of the other gender, at least in terms of social reaction.

For some persons, the gender dilemma is more intense and painful. These individuals, known as transsexuals, actually feel motivated to acquire the physical sex of their orientation. In some extreme cases, persons have resorted to self-castrations and other mutilations in an attempt to accomplish this. Recent years, however, have seen advances in surgery and chemotherapy that make physical changes of sex possible, at least cosmetically speaking.[453] Males surgically converted to females may have vaginas contrived by plastic surgery but, of course, cannot conceive. Similarly, females converted to males can only enjoy sexually non-functioning penises created by surgery. It is usually a male who seeks surgically to become a female rather than the other way around. There are an estimated 2,000 transsexuals in the United States, and 10,000 confirmed transvestites, who more or less, counterfeit the opposite gender on a permanent basis. The process of conversion, or "sex reassignment," as it is known, involves not only the surgery but also hormone therapy, and, in some instances, psychiatric therapy as well. The legal status of such sex conversion surgery is vague, and to date has never been tested in court. When a person undergoes such a sex reassignment, he or she, not infrequently, experiences social condemnation or repulsion, as well as labeling as deviant. This seems to be especially the case where the individual was married and the conversion is traumatic to spouse, children, and family. Transsexuals can experience emotional relief after the gender change, but they can also experience the pain of rejection from family and friends, the categorization as "sexual deviant," and some experiences difficulty in making the complete adjustment to their new gender. Their socialization as a member of the previous sex may provide a residual impediment to their sex role playing. They also must face social discrimination in such areas as obtaining a job, or even retaining their old one. Recently, for example, a male school teacher in New Jersey underwent a sex change and was subsequently fired. A law suit charging sex discrimination failed, and judicial appeal also lost.[454] The transsexual can, in some states, even be liable for arrest for impersonating a female, which may be a vagrancy or disorderly conduct charge. A transexual's credibility in court may even be challenged on the grounds that they are "dishonest anyway, changing sex, creating a new life, erasing the past, and so forth, surreptitiously."[455] Transsexuals, however, can often be resocialized and enjoy a more personally comfortable life with their new gender.

Sexual conversion is perhaps more socially acceptable now than in the past, as evidenced by the fact that it has been the topic of some television dramas, and various books and articles about it have received a sympathetic reception. In general, however, the transsexual remains a sexual curiosity, who by surgically taking on a different gender, represents to most persons, an aberrant variation from the "normal," and, thus, is a sexual deviant. Such a gender masquerade, even when surgically validated, is not without significant problems or social marginality. The transsexual, in effect, must deal with the fact of double identity, and the attendant discomfort resulting from membership in the different social circles associated with each identity. One study has addressed itself to the double identity problem in the transsexual after the conversion operation, and the coping mechanisms used to ameliorate the strain.[456] Inasmuch as the transsexual has ties in some social circles associated with their former gender, they experience some sexual marginality for a time. Transsexuals do not exactly have a double identity as they step back and forth from earlier social circles such as family to their new groups of friends, peers, and employers, etc., and the attendant involvement in different cultures. Transsexuals handle this dilemma by engaging in greater compartmentalization of social circles than do normals. They would appear to prefer "stigma management," and the ensuing risks of ostracism and rejection, rather than the constant anxiety "of being discovered trying to pass." Thus, the transsexual attempts to deal with the incompatibility of old and new circles of acquaintances and the stigmatization by either minimizing contact with either old or new circles, or sharply segregating the two, and in effect, moving back and forth between the two cultures of family and small town, on the one hand, and friends and "night life in the urban underworld," on the other hand.

Some transsexuals who have had successful surgical gender reassignments have encountered social sanctions ranging from stigma and ostracism by family and peers to job discrimination and discharge from the armed services. Some other transsexuals, however, have been more successful in the social reaction to their sexual conversion, and some have even become celebrities of a sort. More than 25 years ago, Christine Jorgensen, the first American to have her gender changed surgically, was a national news oddity. Since then more than 3,000 individuals have had surgical sex change operations, and many hospitals in this country are now prepared to offer such surgery. There are an estimated 10,000 other men and women in the United States who view themselves as members of the opposite sex.[457] During 1980, at least one transsexual ran for Congress, and a former Catholic priest underwent a sex change operation. Perhaps the two best known transsexuals of recent years, however, are James Morris, the English journalist who became Jan Morris through surgical gender reassignment and authored the best selling autobiography, *Conundrum,* and Dr. Richard Raskind who became Renee Richards.[458] Raskind was a 6'2" former football player, Navy veteran, and prominent eye surgeon. Richards is the same thing, only female, and a controversial tennis player inasmuch as other female players think that she is unfair competition.[459] Renee Richards has become a news item, as it were, and a television celebrity by virtue of appearances on the Johnny Carson Show. Given the increased public toleration for transsexuals and the generally wide-spread expertise for accomplishing gender assignment, many more individuals who psychologically are disaffected with their gender may seek sex-change operations in the future.

For some individuals with gender discomfort, but who lack the motivation for an irreversible surgical sex change, cross-dressing or transvestism represents a temporary escape from their biological role. Such a behavioral respite may be little more than an occasional wearing of some items of clothing of the opposite sex (usually female) in private. It may also take on more complex dimensions and involve the total disguise of the opposite sex, both in terms of clothing, appearance, speech, and mannerisms, for extended periods of time; the complete simulation or counterfeiting of gender behavior, as it were. Transvestism is encountered as an institutional behavior pattern in a number of societies, often "as a sanctioned escape for boys unable to face a vigorous male role."[460] It would appear to serve similar functions in our society as well as affording an enriched erotic context, albeit idiocyncratic, for some individuals of ambivalent sexual tendencies, in their efforts to obtain carnal gratification. In some instances, transvestism has attained the status of an art form and affords recognition and a vocation, if not fame and fortune, in addition to the personal erotic benefits. "Comedy drag" or female impersonation has become a very popular form of cabaret entertainment (although as an art form it has been known for centuries), and some of its more successful practitioners have become celebrated and acclaimed performers.[461] As one writer described it:

> Drag is a place where illusion intersects with identity, where performance merges with personality, art with attitude.[462]

COMMERCIALIZED HOMOSEXUALITY

Homosexual gratification, like heterosexual gratification, can be tendered and received with affection and love, or it may be taken violently through rape or coercion. It can also be obtained casually and impersonally such as in the instance of men stopping in at public rest rooms or "tearooms," as they are known, and being fellated on the way home from work by a stranger.[463] Homosexual fulfillment can also be bought and sold within commercial configurations similar to that of heterosexual gratification, although the image of the male prostitute is perhaps not as famliar as that of the female. Male prostitution, although well known historically in many societies, appears to have been more clandestine and less prevalent than female prostitution in this country, although recently some writers have asserted that there are more male than female prostitutes in the United States.[464] Some accounts suggest that homosexual prostitutes are becoming so numerous and prominent in some areas that they are becoming a public nuisance and a "continuing problem." It has been reported, for example, that in one neighborhood in New York, many transvestite prostitutes, some only partially clad, swarm about the street corners and line the blocks. They move out into the street trying to flag down automobiles and when cars stop for a traffic light, the homosexual hookers descend on the vehicles opportuning the drivers and passengers.[465] According to the manager of an apartment complex in the neighborhood, "They light around a car even if it's moving—four, five, six at a time."[466] As he describes them, "They're like locusts."[467] Certainly, movies such as *Midnight Cowboy* have tended to focus more public attention on the male prostitute. Male prostitution often has its genesis early in the life of a boy. Some studies have shown that male homosexual prostitutes may have experienced early homosexual seduction and immediate reward. In time, they learned that they could use sex to "manipulate others and obtain rewards." This coping mechanism followed them to adult life and to their career of prostitution. Other characteristics of such individuals have included being unemployed and/or a drifter, inadequate education and poor vocational skills, and coming from a broken home or home with "little warmth but much rejection."[468] In short, male prostitutes are persons with few roots, no prospects, the need for money, and the sexual knowledge of how to obtain it by submitting to the sexual advances of homosexuals. As some sociologists have pointed out, the etiology of male homosexuality is not entirely or clearly understood. Certainly, such persons cannot always be dealt with effectively in the courts or through social agencies.[469] Because of their generally deprived backgrounds, their homosexual prostitution is a functional, albeit pathological, coping technique for survival. Unfortunately, their homosexual prostitution activities often bring them into constant contact with the police, and their subsequent records frequently prevent them from being able to obtain work or join the military. A problem of considerable concern in recent years is that of the very large number of very young boys, known as "chickens," who are becoming involved in homosexual prostitution.[470] Sometimes voluntarily, and sometimes through coercion, large numbers of boys, runaways and others, are being sexually and financially exploited to satisfy the carnal needs of adults of deviant persuasions.

Homosexual prostitution may occur in several commercial configurations. Some male prostitutes pursue short, debilitating and often stressful careers in "houses" or homosexual brothels.[471] In fact, in some brothels the only "girls" are transsexuals, or rather in most instances, transvestites, who now dress and act as a female but who may be awaiting or wish for surgery to effect sex conversion.[472] Both "straight" homosexuals and transvestite homosexuals may also work as individual prostitutes or hustlers. Male prostitution, like female prostitution, would ostensibly seem to be a matter of economic motivation coupled with homosexual persuasion. The etiology of such sexual deviancy may well invoke causal influences of more complex dimensions. In this connection, some modality of background characteristic pattern has been articulated by one article that attempted a detailed examination of the phenomena based on a study of case histories.[473] The article suggested that the individuals involved shared several background characteristics in common. The parents, and particularly the father, was frequently absent. Their homes were "muted." They lacked affection, and support when growing up and had only limited opportunity for appropriate role learning and development. They also had a problem of identity. As Ginsberg puts it, "He [the prostitute] is simply a prime example of an early life style in which existence did not receive validation" (p. 180). The homosexual hustler may not necessarily be homosexual as some previous authors have suggested. Rather, the individual with the roots of his pathological state in his home environment has never effectively learned to relate to people and can only do so with his body.

SUMMARY

Homosexuality, as a mode of human sexual expression has long tended to elicit intense emotional public reaction. Homosexuality has been viewed as inauthentic sex rather than "real" sex and, accordingly, a "counterfeit" mode of carnal gratification. Homosexuality has been conceptualized as counterfeit for several reasons including the fact that it deviates from the traditional and normatively prescribed heterosexual pattern, that it is often attended by heterosexual role falsification as a means of concealment, and because it may entail an entire counterfeit lifestyle including heterosexual expression and gratification, or marriage, the siring of children, and the seeking of clandestine and furtive homosexual outlets outside of marriage.

Although homosexuality has been attributed to a variety of

factors including mental aberration or psychiatric disorder, glandular imbalance, inappropriate socialization, or the result of some set of traumatic personal experiences, more recently many authorities are asserting that is is essentially a sexual persuasion that has been labeled as an aberration or deviant perversion because cultural objection to it is rooted in Judeo-Christian tradition and ideology. In this regard, homosexuality subverts culture by avoiding mixed set bonding and the attendant complementary and mutual supportive sex role set. The single-sex dyad also violates social custom by rendering reproduction impossible. Additionally, homosexual sexual gratification violates religious proscription and cultural mandate in Western culture by necessitating "unnatural sex acts" such as oral or anal intercourse for carnal gratification.

Homosexuals and their sexual activity are different and, in this society, there is a long standing public tendency toward suspicion and hostility toward them. Within recent decades, polls of public opinion have revealed that a majority of Americans considered homosexuals "harmful to American life." Homosexuals, when discovered, have been fired from their jobs, publicly disgraced, discharged from the military, socially ostracized, forced out of political office, and even subjected to beatings and robbings. Such physical abuse and exploitation of homosexuals has even become endemic in some social situations and locales.

Homosexuality is not condemned or sanctioned to the same degree in all social settings, and in some social contexts such as the creative community is largely tolerated. Some creative occupational settings appear to attract, encourage, and support persons with a decided experimental bent in their sexual inclinations. In some occupations, such as stripping and prostitution, the work appears to be sufficiently unsatisfying and dissaffective, if not degrading, and the clientele often abusive and degenerate, that the practitioners, not infrequently, turn to other sympathetic females for affection, relaxation, and sexual fulfillment. Yet, other occupations, such as naval and military vocations may tend to contribute to or facilitate homosexuality because of the relative isolation from heterosexual outlet, and working and living in close proximity to, and in intimate conditions, large numbers of males. The military sternly condemns homosexuality, however, and zealously attempts to prevent it, or discover its occurrence. If discovered, homosexuality is severely sanctioned. In the past floggings and even death were widespread military punishments. More recently, the military attempts to ferret out homosexuals and separate them from the service, often involuntarily and not infrequently under less than honorable conditions.

Other total institutions such as jails and correctional facilities tend to also precipitate or encourage homosexual activity. Some authorities attribute this to the deprivation of heterosexual outlets, and in this connection, at least one state prison permits conjugal visitations between inmates and their wives as a means of discouraging homosexuality. It has also been asserted, however, that prison populations, being largely composed of lower and lower-middle class persons, who are less capable of sexual fantasy and mental imagery, are less likely than middle class men to be bothered by heterosexual deprivation, and are, thus, more motivated in their homosexual liaisons either by deprivation from meaningful affective relationships, or by a need for sexual dominance. In this regard, homosexual exploitation, including intimidation, sexual abuse, violence, and rape are all endemic to most prisons. This affords an opportunity for sexual and social dominance, and permits the acting out of frustrations and hostility, as well as an outlet for carnal gratification. Homosexual activity is also often endemic to female correctional facilities but the element of sexual violence is often not as evident as in men's prisons. Homosexual activity in prison does not always follow the individual after he/she leaves prison. In many instances, the ex-inmate may revert to a heterosexual mode of carnal gratification, and may even hold contempt for other persons who engaged in homosexual behavior while in prison, even youthful inmates who were coerced into such activity. Thus, homosexual behavior may be viewed as a form of sexual adaptation in prison.

In recent years in the United States, however, the public view of, and reaction to, homosexuality has changed considerably. Many individuals who formerly attempted to conceal their sexual persuasion, including a number of politicians, servicepersons, entertainers, and government officials have "gone public," and have even become militant in defense of their homosexuality. Some admitted homosexual candidates have been elected to public office, and discrimination against hiring homosexuals has been prohibited in some localities, and in work settings.

Even homosexuals in the military have begun to counterattack, as it were, by publically admitting their sexual predilection, protesting and demonstrating against discrimination and recrimination, and by fighting separating from the military. There are now numerous militant homosexual organizations that are actively pursuing the advancement of civil rights for homosexuals. The "gay" church is thriving in many localities. Homosexuals are holding public rallies, protesting, and picketing businesses who discriminate against them. Gay liberation groups are sponsoring conferences, speeches, social activities, and promoting the teaching of homosexual studies. Some homosexual couples are trying to break down the barriers against homosexual marriages, and homosexuality is being redefined by the medical and psychiatric profession as other than a mental illness.

At the same time, some homosexuals are having to submit to various kinds of behavior modification techniques such as group therapy or "aversion" therapy as a condition to parole or as an alternative to incarceration. In spite of a moderated negative societal reaction to homosexuality, the process of admitting a homosexual persuasion, both privately and publicly, and coping with the public response and frequent sanction or discrimination is still a very painful and traumatic personal process.

Carnal gratification is not necessarily a question of either heterosexual or homosexual orientation. For some persons, bisexuality is an equally appropriate posture in terms of sexual activity. Sex surveys have reported that significant percentages of both sexes have had both heterosexual and homosexual experiences, and some do so on a more or less continuing basis. Some entertainers and celebrities have admitted that they are bisexual in persuasion, as have some leaders of the women's liberation movement. There has even been something of a bisexual movement on some college campuses. Bisexuality is but one manifestation of a new ecumenicalism in carnal gratification, although termed a "phony sexual utopia" by some authorities.

Significant numbers of individuals are disaffected by the fact of the gender of their sex, and for various reasons, psychological, social, and physical, think of themselves as more appropriately members of the opposite sex. In effect, they become males locked inside female bodies or vice-versa. Until recently, there was no absolute remedy for such a gender dilemma, although some persons felt compelled to "cross dress," and wear the apparel of the opposite sex. "Gender discomfort" has compelled some persons to dress and appear as members of the opposite sex for extended time periods. Such transvestite behavior may ameliorate the discomfort but if it is more intense and painful, the individual may now seek "surgical reassignment" through hormone treatment and anatomical modification. Some transsexuals may find emotional relief but others may experience the pain of social rejection or the stress of "double identity," as they step back and forth from their old to new life and circle of acquaintances.

Homosexual fulfillment may be obtained commercially as with heterosexual prostitution but it is often more clandestine and less prevalent than its female counterpart. Recently, large numbers of young males, even children, prostituting themselves have received public attention. Some homosexual prostitutes are persons of homosexual genesis while others are simply assuming homosexual behavior for economic gain. In either event, the homosexual hustler may not have learned to relate to others except through his body and the carnal gratification that it can provide to others.

Chapter 8

RECREATIONAL SEX AND CASUAL CARNALITY

Sexual Deviancy in Superficial Context

Sexual behavior may be a manifestation of aggression, hostility, even brutality. It may also be a commodity, bought and sold. Sexual gratification may be part of an elaborate and abstruse exchange relationship. Sexual consummation may be an expression of profound emotion, and affectionate tenderness. It may also, in some instances, represent little more than a mere superficial mode of human carnal interaction. Superficial sex is casual sex. It is, in general, unemotional sex. It involves immediate gratification that neither reinforces, nor is reinforced by, more pervasive and persistent ties of love or attachment. Superficial sex is essentially sex without purpose or goal, beyond the immediate gratification of carnal appetite. In effect, superficial sex is sex for entertainment, after the fashion of that espoused by an early advocate of birth control, Margaret Sanger, who demonstrated for contraception with a motto to the effect of coition "for recreation only."

As will be discussed in a later chapter, even rape cannot be categorized as either casual sex or sex for carnal gratification only. Its motivation is complex, ego involved, and frequently non-sexual. It has traumatic emotional importance for offender and victim alike. Prostituted sex cannot be always labeled, casual, superficial sex, or simply, carnally motivated. The prostitute, by virtue of occupational ideology and emotional posture, can refrain from experiencing sexual stimulation, much less orgasm. The client may obstensibly seek sexual outlet, but his psychological and social requirements may well outweigh his carnal needs. Both prostitute and client may have deeper emotional involvement, albeit not love or affection, than would often seem to be the case, and both may derive satisfactions and meet needs that transcend the superficial and the recreational.

PROSTITUTED SEX AND EMOTIONAL INVOLVEMENT

Prostituted sex, might, however, in some instances, constitute superficial or recreational sex. Perhaps one illustration of recreational sex for sale is the massage parlor. As discussed in an earlier section, the ubiquitous "executive" massage parlor of recent years, obstensibly operates to provide therapeutic and relaxing massage services. This purpose is subverted by using the facade of legitimate health service to thinly disguise the fact that, in actuality, it represents another kind of delivery service—in this instance the delivery of carnal gratification, and accomplishes to provide recreational sex in the form of masturbation of the clients by female masseuses. Some sociologists have expressed curiosity about the seeming success of the massage parlors as they appear to offer only imitative, and thus compromise, sexual gratification, at relatively high prices, in the face of competition with more conventional configurations of prostituted sex. The answer is perhaps more apparent than some realize. Massage parlors offer carnal gratification more closely approaching recreational sex, than do the traditional modes of prostitution, and at this time, recreational sex appears to enjoy a considerable following. For many clients, the involvement in prostituted sex may involve danger, and risks of various kinds including the possibility of venereal disease, arrest, robbery by the prostitute herself, physical attack by persons in the neighborhoods frequented by prostitutes, or even colleagues of the prostitute. There is also the social stigma associated with the self debasement of "whore mongering," as well as the guilt attendant to fornication. The dramaturgical dimensions of the encounter can, in some instances, serve to exacerbate the client's anxieties or dissaffection. The prostitute can either comport herself in such a matter of fact fashion as to dilute any erotic illusion of the client, or else she may effect a contrived role enactment of desire that is patently transparent and, thus, distasteful, or be sufficiently convincing and inject an unwanted element of emotionalism that effectively erodes the recreational aspects of prostituted sexual intercourse. One researcher, who undertook an ethnographic study of brothels from the perspective of being a "john" or client, reported such a contrived erotic performance from a prostitute on his first visit to the brothel he studied. As he recorded the specifics of this theatrical encounter:

> ... She knelt over me with her knees next to my shoulder and her arms on the other side of my body. "Kiss my tits," she said. I did, whereupon she, in my opinion, feigned sounds of passion, making noises such as "uh, uh, uh." ... Then she said, "Oh wow, you sure have got me hot." As if in the grip of great sexual desire she began kissing my neck.
>
> "Who does she think she's fooling?" I thought, assuming subjective command of the situation.[474]

The writer then goes on to describe how absurd he found her entire dramaturgical repertoire of contrived passions and carnal desire. Because prostituted sex tends to involve an element of contrived behavior on the part of both participants, the encounter is never without some emotional reaction on the part of each of them, in regard to the theatrical performance of the other. Such a reaction might consist of annoyance, disgust, anger, pity, or even humor, but seldom is real personal detachment ever accomplished. In the face of all these handicapping elements, prostituted sex seldom provides the relaxed carnal titilation that genuine recreational sex should afford.

THE MASSAGE PARLOR AS QUICK ORGASM ESTABLISHMENT

The massage parlor, on the other hand, is perhaps more tuned in to the contemporary theme of recreational sex.[475] The massage parlor is convenient, in that it is often located in plain sight, on major traffic arteries, or even in shopping centers. Usually ample parking is provided, and they open early enough to cater to the businessman on his way to work, or during his morning coffee break. They also stay open late at night in order to attract the out-of-town conventioneer who may want a rub-down before retiring. Massage parlors tend to effect an illusion of being relatively free from disease, and while they, themselves, may have periodic difficulties with law enforcement agencies, their customers are almost never arrested or annoyed by policemen or vice-squad officers.[476] Massage parlors, sharing much in common with the "quick food" establishments, are relatively fast and uncomplicated as a delivery system. They are direct and straight forward in their business approach. The businessman or traveler wishing a respite from the rigors of the work routine, or the out-of-town visitor seeking some entertaining diversion enters the parlor, encounters a pleasant, if not seductive interior and can proceed immediately to make his appropriate choices, from the line-up of female masseuses, euphemistically called the "meat display," and select his preferred mode of massage from the menu-like listing of establishment repertoire on the wall. Depending on the entertainment investment he wishes to make, and the degree to which he might care to embellish his sexual fantasies, and enhance his carnal indulgence, he may enjoy a particular kind of room, (such as a mirrored one), or bed (the erotic sensation of a water bed perhaps), type of massage (plain or "electrified" by the vibrator), and even in some parlors the degree of attirement of the masseuse (topless, bottomless, or both). In effect, he has set his own carnal table, cafeteria style, as it were. The masseuse gives the massage, providing conversation and light-hearted humor, if desired, or maintains a serious mien and demeanor, if preferred by the patron. The setting and situation is erotic, and facilitates sexual fantasy. The masseuse is attentive and efficient in her epidermal ministrations and this allows the fullest freedom of narcissistic reverie and sensate preoccupation.[477] The masturbation constituent to the massage, affords orgasm, and, thus, the client is afforded sexual gratification in an interesting, relaxed, enjoyable, and recreational manner. The component interaction is completely commercial, and largely devoid of emotional context, save the carnal stimulation of the patron. The patron has purchased casual gratification for his carnal appetites in much the fashion as he might purchase a double-decker hamburger, to go, in way of satisfying gustatory appetites. The massage parlor permits the patron to engage in casual, and completely self-centered diversion, with only the most superficial investment in social interaction and involvement with others. The customer can effectively compartmentalize his sexual gratification in this manner, and detach it from moral or social import and concern. The masseus, similarly, can better avoid social labeling and self condemnation by anatomical and commercial compartmentalization. By only prostituting their hands, and providing masturbation in lieu of more anatomically elaborate and complete sexual services, the masseuses could view themselves at best as only a health technician providing a massage for the "entire" body, and at worse, as only a "hand whore."

SUPERFICIAL HOMOSEXUAL GRATIFICATION

Superficial sex, can in some instances, encompass homosexual behavior. Humphreys in his definitive study of homosexual activities in public places reveals that many homosexual men (and some heterosexual ones) seek, and obtain "instant sex" in "tearooms"—public restrooms—and other public places such as the balconies of movie theaters.[478] These men according to Humphreys, "seek such impersonal sex, shunning involvement, desiring kicks without commitment." These tearooms provide convenient public, yet private, locations for homosexuals to gather and engage in casual sexual activities, that are impersonal, unemotional, and detached from social importance. In short, the tearooms afford recreational sex, of the most superficial variety possible, on demand. As Humphreys puts it, "what they want, when they want it." Homosexuals are not the only men patronizing tearooms. He relates that a number of married men, and many with children, who obstensibly are heterosexual or at least have heterosexual identities, also use the tearooms to obtain recreational sexual gratification on a totally impersonal basis. Again, the tearoom shares characteristics with the "quick" food establishment. Carnal gratification can be obtained on demand, just as easily as one's alimentary appetites can be assuaged with a "quick" hamburger. The near constant availability of carnal outlet, and the short time frame for obtaining gratification are particularly appealing aspects of the tearoom situation to the men who visit there. As one of Humphreys' interviewees phrased it:

> You go into the tearoom. You can pick up some really nice things in there. Again, it is a matter of sex real quick: and if you like this kind, fine—you've got it. You get one and he is done; and before long, you've got another one.[479]

Some men aware of the sexual opportunities for fellatio in the tearooms apparently developed a routine of stopping in on a regular, sometimes even daily basis, to obtain orgasm. For them, the tearoom offered carnal gratification on a kind of drop-in recreational basis. Humphreys wrote of one of his subjects, a physician in his late fifties, who came to the tearoom with great punctuality every afternoon, presumably on his way home from work. According to Humphreys, "This robust, affable respondent said he had stopped at this tearoom every evening of the week (except Wednesday, his day off) for years 'for a blow-job.' "[480] One of Humphreys's respondents claimed that he might even "make the scene," at one of his favorite tearooms more than once a day. One of the significant characteristics of the tearoom sexual activity, on which Humphreys commented, was the general lack of conversation—to the point of near silence. He spoke of spending hours observing dozens of sexual acts, and perhaps not hearing a word spoken.

Other than hearing an occasional unwhispered "thanks," or "not so hard" by the participant, silence generally prevailed. The silence or general lack of verbal interaction attendant to the homosexual encounters, according to the researcher, tended to satisfy the "demand for privacy," "serve to guarantee anonymity," and to "assure the impersonality of the sexual liaison."[481] In short, the tearoom, and the opportunity for homosexual carnal outlet in the form of fellatio, is causal, impersonal, and largely unemotional sex, with even minimal physical effort, that affords gratification on demand, and within a parsimonious time frame. Tearoom sex is a demonstrative form of recreational sexual behavior.

Gay baths, like "tearooms," also serve as the loci of casual and impersonal homosexual activity. Gay baths are becoming increasingly popular because they tend to provide a relatively idealized setting for superficial sexual gratification.[482] In tearooms, there is "almost constant fear of intrusion or arrest," and massage parlors charge exhorbitant fees for masturbation (or perhaps even no sexual services at all). Pick-ups and prostitutes may involve unpleasant settings, danger or hazard, the need for some minimal degree of interpersonal involvement, and may result in being "treated in a demeaning manner." The gay baths, on the other hand, offer the opportunity for impersonal sex while affording "protection; ample, accessible opportunities; a known, shared, and organized reality; bounding of the experience; congeniality; and a comfortable physical setting."[483]

The gay baths may feature a steam room or sauna, shower rooms, snack room, T.V. viewing room or area, discotheque, private bedrooms, and perhaps an "orgy room" or communal area. The patrons undress and wear a towel around their waist. They may then "cruise" (walk about the hallways hoping to make contact with other patrons), retire to a private bedroom, leaving the door open and await a visitor, or they move to the "orgy" room and attempt to become involved in sexual activity.[484] Although anonymity is "far from complete," and individuals may recognize "regulars," there is minimal talk especially in the "orgy" room. In general, other than an expression of thanks, or an embrace or other nonverbal communication after a sexual encounter, there is little conversation.[485]

Thus, in the gay baths, sexual gratification, perhaps with multiple partners, is convenient, casual, relaxed, impersonal, and superficial. With minimal conversation and interaction, much less involvement or commitment, individuals can enjoy orgasm and carnal gratification with detached ease and superficial efficiency.

Even superficial sexual gratification in the protective atmosphere of gay bars is not without some hazard, however. One study reports on the results of 33 venereal disease screening sessions in Denver gay steambaths, and indicated that 11.5% of the men were found to have asymptomatic gonorrhea and 1.4% had latent syphilis.[486] The gay steambaths were "productive locations for detecting asymptomatic gonorrhea and syphilis."[487]

Not all casual and superficial homosexual activity takes place in tearooms or gay baths. An unusual location for such carnal gratification is at truckstops. One study of such sexual behavior has indicated that homosexuals in the city studied would "cruise" the truckstops (i.e. would drive back and forth between various diners and rest areas where truck drivers regularly stopped).[488] This cruising activity generally took place between 10:00 P.M. and 5:00 A.M. The individual drives up to a parked truck with the driver sitting in it and asked something like, "Do you have the time?" Some of the individuals who cruised were unmarried persons, "firmly rooted in the gay subculture," while others were married individuals "whose participation in the gay subculture is limited to the search for sex without commitment."[489] The truck drivers tended to "maintain a heterosexual self-identity and view their homosexual activity while away from home as simply a convenient sexual outlet." The drivers did not report any homosexual involvement when at home, and use their encounters at the truckstops as a sexual expedient. As the researcher, put it, the truck drivers simply looked upon the homosexual activity "as supplements to the sexual outlet provided by wives or girlfriends."[490] Not infrequently, the cruiser and the driver engage in the sexual activity in the sleeper portion of the truck cab. The sexual activity includes "fellatio, anal intercourse, mutual masturbation, and mutual fellatio," as well as "hugging and kissing."[491] It was reported that, "reciprocity is the norm during the sexual exchange." The network for casual sex activity reported in this study is apparently not unique, but rather quite widespread inasmuch as a gay newsletter, *The 18 Wheeler* includes "stories, cartoons, jokes, pictures, and cruising tips for homosexuals who are interested in truck drivers."[492] Here, one has an instance of homosexual individuals, and truck drivers who claimed heterosexual identities, meeting in a furtive and clandestine fashion for the purpose of obtaining casual and superficial carnal gratification through homosexual behavior in an impersonal encounter. Both sought and obtained sexual stimulation and orgasm without emotional involvement.

MASTURBATION AS RECREATIONAL SEXUAL ACTIVITY

It might be argued that masturbation is essentially a recreational form of sexual activity. As pointed out in an earlier section, however, masturbation traditionally has, for many individuals been a sexual outlet that afforded orgasmic relief from sexual tension, but because of the moral onus, and social stigma which attended masturbation, it could hardly be called unemotionally involved, casual, recreational activity. For persons, of both sexes and all ages, masturbation may have been fraught with guilt, and feelings of self-debasement, for surrendering, as it were, to carnal desire, albeit anxiety producing, and ego-threatening, because of concern about social, and thus labeling, as heterosexually maladjusted, or even sexual deviant or pervert (remember Portnoy's mental agonies and torments of the soul). Recent years have seen altered medical opinion which now generally absolves masturbation from harm or dysfunction to health and physiology. In fact it is often prescribed, especially for females and males, alike, as an aid in affecting appropriate orgasmic response and in relieving sexual tumescence where marital heterosexual adjustment is inadequate. Furthermore, moral admonishment and condemnation of masturbation has been largely diluted. In the face of such ideological and attitudinal changes, masturbation has become, in large measure, a value-free form of sexual outlet. It is hardly surprising, therefore, that a number of medical authorities, sexologists, and therapists of various persuasions are now recommending masturbation. Many of the recent best-selling sex manuals (including some for adolescents)[493] even advocate masturbation either as a means of "training," so as to improve and enhance orgasmic response during heterosexual intercourse, or as a means of recreational sexual gratification in addition to providing relief where other means of sexual gratification are unavailable. As the author of *The Sensuous Woman* emphasizes the benefit of masturbation:

> Come on and try it. It won't take you long to realize that masturbation is a happy, healthy, normal act that can contribute to your well being and sensuality enormously.[494]

The author of *The Sensuous Man* also encouraged masturbation, both for its good effects, and because it is "fun." Articulating a variety of benefits attendant to masturbation, he assured his readers that autoerotic sexual activity affords, "an incredible feeling of pleasure and release."[495] It would appear that many persons, both male and female have heeded the advice of sexologists and have espoused masturbation in a more casual and recreational context than in the past, and their autoerotic activity is less anxiety producing, ego-threatening, or potentially guilt laden. As mentioned in an earlier chapter, masturbation is more prevalent among females than in times past, and many have purchased vibrators as a means of facilitating and enhancing their masturbatory experiences.

According to the reports of several researchers such as Morton Hunt, many females do engage in masturbation, with or without the aid of vibrators, for the physical and carnal enjoyment of the activity itself, and apparently experience little or no anxiety concerning the practice.[496] Masturbation also appears to be more prevalent with males than in the past. Boys and girls are apparently masturbating earlier in life than their older counterparts.[497] Males are continuing to masturbate into adulthood, and even after marriage, to a greater degree than in the past, and the frequency of masturbation is also up significantly over earlier generations.[498] The increase in masturbation appears to be related to a desire to maximize carnal gratification rather than because of any diminunization of sexual outlets of other variety. Thus, persons of both sexes seem to be increasingly using masturbation as a recreational means of carnal gratification, as well as a supplemental one.

SEX PLAY AMONG CHILDREN

Perhaps, the prototype, however, of casual, recreational sex is the sex play of children. In our own society of course, children are supposed to be asexual, or at least not have sexual desires, much less sexual capabilities. It is almost a contradiction in itself that our society also has extremely rigid norms that make sexual activities with or among children proscribed and taboo. So strong is this taboo that if children exhibit sexual curiosity or engage in any kind of activity aimed at sexual gratification, they may well be conceptualized, if not adjudged, as mentally disturbed. In short, child sexuality is deemed deviant to the point of pathology. Such is not the case in many other societies, however.

In some primitive and folk societies, the adults may actively encourage sexuality and sexual activity in their children. This process may begin when the children are little more than infants and may involve stimulating their genitals as a way of pacifying them. Parents and kinsmen may massage a child's genitals or even deliberately masturbate it to comfort the child or to quiet it when it frets. Stephens, in his cross-cultural synthesis of family behavior, mentions several societal groups where adults genitally stimulate the children, including the Hopi, the Alor, the Navaho, and the Kaingang.[499] In regard to the latter, he reports, "The sexuality of little boys is stimulated by their mothers by manipulation of the genitals before they can walk . . . "[500] Beyond this, children in these societies may begin quite early in life to engage in sexual play with other children, and to indulge in elaborate and well informed sexual language. Among the Baiga of India, for example, the children, in their normal daily play develop as entertainment, games, such as "Cow and Bull," "Horse and Mare," "Cock and Hen," and "Pig and Sow." All are played with considerable realism and detail and involve surprising physiological knowledge. The Baiga children also play "Houses," in which the boys and girls wander off into the jungle and construct little huts out of leaves and branches. They frequently have their first sexual encounters in these play "houses." Ethnographers of this group report youngsters of nine years old or younger having intercourse. In the words of one such account, the nine-year old Baiga boy told that, "We [he and a similar aged girl] were plucking *mahua.* I was laughing at her. I seized her and had her under the tree. There was no blood. I came to love her and married her in the end."[501] The adults are aware of such sexual play, and may even observe it. They tend to be extremely tolerant of such behavior among the children. If they were inclined to chide the children, they, themselves, might well be subject to criticism from their neighbors who might think them too strict, or even in some cases, jealous of the boy or girl engaged in sexual play with their offspring. Among the Baiga, the adults see the sexual play of children, regardless of degree of intimacy, to be mere recreational diversion, and of no social significance. The children naturally also view it as play and nothing more. In some societies, the adults themselves may even engage in sexual play with the children. Stephens mentions the Kaingang may even have sexual intercourse with the children, in a casual and emotionally uninvolved way, perhaps when a child crawls under the blanket of a family member or kinsman to stay warm in the winter. In such instances, the children may fight the adult in resisting, even scratching the adult. Such experiences are "illicit" but offenders are viewed humorously, rather than as sexual deviants. The children, too, even though they may have been treated roughly or violently, may also well see the incident as humorous rather than traumatic. Such a sexual experience may even whet their appetites, so to speak, for more involved sexual recreation.[502]

Unlike the other societies mentioned where sexual play among children is tolerated, if not encouraged, in our own society, such erotic activity is often severely sanctioned. Children in our society, nevertheless, do engage in sex play usually out of a sense of curiosity. Small children may sometimes make a game out of exhibiting themselves, and examining the genitalia of each other. Not infrequently, this may entail several older children undressing a young child and inspecting its sexual organs. Among slightly older children, the sexual games may acquire more elaborate format, a favorite being "doctor and nurse," where inspection of genitalia can be incorporated into a "medical examination." Chilman asserts that, "Throughout childhood, probably most children engage in these activities—ah! the joy of 'playing doctor.' "[503] She also suggests that children may also engage in exhibitionism, or even homosexual behavior such as mutual masturbation.[504] If, and when, children are caught by parents or other adults while they engaged in such sexual diversion, they may be severely punished, and perhaps even viewed as perverted or disturbed. Some parents may well become agitated and concerned if they hear of a neighbor child who inspected the private parts of younger children. Occasionally, a school-age child who persists in sexual play, and especially that which involves the inspection of young children's genitalia, may well be arrested and taken into juvenile court. He subsequently may have to receive psychiatric treatment, or else be committed to a hospital for disturbed children or, in some instances, a reform school.

In an earlier cited article, the deviant antics of a group of young boys in a hospital for disturbed children was described. Much of the time and energy of these children was preoccupied with sexual play of one kind or another. In fact, almost all of their time was taken up with sexual diversion. Even when they were involved in seemingly more traditional kinds of play, such as making things out of molding clay, their activities had a sexual theme. In this instance, they would create "mickey guns" resembling phalluses out of molding clay. It is interesting to note, that except perhaps for the rather singular preoccupation with sexual themes, these children did little that children in other societies, such as the Baiga, might not do. In this instance, however, these children were viewed as disturbed and severely deviant delinquents. This is not to say that sexual play was the sole factor that accounted for their incarceration. They had a history of delinquent and disturbed behavior, but the sexual play that could have originated in the institutional setting, perhaps as a reaction to boredom and frustration, or at least may have been intensified and promoted by their confinement, tended to reinforce their deviant label and stigma as disturbed children. In short, the sexual play tended to support or corroborate their image as disturbed.

SEXUAL PLAY AS PRECURSOR TO SEXUAL LICENSE

Sexual play among children, in our society, is proscribed because of strong negative moral values surrounding sexuality of any variety. There is further concern that, in addition to sexual play as being morally wrong, in and of itself, it may tend to create a pattern of carnal indulgence in later life. In a sense, the sexual play of today, it is perhaps believed, can lead to the sexual license of tomorrow. Component to the Judeo-Christian tradition, and residual to the Puritan Ethic, is the conceptualization of sexual activity of any variety, outside of marriage, as sinful and degenerate. Sexual activity. according to traditional cultural mandate, and reinforced by religious dogma, should lead to the procreation of children. Sexual interaction outside of marriage, is, therefore, sex without purpose save carnal gratification, and as such, from the traditional view, would represent a surrender, as it were, to lust and lasciviousness. Within this ideological framework, all sexual activities other than heterosexual genital intercourse between a married couple would constitute illicit and deviant sex. In this connection in our society, most such configurations of sexual behavior are, at least theoretically illegal. These illegal sexual variations would include homosexuality, adultery, bestiality, and even oral and/or anal sexual behavior by married persons.

Even though all sexual behavior outside of marital intercourse of a prescribed variety, has been morally, socially, and legally condemned, certain sexual modes and contexts have been particularly offensive to the normative order. These might include sexual activities with socially inappropriate partners such as children or animals, public displays of sexual activities such as exhibitionism, and violent sexual behavior. In terms of the context of sexual motivation, however, casual or recreational sexual activity has tended to particularly run against the ideological grain of our society, and yet there has been a persistent tendency to tolerate it to a degree. Casual sex lacks the redeeming feature of affection or emotion. The romantic myth of Western society has, in some instances, allowed love and passion to justify illicit sexual activity. Even the more offensive and "unnatural" varieties of sex, are perhaps not justified, but at least rationalized, if not excused, on the basis of insanity, mental disturbance, glandular or hormonal disorder, or some other pathological state of mind or body. In short, our society has historically viewed the person who commits an illicit or deviant sex act, as either impetuous and impulsive because of love, or else as a "sick" person. Casual or recreational sex would suggest another category of motivation—that of pure carnal motivation. The individual, so motivated, would not only volitionally give up "control" of his sexual desires and appetites, but would seek and obtain pleasure, enjoyment, and relaxation from sexual stimulation and gratification.

For the devotee of the Protestant and Puritan ethics, even the concept of recreation itself, has a negative connotation. Recreation involves the abandonment of work and productivity, and the subversion of ambition. Pleasure and fun, according to the attendant doctrine, divert one from the true path of purpose and accomplishment. Other than as temporary respite, and, thus, renewer of energy and effort, diversion and amusement has certain basic inconsistencies with the theme of objective effort in Western culture. Where diversion and recreation revolve around carnal gratification, there is an almost total departure from traditional models of normative conformity. Even in today's self-labeled "enlightened" and ostensibly "sexually liberated" times, the public announcement of intention to enjoy recreational sex, and especially outside of marriage would bring a response of raised eyebrows at least, and perhaps sanctions as severe as ostracism, at worst. The announcement of a junior business executive that he routinely stopped in at a nearby "tearoom" for fellatio and a "quicky" orgasm during his coffee break, or that he liked to take a leisurely lunch hour in order to daily visit a massage parlor in the neighborhood, and obtain masturbatory orgasm as a means of refreshing himself for the afternoon's work routine, would probably be viewed as a sexual degenerate. Similarly, a female employee's request for an afternoon off in order that she might spend the time enjoying prolonged sexual gratification with her vibrator might be considered as a manifestation of mental aberration. At a less ridiculous level, even today a married couple that might regularly engage in coitus during the husband's lunch break, or seem to always be in bed when guests call at their home may be humorously, if not contemptuously, referred to as "oversexed." Even single persons who appear to engage in regularized sexual activities without apparent emotional involvement may also run the risk of being labeled "deviant." Aside from the violation of the norm of chastity, the single female, who engages in sexual activities on a regular basis for the sheer carnal enjoyment of it, rather than love, may run the risk of being conceptualized as a "nymphomanic," and the single male, in a similar circumstance, might also be accused of pathological sexual preoccupation.

SEXUALITY IN SOCIALIZATION

In spite of the general societal objection to, and condemnation of recreational sex, there has historically been considerable tacit toleration of sexual activity for the sake of pleasure and entertainment among young people who are courting. Children even in grade school may be encouraged to attend parties with members of the opposite sex. There, parents and adults may permit, if not encourage, games with a content of sexuality. "Spin-the-bottle," and "post office," are venerable devices to introduce young people to progressively more intimate stages of sexual interaction. Hand holding, neck hugging, and kissing between young couples may even be considered as "cute." Unlike some Latin and Mediterranean societies where the *duena* or chaperone constantly attends the unmarried female of genteel birth, and closely monitors and supervises the courtship process, American adolescents are allowed considerable freedom and latitude in their courtship activities. As a result, they tend to move rather quickly to levels of extremely intimate sexual interaction. This is, however, not accomplished without considerable opposition from the adult segment of society, some hazard of societal sanction, and individual conflict and guilt on the part of the individual young people. Inasmuch as young people may have difficulty managing their sexuality because of confused and conflicting societal expectations for their sexual behavior, and as their sexual behavior not infrequently results in problems, they have been labeled by at least one social scientist as a "sexually oppressed" group.[505] Sexual intercourse is considered inappropriate and hazardous for adolescents, but no social support is offered for other forms of sexual pleasure and expression. In theory, adolescents are supposed to refrain from all forms of sexual expression and carnal gratification. Since this is clearly an unworkable proscription, our society has accordingly evolved a two-level normative system in this regard. There is a highly idealized set of normative sexual proscriptions bearing especially on adolescents of the lower and upper class, and at the same time, a more pragmatic view that young people will "do their thing," and the less known the better. The lower class young people are simply seen as beyond normative control in their sexual behavior. Young people of all classes do, indeed, "do their thing" and in this connection, one researcher found, for example, that 60 percent of a sample of college females reported that they had engaged in heavy petting (genital stimulation while in an unclothed state) while they were still in high school.[506] Similarly, more than two-thirds of the men in this country and more than one-half of the women have premarital coitus.[507]

Our society, like most others, make regularized provisions for young persons to meet, engage in premarital social interaction, develop emotional commitments (hopefully based on social compatibility and complementary personality makeup), and ultimately mate, and rear families. These activities are generally termed "courtship." In regard to courtship, however, our society differs from many others in at least two major respects. The time frame that is allocated for the courtship period is unusually protracted. As mentioned above, children may be encouraged to develop a posture of sexuality, and to take an interest in the opposite sex, perhaps as early as elementary school. They may even begin having symbolic "dates" by the time they are eight or nine years old. Regular dating and mixed sex parties may be routinized by the time of the sixth grade for the more socially precocious children, and certainly by the time of junior high school for many. Relatively serious dating and "going steady" may occur during the high school years. Although many young people may marry by the time they graduate from high school, or shortly thereafter, it is socially permissible to wait much longer before doing so, especially if additional educational experience such as college is involved. Young people may continue to date and court beyond college for a number of years. Young "career" people may even defer marriage into their 30s. Thus, a courtship period perhaps spanning up to 20 years is not unknown in our society. In most other societies, young people accomplish to marry many years earlier, usually with the encouragement, if not mandate, of society.

COURTSHIP AS RECREATION

A second major difference in the courtship process in our society as compared to others, is the rationale for the process. Almost universally, courtship is a mate selection process, that may, or may not, allow some degree of personal choice or preference of mate to the participants. Regardless of whether the orientation of the courtship is romantic, pragmatic, or a combination of the two, courtship almost inevitably results in marriage. This is, in fact, its basic *raison d'être*. Thus, courtship is not usually begun, except and unless, marriage is viewed as an exigent probability. In our own society, however, persons may be intensely involved in courtship activities for years on end, with an absolute determination and intention not to marry, at least not for a number of years hence. Courtship in our society fulfills a number of functions including socialization, status sifting or sorting, and personality development. Courtship is recreational in a number of ways. The social activities constituent to courtship, such as dances, parties, and outings are recreational, as is the opportunity for verbal interaction with other young persons of the same age and especially those of the opposite sex. Courtship is a period of sexual socialization, and perhaps even indoctrination, and this, too, is a recreational dimension of the process. The unsupervised "recreational" nature of dating and courtship, however, has encouraged sexual freedom and experimentation, promiscuity and in some instances even sexual exploitation.

Sexual activity, including coitus has been component to courtship, through much of our history, although it would appear that from 1920 on, such activity was more widespread, frequent, intimate, and intense. At different times, various labels for such sexual activity, particularly that which did not include actual coitus have been used to describe it. Such labels have included "sparking," "pitching woo," "necking," and "petting," among others. Petting, as the name used in more recent years, includes all sexually oriented behavior that stops short of actual penetration of the vagina by the penis. Where, at one time, and for many young persons, petting may have involved only kissing and bodily caresses of varying degrees of intimacy, more recently, research by such persons as Hunt suggest, "that it could, in fact, involve partial or total nudity, mutual masturbation, fellatio, cunnilingus, and orgasm for one or both partners."[508]

PETTING AS COMPROMISE SEX AND CARNAL "GAME"

Petting was to assume several functions. Patently, it was an intermediate step in sexual interaction culminating ultimately in coitus, preferably within marriage. In that sense, petting was, more or less, a phase in sexual socializationn. The recipient of such socialization could avoid the dilemma of the unfortunate couples, not infrequently from "sheltered" upper-middle or upper class backgrounds, who in times past, often married and went to their honeymoon bed almost totally ignorant of the mechanics of sexual intercourse. In some cultures, it was anticipated that sexually inept, honeymoon couples might receive last minute guidance and instruction, as it were, through the device of lavishly illustrated sexual manuals. The Japanese traditionally relied on "pillow books," and the Chinese institutionalized the use of sexual manuals termed *fangchung-shu* (literally the "art of the bedchamber") as early as the Han dynasty.[509] In the United States, until recently, however, most sexual or marriage manuals tended to be more expository and clinical rather than pictorial and erotic, and American couples had to wade through considerable verbage in order to derive the carnal instruction they sought. Petting also offered the opportunity to test and nourish romantic conceptualizations of the courting partner. According to Hunt, petting was also "the acceptable middle-class means of expressing erotic and emotional feelings before marriage."[510] Petting, and especially heavy petting to orgasm became a kind of compromise sexual interaction, that took the place of actual coitus. This was especially the case with persons of middle and upper socio-economic backgrounds. The lower class individuals tended to move quickly on to actual intercourse in their courtship activities. The economic exigencies of needing to work, and collaterally seeking to establish a family tended to shorten the period for courtship considerably, and time did not favor protracted and substitute modes of sexual gratification. The middle and upper class also tended to place a premium on virginity, and especially in the female. Petting to orgasm in its various modes permitted the couple to enjoy sexual gratification while preserving the status of technical virginity. Virginity has been traditionally prized in our society for moral, social, and psychological reasons, but of course, never to the extent that it has been, and is, in Japan. Even today in Japan, some brides-to-be may be impelled to obtain a certificate of virginity from a gynecologist to present to their future in-laws, before they can receive their approval for the marriage. Accordingly some of these girls who are not virgins undergo a simple plastic surgery technique known as "hymen rebirth" in which a new hymen is grafted on. In this way, the girls can remove guilt feelings about past sexual experiences, but also lets them enjoy sex before marriage, without fear of not being able to find husbands later in life.[511]

A number of cultures traditionally sought to provide evidence of a bride's chastity at time of marriage by the simple expedient of publically displaying the honeymoon sheets the next morning (presumably with appropriate bloodstains if the bride's hymen had been intact). One informant indicated that this custom was practiced in Greek neighborhoods in this country when she grew up. The mother-in-law would come around the morning after the wedding to pick up the stained honeymoon sheets in order to hang them outside her window. In Egypt, the same function is traditionally accomplished by the device of a *daya* (traditional midwife) or the husband deflowering the wife on her wedding night, with a finger wrapped up with a handkerchief. The bride's mother, mother-in-law, and often other female relatives, are present in the room. The husband (or the *daya*) passes the bloodied handkerchief to the mother and mother-in-law, who then pass it on to the bride's brothers who are waiting outside the room. They in turn show it to the assembled wedding crowd, "amid beating of drums and great jubilation." (Assaad, p. 13)

In addition to being a compromise sexual gratification, petting has also been a kind of "game" between the sexes in American society. As Morton Hunt wrote:

> The boy tried to see how much he could get—and the girl how little she could give—by way of recompense for the time and money he had spent on her, and the better he "made out," the higher was his status among his fellows, while the less she gave in, the more desirable she was deemed.[512]

In this connection, whole youth vocabularies arose to define certain aspects of the game. A female who was too adamant in not giving it, especially if she tended to adopt a posture of manifest sexuality in her day-to-day behavior, might be labeled a "prick teaser." Overly amorous male adolescents might acquire a reputation of being an "octupus," and the whole process of obtaining varying degrees of sexual favors and intimacies from females was labeled with such terms as "scoring." In the face of intense motivation, often probably more social than carnal, many young males became sexually exploitative to the point of violence. Various researchers have indicated that in recent decades, many young females have reported that acts of sexual offensiveness to the point of physical violence and threats by their dates, are relatively common in some instances.[513]

Petting appears to have been very much a part of the courting experience of many Americans, although more associated with the middle and upper educational levels than the lower. Kinsey reported that of the females born before 1900, only 10 percent admitted to having petted to orgasm while in their teens. Kinsey found that in the females born after 1920, 94 percent of those who were still single at 20 had petted, and about one-fourth of those had petted to orgasm. Two-fifths of those single at 25 had done so. The percentage of those who had petted to orgasm went up the longer they remained unmarried.[514] Kinsey found that his married women had approximately eight petting partners before marriage. Kinsey also reported that approximately one-fourth of the males he surveyed had petted to climax by age 25.[515] Surveys of sexual behavior in more recent years suggested that more young people pet but with fewer partners. Hunt, for example found that two-thirds of the under-25 males he surveyed had experienced orgasm by various petting techniques in the 12 months prior to his study. He also reported that more than one-half of his 18–24 single females had petted to orgasm in the past year. Interestingly he found that the number of petting partners for his females was only three. Kinsey had not published figures on number of petting partners for males, but Hunt found that the median number of pre-marital petting partners for the older half of his sample was 15, while the younger half only reported 12. It would seem that young people feel more free to pet, including using a wide variety of techniques to obtain orgasm, but it would also appear that they move on to a routine of fairly regular premarital sexual intercourse after the experience of petting to orgasm with few partners.

PETTING AND PREMARITAL INTERCOURSE AS RECREATIONAL SEXUAL INTERACTION

Traditionally, young people were prone to rationalize "heavy" petting and premarital intercourse, on the basis of emotional commitment. Often, the petting or sexual partner was a "steady" boyfriend, girlfriend, or even a fiancee. Thus, engagement and marriage was imminent and the sexual activities while perhaps premature, were not viewed as promiscuous carnality, but rather as physical expressions of trust and affection. In more recent years, however, some researchers have noted something of a change in ideology concerning premarital sexual activities. Hunt found, for example, that his under 35-year-old subjects (both male and female) were much more prone than were the over 35 group, to approve of heavy petting "even where there is little or no emotional involvement but only such motives as the desire for experience, or for sexual gratification, excitement, or simply for an ego boost."[516] In effect where heavy petting was once more or less reserved for couples in love, it apparently has become relatively routinized, if not institutionalized, as a constituent part of the dating process. Heavy petting is simply a stage in intimacy to which dating will progress if carried on long enough. Young people find it sexually enjoyable, and are, more or less, conforming to contempory norms of appropriate dating behavior, regardless of whether or not there is significant affection between the boy and girl. Petting, and especially petting to orgasm, would appear to have become recreational modes of sexual interaction, and often occur within a superficial context.

Premarital intercourse, in addition to petting, and petting to orgasm has also figured prominently in American courtship patterns. Early research on premarital sexual behavior prompted dire predictions on the part of the researchers in terms of the long range prospects of virginity.

In a study of college students conducted in 1938[517] the researcher found that the rate of premarital intercourse had been steadily increasing for a number of years and predicted that by 1960 virginity at marriage would be practically nonexistent. Subsequent studies after World War II did not support or substantiate the early researcher's prediction of a continuous rise in premarital relations, and even research of recent decades appeared to validate the existence of a significant percentage of virgins of both sexes at the time. What the later studies of the 1940s and 1950s did show, however, was that there had been an impressive increase in premarital sexual activities during the 1920s among individuals reaching late adolescence and young adulthood. This no doubt contributed to the labeling of that decade as the Roaring Twenties. This research however, was not able to document a similar increase in the decades that followed the 1920s in terms of premarital intercourse. An elaborate study of college students in 1959[518] indicated that 57 percent of non-veteran men and only 13 percent of the women had experienced premarital relations. Another study in 1965[519] found that 22 percent of the senior college women had had intercourse but a study by Bromley and Britten as early as 1938 using a comparable sample had shown that 26 percent of the women were participating in premarital sexual intercourse. Other research on college campuses since World War II tended to report on premarital sexual behavior in the general range of between 20 and 30 percent for females and 50 percent for males. On the basis of these college students it appeared that there had been no significant increase, if any, of premarital sexual intercourse for several decades. One of the more prominent researches on sexual behavior was that conducted by the late Alfred C. Kinsey and his colleagues in the late 1940s.[520] Since much of his sample population consisted of middle-aged college educated white urban persons, his findings were subject to some criticism on the basis of bias. Kinsey's data showed 20 percent of females to be non-virgin by age 20 and males, depending on where their education stopped, indicated non-virginity rates of between 50 and 80 percent before age 20. Kinsey's findings from married males and females were quite interesting in terms of the correlation between education, sex, and premarital coitus. For males, 98% of those with grade school education, 85 percent of those with high school education, and 68 percent of the college educated had engaged in premarital sexual intercourse.

The more educated the male the less likely he was found to have experienced premarital coitus. Presumably, this was the result of the highly educated males having had fewer premarital coital opportunities as well as an increased likelihood of using other sexual outlets such as petting to orgasm.[521] For his females on the other hand, 30 percent of the grade school educated, 47 percent of the high school educated, and 60 percent of the college educated had engaged in premarital intercourse.[522] The highly educated female was apparently more likely to have had coital experience because she was older at time of marriage and had had a longer period of opportunity. Also, her educational sophistication made her place less significance on virginity.

THE TREND TOWARD PERMISSIVE PREMARITAL INTERCOURSE

Recent surveys suggest that a somewhat more sexually liberated posture on premarital sexual intercourse now exists. Hunt reported that among white females, nearly 20 percent of his married females have had premarital intercourse by age 17, and one-third of his single sample. By age 25 one-half of his married sample had experienced premarital intercourse, and almost three quarters of his single females. This indication of sexual permissiveness is particularly underscored by the younger females aged 18–24, of which 70 percent of the single white females, and 80 percent of the married white females, admitted that they had experienced premarital intercourse. Kinsey had earlier found that of his females with premarital coital experience, 53 percent only had one partner. Hunt reported that in the younger half of his female sample with premarital coital experience, more than one-half (51 percent) had only one partner.[523] Hunt also pointed out that his males with premarital coital experience in the older half of the sample reported six sexual partners by the time they were married, the premaritally experienced males in the younger half of the sample gave the same median number of sex partners prior to marriage.[524] The recent *Redbook* survey reported that 90 percent of the women under 25 who participated in their study said that they had premarital intercourse.[525] Of the women who were married before 1964, 69 percent had experienced premarital intercourse. For those women married between 1964 and 1969, 81 percent had intercourse prior to marriage, Of those married between 1970 and 1973, 89 percent reported premarital intercourse, while 93 percent of those married after the end of 1973 did so. When the women under 25 years of age in the study are divided into strongly religious and nonreligious categories, a striking difference appears. Of the strongly religious women 75 percent said they have had premarital intercourse while 96 percent of the nonreligious group had experienced intercourse before marriage. Chilman has reported that by 1973, "about 35 percent or more of high school seniors, both male and female, were nonvirgins."[526] Figures for that same year for college students showed that 85 percent of the males were nonvirgins and between 60 and 70 percent of the females. As Chilman further observed that, "it appears that between 1967 and 1974, premarital intercourse rates for white females rose by about 300 percent and for white males, about 50 percent."[527] It appears that the rate of premarital intercourse continues to increase. According to very recent reports, "While statistics on teenage dating habits are still sketchy, they suggest that sexual adventurism among young girls has risen to an astonishing degree."[528] Recent data suggest that "nearly 50 percent of the nation's 10.3 million young women age 15 to 19 have had premarital sex."[529] This figure has doubled since 1971.[530]

That more young people are engaging in premarital intercourse than in the past is undeniable, although it is frequently argued that today's young people are not necessarily more promiscuous than in the past, but rather still inclined to reserve premarital sex for partners with whom there is an emotional commitment. The fact that persons who experience premarital intercourse tend to have relatively few partners would seem to bear this out. The pill and other contraceptive devices, however, are making it possible for young females to completely avoid the danger of unwanted pregnancy resulting from premarital sex. In this regard, inasmuch as birth control pills are being routinely prescribed on demand at many college infirmaries, some coeds are going for their prescriptions practically by the time they register. Young people may be inclined to only engage in premarital intercourse with persons for whom they have an emotional attachment, but they may have a series of partners for whom they have an emotional commitment. In fact, the ideology and philosophy of living together without marriage is alleged to be based on the avoidance of the permanent ties and emotional involvement of marriage.[531] In short, young people in some instances seem to be rejecting the total emotional commitment of marriage for a sexual life style and romantic mode of more transient, and perhaps more superficial character. Bell, for example, has reflected that:

> Finally, it should be recognized that the new sexual values allowing for some premarital permissiveness have developed to the point of competing with the traditional values.[532]

SERIAL ROMANCES AND SUPERFICIAL SEX

Some authors like Hunt, however, reject the concept of a superficial and recreational sexual pattern among young people, citing the fact that partner-swapping and group sex is relatively rare. The new sexual freedom, as he sees it "operates largely within the framework of our long-held cherished cultural values of intimacy and love."[533] Such a view rejects the possibility that serial romances or emotional commitments are being used as a rationale for sexual life style. Many young people are rejecting the idea of marriage and parenthood, at least vocally, and are talking instead about careers, and free unencumbered life styles. For some of these young people, a period of protracted courtship activities, after college or high school, perhaps with a number of partners may be seen as an attractive opportunity to "do one's thing," sexually and otherwise. Premarital coital experience has apparently reached near universal levels in our society in recent years. Component to a trend toward sexual precociousness is the tendency to experience premarital intercourse earlier in life. In this regard, Chilman has reported that:

> By 1973 premarital intercourse was occurring at younger ages than in the past, with about one-fourth of white males and females apparently being sexually experienced by age 15 or 16, and with over 90 percent for black males and about 50 percent for black females.[534]

A very recent nationwide survey of the sex lives of young women in the United States revealed that by age 16, one in five has engaged in sex relations; by 19, two-thirds of the females have engaged in sex relations, and more than 9 out of 10 females have had sex prior to marriage.[535]

Thus, many young persons are becoming sexually active during their dating years and the period of their dating years is lengthening. At the same time, some young people are rejecting the idea of marriage until they have at least had an opportunity to live apart from home and family, and experience an independent and unencumbered life. In the face of these tendencies, the question arises, will these single young people restrict their sexual activities to only those persons with whom they have an emotional attachment? As Donald A. Bloch, a New York psychiatrist and director of the Ackerman Institute for Family Therapy has written on this concern:

> There's a danger of a kind of precocious sexuality that can lead to emptiness if there's no ongoing relationship . . .
> I think the biggest emotional problem these teens have is loneliness —sex with connectedness instead of sex with significance.[536]

Single romances not infrequently give way to serial romances, and even this pattern could no doubt in time evolve into a mode of more casual and more unromantic sex, even sex for recreation, if in fact there is not already a decided movement in this direction.

THE SWINGING SINGLES

Nevertheless, it is to be admitted that the more illustrative pattern of recreational and superficial sex probably is more characteristic of the older single group, and of those persons who are separated or divorced. Hunt observed that both single males and females in the 25 to 34 year old group do have more coital partners per year.[537] It is some of this group along with some of the formerly married that presumably feed the stereotype of the swinging singles set. Admittedly since the great majority of all adult Americans are married, the number of persons involved here is relatively small in proportion to the total adult population, but growing.

Recent years, however, have seen the phenomena of a larger singles group, and especially one that actively seeks to establish an on-going pattern of dating interaction with persons of the opposite sex as opposed to essentially burying themselves within the structure of marital society. This has resulted in ecologically segregated residential areas and dwellings for singles, specialized commercial establishments, such as singles bars, and contrived recreational devices such as singles dances and tours, all designed to maximize the possibility of meeting single persons of the opposite sex.[538] Even specialized institutions such as country clubs and churches are being established to serve a singles constituency.[539] The members of the singles category may not infrequently have experienced social frustration attendant to their present marital status. The never married persons may not have been able to identify a spouse, or at least a suitable spouse, or may even have rejected the institution of marriage as too confining. The divorced or separated person may feel betrayed or disappointed by marriage, or in some instances, feel a sense of freedom at being released from the ties of marriage. For some, singlehood is a transient status until they can remarry, while for others there may be a persuasion, if not a commitment to make it a permanent status. In any event, some feel lonely, many seek outlets for sexual gratification, and perhaps most desire a recreational, if not hedonistic life style, that will either compensate them for, or legitimate and rationalize, their single status. As one Atlanta bachelor phrased it:

> The singles "skindrome" is not a search . . . Its entire premise is to live life to the fullest.[540]

There are approximately 13 million single adults between the ages of 20 and 34 in this country. This is a 50 percent increase in the size of this category since 1960. The number of divorced persons under 35 who have not remarried is now more than 1.3 million, double what it was 10 years ago. Furthermore, the proportion of women who remain single into their 20s is one-third greater today than in 1960.[541] Thus the singles population is not insignificant in size, and is growing. The new singles lifestyle is distinctly different and assertive. It, too, is making an impact on the mainstream of American life.

SINGLEHOOD AND SUPERFICIAL SEXUALITY

Ethnographers of the "singles" culture in the United States have suggested that prominent elements in this emerging life style are the ambience of contrived sexuality and the attendant search for carnal gratification. As one such writer succinctly put it:

> The new suburban apartment buildings for the singles crowd are sexual Disneylands, where the only marriages are those between maximum temptation and maximum opportunity.[542]

The same writer speaks of the singles apartment complex as a "new hot house where sexual indulgences can flourish as never before."[543] The institutions, establishments, routines and behavior patterns, the costumes, and language interaction, all are redolent of sexuality. Presumably, the sexuality provides an encouraging atmosphere that is facilitative of sexual and social fantasies, reassures persons that there are at least theoretically sexual compensations for singlehood, and perhaps most obviously, sets the stage for the search for sex. For some, however, the atmosphere is "plastic." One single female, surveying the singles scene around an apartment complex pool commented, "you know what this place is? It's a playground with deeper voices, that's what it is."[544] The search for sex often begins and ends in the process of looking over the crowd that assembles at a singles bar or other establishment. This process is known as the "meat market ritual." The singles size up the opposite sex and in some instances pair off for more intimate interaction sessions. For the less attractive and less socially adroit, rejection may be the pattern. For those more skilled, physically blessed, and/or more fortunate, the "meat market" may result in contacts, and sexual dates. There is no question but what the singles scene is, in large measure, a sexual market. As one author put it:

> For them, a singles complex seems to represent a sort of sexual super-market—crock full of glittering new goodies to help obliterate painful old memories.[545]

The "meat market" phenomenon is unquestionably dissaffective to many young singles, and some are developing behavioral coping devices to deal with it.[546] Sexual encounters arising from meetings with persons of the opposite sex in singles bars and similar places, is not without hazard. Some females have been assaulted, raped, and even murdered by men they met there.[547] For the majority, however, the singles bar or dance is a functional mechanism for meeting other single persons of the opposite sex, for dates, possibly for sex, and sometimes for romance. The sexual motivation should not be underestimated, however. The theme of such encounters is a simple one. "You cruise, hopefully you connect, and—you go home to bed together."[548]

The sexual encounters resulting from casual meetings in singles bars is, itself, usually casual with only infrequent emotional attachments growing out of it. It is sex for diversion, and thus, in effect, recreational sex in superficial context. The lack of emotional depth in the carnal interaction of the singles scene is echoed in the comment of one single female who observed, "Sex has gotten so cheap."[549]

THE PURSUIT OF SEXUAL HEDONISM

Some contemporary accounts of the single culture tend to emphasize the recreational nature of the attendant sexual interaction, but one recent description even likens the scramble for casual sex to a kind of athletic competition.[550] Mead views the sex-seeking activities as analogous to a contest for single males. She observes that, "The object of the struggle was classically simple: to see which man could take the most girls to bed in a given year." The ecological dimension is an important factor in the singles culture. The large apartment complexes replete with pools, clubhouses, and other recreational appurtenances apparently encourage and nourish single interaction and sexual exchange. Again, as the author phrases it, "The important thing is that the real estate industry has created a new hot house where sexual indulgence can flourish as never before." For many singles, both never married and previously married, the singles culture, ecology and behavior has become, more or less, a way of life. Some individuals still seek a suitable partner for remarriage and devote considerable energy to this enterprise. Others, and especially the males, however, have essentially rejected the notion of marriage and hardly endorse their unencumbered life style. In the words of one divorced male who now staunchly espouses the single life:

> I'm into playin' and lovin' and not givin' a damn for the rest of my life. Comin' home to the same pair of tits, and the same corned-beef hash every night—hell, that just ain't what I was born for.[551]

Life in the singles complexes would appear to revolve around a routinized, and seemingly never ending round of poolside drinks, parties, luaus, happy hours, pick-ups, and one-night sexual stands. It would also appear, however, that life in the singles culture may also be lonely, frustrating, meaningless, and dissaffective. The constant contrived pattern of pseudocourting and the attendant casual and superficial and emotionally meaningless sexual encounters may prove recreational for a time, but such a life style apparently, often represents a facade and is little more than a coping mechanism for dealing with a painful existential reality. As one psychiatrist, who has singles among his clientele sums it up:

> They [the singles] anesthetize themselves with a lifestyle that consists of ritually getting drunk, getting stoned, getting laid. The very nature of their interaction there is one of *not* dealing with anything real or intense, of not dealing with their own feelings.[552]

COCKTAIL LOUNGE AND COMMERCIALIZED CONTACTS

Superficial sex also occurs in commercial configuration as well as within the private behavior patterns of career singles. In many bars, there is a highly routinized, if not institutionalized pattern of behavior for meeting or making contact with persons of the opposite sex, pairing off, and ultimately copulating during "one-night" stands and casual affairs. Such behavioral patterns may involve a sizing-up of potential sexual partners, the employment of an appropriate line of conversation from a more or less regularized repertoire, and some degree of negotiations and "settlements" of gains and losses. Individuals patronize such "market-place bars" because these establishments cater "specifically to young and usually single persons interested in meeting and possibly having sexual encounters with persons of a similar orientation."[553] The goal is sex without emotional involvement or commitment.

Some researchers have documented the function of some "high class" cocktail lounges where married men with a desire for extramarital sexual outlets, and/or for "romantic interludes" with attractive women, could meet, and in many instances, interact sexually with young single women.[554] The researchers found that there were no pathological reasons for visiting the lounge, but, "Rather, these people seemed to visit the lounge because it was a preferred recreational pattern." The men did speak of "extenuating circumstances," such as business or family pressures, or wives who were busy or "cold." Also, they may not have had time for such relationships earlier in life. In any event, they wanted discrete and compartmentalized sexual gratification as a diversion, and for fun.

From the viewpoint of the young women, the lounge permits them to enjoy heterosexual encounters and carnal gratification, as a "substitute" for marriage or while they are still attempting to locate a suitable marriage partner. They simply sought casual "sex and companionship in pleasant and discrete circumstances without having to play a competitive, exploitive courtship game."[555] Both men and women wanted superficial sex and carnal gratification, unencumbered by emotion, ego-involvement, commitment, or social complication. They sought and obtained recreational sex.

According to Roebuck and Spray, inasmuch as the married men must be discrete about their sexual activities with the single women, the women are assured that their reputations will not suffer. According to the "code" of the establishment, the men were mandated to be discrete and protective about the women they picked up and themselves, in terms of "securing safe places of assignation and in preventing pregnancy." The women in turn, indicated that they sought men "who would keep quiet about sexual behavior," and "who did not want to get involved." It was, accordingly, mutually advantageous to keep their sexual activities as clandestine as possible.[556] The women would come alone to the lounge and sit at tables, while the men would sit at the bar. The men would then have a drink sent to the woman and if she assented, he would join her. The bartenders and cocktail waitresses served as go-betweens and provided information to both males and females about the other. Once the woman accepted the man's drink, he joined her and arrangements were usually made for a sexual rendezvous. The high class cocktail lounge served as a commercial mechanism for facilitating casual sexual affairs in the context of respectability but not among strangers. The cocktail lounge, then, was, "a setting in which casual sexual affairs between unattached women and higher class men can be conducted in a context of respectability."[557] Thus, married men and single women who wished to enjoy casual and superficial sex on a recreational basis but maintain discreteness and protect their reputations could meet and pair off at the cocktail lounge. Such behavioral configurations suggest sex primarily for fun and relaxation, and, thus, in a superficial context.

THE RENTED COMPANION AND SUPERFICIAL SEXUALITY

Pairing off for companionship and possible sexual gratification may, in some instances assume more direct commercial characteristics. At least one author has described the recently emerged "escort business," where young women (and sometimes men) allow themselves to be hired for an evening as an escort or symbolic date to some man (or woman).[558] In such instances, the pairing off is for a fee, and obstensibly is not for the purpose of sex. The customers of such services are not infrequently middle-aged traveling businessmen who find themselves in a strange town and want to sightsee, eat at gourmet restaurants, and generally "do" the town but wish female companionship, and a sympathetic ear. The possibility of sexual interaction is not indicated. The men want company, and to see and be seen with an attractive young female and don't mind paying for the privilege. In some agencies, the man can select from an array of pictures, and can even pick a woman who has interests and entertainment preferences similar to his. In theory, the couple enjoy an entertaining evening out on the town and lively conversation. In many instances however, before the night is over, the woman may likely offer to have sexual relations with the man—for an additional fee, or "tip." This, of course, makes her a technical prostitute, but this is a difficult charge to prove given the circumstances, and, furthermore, the woman, unlike a regular prostitute, does not offer to sleep with every customer—only those that she prefers. The escort profession provides the men with an instant and temporary companion, and often with casual, superficial sex, without danger of emotional involvement. The woman can make money, have a nice meal, and meet men, some of which are acceptable as sex partners, for a fee, and even in some instances, are potential boyfriends or husbands. As one escort put it:

> Then I get a free dinner, a good one, every night, and if I happen to get lucky and go out with a dude I dig, well, we can ball later.[559]

Although escort services cater mainly to middle-aged men, they sometimes have other clientele. Occasionally, younger men not adept at meeting women may settle for an artificial "date" and even in some instances females may seek male escorts. In this connection, this author and a colleague in 1972, undertook a pilot study of an escort service for females in a large city in a Middle Atlantic state, including some in-depth interviews with several of the male escorts. Our investigation revealed that many widowed and divorced middle-aged females will sometimes pay for the company of a charming and urbane gentleman who will take them out on a date, at their own expense. It also appeared that the ladies also sometimes arranged for some carnal recreation as well. In all instances, the client buys what he does not have free access to, and receives a purchased product—

contrived and superficial social interaction with a person of the opposite sex, and on occasion, recreational sexual gratification with a pseudo-lover, for a price.

SUMMARY

Although much sexual behavior involves an emotional symbiosis or social exchange process, some sexual behavior seeks only individual carnal gratification and, thus, only the reciprocal satisfaction of sexual appetite is involved. Such sex is casual, unemotional sex for entertainment only. In most instances, it represents little more than a mere superficial mode of human carnal interaction. Inasmuch as rape and even most kinds of prostitution have an emotional and complex ego-involvement component to the interaction, they do not qualify as superficial sex, however, in spite of the fact that there is a lack of love, tenderness, or affection for the sexual partner.

There is one type of prostituted sex that may well qualify as a superficial context—the massage parlor and its often constituent offering of masturbatory services. The customer seeks erotic stimulation and carnal reverie afforded by the epidermal ministrations of the masseuse, who may be topless, bottomless, or both, and who affords relaxed, and completely narcissistic sexual gratification to the customer as she provides "local" massage and attendant orgasm. The absence of inter-genital intercourse may tend to relieve the customer of normal concern with the fear of contracting venereal disease often associated with brothels. Inasmuch as massage parlors are not infrequently located along main arteries of traffic and interspersed among more conventional businesses, even situated in shopping centers, in some instances, the patron can feel more secure concerning the hazard of robbery or assault. The masseuse can deal with her stigmatized identity through the device of anatomical compartmentalization. The masseuse who gives "locals" can perceive herself as only a "hand whore" and not a genuine prostitute. Similarly, the customer can think of the masturbatory services he receives as only an erotic massage and orgasmic relief and can, thus, avoid adulterous guilt and the self- or social-image of "whore mongering."[560] He is simply receiving a healthful and sexually stimulating total massage. The masseuse, on the other hand, can view herself as simply providing a health and relaxation service rather than as a prostitute. By restricting the sexual services offered to masturbation only, and by effecting an anatomical compartmentalization in terms of self-identity, the masseuse can maintain an image of herself as health technician at best, and at worst, as only a "hand whore." The entire episode provides detached, casual, and recreational carnal gratification, within the context of an ephemeral interactional encounter.

Superficial sexual gratification can also occur within a homosexual context. Studies have shown that considerable homosexual activity takes place in various public places such as movie theaters or public restrooms known as "tearooms." Here, individuals can encounter strangers and engage in impersonal, casual, recreational sex of the most superficial variety possible, without social involvement or commitment. Not only homosexuals, but also some individuals who maintain heterosexual identities, also avail themselves of the convenient, carnal gratification on demand, character of the "tearoom." Some persons who claimed heterosexual persuasion reported stopping at a tearoom on a regular basis to obtain fellatio and orgasm. Such sexual encounters generally involved an almost total absence of conversation revealing the socially sterile superficiality of such a sexual pattern.

Other loci for superficial homosexual activities include gay steambaths and truck stops. In the instance of the former, the individual pays admission, dons only a bath towel around the waist and either wanders around the halls of the establishment or the "orgy" room seeking impersonal sexual encounters or retires to a private bedroom and awaits the visit of a stranger who will provide him with orgasm and superficial carnal gratification. In the instance of the latter, the individual drives to truck stops or roadside rest areas and finds truckers who are in the mood for quick and uninvolved sexual release. The sexual activity may well take place in the sleeper portion of the truck cab. The truckers who generally maintain a heterosexual identity enjoy superficial carnal gratification without commitment or other than minimal social interaction, and the homosexual also obtains anonymous sexual fulfillment without emotion or involvement.

Masturbation, particularly in the more contemporary context where it is encouraged as recreation, an efficient means of tension release, or as training for other forms of sexual activity, and where it tends to less frequently generate feelings of guilt, concern, or anxiety, has become, in large measure, a "value-free" mode of superficial sexual gratification. Masturbation is espoused by many medical authorities and sexual therapists as beneficial and "fun," and there has been a significant increase in masturbation, sometimes aided by mechanical devices such as vibrators, in terms of individuals beginning to masturbate earlier in life, continuing to masturbate later in life, as well as in frequency. These trends in increase appear to be the use of masturbation as a recreational and supplemental mode of carnal gratification as opposed to a diminunization of sexual outlets of other variety.

Universally, children engage in various forms of sexual play for fun and recreation. Playing doctor is a traditional form of sexual game and mischief in our society. Some modes of sexual play among children, however, such as the excessive use of profanity or any over-preoccupation with sexual objects or activity, might in some instances be viewed as pathological and the principals treated accordingly.

It would appear that sexual play is culturally condemned in general because it is often seen as a precursor to unbridled sexual license and lack of control in the area of sexual gratification is antithetical to the value system of Western industrialized society and the Protestant ethic, as well as traditional Judeo-Christian ideology. Superficial sex, being socially uninvolved, recreational sex would, accordingly, be one of the more reprehensible modes.

There is something of a contradiction in our cultural values, however, in that children are encouraged to develop a posture of sexuality quite early in life, and dating, romantic games, and even erotic activities such as neck hugging or kissing may be promoted by adults. When children pass puberty, however, all forms of sexual outlets and sexual activities ranging from masturbation to heterosexual intercourse are formally prohibited and often severely sanctioned. On the other hand, such norms are widely violated by young people and such deviancy is often tacitly tolerated by adult society. Society tends to close its eyes to the actual sexual behavior modes of young people and continues to pay lip service to an idealized and totally unrealistic set of sexual norms.

Even though sexual activity among young people is formally proscribed, and dating is often the behavioral context in which sexual activities occur, dating among unmarried persons is, nevertheless, encouraged and facilitated by society. In this regard, dating may begin even before puberty and continue until the time of a fairly late, deferred marriage, perhaps even in one's 30s. Thus, the period of courtship in our society may span up to 20 years, as compared with a much shorter period in other societies. Again, unlike other societies, where courtship almost inevitably leads to marriage, in the

United States, courtship may involve many partners, and is often essentially a recreational pattern rather than preliminary to marriage. Courtship in our society may also fulfill a number of other functions including socialization, status sifting or sorting, and personality development not to mention sexual socialization and indoctrination. But it is mainly recreational for many individuals, in that it is attendant to other recreational configurations such as dances, parties, and outings, as well as providing an opportunity for sexual stimulation and interaction. Such carnal behavior could include a variety of erotic activities including kissing, bodily caresses of varying degrees of intimacy, partial or total nudity, fellatio, cunnilingus, or mutual masturbation.

"Petting," which may involve some combination of the sexual activities above, but which usually results in orgasm for one or both partners is a particularly institutionalized sexual pattern in courtship, especially with individuals of middle and upper socio-economic background. Although the lower class couples move on more quickly into actual coitus, the middle and upper-class individuals, who traditionally placed a premium on virginity, have tended to use petting as a mechanism of compromise sex which permits the couple to enjoy sexual gratification while preserving the status of technical virginity.

"Petting" also sometimes assumes the form of a game with the male seeking to maximize the degree of sexual intimacy that he can accomplish with the female—to see how far he can go, as it were, and the female seeking to withhold her sexual favors as much as possible —or see how little she can give. The male, accordingly motivated to succeed may become overly amorous or even sexually exploitative to the point of violence.

Petting is very much part of the sex experience of most adults today. Of females born before 1900, it has been reported that only 10 percent admitted to having petted to orgasm while in their teens. More recently, studies have shown that at least two-thirds of the males under 25, and more than one-half of the females under 25 had petted to orgasm. Where at one time, young people engaged in "heavy" petting as a component of emotional commitment, in more recent years, some studies of unmarried young people have indicated that they tend to approve of heavy petting on the basis of such motives as the desire for experience, sexual gratification, or other similar reasons. In effect, petting has become a recreation, and, thus, superficial, form of carnal gratification.

Premarital intercourse, in addition to petting, has also figured prominently as a sexual configuration in American courtship patterns. Although results of studies both before World War II, and after the war but before 1960 are mixed, the results indicated that slightly more than one-half of the college males and between 10 percent and 25 percent of the college females had engaged in premarital intercourse. By the early 1970s, however, studies of college students suggested that 85 percent of the males and between 60 and 70 percent of the females were nonvirgins. The so-called sexual revolution which some asserted occurred during, and immediately after, World War II, appears to have been more a part of the social value changes of the 1960s and 1970s. Although it is true that a significant proportion of the premarital intercourse of recent decades has involved relatively few sexual partners, and has occurred within the context of an emotional commitment, the pill and other contraceptive devices are making it possible for young people to engage in premarital sex without fear of unwanted pregnancy. Given the fact that many coeds now routinely seek contraceptive prescriptions by the time they register for college suggests a much greater tendency to engage in casual sex. Young people may still tend to have one sexual partner at a time, as it were, but it is now a series of sexual partners.

The young unmarried group appears to be becoming more sexually precocious, more sexually active and more sexually permissive. One recent nationwide survey of the sex lives of young people revealed that nine out of 10 of all females have had sex prior to marriage. Without question, young people are increasingly engaging in premarital intercourse within a recreational and thus superficial context. Sex is becoming enjoyable for its own sake.

If the young unmarried are becoming more sexually active, so, too, are the adult singles, both divorced and never married. An entire subculture has grown up around the so-called "swinging singles," including special housing areas, clubs and bars, and distinctive recreational patterns. Although singlehood may be a transient status, for some it is becoming a persuasion, or commitment to a hedonistic life style. Some feel lonely but others seek a variety of sexual outlets for recreational carnal gratification. The swinging singles subculture is redolent of sexuality and facilitates and encourages both sexual fantasies and activities. Meeting and subsequently engaging in sexual intercourse is accomplished in highly superficial contexts including casual meetings in bars and at parties. The name of the game is sexual variety, if not exploitation, and some individuals seek to maximize their sexual conquests as a kind of contest or goal. The pursuit of recreational sex component to the unencumbered life style in such a situation becomes a central preoccupation.

Even, for married males (and sometimes married females) who seek extra marital sexual outlets for relaxation and recreation, which do not involve emotional commitment, there are certain types of cocktail lounges with ritualized, if not institutionalized, behavioral patterns for meeting attractive single persons of the opposite sex who become willing sexual partners on an ephemeral and superficial basis. For those who seek attractive companionship for a brief period, "escorts" can be hired and company with a person of the opposite sex can be obtained, even if the social interaction is contrived and superficial. In some instances, even sexual gratification on a recreational basis with a pseudo-lover, can be had, for a price.

American sexual values would appear to be moving, in many instances, more in the direction of sexual gratification that is narcissistic, casual, recreational, and superficial, much in the way that one author has spoken of a "Hot Sex" society that:

> ... treats a man or a woman solely as a series of anal, oral and genital orifices to be filled, exhausted, emptied or violated.[561]

The same author goes on to say (on p. 14):

> For the Hot Sex male, any playmate will do. Sex is something one does to a female, or—phrased in a slightly more subtle way since the demise of Victorian prudery—sex is something one does for a female. Personal physical pleasure is the prime concern; sensitiveness and responsibility are minor. Hot sex relationships are casual in their impersonalism.

Superficial sex may only represent a life style more liberated from the dictates of tradition and cultural ethnocentrism, as well as a new ability to indulge the sensate appetite without guilt or self-recrimination. On the other hand, superficial sex, in spite of its recreational quality is essentially one-dimensional sex without benefit of emotional reciprocity and accordingly is a lonely enterprise. Whether such narcissistic, socially mechanical, and impersonal carnal gratification obtained from sexual partners who are more plastic than real in their existential interaction will prove satisfying, much less provide personal and emotional growth remains to be determined.

Chapter 9

ADULTERY, GROUP SEX, AND PROSTITUTION

Sexual Deviancy in Symbiotic Context

Marriage, as an institutionalized relationship, subjects to regulation and routinization the attendant behavior of the participants and invokes reciprocal obligations on the part of both principals. The reciprocal obligations contained implicitly, if not stated explicitly, in the marriage contract concern themselves not only with economic requirements, but also with others such as the sexual obligation. In this regard, marriage has been defined as a "socially legitimate sexual union."[562] In the sense of serving as a functional device for the channeling, regularizing, and legitimating sexual behavior, marriage can be said, in a sense, to be built on a sexual foundation. Furthermore, the privileges of sexual gratification are tied to the other reciprocal obligations of the marriage contract, thus as one authority has stated "it [marriage] imposes obligations in return for sexual gratifications."[563] Along with the reciprocal sexual obligations goes an obligation of sexual exclusiveness. Thus, marriage encompasses a complex pattern of exchange behavior, including the exchange of sexual gratification in concert with other kinds of reciprocity activities.

MARRIAGE AND SEXUAL EXCHANGE

As an exchange relationship, marriage can also be conceptualized as a kind of social symbiotic relationship between a man and a woman. There would appear to be two main normative elements associated with the sexual dimension of marriage, both affected by appropriate social proscription and prescription and maintained by sanction, both legal and informal. The first of these normative elements is the concern with marriage affording the opportunity for sexual gratification on the part of both marital partners. In this regard, society in its goal of insuring and legitimating sexual outlets for married persons, goes so far as to even dictate the specific modes and methods, by which sexual gratification may be obtained. Such specifics may even include the articulation of sexual techniques, coital positions, and other behavioral particulars attendant to heterosexual gratification. In our society, as in many others, the violation of either the normative specifications for appropriate sexual gratification or that of the prerogative of sexual exclusivity constitutes social deviancy and can invite informal social castigation, if not the application of legal sanctions. Indeed, sexual intercourse, itself, in our society is considered so fundamental and essential to marriage that in many states, physical impediments or willful abstention from intercourse may be grounds for divorce. Included among such grounds are impotence, malformation preventing sexual intercourse, and refusal of sexual relations with the spouse.

THE NORMATIVE DIMENSION OF MARITAL SEX

In regard to the normative control of sexual mechanics, it would appear that some of our societal specifications for appropriate and socially approved marital sexual activity may be rooted in Judeo-Christian theology and writings as well as early church history. The so-called "normal," "missionary" or "American" coital position, for example, with the female supine, on her back, with the man above and facing the female, has been traditionally considered to be so normatively correct that other sexual positions, until relatively recently, were considered to be sexual perversions. It has been reported that "there was a time in the history of the Christian Church when the utilization of any other except the present-day position was made a matter for confession."[564] In some states even today, for married couples to employ other than the "normal" coital position could theoretically place them in violation of legal statute. Coital positions, like other mechanical aspects of sex, are culturally relative. Malinowski, for example, has reported that among the Trobrianders in the southwestern Pacific, the English-American sexual position is so unnatural that they humorously and derisively referred to its use as the "missionary position."[565]

Traditionally not only have coital positions other than the "American position" been socially condemned, but also forms of sexual gratification other than inter-genital activity. This, of course, rendered sexual variations such as masturbation, and oral and anal sexual gratification unnatural, perverted, and, thus, often illegal. Also traditionally viewed as inappropriate, if not perverted, were such practices as nudity in marriage and especially when sleeping, manual manipulation of the spouses' genitals, and oral eroticism. A combination of ignorance of the subleties of sexual anatomy and physiology, Victorian and Puritan morality, and preoccupation with a kind of model conformity tended to make most Americans relatively sexually unsophisticated and quite conventional in their married sexual behavior.[566] The Kinsey studies in the early post-war years provided a general picture of the American, and especially the American of lower and lower-middle socio-economic background, as relatively rigid in their conformity to the norms of conventional sexual behavior, and certainly not as innovative or experimentive in the vagaries of sexual activities as the persons of the upper level. As reported by the studies, for example, nude coitus was practiced by 90 percent of the upper level males as opposed to only 66 percent of those who never went beyond high school, and 43 percent of those who never went beyond grade school.[567] The lower level male only attempted manipulation of the female genitalia in 75 percent of the cases, and only 57 percent of the females spoke of manipulating the male genitalia. Less than 45 percent of the males of any educational level reported mouth contacts with the female gentalia. It was also reported from the Kinsey studies that "throughout the population as a whole, a high proportion of all the intercourse is had in a position with the female supine, on her back, with the male above and facing the female."[568] Only 64 percent of the females in the study had even experienced orgasm at least once before marriage.[569] Some researchers have even reported the ultimate sexual naivete of some married couples. One study of wives who remained virgins after marriage even told of some couples that were even ignorant of how sex took place, or even that married couples "customarily did such things."[570] Thus, the Kinsey era American married couple appears to have been relatively strict in their observance of the traditional sexual taboos and norms attendant to sexual activity in marriage.

Although legal norms were seldom invoked for violations of such social conventions, there were some cases of divorces being granted because of "unnatural sexual demands" being made by spouses, and in a few instances there were even cases of legal indictments and prosecutions for unnatural sexual practices within marriage.[571] In large measure, however, it was the informal social pressures combined with a sexual naivete born of provincial origin that perhaps prompted most couples to avoid sexual experimentation and to confine their carnal gratification to traditional and conventional techniques and outlets. Married individuals did not want their spouses to label them as deviants for having initiated sexual experimentation, nor did they want to face their own self-labeling.

Sexual Liberation and Contemporary Marital Practices

In the decades since the Kinsey era, however, various waves of sexual emancipation and liberation have washed over our society, and the media has provided both educational enlightenment and vocal encouragement of sexual exploration. The result has apparently been a much relaxed situation within marriage in regard to sexual variety and a general concern with maximizing sexual gratification within marriage. One recent sexual survey conducted by *Redbook* reveals some illuminating findings.[572] Whereas only about 50 percent of the women interviewed by Kinsey and his associates reported experience with fellatio and cunnilingus, close to 91 percent of the females in the *Redbook* survey indicated that they have experienced oral-genital sex, both giving and receiving it. Of those 91 percent, 40 percent engage in it often. In the Kinsey study, anal sex was considered to be too taboo to even bother asking about. In the *Redbook* study, approximately half of the women in the survey reported that they had experienced anal sex. Nevertheless, in some medical quarters, oral sex is still considered to be sufficiently dangerous, as well as perverted, as to be officially condemned. The Associated Press, for example, in 1973 reported that one Virginia woman and possibly several others may have died from an air embolism in the circulatory system.[573] The air bubble, it was charged, resulted from cunnilingus, or as a State Department of Health official put it, a form of "love play" or "sex practice now gaining in popularity among young people." The Health Department official suggested that as many as 14 women may have died from this cause and warned against it. As the official put it, "This is a serious matter. My understanding is that this is becoming a widespread practice among young people." The official went on to say that such deaths will increase if the practice continues to grow.

Similarly, as with oral sex, there appears to be somewhat more of a tendency for contemporary married couples to experiment with anal sex to a much greater degree than in the past. Although Kinsey discussed the physiology of anal sex, he did not report the frequency of anal insertion among women.[574] In the more recent *Redbook* survey on female sexuality, however, it was reported that 43 percent or almost one-half of the respondents indicated that they had tried anal sex. Some 10 percent reported that it was "very enjoyable," and another 31 percent said it was "somewhat enjoyable."[575] Although it was not as popular as other forms of sexual expression, there was clearly a willingness for couples to experiment with sexual activity in an uninhibited way in the search for variety and gratification in their sex lives.

The *Redbook* survey also suggested that married women are becoming more sexually aggressive, something of a contrast with the passive Victorian "respectable" woman. The great majority of the women responding—almost 78 percent—described themselves as always or usually active partners. The survey would also seem to suggest a contemporary tendency to intensify or maximize carnal gratification in marriage. In the survey, 30 out of every 100 women acknowledge having sex after smoking marijuana, and 63 percent of the women under 20 reported combining sex and marijuana. There was also mention of the use of various devices to "enhance" the sexual experience, including vibrators, oils, feathers, and phallic objects. A total of 75 percent of the women surveyed indicated they have masturbated since marriage. The picture that emerges is that of a married female with much widened sexual horizons and not particularly troubled by the traditional label of deviant applied to sexual innovator.[576] In fact, some authors today are suggesting that the married female may actually enjoy the role of sexual innovator, if not sexual instructor to her husband. As Morton Hunt, for example, puts it:

> A generation or more ago it was almost always the husband who suggested some novel activity—rear-entry coitus, say, or fellatio, or watching the action in a mirror—often to the alarm of the naive wife, who feared her mate might be giving voice to some perversion or

abnormality. Today the young wife is as likely as her husband to have heard and read about these and even far more fanciful novelties, thanks to the bumper crop of best-selling sex manuals, candid magazine articles and exotic novels and to the new openness of talk about such things among her peers. Moreover, she is nearly as likely as her husband to regard such things as normal, intriguing and worthwhile.[577]

SEXUAL EXPERIMENTATION IN MARRIAGE

Morton Hunt, in his research, found that sexual experimentation in marriage is widespread and often intensive, for couples of various socioeconomic backgrounds. The new publishing freedom for sex materials has literally been an eye-opening experience for many couples who hitherto have been stuck with a relatively limited sexual repertoire. The new sexual openness and experimentation has not been confined only to the younger generation of married couples but, in many instances, is infecting middle-aged and even older persons who now are enjoying new plateaus of carnal gratification and express considerable pleasure with their new outlook and activities. In general, Hunt's findings and the results of other research all suggest that married couples engage in coitus and other sexual activities more frequently than in some times past. They are more likely to engage in a much wider variety of sexually gratifying behaviors even those formerly or perhaps still socially, if not legally, condemned. The flood of sex manuals and books of sexual ideas such as *The Sensuous Woman* and *The Joys of Sex* are apparently providing inspiration and thrust for the increased libidinous activities of many married couples. Wives as well as their husbands are initiating sex, and deriving satisfaction from both conventional and innovative sexual behavior. Perhaps most importantly, these married couples are not conceptualizing themselves as deviants or perverts even though they are engaging in sexual vagaries often formerly classified as unnatural or bizarre. It would seem, then, that in the space of a few short decades, for many married persons, the social norms governing sexual behavior within marriage have in large measure lost their applicability, if not their former meaning and impact. In the face of eroding sanctions for violation of such norms and a much increased public permissiveness, if not support of, wide latitude in individual prerogative in carnal gratification in marriage, it might be expected that such normative dictates will be largely ineffective in the future, if not completely fade. The new liberated sexual posture is not without its dysfunctions, however. Some psychiatrists have written recently of the "new impotence"—a tendency of some males, particularly those of traditional sexual attitudes, not to be able to function sexually effectively, or to lose their sexual desire under the impact of some women's newly acquired sexual self-assurance, assertiveness, and more demanding sexual stance.[578] Older men or at least old-fashioned men, like old dogs, apparently cannot always learn new tricks, sexually speaking. In this regard, males, perhaps burdened by the residue of the double sexual standard, seem to be experiencing more difficulty in adjusting to the changing concepts of sexual normalcy and today's reluctance to label as sexually inappropriate, much less deviant, that which was viewed as unnatural or perverted in the past.[579]

OTHER DEVIANT VARIATIONS WITHIN MARRIAGE

Coital position and mode of sexual stimulation are not the only carnal parameters which are socially monitored and controlled. Other sexual variations and arrangements are also proscribed and violation of such proscriptions may well result in serious sanctions. Almost universally, there are social efforts to insure that babies are born within a marital unit in order to insure that there is someone charged with the social responsibility of the child. In the absence of a marriage of the couple, the child is "illegitimate." Although the child frequently bears the stigma of "bastard," the parents may also experience stigma and be punished for their transgressions.

In this society as with many others, traditionally pressure has been brought to bear on the parents of the illegitimate child to marry. The so-called "shot-gun" marriage has long been component to our rural (and not infrequently urban) culture. Inasmuch as the illegitimate child is evidence, as it were, of sexual activity on the part of the couple, there is *prima facia* evidence of their sexual deviancy. They are guilty of fornication and the baby is the proof. In the instance of the female, she is often publically stigmatized as unchaste and subject to informal sanctions. Like Hawthorne's Hester Prynne, the female wears a symbolic "scarlet letter" and may be treated accordingly. If the female is under the legal age of consent the male might be charged with statutory rape. Often, this is the pressure to marry his sexual partner. Even if the female is over the age of consent, if the male refuses to marry the female he could in some states, be charged with bastardy, or siring an illegitimate child. The general tendency is to encourage marriage on the part of the couple or to at least insure for the financial support of the child.

There is seldom a legal punitive posture on the part of public officials. There are even exceptions to this, however. At least one Federal District Judge has threatened to send a defendant to federal prison if she bore an additional illegitimate child.[580] The defendant had stolen a government check and defrauded some money but she also had three illegitimate children and it appeared that this situation was a factor in her theft. The judge sentenced her to probation on condition that she would not become pregnant. If she had any more illegitimate children, the judge would revoke her probation and send her to prison.

The extremely high number of illegitimate pregnancies in this country has tended to moderate the pressure for the young couples to marry, and are sufficiently common that some states are modifying their statutory rape laws to exclude young males who impregnate females, who are under the age of consent, but approximately their own age. Abortion or placing the illegitimate child up for adoption have become popular alternate means of resolving the dilemma. Such illegitimate pregnancies not infrequently result from meaningful emotional and symbiotic relationships between a couple and neither reacts to the situation in a superficial and detached fashion. Although illegitimate pregnancies have traditionally been considered to be the female's problem, now increasingly the "unwed" father is also being viewed as experiencing guilt, anxiety, and other serious psychological problems. With 600,000 teen-aged boys becoming unwed fathers each year the problem is not insignificant. As a result, there are now counseling and therapy programs for boys as well as girls who violate the social norm of precipitating pregnancy outside of marriage, as a means of ameliorating their burden and facilitating an appropriate means of handling the situation.[581]

Other sexual activities, sometimes (or at least traditionally) defined as inappropriate, if not deviant, include sexual intercourse during menstruation,[582] sexual intercourse during pregnancy,[583] and even, in some instances, being voluntarily childless or, conversely, having too many children.[584] Impotence can be a legal grounds for divorce in some states, and represents role failure, as it were. Accordingly, such a condition may be viewed, at least by the victim, as a kind of disvalued condition, and, thus, deviancy. Only recently did the Vatican rule that sterilized men can enter valid marriages.[585]

Previously, a sterilized or impotent man could not be validly married, religiously speaking. To have done so would have constituted a violation of Catholic doctrine and thus, sin and deviant behavior.

BIGAMY AND POLYGAMY AS MARITAL DEVIANCY

In the United States, as in most Western societies monogamous marriage, is socially and legally prescribed. Violation of the law usually brings a stringent jail sentence. In spite of the possible sanctions involved, there are significant numbers of bigamy cases each year. Generally, instances of bigamy assume two configurations. In one, a female frequently marries a series of men, neglecting to obtain divorces from present spouses when she remarries. The female obtains money from the various husbands and is, in effect, operating a swindle or confidence game. This particular pattern is more prevalent during time of war or national emergency when there are many servicemen who engage in hurried courtships and "quicky" marriages before being shipped to another part of the country or another country. This, of course, makes it easy for an unscrupulous woman to marry a series of servicemen, obtain a military allotment and other funds from each, and more easily keep her bigamy secret from all. In some cases, the war is over before the woman's racket is discovered.

In the other pattern, it is a man who becomes romantically involved with a series of women and marries them without divorcing his current or earlier wives. There are some bigamous males who have been involved in a financial exploitation racket like the females, but this is much less common than the multiple romantic involvement. The bigamous male is not infrequently middle-aged and apparently enjoys his multiple romantic "conquests." He may not be able to obtain divorces from earlier wives but cannot resist subsequent marriages. Bigamists who end up in prison sometimes complain that they simply liked women too much. Perhaps the most unusual pattern of bigamy, however, is the so-called "Pennypacker" pattern in which a man has two or more wives and families and maintains them in different homes, usually in different communities, with both (or more) families ignorant of the existence of the other. Here the bigamous man leads a kind of schizoid marital life dividing his time, energy, and finances between two or more communities, families, and existences, playing the correct and appropriate roles as husband

and father, but deviating from the norm by having multiple wives. When discovered, these men usually face financial ruin, social disgrace, and prison, and their families are frequently shattered. Some individuals undertake such marital adventures any way and assume the danger of being caught for the gratifications involved.

The Pennypacker label derives from the stage comedy, "The Remarkable Mr. Pennypacker," which portrays a bigamist with two wives and two families in two different towns who blithely goes about his business meeting his responsibilities as husband and father in both locations. The humor of the play derives from the amusing antics of the protagonist in trying to keep his arrangement secret from each of the two families. The Pennypacker arrangement is not infrequent in real life and has been a featured plot in movies and T.V. shows including a Lou Grant T.V. episode and an Alec Guiness movie, *Captains Paradise.* Truth is stranger than fiction, however, and only several years ago, when a famous American multi-millionaire died, it was revealed that he had maintained two families in two different communities. Litigation concerning the distribution of the estate was heated and protracted.

Closely related to bigamy is the practice of polygamy, but here, the multiple spouses are aware of the arrangement and may live in the same household as a single family unit. This deviant marital arrangement has been historically associated with various cults and utopian movements and communities throughout American history, but most particularly with the Mormon Church. The Mormons openly practiced polygamy as part of their religious ideology until 1890 when the Church of Latter Day Saints outlawed the practice as an accommodation to society and to avoid continued persecution. A number of persons continued to practice polygamy against religious and social law and many were punished for it. Some retreated into isolation and defied the law, while others flaunted their practice and fought in the courts. Over the years, there have been law enforcement raids on polygamous settlements, prosecutions, and efforts to break up the family units and even put the children in foster homes. Polygamy has persisted, however, and today there are an estimated 35,000 practicing polygamists, or "pligs" as they are locally labeled, located in parts of Utah, Arizona, and Colorado, and in Mexico.[586] Authorities have, in effect, given up on trying to stop the practice and there have been no prosecutions for polygamy in more than 15 years. Other than violating the social and legal proscription against plural spouses the "pligs" tend to be quite "strait-laced" otherwise, usually not drinking or smoking, or engaging in intercourse during pregnancy, lactation, or menses. Furthermore, according to the "law" of purity which most practice, a husband does not even approach his wife for sex unless she invites him, and this is only when she desires another child. Thus, the polygamists are circumspect in their sexual activity to the point of being deviant to the general norm, in addition to being deviant in number of wives.

Marital Adultery

In spite of an apparent dramatic change in social values concerning sexual variation, and especially within marriage, some persons would appear to find the opportunities for sexual gratification attendant to the symbiotic relationship of matrimony, to either be inadequate or inappropriate. In such instances, sexually dissaffected members of a marital dyad may, in such instances seek alternate outlets for sexual gratification. Even in an earlier decade, the Kinsey studies suggested that approximately one half of all married men, and one quarter of all married women, by age 40, had sexual intercourse with a partner other than their spouse. A recent national survey conducted by *Redbook* indicated that the percentage of wives admitting infidelity was somewhat higher than the earlier researcher showed. *Redbook* data showed that among one age group (the 35–39 year old wives) the percentage of those involved in extramarital activity was 38 percent.[587] Within that age group, 47 percent of those who were wage-earning wives said they had intercourse with men other than their husbands. Morton Hunt's recent study of sexual behavior suggested that "the picture is thus one of rather little change since Kinsey's time in the incidence of extramarital behavior by males."[588] In regard to females, Hunt concluded that some of Kinsey's data was misleading because of sampling bias and certain problems connected with separated and divorced women being included in his white female category. When Hunt attempted to rebalance Kinsey's data, he found that the actual percentage of married women extramaritally involved by 45 was really 20 percent rather than 26 percent. In this connection he found no general change in rate of infidelity "of any consequence except below age 25—where, however, the change is of historic dimensions."[589] Where Kinsey had only reported 9 percent of the married women under 25 admitting to extramarital coitus (and even Hunt's rebalance was only 8 percent), Hunt's recent data suggested 24 percent of the 18 to 24 year old married females had committed adultery. Thus, in this age group the incidence of extramarital intercourse is three times as widespread among married women as at the time of Kinsey's study. Given this fact, Hunt concludes that, "in the next 20 years or so, overall female experience will double or triple, bringing it more or less to the same level as overall male experience."[590]

Although the research figures from the various studies are not always consistent, there does appear to be some degree of increase in adultery among all married persons, and the tendency to seek carnal gratification outside of marriage would seem to be accelerating, especially among the younger females. A variety of factors may be involved. There clearly has been something of a revolution in terms of sexual values and ideologies, as well as the erosion of traditional moral values and social proscriptions concerning adulterous sex. Persons generally, and especially the younger generation, would appear to be genuinely less rigid in their sexual outlook and behavior. The recent changes in our divorce laws, and especially the "no-fault" divorce arrangements in some states have, in effect, taken the legal onus off of adulterous behavior and thus have removed a former "penalty" for extramarital sexual behavior. Divorce itself, even if motivated by adultery does not carry the traditional social stigma, and for that matter neither does adultery itself. Although adultery would manifestly suggest a sexual dissatisfaction in marriage, this may not always be the case. It has been asserted that this may more often be the motivation for men seeking adulterous unions, than for females.[591] Adultery may be a function of the situation for some men. The traveling man, for example, in the loneliness and dissaffection of his routine may experience an exaggerated sexual deprivation. He may also simply seek companionship. Sex away from home, may also be a means of a man experiencing some form of aberrant sexual gratification, which he may feel would be distasteful to his wife, or dangerous to his job and career. In effect, he is freed from the taboos of his normal situation, and can indulge his carnal fantasies.[592] The male who seeks sexual gratification outside of marriage may also be seeking the type of interpersonal response and ego support he needs, in addition to simple sexual outlets. In effect, the errant husband may seek extramarital sex because of sexual dissaffection in marriage, but it may be a deprivation based on the emotional or psychological component of sex as well as just the mechanics. It is asserted, however, that women turn to extramarital coitus not so much because of "flagging sexual interest at home," but because of "disappointment in their marriage as a whole relationship" rather than with its sexual content."[593] Thus, infidelity is a symptom, rather than syndrome, of an unhappy marriage. It may well be that because of cultural conflicts, and role strains today for many women disenchantment with marriage may result, and in some instances manifest itself in adulterous activity. According to some definitions, adultery can occur in the mind as well as in deed. Pope John Paul II did recently admonish men not to "lust" after other women inasmuch as their erotic thoughts would be tantamount to "committing adultery in the heart." The Papal pronouncements might make some recall former President Jimmy Carter's statements about lust which appeared in a *Playboy* interview. Interestingly, the Pope also proscribed looking at one's own wife in a lustful manner.

OPPORTUNITY STRUCTURE AND ADULTERY

It has also been suggested that opportunity for extramarital involvement is a critical factor in infidelity.[594] Perhaps no where is this opportunity structure more prevalent than at work. It would appear that certain occupations or occupational situations provide opportunity for infidelity. Work throws persons of the opposite sex together, as peers, practitioner and clientele, or superior-subordinates.[595] The work place setting may not infrequently, present both persons in their best light—the important, aggressive, distinguished executive and the pert, well-coiffured and stylish, young, understanding secretary, for example. Propinquity breeds familiarity, relaxed interaction, and ultimately, intimacy. In such intimacy, adultery may flourish. Water cooler romances are legend in our society and the so-called "office-wife," often with attendant relatively permanent sexual liaison, is alleged to be quite prevalent in our society.[596] More married women than ever are working, and with such work, comes the possibility of emotional and intimate involvement with other men, and the opportunity to engage in extra-marital sexual activities with them. (Recall the *Redbook* data which showed that 47 out of 100 married working women in the 35 to 39 age category said they have had intercourse with men other than their husbands). Some areas of work afford an opportunity structure that may be conducive to sexual activities and may also generate a value system or rationalizing milieu that may facilitate such behavior. Such occupational contexts may encourage or nourish adultery.[597] The entertainment business, allegedly a stressful vocational setting for many, also promotes a contrived interpersonal familiarity if not intimacy, and a narcissistic superficiality in relationships. What can begin as a superficial contact with an individual of the opposite sex may, however, quickly develop into an on-going sexual involvement of neurotic and compelling interdependency. Ego support and the maintenance of self-image may well simply mandate the symbiotic sexual relationship with another. Politics, and especially Washington politics, often constitutes a context that precipitates and sustains such a symbiotic sexual relationship. The sexual liaisons that not infrequently occur between political officials and career females on the scene afford exchange benefits of significant worth to both. The Wayne Hays—Elizabeth Ray episode might be an example of such a mutually beneficial symbiotic sexual relationship. As one writer described the Washington sexual scene:

> Capital Hill attracts thousands of women, many of them young, attractive and single, who are involved in politics, who sometimes come to regard power as related to sexual gratification. For some of them, an affair with a member of Congress—their employer or someone else's—can become a sort of political and social status symbol as well as a diversion.[598]

Night work routines such as in a medical setting like a hospital, or a factory is also said to promote sexual affairs.[599] Similarly, isolation or a more private work setting may also facilitate sexual interaction. Where there is opportunity structure which facilitates it, a rationalizing culture or value system which justifies or helps rationalize it, and where there is stress or unhappiness, there is not infrequently adulterous behavior. In many instances, adulterous-type sexual deviancy is related to stress. According to one authority:

> . . . Perhaps stress elicits a generalized latent tendency toward promiscuity in some women, while in other cases the nature of the stress itself was such that it "called for" this type of response. In any event, the appearance of sexual promiscuity within the context of developmental stress is common.[600]

All in all, adultery or "playing around" as it is sometimes called, is often a function of stress, insecurity, marital disequilibrium, or a neurotic search for some elusive goal or state of mind requisite to a satisfactory concept of self.[601] Adultery may well often result from personal or marital stress but it may also precipitate marital or personal stress. Research has suggested that "adultery is the cause of nearly half of the problems that marriage counselors deal with." Furthermore, adulterous affairs very often involve the participants in a particularly stressful symbiotically emotional fashion.[602]

Adultery may assume the form of relatively ephemeral sexual and emotional involvement such as "one-night stands" or slightly more prolonged dyadic sexual relationships such as "affairs." In some instances, however, the extra-marital sexual interaction may encompass a relatively long-term, enduring, and emotionally symbiotic relationship with a "lover"—a mistress or paramour. In some societies, allegedly the Latin American countries, mistresses are institutionalized arrangements among certain segments of society. In the United States, there is also evidence that a significant number of individuals have "permanent" mistresses or paramours and such an arrangement has been the theme of numerous books, television dramas, and movies. The mistress becomes a surrogate, substitute, and supplemental wife, and the mutual emotional involvement and interdependence and symbiotic relationship is often quite intense. The sexual component of the relationship can often only be the foundation for other interactional components. As one mistress articulated it:

> He wants me to go through the book and that's OK with me. He asks me to do things he'd never ask his wife to do—like triolism or group sex. He is really grateful that I agree to these things. If he's a dirty old man then I'm a dirty old woman because I enjoy it too. He's proud of my ability in bed and he wants to show me off by having others there. With me he can have fantasies he can bring into the relationship.
>
> We use each other in a kind of partnership. He's terribly concerned about whether he does satisfy me and takes a great deal of trouble to make sure he does.[603]

Inasmuch as the mistress relationship is a kind of idealized relationship because of the erotic excitement and because it usually operates with a time and circumstances context perhaps more conducive to romance and glamour than the marital routine, many mistresses indicate that they see such as preferable to that of wife. Again as one mistress expresses it:

> I prefer to be a mistress. I wouldn't marry my lover even if he left his
> wife. I prefer being the other woman—it's a more exciting caviar
> relationship. You're not taken for granted as you are when you become
> a wife.[604]

If the status of mistress and the attendant sexual and social interaction can be carnally gratifying and emotionally fulfilling, it can also be emotionally devastating, especially in the event of a break-up, perhaps even more so than marriage. The stress, frustration, self-doubt, and trauma of mistress-hood is such that recently some mistresses have organized themselves into a group called "Mistresses Anonymous," for the purpose of mutual support, advice, and self-help.[605]

Finally, it must be assumed that under the impact of new carnal propaganda in our culture urging a liberated and uninhibited sexual life style that many females, and especially young females, released from the formerly held double standard may seek to actualize a more hedonistic ideology and turn to extramarital sexual gratification as a means of better realizing their existential potential and maximizing their sensate pleasures. This would seem especially suggested in light of *Redbook's* findings that married women involved in extra-coital activities are not necessarily less satisfied with their marriage than are the non-adulterous wives. Many of the extra-coital wives rated their marriage and marital sex good, but still sought adulterous, carnal extra-marital outlets.[606] Regardless of the rationale, and in spite of the new permissive sexual values demonstrated by some members of society, infidelity is still a deviant departure from the marital role prescribed by custom and law. Adultery violates religious and civil mandates and breaks the bond of conjugal trust. It is deviant behavior by the standards of spouse or society, or both. Violators are not still stoned or even made to wear the "scarlet" letter, but in most primitive and folk societies, are still treated harshly. Even in our society, the adulterer may, in some states and circumstances, still be subject to criminal prosecution, and furnish grounds to be divorced by spouse, including a retributive economic settlement. The adulterer may also experience informal social sanctions in job and career, in community and neighborhood, and from friends and family as well as suffer the social stigma of being labeled as adulterer, if not sexual degenerate. In some instances the negative public reaction may be intense, as in the case of Ingrid Bergman and her infidelity with Roberto Rosselini.

GROUP SEX AND SWINGING

Some instances of extramarital sexual gratification may be brief and superficial. Others, however, may involve more emotional intensity, and be of longer duration. Some such relationships may develop a semi-permanent structure symbiotically not unlike marriage itself with a reciprocal exchange of needs and appropriate responses. Men may maintain mistresses (or women, paramours) for long periods of time. In some cases, however, even such semi-permanent symbiotic sexual arrangements may not necessarily serve to satisfactorily provide for carnal needs, real or fantasy. Here, the individual may have to enlarge the circle of persons in the symbiotic sexual network in order to afford an even wider array of carnal outlets. In recent years, a new such variety of extra marital sexual deviancy has appeared, with increasing and widespread frequency. This new form of sexual misadventure is group sex, wife swapping or "swinging," as it is more popularly known.[607] Swinging has become a relatively prominent form of sexual deviancy in American society and it has been well publicized in numerous books and films such as *All the Loving Couples,* and *Bob and Carol and Ted and Alice.* Such films have tended to familiarize, if not popularize, the "sport" with the public. Some swingers have even affected a stance of indifference, defiance, or militancy in the face of public repulsion. One group of swingers even held a national convention.[608] Cosmopolitan in orientation, swingers often look outside their circle of regular intimates for participants in their sexual soirees.[609] To this end, several swinger magazines are published with news of single swinging gatherings and events, not to mention personal ads and notices featuring pictures, postures, and particulars for the rest of the faithful to pursue in window-shopping fashion. On the surface, swinging would appear to be a form of sexual activity oriented toward fun or recreation and an opportunity for personal sexual gratification in what is perceived to be more stimulating but socially sanctioned situations. At a deeper level, swinging must be viewed as a means of providing an opportunity to fulfill sexual fantasies with social facility and the swingers of more sophisticated taste and fuller experience have turned on to sexual experimentation of a broad spectrum of idiosyncratic taste involving costuming, unusual combinations of sexes (and animals), and a whole repertoire of sexual "cultures" including French (oral) and Greek (anal). Swinging, as a purported recreational pattern, often assumes routinized and ritualized configurations and can offer diversion (albeit of a deviant, and sometimes pathological nature) to as many as several million married Americans, by some estimates.[610] Swinging, in essence, is consensual adultery and permits a structured form of family deviancy for ostensibly recreational purposes, but which allows the couples involved to violate traditional sexual norms while monitoring each other's behavior. Thus, although the deviancy occurs within a permissive context there are, in fact, sanctioned limits. Swinging allowed an expanded exchange network of sexual gratification without the need for clandestine extra-marital activity, and obstensibly without threat to the unity of the basic marital dyad. In effect, having one's cake and eating it too. Swinging also, however, involves something more than direct sexual symbiosis. Swinging is an attempt to exchange other services and meet other needs. As one researcher has phrased it:

> We agree that swinging for many couples fulfills the husband's needs. However, these needs we found to be intimately connected to juvenile fantasy fulfillment, which abounds in American society, rather than to neurotic predilections. Furthermore, swinging in some cases could fulfill a husband's homosexual needs if he so desires. Two other strong possibilities suggest themselves, both of which are a far cry from the triteness of continually belaboring the term "latent homosexuality." Jealousy, or more aptly the desire to retain one's ego image, increases the male sexual interest following group sex. Second, our data indicate that swinging often satisfies social needs more completely than it ever satisfies sexual needs for many swinging couples.[611]

Swinging represents a desperate, and from a social standpoint, pathological effort to satisfy carnal and other needs within the context of a contrived social system with reciprocal and symbiotic exchange of appropriate physical and emotional gratification.

Bestiality as a Variant in Swinging

The extent of the pathological depths to which swinging activity may descend was perhaps well illustrated by an account of two swinging couples who turned to bestiality in order to satisfy the carnal catholicity of some of the group.[612] In this instance, the story is told of a married couple that had originally sought diversion, variety, and perhaps self-reassurance who became involved in swinging. As the wife became increasingly disenchanted and dissaffected, the husband became more and more dependent on the variety of carnal gratification offered by the activity. The wife turned to alcohol as a means of coping with the unacceptable reality of herself involved in sexual experimentation that was personally distasteful and socially despicable. Ultimately, the vagaries of heterosexual gratification afforded through swinging were not adequate to satisfy the carnal appetites of the husband. The husband sought new and bizarre sexual variety in the form of vicarious carnal gratification derived from observing his spouse engaged in bestiality. He looked for another swinging couple with sexually innovative tastes similar to his own. He and his wife visited the other couple for a weekend of sexual novelty and while the wives took turns serving as sexual partner for a collie dog, their husbands looked on apparently deriving vicarious sexual gratification from the event. The other wife who had enjoyed observing the sexual spectacle herself, apparently also took sexual pleasure from participating in the act. For the first dissaffected wife, however, it was the ultimate act of sexual degradation. Reduced to engaging in sexual intercourse with a dog for the carnal titilation of her husband and other swingers, the wife's former enthusiasm for the sophistication of sexual innovation and variety was replaced by loathing for her spouse, and self-disgust. Swinging, in this instance, had also failed to appropriately provide for her sexual or emotional needs, much less her wants.

CARNAL GRATIFICATION AND ECONOMIC EXCHANGE

The satisfaction of the sexual drive, at least in terms of rather immediate carnal gratification, may not always be obtainable on the basis of mutual affective interaction and the exchange of emotional support. Nor are appropriate sexual outlets necessarily residually available as a result of constituent participation in a work unit based on mating and progeny. This may be particularly the case in other than a peasant or primitive society, where a variety of factors may all operate to produce situational disequilibrium in terms of availability of opportunity for regularized sexual gratification. These factors may include the complex division of labor, high rate of population mobility, and societal values emphasizing personal preference and emotional motivation rather than group concern and rational consideration, which are extant in such societies. As in the instance of other goods and services normally available, component to the mutual discharge of group responsibilities, within the village or kinship unit of the peasant society, sexual fulfillment may become a commercial commodity, involving the exchange of tangibles in barter in the marketplace of the industrial or urban society. Many services, informally rendered within the group as a result of inter-locking networks of mutual responsibilities in the agrarian setting, become transformed into units of economic exchange in the fluid social system of the complex society. Protection, in the form of family and clan linkages of mutual support, aid, and revenge obliga-tions, give way to the need for professional protectors such as police and sheriffs, paid for by tax revenues, and private security guards who charge specific fees for specific protective services. The nurtura-tive context of watchful and emotionally concerned kinsmen gives way to the need to exchange economic value in the form of wages and tuition fees for the temporary and formalized child care afforded by commercial baby sitters, career nurses and governesses, and nurs-eries and day centers open to all, for a price. Sexual gratification must, in similar circumstances, often be obtained through formal economic exchange, with elaborate gradations of price for services rendered and even the sexual experience itself quantified for ease of economic pricing and sometimes embellished with appropriate dramaturgy as a means of adding commercial value to the product.

The complete quantification of physiological sexual response as a manifestation of total commercialization of service is perhaps no-where better illustrated than in Jack Richardson's engaging account of negotiating with a whore in Las Vegas.[613] After a preliminary and perfunctory conversation of pleasantries and an agreement on ser-vices desired and available, the prostitute brusquely interjects, "But we've got something to discuss first." The customer, sensitive to the need to establish price at this point, inquires; the prostitute tells him, "A hundred dollars." Taken aback and perhaps slightly stunned by the inflated flesh marketplace of Las Vegas, the protagonist naively asks, "A hundred dollars? That for the night?" But the prostitute is the complete professional dispensing a carefully metered economic commodity for carefully priced monetary value. She knowledgeably replies, "No, Jack, you know better than that. This is Vegas. It's a hundred a pop." Because the author of the article had, in fact, been a big-time winner at the gambling tables, he did partake of "two pops' worth" of sex before the prostitute finally departed. In an earlier time, prostitutes like other artisans, might have been inclined to sell a complete sexual experience in its gestalt entirety, but as society began to march to the throb of machine, the assembly line, and the time clock, even prostitutes got in step with industrial society and often charged by the hour. The analogy of prostitution and assembly line work may not be completely without foundation. It was reported several years ago, for example, that a brothel in Stuttgart, West Germany rented a background music service and requested a "light industrial" music program. The prostitute in Las Vegas, however, articulated a pricing policy more redolent of some of the more recent commercial orientations such as "portion control" in restaurants as a means of maximizing inventory efficiency.

PROSTITUTION IN HISTORICAL CONTEXT

Actually, prostitution did not await the coming of the industrial revolution. By neolithic times, prostitution was a well-established service occupation in the Mesopotamian city-states. Prostitution apparently arose initially as a component of religious ceremony, possibly the continuation of earlier fertility rites.[614] Temple prostitution, required of young women in numerous early societies, such as Egypt, Phoenicia, and Babylon was apparently functional in several ways. The females could more readily accumulate money for their wedding dowry and the transient males in the cities could be sexually accommodated. Various religious symbolisms also attached themselves to the sex acts that were prostituted. Prostitution was sufficiently institutionalized as a service occupation by the Greek era that there were both brothels for profit and some run as state establishments, called *Dicteria*. It is claimed that, because of the many arranged marriages based on convenience or property rather than love, Greek husbands sought sexual outlets outside of marriage, and in the eyes of many, commercial sex was viewed as preferable to adultery. Prostitution was not infrequently offered along with other services such as singing, dancing, musical instrumentation, and story telling in Greece and Rome. There were both full- and part-time prostitutes operating in regular brothels as well as independent entrepreneurs offering their services behind the guise of public baths or other commercial establishments. It has been suggested that in Rome, particularly, the cultural preoccupation with carnality in all the belle arts, and everyday life as well, plus the abundance of female slaves and women of the lower economic levels, made the flowering of prostitution inevitable. Many females from the rural areas and provinces could not be absorbed into their own local social structures and many ended up in Rome consequently, not unlike some of our own big cities today. Such factors may well have been significant contributing elements but the vast number of transient males in Rome were also a major consideration in widespread prostitution. Rome was the crossroads of the empire; at any given time there were thousands of workers, slaves, soldiers, travelers, and traveling merchants coming and going, for the most part single or separated from spouse or other regular female companion. Prostitution became a practical necessity, trading the sexual favors of the female surplus population for economic value to the transient male population. Throughout history, large concentrations of males, such as in mining, lumbering, and other "boom" towns, as well as military camps, have necessitated and attracted prostitution. In some ways the situation in some parts of the world today is no different from the times in imperial Rome. In 1970, in France, there was some political agitation to legalize prostitution with state-supervised brothels. Venereal disease and health concerns, the elimination of sexual crimes, and the helping of "timid young men to overcome sexual complexes" were all listed as reasons for the desire to legalize prostitution. Another less discussed reason, however, was the existence of 3 million foreign laborers in France at a time when "many French women [were] reluctant to go to bed with them."[615] Similarly, the building of the Alaskan pipeline has attracted its share of prostitutes even in spite of concerted efforts to keep them away from the construction sites. The concentration of men with high wages and no heterosexual outlets has tended to draw the prostitutes magnet style. One prostitute, posing as a magazine saleslady, was reported to have made $5,300 in four days around a construction site in Deadhorse.[616]

PROSTITUTION AND THE MILITARY

It is the military, however, today or in Roman times, that frequently serves as the most effective catalyst in promoting prostitution. In times past, as today, many armies had prostitutes or "camp followers" as they were known, who marched with them. The famous ballad, "Greensleeves," is about prostitute camp followers. The Germans and the Russians in World War II, had prostitute units that traveled with their military. The Japanese Army had "comfort battalions." From the time of Greensleeves to the girls of the Japanese comfort battalions, such females have provided sexual services, female companionship, and also discharged other responsibilities such as nursing wounded and sick men, and cooking. In turn, they have received food, shelter, protection, income, and other valuable considerations. The American military formally often had to eschew a formal policy of tolerating, much less encouraging, prostitution during World War II, because of the public sentiment of the "folks back home." Informally, however, the military authorities tended to supervise or maintain brothels for their personnel in all of the theaters of the war including China-Burma-India theater, European, and the Pacific theaters.[617] During the Vietnamese conflict, the South Vietnamese government with the tacit agreement of the U.S. military established a prostitution quarter in An Khe and other places and undertook some degree of regulation of at least the clientele. For American servicemen going on "R and R" in Taiwan, there was an information pamphlet with advice on how to rent a girl from a bar. The pamphlet instructed, for example:

> Her [the prostitute's] company can be bought from the bar for a 24-hour period for U.S. $15.00 . . . Do not purchase the company of a girl for more than 24 hours. They seldom look as good in the morning as they did the previous night . . .[618]

The military situation tends to attract prostitution for several reasons. First, there is the obvious element of demographic concentration that means a preponderant male population. The military culture emphasizes manliness and especially sexual aggressiveness. Both of these values, combined with the general youthfulness of the male military population make them especially prone to want to exercise their maleness, and prostitutes are generally the only available sexual outlets. The military memeber also seeks "relaxation after the rigors of bivouac, combat, or a sea voyage."[619] Inasmuch as military personnel face deprivation, if not potential death or maiming, they not infrequently develop a significantly fatalistic and hedonistic orientation to life. As Winick and Kinsie put it, "The imminent possibility of death seems to lead many participants in a war to feel that they ought to enjoy themselves while they can."[620] Thus, for the soldier or construction worker physically and psychologically separated from spouse, lover, or girlfriend, and facing deprivation, danger, and loneliness, the prostitute provides temporary companionship and commercial outlet for sexual gratification. The prostitute, in turn, is well paid for her carnal services and can be self-supporting, where she might not otherwise. It is interesting to note that many women engage in prostitution, out of choice rather than coercion. Several years ago the Detroit City Council set aside $151,191 for the purpose of rehabilitating prostitutes. The money was to be used for retraining and job counseling. After a year the program was terminated when the Council could not identify a single prostitute who wished to be rehabilitated.[621]

PROSTITUTION AND INTRINSIC SATISFACTION

Prostitutes do more than derive economic sustenance from their sexual work. Few claim to derive sexual satisfaction from the work, but some do assert they enjoy the attention they receive from men, and their perceived ability at "turning a man on more than he's been turned on before."[622] It has been claimed that they derive a variety of psychological, albeit perhaps pathological, satisfaction from their work. Some authorities such as Winick and Kinsie, claim that the lack of sexual response on the part of most prostitutes is psychologically functional for many.[623] They have asserted, for example, that, "Their lack of response may be one means by which they can express superiority to or contempt for customers. Without the woman yielding she has forced her customer to respond in the form of his ejaculation.[624] A number of other benefits have been said to accrue to the prostitute because of her work. It is said that some prostitutes find the life adventurous. Some women, it is claimed, may obtain a "nonsexual goal" through their work. It is even asserted that some prostitutes "may discover a true romance" through their vocation. Others may simply be able to "act out a neurotic impulse." In any event, for some prostitutes the economic remuneration may be quite lucrative, and for some females, who, for various reasons, may not be able to hold down a conventional job, prostitution, either full-or part-time, may be the only, or at least a preferred, way of earning a living. As has been seen from news accounts from Washington, D.C. lately, for some women who are not able to effectively type or answer the phone, the provision of sexual services for monetary reward is sometimes an expedient means of enhancing one's salary. Even the achieving of temporary goals, monetary or otherwise, may, it is suggested, be accelerated by prostitution.[625] In some instances, even previously respectable females have taken up prostitution as a side line or at least temporarily as a means of relieving some chronic or pressing economic burden. From time to time, one reads in the newspapers of college girls who are arrested for prostitution when they attempted to raise money for tuition or to supplement their spending allowances from home and were apprehended because of amateurish ineptitude. A classic example was the case of 15 housewives from a Long Island, N.Y., suburban community who were arrested for prostitution several years ago.[626] The women, 20- to 45-years-old, "were by their own account, merely trying to cope with a classic suburban problem: keeping up with the Jones despite a limited budget." They frequented local bars and restaurants, seeking customers and extra income. In some instances, the husbands did not know of their wives' moonlighting efforts, but in at least one case, the husband not only knew of his wife's prostituting activities, but even babysat with the children. He was aware that his income was insufficient for their needs and that his wife was simply doing what she was in order to help. There have even been reports of a group of physicians' wives in a middle-sized Southern city who became part-time prostitutes as a means of amusing themselves as well as acquiring some extra "pin" money for their personal shopping.[627] Sometimes women will even resort to partial prostitution as a means of enhancing their income. As seen in an earlier chapter, the masseuse in the "executive" massage parlor may not infrequently "hustle her hand," and provide "locals" for her clientele for handsome fees and tips.[628] By restricting the anatomical extent of their prostitution, self-labeled "hand-whores" can provide masturbation services and still generate the high income necessary to afford the economic style of life to which they aspire and have often become accustomed, including the "steaks and cocktails" to which they often treat themselves and their boy-friends.

PROSTITUTION, DEMOGRAPHY, AND SOCIAL SETTING

In Rome and at other times and places, prostitution was something of a demographic necessity. In an earlier period in the United States, prostitution was also a demographic necessity and, thus, something of a practical, albeit, deviant, necessity. The vast waves of immigrants that inundated this country were predominantly males, with minimal prospect of ever bringing women from the old country to be their wives. A female mortality rate, somewhat higher then than now, also added to the unbalanced ratio of males to females. As the country moved westward, men constituted the majority of the vanguard. Even as more women migrated to the frontier, many of the male population never had the economic resources appropriate to marriage. Thus, many of the western and frontier communities had essentially male populations for whom there were few heterosexual outlets for many other than the ubiquitous cow-town bordellos and the prostitutes' cribs in the ethnic ghettos. The musical play and later movie entitled *Paint Your Wagon* revolved around a theme of largely all-male town population and a minimum number of females to serve as sexual outlets.

During the frontier period, or into the Victorian era, and, in fact, until recent times, it was widely believed that "male lust" required a sexual outlet, and that in the absence of prostitution, sex crimes and depravity forced on "decent" women would result. Prostitution, then, was seen as a necessary sexual escape valve, protecting the unmarried females of virtue and even, in some instances, the married woman from the excessive sexual demands of her husband. Such a rationalization for prostitution persists in some quarters today among prostitutes, clientele, and public. With the various waves of female emancipation and liberation and the general trend toward sexual freedom and public enlightenment, it may well be that by earlier standards the number of virtuous females has much declined, and it would seem that non-marital and non-commercial heterosexual outlets for "male lust" have expanded significantly both in terms of range and number. In such a situation, it might be expected that prostitution would have largely disappeared as a vocational practice because of insufficient demand. Such, apparently, here and abroad, is not the case. In most of the European countries, literally hundreds of thousands of prostitutes roam the streets and caberets looking for clientele. In Rome, for example, as many as 2,000 streetwalkers sometimes gather around soccer matches seeking customers.[629] In Germany, prostitution is such big business that one firm is offering to sell limited partnership shares in its chain operation. The money raised through the sale of these shares will be used for expansion.[630]

In the United States also, prostitution continues seemingly unabated by law enforcement pressures and undiminished in the face of widespread sexual promiscuousness. Although many prostitutes have left the streets and moved to the bars and hotels, nevertheless, streetwalkers do still create a public nuisance in some areas. Apartment house dwellers in some large cities, for example, have in recent years complained about the prostitutes, their pimps, and their clientele who loiter about, if not live in, the buildings as well as the general noise and disturbance which the prostitutes generate in the course of their business.[631] A new and particularly annoying trend to some large city dwellers is the tendency of some prostitutes to walk the neighborhood streets "early in the morning, in time to catch [the] patronage of early rising construction workers."[632] The streetwalker, has in many cities, at least been forced to be more unobstrusive and, thus, wary of vice officers in mufti. Also, the brothel, at one time a prominent establishment in most communities of any sophistication, has diminished both in numbers and elegance on the American scene. Many brothels were venerable masculine institutions in their communities and often attained regional and even national fame (or infamy, depending on one's point of view), and some could even boast of having entertained celebrities and politicians of national prominence.[633] Some brothels were little more than dingy hovels or shabby rooming houses in the slums, in some industrial town, while others were plush genteel mansions of popular architecture and stunning decor. Like the physical surroundings, the women who staffed the brothels ranged from derelict crones, to exquisitely beautiful women, and the clientele and their pocket-books matched accordingly. In some cities like New Orleans, whole sections of town, like Storyville, were devoted to prostitution. The "cathouses" of Storyville were so famous and attracted such large clienteles, that many later famous dixieland jazz musicians were able to launch their careers as piano players in the brothels.[634]

America was and is a mobile society, and often the brothels disappeared as population shifts occurred, and the pressure of local law enforcement agencies coupled with the high cost of "protection" forced many out of business. By the time of World War II, the prostitutes were following the servicemen to their camps and often set up business just outside the camp in trailers. Since then some enterprising prostitutes have even attempted to operate rolling brothels in the form of pickup trucks with covered sides, and a mattress in the back.[635] In more recent and affluent times, private yachts have appeared as floating brothels.[636] Where at one time, taxi dance halls and dance studios served as "covers for prostitution,"[637] in more recent times prostitutes may more likely hide behind the guise of "public artists studios," "escort services," or the ubiquitous "massage parlor."

PROSTITUTION AS OCCUPATIONAL SPECIALTY

Although prostitution is usually classified as a deviant or criminal vocation, it possesses all of the general characteristics of an occupation including a system of rewards, occupational recruitment and socialization, expected role behavior, structured relationships with clientele and colleagues, and mechanisms of control. Contrary to popular stereotype, prostitutes are not the victims of white slavery, and a great many apparently find their work sufficiently rewarding economically, if not intrinsically to make it a life's career. Prostitution is a lucrative vocation, relatively speaking, whether street walker or executive call girl, although the prostitute is not "working" all the time and must, accordingly, price her services sufficiently high to cover her nonwork time. She also has extraordinary expenses—for example, tips, payoffs, court fines, lawyer fees, medical bills, beauty shop costs, and clothing expenses.

In this sense, it must be recognized that prostitution is much more than the simple act of permitting the male customer the use of her sexual organs temporarily (or whatever service she renders) for a fee. Prostitution is a complex service and requires training and an elaborate web of assistance from others. The successful practice of any occupational specialty, and especially a complex one, requires appropriate socialization, including both the transmission of skills and ideas, as well as a change of status. The transmission of occupational skills includes, among other skills, the teaching of regular technical skills. In the case of prostitutes, they are "turned out," or apprenticed.[638] They must acquire a broad repertoire of sexual approaches and techniques, including sexual positions, practices, and responses. They must become familiar with oral genital sexual techniques, as well as appropriate orgasm control. As James Bryan puts it, "You teach them to French (fellatio) and how to talk to men."[639] Transmission of occupational skills also includes the learning of "tricks of the trade." Examples here might include learning deceptive responses to the male clientele's sexual efforts, protecting themselves against veneral disease and pregnancy, gracefully obtaining their fee in advance from the client and avoiding detection and arrest by law enforcement officers. A prostitute must also acquire the appropriate social skills such as the requisite social graces and role behavior that will permit her to pursue her trade effectively. Again, Bryan indicates that:

Training may also include proprieties concerning consuming alcohol and drugs, when and how to obtain the fee, how to converse with the customers, and occasionally, physical and sexual hygiene.[640]

Not to be neglected in the prostitute's education is the internalization of an appropriate occupational ideology. The prostitute must acquire new ideas and values if she is to operate effectively in her new occupational endeavor. She must, for example, develop "professional" detachment or impersonality. In most instances, she will be encouraged not to experience sexual orgasm with the client. She must also learn to be exploitative inasmuch as others will attempt to exploit her, and that people, and especially men, are corrupt or corruptible; thus, prostitution is "no more dishonest act than the everyday behavior of 'squares'."[641] In this way, she can maintain a rationalization of her work that is essentially supportive of a satisfactory self-image.

PROSTITUTION AND THE SYMBIOTIC NETWORK

Armed with her detailed skills and abilities acquired through occupational socialization, the prostitute still is not able to dispense her elaborate services without, for the most part, an extensive network of co-workers either directly assisting or providing ancillary services. The brothel of past times and present, for example, often houses an elaborate work system, including cooks, maids, musicians, bouncers, prostitutes, and the madame who often serves as manager and general trouble shooter.[642] When the prostitute leaves the brothel to pursue her trade as a call girl, she still is not working alone, strictly speaking. She, too, is often part of a work system, involving concerted team effort. Her co-workers may include bell hops, cab drivers, bartenders, pimps, and even the attorney or retainer who will bail her out of jail when arrested.[643] Even in the newer configurations of escort services and massage parlors, the prostitute must still rely on other co-workers including receptionists, establishment managers, bouncers, and attorneys, to name some. To do her work, the prostitute must rely on the parasitic, and thus symbiotic, services of other service specialists—the cabbie or motel desk clerk who refers the customer, the managers who handle the "front" and carries out the initial negotiations, and even the attorney who handles the problems of licenses and pay-off and perhaps bails her out when arrested. Prostitution, then, in effect, represents a highly complex service delivery system with numerous persons working symbiotically as a work team. Prostitutes are, according to one study, also involved in symbiotic linkages with law enforcement agents, as well as confederates.[644] In the situation reported, the police vice squad officers are described as both the legal nemises of the prostitutes but also, on occasion, their friends and confidants. The prostitutes render information services to the officers, and the officers, in turn, provide assistance to the women from time to time. As the authors (p. 228–229) phrase it:

> Vice officers not only arrest prostitutes, they help them. Vice officers drop or reduce charges in exchange for information, help prostitutes' friends in court, provide inside information on the disposition of charges, and help prostitutes solve their personal problems.

Thus, the authors describe a pattern of symbiotic accommodation and cooperation between prostitutes and vice officers. The two occupational groups work together in much the same way as does the prostitute work with many other occupational groups such as bartenders, club and lounge owners, pimps, drug pushers, and cab drivers, just to name a few. In this way, a kind of occupational ecological balance is effected and maintained.

Prostitute and client also enjoy a kind of symbiotic relationship in terms of the respective roles each play and the services rendered for value received. From the standpoint of the prostitute, she receives more than merely money from her clientele. As previously discussed, some prostitutes derive intrinsic satisfaction from their work based on the fact that they can "turn men on," and that they are erotically attractive to men. Some authors have asserted that, ". . . because they perform a necessary function for the maintenance of the double standard, they are not without some oblique prestige."[645] Some prostitutes enjoy the fact that they have celebrities or famous people as well as prestigious occupational types such as lawyers and physicians as clientele. It has also been asserted that some prostitutes become involved in lesbian relationships with other prostitutes, and that by rationalizing that "men are ultimately paying the bills for such liaisons," ". . . a dimension that heightens the pleasure afforded by the relationship itself" is added.[646] Some psychiatrists even contend that prostitutes "may be avenging herself on every man for the love she had expected to get but did not receive from her father."[647] In any event, it suffices to say that prostitutes obtain more than money from their clients; they derive various residual neurotic or ego-enhancing benefits as well. In that sense, the prostitute cannot do without the client, economically or psychologically. The economic symbiosis should, however, not be minimized. In foreign countries like Vietnam, prostitution expanded rapidly to service the needs of the American GIs, and, in time, the prostitutes and often their relatives became very much economically dependent on the revenue from prostitution. When the GIs left, the economic impact was severe on prostitutes, their illegitimate children, relatives, and the entire economy.[648] Like a performer who enjoys a symbiotic relationship with an audience, the prostitute enjoys a symbiotic relationship with the client.

PROSTITUTION AND SYMBIOTIC EXCHANGE

The client derives more than simple sexual gratification from the prostitute. In some instances of the past, where demographic situations had men greatly outnumbering women, prostitutes were "necessary" as a means of providing an expedient heterosexual outlet for the predominately male population. In contemporary times, however, prostitution flourishes even in areas where there is no real shortage of women. Furthermore, with the much increased level of sexual permissiveness today, there is presumably no real shortage of females who might be potential sex partners. On top of all of this, it should also be stressed that many clients serviced by prostitutes are married. The prostitute, then, must deliver more than sexual gratification. The prostitutes, first of all, offer sexual variety. She herself, as simply a different person from spouse or habitual lover, offers variety in the form of another sex partner. She also offers variety within her sexual services. Some married men, so writers like Winick and Kinsie have suggested, seek more diversity in sexual procedure than perhaps their wives are prepared to deliver.[649] In spite of the increasing sexual sophistication of many American women, it would appear that many married couples restrict their sexual activity to genital coitus. Prior to World War II, the standard sexual service offered by most prostitutes was coitus. Today, however, the service most requested of prostitutes is fellatio, and the average prostitute will have a repertoire which includes anal intercourse, cunnilingus, fellatio, genital coitus and various combinations and permutations of these practices. In the 1930s only 10 percent of prostitutes' customers wanted some form of oral saisfaction; today it has been reported that as many as nine out of 10 men ask for it.[650] Prostitutes may have to offer a wide variety of sexual services, some bizarre even by pathological standards. Prostitutes, for example, may have to participate in a range of behavioral perversions such as beating or whipping the client or being beaten by the client (this practice is known as "dumpings"). Some prostitutes even specialize in "dumpings," exacting high fees and payment of any attendant medical or dental bills.[651] Prostitutes are often requested to assist a client with his bizarre fantasies which may require her to wear certain kinds of clothing, lingerie, or foot wear. She may have to pretend to be dead while the customer has intercourse with her or even let the customer pretend to kill her. The customer may insist that she be tied up or tie him up. The prostitute may be requested to use obscene language, bite or scratch the client, or whip him, if not let him whip her.[652] Many prostitutes, however, do have limits beyond which they will not go. As one expressed it:

> That time I went along with the customer. Othertimes I flatly refused. I refused to be covered with black shoe polish for one of Bea's Johns, despite his protests that it would come right off. I refused to wear a collar and leash and be led around an apartment and eat crackers from a dish on the floor, although I did consent to lead the John in that way, which partly satisfied him.[653]

Some prostitutes indicate, however, that many of their clients are as much interested in conversation and companionship as in sex, and in this sense many prostitutes claim that by providing therapy for married men, they are "holding marriages together." In this sense, their "therapeutic" services cast them in a kind of symbiotic relationship to some marriages in a manner similar to the mistress or paramour. The socially prescribed sexual relationship attendant to marriage may only be able to survive where a socially proscribed ancillary and supplemental sexual extra-marital relationship can be effected. Prostitution may support and facilitate business to the extent that commercial deals are sometimes "sweetened" and, thus, facilitated by added inducement of prepaid prostitutes. The traveling businessman (as in the case of Willie Loman of *Death of a Salesman*) may have to depend on prostitutes for sexual outlets in the considerable time he is away from home and spouse. Even government apparently requires some element of prostituted sex to keep the politicians going, as the recent scandals indicate.[654] In England recently, there was the suggestion that a chain of government-supervised houses of prostitution be made available "for the use of politicians and diplomats throughout Europe."[655] In the face of scandals and security leaks resulting from politicians and government officials, it was felt that the establishment of "safe houses" would be functional to both the government and the individuals involved. Thus, "those politicians who wished, could avail themselves of the services offered without jeopardizing either their career or their governments." Actually, politicians have been reported to be heavy users of prostitutes. One recent study of high-priced prostitutes showed that "60% of their clients are political leaders or powerful corporate chieftains who usually prefer 'kinky' sex" including fetishism, exhibitionism, voyeurism, and flagellation while held in bondage. The prostitute-client relationship is symbiotically attractive, however, because, as the researchers put it:

> Through prostitution, politicians and power brokers get unusual sexual needs gratified. The arrangement provides a convenience in that neither the powerful figure will expose the call girl nor the reverse.[656]

The prostitute-client relationship cannot be considered casual or superficial in its dynamics or trivial in its ego involvement, social importance, and consequences for self. Both individuals often bring strong emotional postures into the encounter. Aside from latent (or manifest) hostility and disgust toward the client and his carnal *desiderata,* the prostitute may well also experience self-hatred and disgust, with a resulting defective image of self as a result of their vocation. An example of such self-condemnation was cited by one group of researchers in the words of a prostitute who observed:

> I will rot in hell for what I am doing. If you don't know what you are doing is sinful, then it is not so bad. But it is an unpardonable sin if you know what you are doing is sinful and keep on sinning.[657]

Presumably, as a result of such an unsatisfactory conceptualization of self, prostitutes are frequently drug abusers, if not addicts, or alcoholics and such reliance on drugs is essentially a coping mechanism. Prostitutes not infrequently neglect their health and often have physical and mental health problems. Prostitutes are reported to be unusually self-destructive and have a suicide rate somewhat in excess of the average.

The prostitutes' clients may also experience hostility or disgust toward her. They may additionally have feelings of guilt, and anxiety, and even hostility toward themselves. In some instances, they may experience hostility toward their spouse or girlfriend (attributing their spouse's failure to provide them with appropriate sexual satisfaction as a major factor in their reasoning to have sex with a prostitute). The clients of prostitutes sometimes seem especially anxious and concerned about the possibility of detection and the social consequences. In Buffalo, N.Y., a police effort to deal with prostitution involved the strategy of arresting the clients, and having the local newspapers print their names and addresses. Even though the offense was only a misdemeanor and carried a relatively small fine, those arrested were greatly distressed because of the publicity. Publicizing their arrest could lead to loss of jobs, divorce, or family disgrace. Some of those arrested were fired or experienced marital disruption, and other serious social consequences. One arrested individual asked the policeman to shoot him, because "he said he was disgraced and might as well be shot."[658] In Trenton, N.J., one prostitute's customer arrested who had his name published in the local newspaper committed suicide.[659]

The prostitute-client relationship then represents more than mere casual sexual gratification. It is a complex relationship affording a variety of interpersonal benefits. As one prostitute phrased it, "we sell orgasms, illusions and emotional support,"[660] and as one researcher said of the clients patronizing of a prostitute, ". . . any one visit to a prostitute is so complexly motivated that it can almost be said to be over-determined."[661]

MEDICAL PROSTITUTION AND SEXUAL SURROGATES

Interestingly, since the advent of the Masters-Johnson studies and subsequent therapy programs, some marriage therapy programs have used surrogate partners or "sexual therapists" as they have become known.[662] Generally they are single sexually well-adjusted females who engage in sexual activities with men who have sexual problems. As one therapist described her work:

> What I'm doing is technically prostitution. But I'm convinced that
> helping men out of their hangups is valid important work.[663]

The sexual therapist becomes a substitute for the spouse or girlfriend (or boyfriend). The individual with the sexual difficulty or dysfunction (premature ejaculation), for example, will work with the surrogate over a period of time in a carefully paced, step-by-step, sexual re-socialization which may spend considerable time on such preliminaries as "sensate focus," "shaking," and touching. The relationship is supposedly clinical and the individual can feel relaxed, secure, and less anxious than with his regular sex partner. The surrogate is constructive not critical of the patient's sexual performance. As he learns the proper technique, he supposedly also acquires self-assurance and confidence in his ability to engage in sexual intercourse. Although the relationship between surrogate and patient is supposedly impersonal, both have an emotional investment. The surrogate is attempting to resolve the patient's sexual difficulty and is, presumably, ego-involved in her success. There is also the stress to succeed. The goal of the therapy is to have the patient reach the point where he can function satisfactorily as a sexual partner with her and, subsequently, with other females. Reaching such a point requires time, mutual effort, and teamwork, as it were, all of which tend to contribute to an interpersonal involvement, even if relatively minor. The situation is stressful for both, and the patient may be particularly anxious about the encounter. Because the therapy sessions are so emotionally stressful, and the client is being "pressured" by the therapist, the patient sometimes attempts to resist or sidestep the pressure, and not become involved,[664] such as some patients who resist psychotherapy. Apparently, the relationship between sexual surrogate and patient is sufficiently intense, ego-involved and with constituent pressure as to be threatening to one or both, suggesting a symbiotic relationship even if clinical and ephemeral.

In addition to sexual therapy involving actual sexual surrogates, there are numerous instances where sexual activity becomes part of medical, psychiatric, or counseling therapy, even if a deviant and unethical remedy.[665] The scenario is common and simple. A female in the throes of marital discord seeks marriage, medical, or psychological counseling. The patient develops an emotional dependence on the counselor, perhaps there is even a mutual attraction and emotional interdependence. The patient is psychologically vulnerable and the unscruplous therapist or the counselor who forgets decorum and responsibility can exploit the patient and enter into a sexual relationship. The therapist may rationalize his action by arguing that he is "solving the client's immediate problem by providing a responsible and secure sexual outlet, or freeing the client from unfounded fears and inhibitions," aside from being sexually exploitative, unethical, if not illegal in some contexts, such behavior is socially reprehensible and deviant, inasmuch as the practitioner violated an obligation of trust and confidence with the patient.

SUMMARY

Marriage involves a variety of reciprocal obligations including the exchange of sexual gratification in concert with the other kinds of reciprocity activities. Marriage is accordingly, a "socially-legitimate sexual union." Inasmuch as marriage is an exchange relationship, it may be also conceptualized as a kind of social symbiotic relationship between a man and a woman. The sexual dimension of marriage is regulated by two normative elements, one, the prerogative of sexual exclusivity and second, the specification for appropriate sexual gratification.

The latter element encompasses a complex and convoluted set of norms prescribing or proscribing a wide range of sexual techniques, procedures, mechanics, and modes of gratification. Included within the regulated behavior are such components as coital position, genital manipulation, oral-genital contact, and time, place, and circumstance of sexual activity to name some. Traditionally, couples in the United States were relatively circumspect in their carnal behavior, and systematic studies such as those of Kinsey et al. suggested that couples were, in general, relatively conventional in their sexual behavior, relying on the traditional male-above-the-supine-female coital position and penile-vaginal penetration for their sexual gratification. Only a relatively small percentage were daring enough in their sexual experimentation to venture far from the bounds of socially-defined sexual conformity. According to Kinsey, for example, less than one-half of all of his males had ever utilized oral-genital contacts, and only two-thirds of the females had ever experienced orgasm at least once before marriage.

In recent decades, however, with the coming of "sexual liberation" and a much liberalized view of variations from traditional sexual conformity, sexual experimentation, albeit still socially deviant by some standards, within marriage became much more wide-spread. Variation in coital position, oral-genital sex, masturbation, the use of vibrators, and even anal sex became relatively common. In a recent survey, for example, 91 percent of the females reported having engaged in oral sex with almost 50 percent of them reporting that they engaged in it often.

Although such sexual experimentation is somewhat more com-mon among younger couples, middle-aged and even some older mar-ried couples have been willing to enlarge the scope of their sexual repertoire, and have been reported to be enjoying new plateaus of carnal gratification and increased pleasure with their new outlook and activities. Such sexual innovation and experimentation is still considered socially deviant, if not perverted, in some quarters and often is still classified as illegal, although seldom prosecuted. Al-though some persons are experiencing anxiety, guilt, and doubt con-cerning their sexual vagaries formerly classified as unnatural or bizzare, most married couples involved in carnal exploration are not conceptualizing themselves as deviants or perverts. This new liber-ated posture has had one dysfunction, however, in precipitating a "new impotence" among some men who have been unable to cope with the higher levels of sexual performance being demanded by many females.

Coital position, and mode of carnal stimulation are not the only aspects of sexual behavior subject to control and proscription. Un-wanted pregnancy or birth may elicit both social stigma and legal sanction for one or both of the sexual partners. In a society that prescribes monogamous marriage by both religious and legal man-date, bigamy or polygamy are considered deviant and a criminal offense punishable by severe sanction.

When the exchange of sexual gratification in marriage is deemed inadequate or inappropriate by either partner, inequitable, or does not insure value given and received, the aggrieved partner or partners may sometimes seek alternate sexual outlets that would be either complementary or supplementary to their own carnal needs. This may take the form of casual sexual liaisons with one or more persons over time, or it may evolve into a more institutionalized arrangement such as a mistress or paramour. In either event, the sexual exchange network has simply been widened to include an additional person with sexual input and appropriate equitable expectations. Such an arrangement may restore a kind of sexual symbiosis to the marriage, such as the classical *ménage à trois* arrangement. In some instances,

persons have even maintained several spouses and families at different addresses and attempted to live a harmonious multiple married
and sexual life (as long as no one but them discovered the facade).
For other persons with perhaps deeper, more erotic, and more compulsive sexual needs and desires, other more elaborate and innovative
arrangements, even at the risk of deviant, if not aberrant, labeling are
sometimes sought. The rise of spouse swapping, swinging, sex clubs,
and other forms of avocational permissive collective sexual activity
represents efforts to widen the sexual network sufficiently to indulge
the fullest range of sexual appetites and fantasies. Some extra-marital
adulterous activity may involve relatively short-termed episodes of
emotional and sexual interaction—"affairs," as it were, while in
other instances, the adulterous behavior may assume the form of a
semi-permanent sexual liaison with one individual, a "mistress" or
"paramour," who becomes a kind of substitute or supplemental
spouse. Not infrequently, work and its attendant routines provides
a facilitative opportunity structure for adultery. The 1974 *Redbook*
sex survey revealed, for example, that more than 50 percent of wage-
earning wives in the 35–39 year old category said they had intercourse with men other then their husbands.[666] Adultery is not only
apparently becoming more common, it is also becoming more tolerated as a result of the newer sexual values, and as evidenced by the
"no-fault" divorce laws in many states. Adultery is still a major
factor in marital disequilibrium, however, and is still technically
against the law in some areas. It is still regarded by many as a
violation of social and religious sexual norm and stigmatized and
sanctioned accordingly, in many instances.

For some situations and individuals, the network of sexual alternatives outside marriage has moved to encompass commercial sex in
its many vagaries. In all instances, the non-marital options, too,
extract their cost and dilute their benefits. Each participant derives
perceived value, albeit deviant value, from the sexual recipient. The
prostitute earns her monetary fee by offering expedient sexual gratification to the mobile male who values time and efficiency (not unlike
his affection for the "fast-food" service establishment). The single
female clerical worker in Washington gives sexual vigor and the
bloom of youth to her political paramour, but derives value of different type in return. As one writer put it, "For some of them [the
females], an affair with a member of Congress—their employer or
someone else's—can become a sort of political and social status
symbol as well as a diversion."[667] The "casting-couch" approach to

stardom is not without promise. Even the swinger trades neurotic needs, psychological "hang-ups" and distorted fantasies with his advocational fellows, giving and receiving in kind. All such forms of extramarital sexual outlets obviously function to fulfill significant needs, even if socially perceived to be pathological, and because of this functionality, the participants and recipients do not always necessarily conceptualize themselves as deviant, much less criminal (adultery like prostitution is illegal in most states).[668] Institutionalized sexual arrangements such as prostitution may often endure harmoniously with both the business community and family, and wives, not infrequently are aware of, and tolerate, a mistress for reasons they deem rational and personally beneficial.

Prostitution, a historically institutionalized sexual exchange arrangement, has been labeled and sanctioned as deviancy, but has persisted in the face of social need for nonmarital sexual outlet. Prostitution has been functional in a variety of demographic and social contexts and continues to serve as a symbiotic, alternate sexual mechanism. The prostitute sells more than mere sexual gratification, and serves a variety of functions in providing her services; her own needs and rewards are far more complex than simply financial. The client, likewise, derives a complex set of non-sexual as well as sexual gratifications from his interactional encounters with the prostitute. Prostitution often involves an elaborate occupational network of supportive vocations, and the prostitute-client dyad, itself, with the complex interchange of rewards, gratifications, and interpretive meanings, represents a symbiotic relationship of rich emotionally charged and symbolic content. Even swingers are not necessarily sexual pariahs. Inasmuch as their occupational and social contributions may sometimes tend to balance out the stigma of their avocational sexual caprices, they too, may endure in the community symbiotically over time. Toleration is not normative acceptance, however, and regardless of the new frontiers of sexual permissiveness, and perhaps more particularly in terms of extra-marital sexual activity, sexual outlets, alternate to marital varieties, are still socially proscribed. Even if enforcement is less than vigorous, sanctions are seldom severe, or uniformly applied, nevertheless, the name, the fame, and the shame of social deviancy still apply.

Chapter 10

INAPPROPRIATE AGE AND KINSHIP IN SEXUAL PARTNERS

Sexual Deviancy in Disparate Context

George Peter Murdock, in his treatise, *Social Structure,* concluded that the selection of sexual and marriage partners in human societies is governed "in accordance with a limited number of fundamental criteria, some of them negative and some positive." These fundamental criteria are culturally derived and provide the basis for many of the prescriptive and proscriptive sexual norms operant in all societies. Murdock conceptualized these criteria as a series of continua of differential characteristics ranging from maximum attraction to maximum repulsion or least attraction. Each criterion is socially judged within a gradient framework. Sexual partners of inappropriate criteria or characteristics are accordingly viewed as undesirable or unacceptable and are often forbidden by social norm. Violation of such a norm represents a serious disruption of social equilibrium and may elicit severe sanctions. Inasmuch as norm violation of this variety involves sexual partners of distinctive dissimilarities to a degree of social unacceptability, it can be viewed as sexual deviancy in disparate context.

Among the laws of sexual choice, Murdock listed, THE NEGATIVE GRADIENT OF ETHNOCENTRISM with gradations ranging from the lower animals to persons with similar cultural differences. Even in relatively pluralistic societies such as our own, there are strong ethnocentric biases operating in defining socially acceptable sexual and marriage partners. Strong informal pressures may be brought to bear on individuals to avoid sex or marriage with persons of significantly different social class, ethnic, or other subcultural background. Marriage across religious lines, in some instances, may be discouraged and informally sanctioned. The most obvious example, however, of this principle of sexual avoidance in our society were the miscegenation laws of times past.[669] The violation of laws prohibiting inter-racial marriage were vigorously sanctioned and offenders often severely punished. The controversy about the equitability and morality of the miscegenation laws even provided the inspiration for two best-selling novels by well-known authors Pearl Buck and Sinclair Lewis.[670] Ultimately, the United States Supreme Court ruled that miscegenation laws were unconstitutional. Even today, however, in many instances there are strong informal pressures sometimes brought to bear on individuals in an effort to discourage inter-racial dating and mating, and where the residual informal norm is violated, some individuals experience strong social reactions including sanctions such as loss of job, ostracism by peers, rejection by family, or loss of some social privileges.[671]

Murdock also spoke of THE NEGATIVE GRADIENT OF EXOGAMY, which embraced the various incest taboos. This criteria of sexual avoidance will be discussed in detail later in the chapter. Additionally included as a principle of sexual avoidance is THE NEGATIVE GRADIENT OF ADULTERY, which more sternly opposes adulterous liaisons with spouses of kinsmen than with non-related persons. A fourth criteria of sexual avoidance is THE NEGATIVE GRADIENT OF HOMOSEXUALITY, which seeks to "confine marriage and sex relations to persons of complimentary sex," a topic which was addressed in an earlier chapter.

Other laws of sexual choice and avoidance include THE POSITIVE GRADIENT OF PROPINQUITY, which is based on the attraction of physical nearness and opportunity. Beyond this, Murdock speaks of THE POSITIVE GRADIENT OF KINSHIP which emphasizes the attraction of endogamous kinship unions where the incest taboos do not specifically prohibit them.

Finally, Murdock describes THE POSITIVE GRADIENT OF APPROPRIATE AGE. Basically, differences in age between sexual and marriage partners are to be minimized, with persons of the same generation being the preferred partners. Where one partner is older, this gradient encourages that it be the male rather than the female.

The principle of inappropriate age between sexual partners rendering the relationship deviant is constituent to various other types of sexual norms and is a seminal component in the interpretive context of sexual deviancy. Accordingly, inappropriate age is an important consideration in the social control of sexual behavior and merits detailed examination.

SOCIETY AND THE AGE OF SEXUAL CONSENT

Among the many aspects of sexual behavior subject everywhere to social normative control is the specification of appropriate age variation for sexual partners. Although there is clearly physiological rationale for proscribing sexual intercourse with persons below certain ages of genital maturity, many of the norms prescribing and regulating the age diversity in sexual partners are more social than physiological in rationale. Pre-pubescent females, for example, would seldom be able to genitally accommodate a mature male without possible anatomical harm, and, certainly, children of that age could not generally conceive or carry a baby to term. Similarly, pre-pubescent males would not normally be able to function effectively as a heterosexual partner. After the onset of puberty, however, young persons of both sexes are usually able to satisfactorily engage in sexual relations and to sire and bear healthy offspring (many medical authorities believe healthier babies result from parents older than barely past puberty).

In many societies, young people and especially females, can appropriately marry within a short time after reaching anatomical maturity. Even in our society in times past, and especially in rural and frontier areas, many females married in their early to middle teens (marriage as early as 13, although not common, was not viewed as aberrant). Nevertheless, in our society all states have legislated the age at which both male and females may marry and the age at which females may voluntarily engage in sexual relations with a male; these age limits are usually several years beyond puberty and anatomical maturity. The age at which young people can marry is, however, subject to variation from state to state and also is often different for males and females. Age variation may also be a function of whether the young people have their respective parents' permission and if the girl is pregnant.

The age requirements for marriage and for voluntary sexual

consent in females are not necessarily the same and are not legislated for the same intent. Minimal ages for marriage are presumably based on certain assumptions concerning the social maturity of the couple, their ability to effect a successful cohabitational union, and to be economically self-supporting. The age of marriage, not infrequently, approximates the age at which young people might be assumed to be concluding their basic educational experiences (high school or trade school) and, thus, ready to enter the job market. The age of sexual consent for females rests on other assumptions. Here, the concern is that a female below a certain chronological level of maturity may not necessarily be completely aware of the possible consequences and social importance of engaging in sexual intercourse. It has been traditionally assumed, (or at least, many lawmakers have so asserted), for example, that the immature female may not necessarily be aware of the dangers of venereal diseases or the possibility of anatomical discomfort or harm. Additionally, she may not fully understand the intricacies of conception, or the social consequences of pregnancy and bearing a child out of wedlock.

Perhaps the most quintessential assumption underlying the enactment and enforcement of statutory rape laws, however (regardless of how anacronistic such a supposition may have been rendered by contemporary norms of sexual permissiveness) is the belief that the immature female may not realize the full social importance of losing her virginal status in a society which has traditionally placed extremely high value on female chastity before marriage. As one judge has expressed it:

> ... The purpose of the lawmakers in its enactment (the law on age of sexual consent) is manifest. Experience has shown that girls under the age of sixteen, (the age of consent in that particular state) as the statute now reads, are not always able to resist temptation. They lack the discretion and firmness that comes with maturer years.[672]

STATUTORY RAPE

Interestingly, however, there is great diversity from state to state, in terms of legally conceptualizing the age at which this "discretion and firmness" appears. In Delaware until 1973, the age of consent was seven years old (this was changed to 16 in 1973). At the other end of the continuum, Tennessee places the age of consent at 21 under certain circumstances. In most of the other states, the age of consent generally varies between 12 and 16. In some of the states, the age of consent can, itself, vary based on such factors as previous unchastity. The act of sexual intercourse with a female below the age of consent constitutes statutory rape. Just as consent is legally immaterial, so, too, is the question of resistance on the part of the female. It is also immaterial inasmuch as it is held that "the law resists for her."[673] Because of the legal penalties attaching themselves to the act of sexual relations with an under-aged female, the euphemism of "San Quentin Quail" is often applied to girls below the legal age of sexual consent with whom some males have sexual relations. Although the prior unchastity of the girl can, in some states, have a bearing on the age of consent, in general, the sexually delinquent background of a female under the age of consent does not negate or dilute the crime of statutory rape. There have even been instances of individuals being sent to prison for having sexual intercourse with prostitutes who also happened to be below the legal age of sexual consent.[674] In some states, a female may legally marry at an age younger than that at which she may voluntarily consent to engage in sexual relations with a male.

Generally speaking, the age of consent laws were designed primarily to protect females, and they do, in fact, apply almost exclusively to females. There are some exceptions, however. In some U.S. jurisdictions, an adult female who uses enticement as a means of having sexual relations with a youth may be prosecuted for statutory rape. In the state of Colorado, for example, if an adult woman accomplishes sexual intercourse with a boy under the age of 18, by "solicitation, inducement, importuning or connivance," she may be charged with rape. Even a prostitute who sells her sexual services to a male under 18, may be charged with rape, if he was "of good moral character, prior and up to the time of the commission of the offense."[675] In some states, a boy under 14 is presumed to be physically incapable of committing rape, unless his "physical ability to accomplish penetration is proved as an independent fact and beyond a reasonable doubt."[676] In an interesting case in England several years ago, a female school teacher was accused of seducing and having a sexual affair with an 11-year-old school boy and was tried for the offense. The boy testified concerning their affair and offered "detailed descriptions of his young school teacher's body." The jury ultimately found the teacher innocent of sexual offenses but the judge "refused her costs, for he considered that she had brought the case on herself."[677]

The various statutory rape laws were originally legislated to protect young females (and in some instances young males) from sexual exploitation by carnally motivated males who would not honor the informal norms respecting the chastity of young unmarried females. Such laws were also designed to protect the young females from their own carnal curiosities, inclinations, and impulses. To avoid the prospect of illegitimate babies born to unmarried adolescents and children, and the possibility of young females being less matrimonially marketable because of lost virginity, the statutory rape laws tended to insulate them from the sexual advances of older males by making them legally and, thus, socially dangerous as a sexual partner. Perhaps allied to the statutory rape laws were the seduction and breach of promise laws of an earlier day (in some states such laws are still on the books). These laws were designed to protect the older (above the age of consent) unmarried females from sexual exploitation by carnally depredating males who might use romantic guile or even spurious promises of marriage as an inducement for sexual relations.

All of these laws suggested a strong social concern with protecting the unsophisticated and unmarried female against sexually predatory males, and in aiding unmarried females in maintaining their virginity until marriage. The effectiveness of such laws, including statutory rape laws, has tended to be eroded in recent decades by a number of factors including a generally more sexually permissive posture on the part of society, the social emancipation (or "liberation") including sexual emancipation of women, a significant decline in emphasis on and the value of female virginity at marriage, somewhat lesser importance placed on marriage itself, and the occurrence of courtship and marriage at an increasingly earlier age. Sexual permissiveness has encompassed even statutory rape.

The legal sanctions for statutory rape are usually quite severe. Penalties vary from state to state and, not infrequently, also vary depending on the age of the victim. In general, the older the victim, the less severe the penalty. In most states, long prison terms are often given to persons convicted of statutory rape. In some states, and especially where the victim is particularly young, under 14 or 12, for example, even where the consent of the female was obtained, the maximum punishment is death.[678]

In some juvenile court jurisdictions, cases of teenage girls below the age of consent who are caught having sexual intercourse with older boys or men, have become so common as to make conviction and the application of severe jail sentences to the offenders counter-productive. In one U.S. juvenile court jurisdiction, statutory rape with consenting females was quite common, and the judge accordingly relied on a relatively routinized process of criminal justice. The offender was given the opportunity to plead guilty (which they were usually delighted to do), and the judge would give them a suspended jail sentence, probation, and a $500 fine. The $500 then reverted back to the juvenile judge for use in improving the effectiveness of his various delinquency control programs. The female victim was then usually charged and convicted of sexual delinquency and either placed on probation, required to obtain psychiatric, or other therapeutic guidance, and in cases of repeated sexual delinquency, sometimes sentenced to a juvenile correctional institution.

The large number of teenage female runaways and "flower-children" roaming about the country, staying in "crash pads," living in communes, and often fornicating with various males has, perhaps, also impacted on the enforcement of statutory rape laws. In the face of this situation, and a generally greater degree of sexual experimentation at an earlier age among many adolescents of both sexes, the strict enforcement of statutory rape laws has been rendered less frequent and effective.

In this regard, the statutory rape laws are, in some states, precipitating an interesting transformation in social concern. Originally intended to punish adult males for having sexual relations with under-age girls, the statutory rape laws have more recently, not infrequently, indiscriminately attached to adolescent males who had voluntary sexual intercourse with a female of their own age level. With the increase in sexual activity among young people, and the increasingly lower age at which teenagers are engaging in sex, many young males are in violation of the statutory rape laws by having sex with their girlfriends. In this connection, it has been recently reported that "20 percent of 13-14 year-olds in the United States have had sexual intercourse."[679] Many a parent of a young female teenager, shocked and angered to discover that their daughter had engaged in sexual intercourse with a young boy, have been prone to push for prosecution of the boy for statutory rape, to the distress and dismay of the boy's parents.

There was enough concern about such a situation in New Jersey that two feminist groups in the state urged reform in the rape code including the section on statutory rape. They believed that the law should be brought "up to date with the sexual habits of teenagers."[680] The change in the law would help strengthen "protections for actual rape victims," by making it easier to obtain convictions. The reform would also "exempt consenting youngsters from statutory-rape charges—often brought by irate parents." As a leader of one of the women's groups seeking reform put it, "A rape prosecution is too high a price to pay for adolescent sexuality."[681] The New Jersey legislature changed the law and lowered the age of consent for sexual intercourse from 16 to 13, and additionally legalized sex between children even younger, "if there is less than four years difference in their ages."[682] There was an understandably very vocal negative reaction from many parents, teachers, and clergymen. The New Jersey legislature did restore the age of consent to 16, however, for instances of adult males and adolescent females but, in effect, kept the age of consent at 13 if the male were no more than four years older than the female (in fact even if the female were under 13, and the boy were less than four years older, there would still be no statutory rape offense).

It has been widely reported and recognized that sexual activity among young people is widespread and is occurring at an increasingly young age. Attendant to this sexual precociousness, female victims are not infrequently reluctant to testify or otherwise assist in the prosecution of statutory rape charges against their boyfriends. In view of the situation, and because of the publicity involved, parents are often less inclined to want to prosecute than in times past. Law enforcement officials and district attorneys are, in some instances, less inclined to want to push prosecution because of the difficulty in getting convictions and the generally mitigating circumstances extant today. Where sexual intercourse between a girl under the age of consent and an older boy results in pregnancy, the parents of the girl, and, indeed, the girl herself, may be more inclined to encourage marriage for the couple rather than push for prosecution of statutory rape. Interestingly, in some states (at least until a few years ago) the only way to obtain a legal abortion was in connection with rape. Thus, where the parents of a pregnant girl under the age of sexual consent did not wish to force the couple into marriage but, instead, wanted their daughter to have an abortion, it became necessary to charge the boy that impregnated the girl with statutory rape in order to have the district attorney authorize the abortion.[683]

Women, now, seek more independence, including sexual independence, and, thus, tend to eschew "protective" sexual laws which interfere with their perceived prerogatives. The double standard is rapidly being diluted in the wake of the current women's liberation movement and the absolute value placed on female virginity at marriage has increasingly become a matter of relative social toleration and personal indifference to many married couples. Seduction and breach of promise laws have long been outmoded in the face of women's ability to compete in the job market and to support themselves, not to mention females often opting to remain single as a means of pursuing a career. As young persons of both sexes continue in the trend toward sexual precociousness at an earlier age, and with increasing emphasis on women's sexual independence, the laws on sexual age of consent for them may undergo modification, and the stringent enforcement of statutory rape laws and the attendant severe penalties may well give way to a more flexible interpretation of the societal need to offer sexual protection to the socially inexperienced.

THE CHILD AS SEXUAL VICTIM

If there has been some softening in regard to the enforcement of statutory rape laws and some modest decline in social concern with sexually protecting the underage adolescent female, even against her own sexual persuasions, there has been little lessening of social concern with the child victim of rape and sexual abuse. Sexual crimes have undergone a dramatic increase in recent years. In 1972, for example, the reported figure of 46,430 forcible rapes, and 47,507 other additional types of sexual offenses represents a 70 percent increase since 1967.[684] A significant number of all sexual offenses are directed at children. In one large city, for example, 24 percent of all sexual assaults were on children under 14. Some estimates place the number of sexual assaults on female children from 4 to 14 years old at between 200,000 and 500,000 cases per year. There is reported to be an average of 5,000 cases of incest annually. Estimates of sexual assaults on male children are, for the most part, unavailable, but one report showed 30 boys receiving emergency room treatment for sexual assaults in one city.[685] It is entirely possible that many sexual assaults on children are never reported. Brant and Tisza, for example, in a study of child abuse based on pediatric emergency room records and on clinical experience in a children's hospital, suggest that only a small percentage of such cases are fully reported. Out of 56,000 emergency room cases involving children during their year of study, 52 instances of possible sexual abuse were found. Fewer than five of these, however, had been actually reported to the hospital child abuse team.[686] They also found that in approximately 25 percent of the cases, the attending professionals had not "considered the diagnosis of sexual abuse."[687] They suggested that sexual abuse is often a reflection of family pathology. Also, they found that sexually abused children "are at high risk for repeated misuse," and that "children of parents who were misused are at risk for sexual misuse."[688] Their findings also indicated that many of the sexual abuse cases "involve children in foster placement." In effect, the underreporting of sexual misuse cases involving children is the failure to recognize the constituent patterns involved and an unwillingness "to entertain the possibility that the situation may exist." As the researchers put it:

> . . . Social and cultural taboos and values, personal anxiety, and ignorance may contribute to failure to recognize these cases in emergency settings.[689]

This lack of reporting may be based on the fact that most sex offenses against children are committed by persons with whom they have had a relationship before the offense. Such persons may include family members or relatives, family friends, neighbors, or teachers. Many reported sexual assaults on children may not necessarily find their way into official data inasmuch as there is no central or national system for recording sexual offenses against children. Since children who are victims of sexual assaults may know the offenders well and enjoy a significant, if not an affectionate relationship with them, force and coercion may not necessarily be involved.

Not all child victims of sexual offenses are willing participants, however, nor do the children necessarily only suffer minimal harm. Many children are forcibly raped or otherwise sexually abused. In a study of rape in Denver, it was reported that 1 in 8 of the 200 victims studied were children under 15.[690] As victims of forcible rape or other sexual abuse, children may suffer significant physical damage including damage to the sex organs, hemorrhages, and general body damages such as bites, bruises, abrasions, lacerations, and broken bones. They may also become impregnated or contract venereal disease.[691] Children may also sustain considerable mental trauma as a result of being the victim of rape or other types of sexual assault. The trauma can result from the actual event itself and the fear and pain associated with it, or it may derive more from the subsequent events such as medical treatment or hospitalization, interaction with law enforcement officials, or from the concern and anxiety in the home itself. Inasmuch as the sexual offender may be a family member or friend, the child may experience trauma in connection with anxiety or guilt in connection with what happens to the offender and the subsequent impact on the relationship between the child and the perpetrator.

VICTIM PRECIPITATION IN SEXUAL OFFENSES AGAINST CHILDREN

As with other kinds of sexual offenses, child victims of rape and sexual assault are also not infrequently contributors to the crime and sometimes have a history of sexual precociousness. Various studies of the role of female victims in sex offenses have suggested that the children played a cooperative, if not contributive, part in the crime. In one study of almost 2,000 court cases, the victim was "non-objecting," and in another study of 73 court cases, 60 percent of the female children were "fully participating." Such victims have been described as "encouraging" the offender in between 66 to 95 percent of all sexual offenses. One study of 185 court cases even suggests that the female children may even be the "seducers" in the crime in a kind of Lolita fashion.[692] In one case reporting a man who was involved in a sexual relationship with his 10-year-old step-daughter, it appeared that the daughter had been having sexual relations with her step-father since she was seven and had been involved in sex play with him since age five. He was prosecuted and sent to prison for statutory rape. After six months he was released, returned home, and again began having sexual relations with his step-daughter. The girl had a history of sexual abuse in which she appeared to have been involved. At age five she accused an adult male cousin of sexually molesting her, and at seven accused a school janitor of doing the same. The janitor indicated that she had initiated the sexual activity by asking him to let her play with his genitals. Even when she was ultimately taken to a psychiatrist, the girl was "friendly and flirtatious" with him.[693]

In one study of 64 cases of pedophilia offenses in Finland, it was demonstrated that almost half of the cases involved precipitating behavior on the part of the victim. This precipitating behavior involved several patterns including the offender knowing the victim, the victim initially visiting the offender (sometimes even bringing along a playmate), and the victim taking "some kind of initiative in the offense itself." The offense was often linked with bribery, the victims "became the object of the offense more than once," and there were "often several victims."[694] Furthermore, there was no aggressive behavior linked to the victim-precipitated offenses. The children simply became willing and often eager, participants in their own sexual victimization. As the researcher describes it:

> ... the pedophilic situation (is). ... often such that both the offender and the victim meet on a plane of mutual understanding. On the child's part, it is unbounded sexual curiosity, which seeks support and satisfaction from adults. The offender, again, does not have to adapt himself to the level of a child, since his own mentality is already infantile.[695]

Some authorities have suggested that such children who cooperate with their sexual abusers may have acquired such a posture as part of their socialization process. It has been charged, for example, that some mothers encourage their young daughters to be "flirts" or to be "sexy." One mother was reported to have taught her six-year-old daughter to do a striptease act for company. Parents are also sometimes accused of not inculcating appropriate norms of modesty into their children and especially their female children. Parents are sometimes said to inadvertantly stimulate their children sexually, such as the mother who was reported to have warned her young daughter to "avoid men because of the sexual consequences." It has been suggested that such a warning was sexually stimulating inasmuch as it acquainted the child with "the possibility of sexual relationship with adult men." Even fathers roughhousing, wrestling, or fondling their daughters is said, in some instances, to stimulate the children sexually.[696]

INCEST AND UNDERAGE VICTIMS

The offense of sexual abuse, assault, or rape is often compounded by the charge of incest, which in this society is perhaps even more repugnant to the public sense of morality than is sexual abuse against children.

Incest is one of the most complex instances of deviant sexual behavior, in terms of social definition and context, and the proscriptive norms against such behavior are subject to elaborate social and cultural[697] variation. When the two are combined, public reaction is overwhelmingly and often violently negative. The attendant social sanctions are extremely severe. A case reported in 1968 in Oklahoma, for example, involved a middle-aged oil field worker and part-time pastor, who was convicted of raping his 15-year-old daughter. He was sentenced to 99 years imprisonment. A total of 10 members of the jury panel actually voted to give him the electric chair. Two years later his daughter confessed that she had lied about the rape because she was angry with her father because he had beaten her mother.[698] Although rape, in general, tends to elicit severe legal sanctions, rape of children and adolescent females is especially likely to result in harsh punishment. The average time served by federal and state prisoners, in one study, indicated that convicted rapists serve longer than men sentenced to prison for robbery, manslaughter, and aggravated assault—longer than any offense except murder. One man, convicted in Texas in 1969 for raping an 18-year-old high school girl, received a sentence of 800 years.[699]

The crime of incest, however, and especially where it involves forcible rape, or statutory rape, of an under-age daughter, is perhaps one of the most socially repulsive and condemned of all sexual offenses. Sometimes, however, the incestuous senario occurs only in the mind and fantasy of the presumed victim. Although actual incestuous involvement is somewhat more common than had been previously thought, some clinicians report that children not infrequently fantasize sexual molestation and incestuous encounters with parents.[700] The child may wish to "punish or torture a hated adult" and, thus, makes a false accusation. The child might be psychologically disturbed, unable to distinguish fantasy from reality, have "erroneously interpreted" a childhood fantasy as reality, "feel guilty for some matter unconnected with sex and use the accusation as a vehicle to express the guilt," or have simply experienced an "overstimulating"[701] family setting. In any event, the clinician or therapist can experience frustration and uncertainty in attempting to determine validity of a child's claim of incestuous sexual molestation. Such uncertainty in discriminating between fact and fantasy may well be one factor in minimizing the number of incest cases referred to legal authorities.

It has long been assumed that incest was a relatively infrequent mode of sexual deviancy in our society, and was largely confined to certain lower socio-economic portions of the population. There is some recent indication, however, that incest may well be somewhat more widespread than was formerly believed although accurate statistics on the incidence of incest are not available. Some current estimates would seem to be ridiculously high. At least one author, for example, has suggested that perhaps one in five women has been victimized by incest (this author also speaks of other estimates as high as one out of every three men and women).[702] Because of increased public awareness of the existence of incest and concern about the victimization of children, there has recently been a plethora of books on the subject.[703]

Although traditionally incest offenders have been subjected to extremely severe legal and social sanctions, more recently some researchers and therapists are calling for more of a medical or counseling response to incidences of incest. Giarretto, for example, argues for a "humanistic treatment" of father-daughter incest.[704] The punitive response to incest often destroys the family and does irreversible harm to the various family members. The father can be jailed and lose his job, the wife may be reduced to welfare, and the family's finances totally destroyed. Additionally, the entire family may experience social stigmatization and the rejection of friends and relatives. The daughter will likely experience trauma and guilt, and the wife may experience feelings of failure as a wife and mother, possibly jealously toward the daughter, and even guilt herself if she felt some contributory role. Instead, Giarretto urges a more constructive program that attempts to support the family, and through counseling and therapy sessions, have all of the family members achieve a more valid self-assessment of themselves and confront the family situations that may have precipitated the incest. The family can better come to grips with the fact that they all may have had some contributory part. Where the punitive response often tends to destroy the family, the humanistic approach attempts "to help the family reconstitute itself as quickly as possible, hopefully around the original nuclear pair."[705]

Other researchers have pointed out the "victim-perpetrator" model that has enjoyed wide acceptance in incest offenses is "too simplistic for the complex and distorted intrafamilial relationships seen in many cases of incest."[706] Furthermore, it is asserted that the application of this model "can lead to destructive rather than constructive interventions and to further victimization of the child by well-intentioned legal and social service personnel." The author goes on to write that in one mode of incest offense, "endogamic" incest as he terms it, the offense can be concealed over a long period of time;

thus, the offense can seem incongruous for the family. The parents in such families are "immature and their lives are filled with personal losses, actual and psychological."[707] Incest is tolerated over a period of time because all of the family members fear separation and incest is "tension-reducing."[708] Force is rarely used, and often the sexual abuse is protracted and progressive. The father may well be able to effectively rationalize his behavior, and display an interest in the child "not only as a sex object but also in other aspects of the child's life."[709] The child may be "seductive" and seek to gain the attention of grown-ups in ways that are sexually arousing. The child has learned to be "seductive" as a "means to obtain nurturance." Because of the child's affectional neglect and the interactive efforts of the child to be warmly involved with the father, there may be a predisposition to incest and the child can actually find the sexual behavior pleasurable, albeit with considerable ambivalence. At least the child assents to the sexual involvement because it is a " 'special activity' with an admired adult." Here, the therapist recommends that punitive legal intervention is not necessarily always the most effective approach. Rather, he encourages psycho-therapeutic intervention based on an "understanding of the family dynamics," inasmuch as, "endogamic incest is a victim-victim interaction and, as such, is an exploitative relationship."[710] Therapeutic intervention, he believes, "better recognizes the realities and meets the needs of incestuous children and parents."[711] Thus, even sexual offenses as traditionally and socially reprehensible as incest are being reconceptualized by some authorities as medical and psychiatric problems rather than as punishable crime.

Incest comes close to being the universal crime. With the exception of a few instances in the past where brother-sister marriage was mandated for the royal families of some of the dynasties of ancient Egypt,[712] and for a time among some of the royal families of Hawaii, incest is a universal taboo. The norms of sexual exogamy of which incest is the most explicit, is generally extended to kinsmen more distant than the nuclear family. It is subject to gradations of severity, however, and the closer the degree of kinship of the offenders, the more serious the offense. It is also usually considered more severe when there is a considerable disparity of age, and especially if the older participant is male. Thus, father-daughter incest is normally considered to be more reprehensible than brother-sister incest. Curiously, the literature on incest has tended to neglect the father-son incestual mode, presumably on the assumption that there was an extremely low incidence of such sexual deviancy. One set of researchers, however, take some issue with such a presumption and assert that ". . . it seems reasonable to expect that the frequency of father-son incest in the overall child psychiatric clinic population is higher than has been assumed."[713] They reported on cases of father-son incest in six families in which 10 sons were involved in an incestuous relationship with a natural father or step-father. The researchers reported that:

> The fathers generally had histories of alcoholism, sociopathy, or both. Four fathers were known to be violent and physically abusive with the children. They often had a history of poor judgment and impulse control. None was known to be homosexually involved with other than immediate family or close relatives.[714]

In several of the cases, the mother of the victimized child knew about the sexual abuse but was unable to do anything or protect the child. Unlike cases of father-daughter incest where the daughter ". . . often feels anger and resentment toward both parents, the father as perpetrator and the mother as nonprotector," the sons in these cases tended to express "intense negative feelings, even homocidal wishes, toward the father," but did not view the mother as a nonprotector.[715] In some of the cases, both male and female children were abused, but in the other families only the sons were the victims of the father's sexual abuse. The researchers admit that this is a small number of cases, but they believe that father-son incest "appears to be a more frequent clinical entity than was thought previously."[716]

Mother-son incest, however, may well have been the most reprehensible of all incestuous modes. Admittedly, it is relatively rare, or at least rarely reported. It does occur, however. Recently, for example, in Virginia, a 19-year-old marine and his 42-year-old mother were arrested and charged with incest.[717] The young marine and his mother had accomplished to obtain a license and had been married and were living together. The marine was also charged with sexual offenses against his four- and five-year-old half-sisters. The boy and his mother were found guilty of "unlawful marriage," a misdemeanor, and given suspended six-month jail sentences, but the judge also passed on evidence to a grand jury that might result in felony charges of incest. Subsequently, the couple was convicted of incest and both given five year prison terms, suspended on provision that they never see each other again. The young man was also discharged from the Marine Corps because of the conviction. Within a few weeks, the couple moved in together again and, later, warrants were issued for their arrest on charges of probation violation. The trial judge then revoked his suspension of their prison terms. They would be eligible for parole after serving a year to 15 months of their jail sentence.[718]

Brother-sister incest, although apparently relatively infrequent, has also surfaced in the national news in recent years. In 1979, in New England a brother and sister aged 22 and 24, respectively, separated since infancy, and raised by two different sets of adoptive parents, were reunited after many years, promptly fell in love, and subsequently got married to the consternation of both sets of adoptive parents and the real parents, all of whom became involved in the case. They were ultimately arrested and, in court, pleaded guilty to charges of incest. They were fined and placed on probation, and the man also received a suspended one-year jail sentence because of some other minor charges unrelated to the incest charge.[719] There have been some well-known individuals in history who allegedly were involved in incestuous relationships with their sisters, including Lord Byron and Wordsworth.[720]

Interestingly, at least one historian has asserted that in the nineteenth century there was a strong element of latent incestuousness involving the mother and her son in many families.[721] Furthermore, Strong contended that this latent incestuous attachment was encouraged. In that era, relations between husband and wife were strained, and sexuality was discouraged. Women, "turned to their children for the emotional satisfaction and sense of relation necessary for human existence."[722] The relationship between mother and son was warm and emotional with each holding idealized concepts of the other. As Strong describes it:

> There was an entirely different quality in the relations of the mother to her son which led, it appears, to an increased rather than decreased emotional, almost erotic, attachment of the son toward his mother as he grew older. This attachment may be described as latently incestuous, that is, it was an attachment that possessed markedly romantic and erotic components, although consciously it never was identified as incestuous or even tied to actual incestuous acts.[723]

This reciprocal romantic and even erotic relationship between mother and son was either not recognized for what it was, or was tolerated as harmless and not socially disruptive.

Although it has been demonstrated by Eva Seemanova, a Czechoslovakian researcher, that a child born of an incestuous union would stand a much enhanced probability of abnormality than one that was the product of a non-incestuous union, the proscription against incest appears to be universally based more on social considerations than biological ones.[724] In this connection, the rationale for the incest taboo is open to controversy from both psychiatric and anthropologic points of view. Without going into a detailed exposition of the intricacies of such explanations, it suffices to say that at an operational level, incest taboos apparently serve to "prevent disruptive sexual rivalry," or "role confusion within the nuclear family," or both, depending on the particular view of the theorist involved.[725] Regardless of the theoretical rationale, incest represents one of the most repugnant forms of crime and deviant behavior in our society. The social and legal sanctions attendant to incest are quite severe but in spite of the formal punishments and informal sentiments proscribing such behavior, violations of the norm do occur and with significant frequency. It has been estimated that more than 800,000 cases of incest have occurred over a 15-year period with perhaps a quarter of these being instances of father-daughter incest.[726] Incest is considered to be such a socially and psychologically pathological act that many often consider the perpetrator, if not the victim, as both being mentally disturbed or deficient, and certainly the stereotype of incestuous persons is not infrequently that of "degenerate" hill people. Incest does, in fact, frequently attract a psychiatrically as well as sociologically pathological label. A father who commits incest with a daughter is guilty of a variety of norms, legal and social. He would have committed adultery, fornication, incest, and usually statutory rape. He would be considered a sexual degenerate and guilty of the sexual exploitation of children. Additionally, he would be a failure in discharging his role as protector of his family and especially his children. It is interesting to note that some of the most derisive profanity in our language makes reference to incest participants.

Incest also carries an additional sanction in the form of the burden of religious guilt which many offenders experience. According to inmate informants of mine, when incest offenders are convicted and sent to prison, the inmates can usually recognize them because these "fish," as new inmates are known, invariably carry a Bible.

Father-daughter incest has received considerable attention in the clinical and criminological literature.[727] In one such study based on case materials of 27 incest offenders, the men studied did not appear to be "degenerate."[728] They were generally of normal intelligence, had made "an acceptable occupational and social adjustment" prior to the offense, and had no record of adult sexual perversion. They were not seen as "conspicuously promiscuous." In these cases, incest seemed to have been precipitated by a variety of situational factors. Father-daughter incest seems to be especially prone when the father is approaching middle age and when the daughter is an adolescent. This is not infrequently a period of considerable marital stress for such men. Additional stress factors may intrude such as marital disharmony resulting in the wife adopting a sexually withholding or hostile posture, the death of the wife, or some other disruptive contingency. In such situations, the father may seek the emotional response and support of the daughter, or the daughter may have to assume many of the mother's family responsibilities, if not role. The father may even see in the daughter a reflection of the wife at a younger age, and, thus, substitute the daughter for the wife who is either dead or has rebuffed him. The father becomes the sexual partner of the substituted daughter and may prevent her from dating young men because of his own jealousy. The daughter can, at least at first, be a willing participant in the incestuous activity, either because she is flattered by the father's sexual attention and enjoys succeeding in a kind of rivalry with her mother, or because she simply feels obligated to accede to her father's wishes due to fear, respect, affection, or other reasons. The daughter can, in time, however, rebel and expose the incestuous relationship. The mother, who has, in effect, been transformed into a menacing mother, can also rebel and expose the incest. The offending father may have effectively been able to rationalize his sexual deviancy by blaming his wife's inadequacies or deficiencies in discharging her marital and familial responsibilities or her sexual aloofness. The entire incestuous scenario must be viewed as inappropriate family role behavior, and the situational elements facilitative to incest would seem to be obvious.[729]

The insecure father reaches middle age and experiences stress and anxiety because of his age and his unsupportive spouse. As his daughter reaches adolescence and develops a youthful attractiveness, his stress can be even reinforced. In some instances, the husband may seek a sexual affair with a young woman outside of marriage. In other cases, especially if the wife is dead, absent, or totally neglectful of him, he may even vicariously "court" his daughter, seeking his lost youth, and, in time, actually initiate a sexual relationship with her. At this point, the father may be playing the conflicting roles of sexual suitor and protective father. The daughter, who may enjoy the rivalry with the mother, may have assumed a seductive or provocative role stance toward the father. The mother, refusing to accept the fact that she has been bested in a sexual rivalry with her daughter or hoping for a reconciliation, if not to actually win back the husband's affection, or perhaps fearful of the social and economic import of exposing her husband's behavior, may not admit the incestuous relationship to others or to herself. She may be indifferent or even help to conceal it for a period of time. For a variety of reasons, incest may be more tolerated within a family unit, at least for a time, than it is by the public outside the family.

Incest, in general, appears to be somewhat more prevalent in lower or lower-middle class families than among persons of relatively higher socioeconomic status. Perhaps the husbands are better equipped to handle stress and anxieties brought on by middle age or family disequilibrium, or at least, they are better able to direct their frustrations into more socially acceptable sexual channels. The middle and upper-class wives are also probably more financially and socially secure, and, thus, less inclined to tolerate incestuous behavior between husband and daughter, or to permit the familial circumstances that might precipitate or facilitate incest. Incest does occur within all socioeconomic status levels, and often with devastating results for intrafamilial relationships and for the participants in terms of psychological and social costs and legal sanction. Even with today's much liberalized social views on sexual activity and social control, incest does not appear to have been viewed within any more permissive context than in the past. In the final analysis, incest represents an inappropriate system of triadic role interaction that is dysfunctional to the family, and pathological in configuration; it is usually conceptualized as social deviancy of the most reprehensible nature.

PEDOPHILIA

Incest offenders are generally considered to be among the most "degenerate" and lascivious of all sexual deviants, even more so than the rapist. But they would, however, appear to share this unenviable status with the child molester and pedophiles. Sexual offenses against children vary greatly in terms of motivation, etiology, and nature of the actual offense perpetrated. In one study of sex offenses against children aged five or less, it appeared that the great majority of the offenses were directed against female children.[730] Of the 60 male offenders studied in this project, about one half had experienced a home broken by divorce, separation, or death of a parent early in life. Additionally, the men reported that they enjoyed "rather poor relations with surviving or original parents." Most of these sexual offenders had a history of sexual play in childhood. Close to 70 percent had engaged in sexual play as children, with other children or in the case of 23 percent of them, with adult males. These men were also found to have been members of "antisexual fundamentalists sects." Contrary to popular belief, these sexual offenders were not "senile deteriorated" men, but for the most part, were relatively youthful, with a median age of 27. Furthermore, the majority of the married offenders had children (some of these men had committed sexual offenses against their own children). This group of sexual offenders had a relatively high percentage (57 percent) of individuals who had experienced homosexual activity after puberty. They also had a relatively high (22 percent) incidence of post-pubertal sexual contact with animals. The offenders, as compared with other control groups, had a higher percentage of men who had engaged in cunnilingus, and anal coitus with both females and males. In general, these men had experienced 43 percent less premarital coitus than is usual for men of their socio-economic background and age group, indicating, perhaps, some difficulty in working out an adequate heterosexual adjustment with adult females. It also suggests an "undeveloped heterosexual premarital experience." This conclusion is supported by the fact that a significant number of the group had never married and a number of others had experienced divorce and multiple marriage.

The child offenders in this study were generally under-educated with 60 percent having not gone beyond grammar school. More than two-thirds of the group were unskilled and semi-skilled workers. Of the men, 12 percent were feeble-minded and another 32 percent rated below the category of average intelligence. There appeared to be a compulsive element in the pattern of these sex offenders in that there was frequently a history of repeated sexual offenses against children. Furthermore, the majority of the offenses were committed while sober, suggesting that there was not a factor of "periodic alcoholic breakdown of impulse control." As is frequently the case with child molesters, there was a strong tendency to deny or partially deny the offense, or to at least minimize the character of the event. Where it was admitted, there was often a lack of "logical coherence," such as the comments of one offender who said, "I didn't do it and besides she was big for her age."[731]

From the study, the researchers were able to articulate four general categories of child-offenders. These include those men who may, or may not, prefer children as sexual partners, but do have a history of repeated sexual activity with children. A second category is that of mental defectives who are generally incapable of "developing any adequate sociosexual relationship with adults." A third category is composed of those offenders who appear to be "sociosexually underdeveloped." In effect, their lack of sexual sophistication makes them failures in their interaction with adult females, and, thus, they turn to children as a last resort. Finally, there are those offenders who appear to have sexually molested children as a result of severe alcoholic involvement. As the researchers put it, "The alcohol seemed to release potentials which were not readily apparent in their prior behavior."[732] There are instances of adolescents engaging in acts of child molestation or sexual abuse of younger adolescents.[733] Presumably, such individuals would be most similar to the third category of offenders.

Other authorities on the topic of child molesting have suggested other categories of offenders.[734] McCaghy has suggested that such offenders can be differentiated into categories based on certain "offense-situational" factors. He mentions, for example, incestuous molesters, who may engage in initial "caressing contacts" with blood relatives, usually female, living in the same home, and subsequently move on to genital-genital, and oral-genital contacts. McCaghy believes that alcohol may often be involved in such cases. He also describes molesters who work with children. These are often middle-class individuals who are employed in "child-centered" occupations or volunteer activities, and, thus, have a wide range of exposure to children and an opportunity structure for sexual offenses. Such offenders, he believes, may often be homosexual offenders, and/or may have an affectionate or "love relationship" with the child. Another type of offender is the asocial molester who may have a criminal record of non-sexual offenses, and who has "little compunction over violating the law regarding either sexual or nonsexual conduct." Molesting incidents are likely to be "opportunistic and spontaneous," and, not infrequently, alcohol-induced. Such offenses are seldom serious, and not likely to be repeated.

Also mentioned by McCaghy is the aged molester who is in some way similar to the child-centered molesters who work with their victims, in that the children victims are often passive or cooperative, and there may be an affectional relationship between the two. The aged molester is usually retired from an unskilled or semi-skilled job, and there may be a biological factor such as impotency or brain deterioration. In most cases, however, the individual has few adult friends and simply comes to identify closely with the children he sees on a frequent basis. The career molester perhaps comes closer to fitting the stereotype of the child sexual offender than do the other types. There is usually a record of repeated molesting charges, and the child victims are usually strangers to the offender. Such persons may have both homosexual and heterosexual contacts with children with the actual sexual acts committed usually being oral-genital contacts as opposed to simple petting or fondling. Such individuals are usually able to ingratiate themselves with the children through gifts, or perhaps with a pet such as a puppy or monkey. Such a person usually only seeks sexual gratification and no other interest, affectionate or otherwise, in children. Finally, McCaghy writes of the spontaneous-aggressive molester where the offense includes violence. The victims are usually strangers, and there is seldom any attempt at persuasion or at soliciting cooperation. The offender simply forcibly seizes the child, perhaps abducting it in an automobile, and physically makes the child participate in the offense. Not infrequently the sexual offense includes attempted coitus. The offender simply treats the child as an adult and tends to disregard the age of the victim. One offender questioned by McCaghy about his crime simply said, "I saw her walking alone on the street late at night. It was late and she was alone. It wouldn't have made any difference what age she was."[735] The stereotype of the pedophile may be that of a retarded or infantile, lower-class male but in actuality, pedophilic tendencies have been known to occur with males of all walks of life, including celebrities. Many famous persons married teenage wives, and many have been romantically involved with young girls.[736] When Errol Flynn died, "his constant companion was a girl of 17"(p.248). John Ruskin, the English writer, was reported to have fallen in love with a 10-year-old, and Edgar Allen Poe married his 14-year-old first cousin. More recently, Polish movie producer, Roman Polanski, pleaded guilty to seducing a 13-year-old girl. The pedophilic episode can be viewed as a "surrogate activity" or a result of stress. One study, however, demonstrated that a number of normal males were sexually aroused by photographs of nude six- to eight-year-old girls. The Lolita complex may be more widespread than one is led to believe.

Perhaps because the public reaction to child molesting is so negative and the legal sanctions so severe, many offenders when apprehended, are reluctant to accept and admit the deviant label. It may also be that the repulsive and degenerate image of the perpetrator of sexual offenses against children is simply so socially repugnant that the offender himself, may be unwilling to incorporate it into his own self-image. There is, for example, a case of a defendant in Wisconsin who entered a store and attempted to rape an underage female at knifepoint. Failing in the attempt, he took some money and goods and left. Unwilling to be branded with the label attendant to attempted rape on an underaged female, he instead bargained to plead guilty to the crime of armed robbery, which had a longer prison term as punishment.[737] McCaghy, who has studied child molesters and their own explanations for their offenses, has reported a tendency on the part of these individuals to deny the crime, to ascribe their behavior to alcohol, and to dissociate themselves from others who molest children.[738] The label "child molester" is apparently sufficiently threatening to the self-identity of men that they attempted to cope with the situation through a process of "deviance disavowal." The label is an uncomfortable one. As McCaghy points out:

> Regardless of a child's seductiveness, aggressiveness, worldliness, or wile, an adult who performs any sexual act with the child is without recourse before the law.[739]

Such an offender, in the eyes of the public and the law, is a criminal, and likely a "psychopath," if not "sex fiend," for according to community values, child molesting is deviant behavior, for which no "rational man has an excuse." Faced with the stigma of having committed a reprehensible crime that is socially "inexcusable," the offender must cope with his label and rationalize or explain his behavior. In this regard, the individual may use excuses ranging from "frigid wives" to "torrid children." Some simply deny the offense as a means of maintaining an image as "normal." Many child molesters, however, incorporate drinking into their explanation and attempt to suggest an involuntary loss of control in connection with the offense. Interestingly, McCaghy also found that those offenders denying the crime, and those who relied on alcohol as an excuse, were more likely to be negative and derogatory in their opinions of other child molesters, and more severe in their condemnation of such offenders.[740] These findings suggest that their efforts at deviancy disavowal are at least partially effective, at least in the sense of their ability to successfully rationalize their behavior to themselves as largely the result of their drinking, if they, in fact, even admit their offense to themselves.

Not all child molesters, however, appear to reject the label. One study of a group of pedophiles in Europe was based on the responses of persons with a sexual preference for children, who were attending a conference on sexual reform.[741] The results of the study suggested that these individuals are generally young for the most part, unmarried, and have a level of education higher than that of the average population. They became aware of their pedophilia at an early age and had their first pedophile contacts in the same period. They expressed preference for boys and girls of certain age ranges, and the majority were involved in a pedophile relationship at the time of the study. Close to one half of the group had been apprehended and sentenced, and more than one third had voluntarily started psychiatric treatment (perhaps as part of a sentence). Interestingly, the researcher found that "very few want to get rid of their pedophilia."[742]

AGING AND SEXUAL OFFENSES

Older persons, according to Bernard, are often "emotionally isolated and regressed." They may seek affection and response from younger persons. Older females may be able to hug and fondle children because it is more "natural" for them to do so. For the older male, however, there is the likelihood of being labeled as a child molester in a similar situation. Organic brain disorders, senility, or even absentmindedness may cause elderly men to be less socially conscious of social proprieties and expected behavior. A failure to remember to zip one's fly after urination, for example, might, in some instances, be conceptualized as exhibitionism.

There is evidence of prejudicial attitudes toward older people in our society, and in connection with these attitudes is a tendency, perhaps, to overreact to the older person's deviancy. This appears to be especially the case of unnatural sexual acts committed by elderly men. The geriatric sex offender is particularly offensive to societal standards of morality and proprietous sexual behavior, and, thus, becomes the "dirty old man" stereotype. The public reaction to such private patterns of sexual deviancy committed by the elderly, often "exceeds that evoked by, say, a similar act by a younger person."[743] The elderly person, then, can become a sexual offender as much by virtue of disparate age as by sexual act. In this connection, it appears that some older men are especially vulnerable to charges of sexual deviancy because of the public predisposition to judge the sexual impulse in the elderly as deviant. As Whiskin phrased it in an article dealing with sexual deviancy among the elderly:

> Most curious, however, is the general public's belief that older persons do not have sexual desires or needs for sexual expression or, if they do, it is improper for them to do anything about it. It seems that any evidence of sexual activity in older persons is considered abnormal, or, at least, inappropriate.[744]

VICARIOUS PEDOPHILIA

The number of persons with sexual preferences for children, even if not actually implemented, must be large in view of burgeoning market for "kiddy-porn"—pornography featuring youngsters engaged in sexual behavior with other children or with adults. Examples range from periodicals like *Lollitots,* that feature preteen girls showing off their genitals in pinup pictures, to 8-mm films depicting a 10-year-old girl and her 8-year-old brother engaged in fellation and intercourse. The variety of sexual activity featured in such "kiddy-porn" encompasses a wide array of carnal appetites as suggested by the titles of some other periodicals in the field—*Naughty Horny Imps, Children-Love,* and *Child Discipline.*[745] There are child porn periodicals and films for persons of wide sexual taste. *Young Stud* or *Chicken Supreme,* for example, depict young boys masturbating or engaging in homosexual acts. Films like *Children Love,* on the other hand, feature boys and girls having sex with each other, or those like *Young Lolitas* or *Youthful Lust* show 6- to 11-year-old girls having oral sex with adults of both sexes. Police in Los Angeles estimated that in 1976, 30,000 children in that city alone were sexually exploited by adults for pornography purposes.[746] Recently, even physical violence to children is appearing as a theme in the child-porn media. It has been reported that various underground sex magazines are "heavily stressing incest and pedophilia," and there have been a number of arrests around the country of persons involved in recruiting children into pornography work, for producing the pornography, and for sexually exploiting the children they recruited.[747]

COMMERCIALIZED JUVENILE SEX

Disparate age as a factor in sexual deviance, also manifests itself in commercial configurations. In a heavily economically-oriented society, it is not surprising that sexual gratification is a commodity that can be bought and sold like other products. Even though historically (and into the contemporary period) there has been very strong religious and social opposition to prostitution, and vigorous legal (and extra-legal) efforts to extirpate the practice, such opposition has been far from successful. In spite of efforts to the contrary, prostitution has persisted, and even flourished, in some contexts. This has been facilitated, in some instances, by political corruption, ineffective law enforcement, and the belief among some segments of the public that prostitution is functional and, therefore, a necessary evil. Such contributing factors and values would seem to suggest that our society has had a significant toleration for prostitution in its myriad forms, or at least a singular lack of complete effectiveness in controlling or minimizing it, much less suppressing it.

It appears, however, that prostitution is not always confined to the adult ranks, and when it occurs among those of age categories that are culturally supposed to be sexless, it is often a traumatic revelation for the public. As Whiskin has pointed out in his article, there are instances of innovative sexual entrepreneurship even among very young children. He speaks, for example, of a " 'ring' of 7- to 10-year-old girls who made a considerable amount of money from older men whom they allowed certain liberties for a fee of 25 cents." Sexual activity of the wildest possible variety is known to occur with some relatively young persons, and some children are quite sexually precocious at an extremely early age. As brought out earlier in this discussion, in instances of sexual offenses against children, the children themselves are not infrequently cooperative participants, if not the seductive initiators of the sexual activity. Some children are, in effect, starved for affection and to obtain it will sometimes allow an adult to engage in sexual activity with them, as a means of obtaining it. Seductiveness becomes an easily acquired talent for children where the motivation is great. Beigel, for example, has written:

> They (children) soon learn how to turn on the charm to signal their readiness to a potential seducer. In truth, they go about seducing their seducers.[748]

For some children who are prepared to exchange sexual favors for affection and emotional response, the transition to exchanging sex for money is not great. The runaway adolescent, unhappy in an emotionally barren home situation, may run away, and, perhaps be befriended by those who first provide the food and shelter, along with the affective response and support she seeks. In due time, however, the new friend may extract his price in the form of coercing the girl into selling sexual services, and turning over her income to him.[749] In our society, the pimp is more detested than the whore because of the exploitative nature of his parasitic existence.

Particularly repugnant to the general norms of community morality are those persons who financially exploit the sexual favors of children. In this regard, however, child prostitution is by no means uncommon in contemporary American society and may well be on the increase, in addition to assuming new configurations such as male children taking up careers selling sexual services. A recently published overview of this problem points out that there are child prostitutes of both sexes in our society, most of whom have been coerced by adults, sometimes even parents, into their carnal livelihood.[750] The wide-spread existence of child prostitution is suggested by the emergence of slang words for such children, "baby pros" for female prostitutes, and "chickens" for male prostitutes.[751] For those of more catholic sexual persuasion, the younger purveyors of sex are particularly tempting, but the risks are high inasmuch as society often reacts in a most negative fashion to even consensual sex involving children, regardless of whether it is bought and paid for. Still, where there is demand, there is supply, regardless of risk, and the "baby pros" and "chickens" will undoubtedly continue to be made available to those of debauched sexual appetite, in the face of public indignation and severe social sanction. Relatively unknown to the public in general, child prostitution, because of the tabooed disparate age context, represents sexual deviancy of a particularly condemned variety.

Disparate Age in Heterosexual Dyads

The violation of social norms proscribing sexual activity between persons of disparate ages encompasses more than statutory rape and child molesting. At an informal level, at least, even the marriage or voluntary sexual relations between two adult persons of great age difference may evoke criticism, if not stronger sanctions. When the late Justice Douglas of the U.S. Supreme Court married again after several former marriages and divorces to a woman in her early 20s, he was subject to severe public criticism. This included an attack from the then Congressional Minority Leader, Gerald Ford, who proposed impeachment for Justice Douglas. Other members of Congress, including Robert Dole, charged that Douglas had used "bad judgment," and Colorado Congressman Byron Rogers suggested that Douglas should be "retired under a law allowing for the removal of a judge 'permanently disabled from performing his duties.'"

In France several years ago, a 30-year-old teacher was brought to trial for having an affair with a 16-year-old student. She subsequently committed suicide because of the condemnation.[752] Several years ago, a 29-year-old school art teacher in New York married one of her students, an 18-year-old, two months after he graduated. She was subsequently suspended by the school board who, "found fault with her association with the student prior to his graduation" and other assorted minor complaints. She later sued the school board because of her suspension, and ultimately accepted a settlement for dropping her lawsuit.[753] Movie stars, politicians, and celebrities, who not infrequently marry or have affairs with persons outside of their immediate age range, are often the targets of public ridicule and scorn. In many instances, both parties to the marriage or sexual affairs are subject to deviant labeling. If the man is much older than the female, he may be called "an old fool," "dirty old man," or even "sexual degenerate." The woman may be accused of being an opportunist, "gold digger," or even a prostitute. If the female is much older than the man, she may be accused of "robbing the cradle" or being some kind of sexual deviant herself. The male, in turn, may be called a gigolo, a person trying to "use" the older woman to some personal advantage, or accused of having perverted tastes. Underlying such labeling is the assumption that there are upper and lower (especially upper) age limits on sexuality. The very young, and the very old are simply assumed to be "sexless" or at least assumed that they are expected to be so.

It is difficult for the public to accept the idea of an older person having any sexual attractiveness for a much younger person and even for the older person to have sufficient sexual motivation so as to seek out younger partners. One interesting such incident was a news report about a 21-year-old California man who announced that he was planning to marry his 77-year-old step-grandmother (his father's widowed stepmother). He contended that, "When there is deep love there is no need for sex." Although such a marriage was legal inasmuch as the pair were not blood relatives, they were no doubt greeted with considerable social derision, if not scorn, and probably assumed to be mentally deranged.[754] When two adult persons of disparate age do engage in sexual activities, within marriage or otherwise, society is often dubious of the manifest sexual motivation and tend to view such sexual dyads as being inappropriate, if not perverted.

SUMMARY

Although society retains much of its traditional posture of chivalrous protection of the young, unmarried female and continues to retain, in most states, laws specifying an appropriate "age of consent" for coital activity for them, replete with severe sanctions for males who violate the statute, it has become increasingly ineffective in accomplishing the aim of such legal efforts. It may well be that statutory rape laws have become as anachronistic as some of the other long-standing social proscriptions of sexual behavior. Statutory rape laws were never completely effective in earlier periods. As previously pointed out in the discussion, there was great variation in the legally prescribed age of sexual consent from state to state, ranging from seven in Delaware to 21 in Tennessee. Even among those states with more rational age requirements, the actual age requirements varied from 12 to 16. Various states made allowances for certain exceptions to these age specifications, depending on certain circumstances. Thus, there was no uniform presence of the law on such uniformity, neither was the original purpose completely accomplished nor was justice necessarily served. Again, as pointed out earlier, there have been instances of adolescent males being convicted of statutory rape for having had sexual intercourse with sexually experienced women several years older, but still under the legal age of consent. There have even been cases of statutory rape convictions where the under-age woman was a prostitute. In the face of such legal incongruencies, many judges have simply employed various subversions of the statutory rape laws to effect justice but retain the socially intended protection of such laws. The events and trends of recent years, however, have tended to erode the original purpose of statutory rape laws.

For a number of years, the average age of marriage for both males and females has been dropping. Concomitantly, the age of courtship and dating and sexual experimentation has likewise been dropping. Children and adolescents of both sexes have increasingly become sexually precocious at an earlier age. The sexual revolution of recent decades has had its impact on teenage culture. Sexual activity, even to the extent of actual coitus, is increasingly becoming the rule rather than the exception. A study conducted several years ago by Planned Parenthood Federation of America estimated that by 1974 more than half of the nation's 11 million women between the ages of 15 to 19 had had sexual intercourse. The study also revealed that one million teenage women become pregnant each year, and that this group accounts for 20 percent of all the births in this country. More than 30,000 unmarried girls under the age of 14 become pregnant every year.[755] In the face of such widespread sexual activity among young females, the vigorous and relentless enforcement of statutory rape laws would be dysfunctional in that it would result in the arrest, conviction, and criminally stigmatizing of a substantial segment of American male youth. Some states, sensitive to this problem and the handicap it imposes in enforcing the intent of the statutory rape law, have moved to make the age of the male offender a consideration, and, thus, exempt teenage males. In New York, for example, the statutory rape law has been amended "by stating that no male under 21 years of age could be indicted or convicted for statutory rape."[756] A few other states also take the age of an offender into account. In all likelihood, other states will join New York in modifying their statutory rape laws to exempt teenage males, in effect, as a means of decriminalizing the relatively endemic sexual activity among young people today.

Statutory rape laws, even as they are only applied to adults, however, are not without problems of enforcement. The counterculture of the late 1960s and 1970s had its wandering hippies, flower children, and countless runaways. From this mass of socially and geographically displaced young people came the so-called street girls —teenage drifters that wandered the streets looking for a man to take them in for the night and ready to exchange sex for bed and a meal.[757] The number of such vagrant females, often under the age of legal sexual consent, was, and is, substantial. Since the girls generally interacted with adult males, either in an actual prostitution relationship, or on a temporary "shack-up" basis, such activity clearly represents a violation of the letter and spirit of the statutory rape law. Conviction is difficult, however, since the girls are cut off from family and friends, and there is seldom anyone to make a complaint. The girls, themselves, wish to avoid legal entanglements, inasmuch as the arrest of their sexual partners might mean their own incarceration, or being returned to the home from which they ran away. The girls, if deprived of their pandering sexual relationships with men, would be hard pressed to economically survive. Law enforcement agencies have often been reluctant to arrest and convict for these reasons and for the additional concern that a staggering number of males, who would have to be arrested and convicted, would over-load the courts and jails. Furthermore, given the promiscuous background and socially disreputable lifestyle of the girls, convictions would be more difficult to obtain. Even in instances where street girls have actually been raped, they have been reluctant to report it because of fear of their own arrest and/or being returned home. In spite of the tender age of the girls, forceful rape convictions are difficult because of their unsavory history. In effect, such females have become a kind of social junk, and given their socially viewed sexual immorality, have, in effect, not been seen worthy of having their virtue protected since they have been perceived as having none. Statutory rape convictions would simply be too costly to the social equilibrium in the long run, in proportion to such social good as might be accomplished.

In the future, the number of runaways and vagrant youth is not likely to diminish significantly, even though the hippie counterculture may be fading away as a discernable entity. The divorce rate, the large number of broken homes, the difficult job market, increasing stress and disequilibrium in the home, and other societal conditions and trends may all contribute to an increase in "street-girls" in the future. Given the large number of such socially detached promiscuous females in the community, and the equally large number of sexually active females still living within the framework of a family, it is most unlikely that a statutory rape law can remain a viable and effective social proscription.

Many young people, and especially females, are quite vocal in their demands for freedom and independence. Many states have already lowered the age at which young people are accorded adult status to 18. There will likely be strong pressures in the years ahead to lower the age still further, perhaps to 17 or even 16. Since a number of young people are actually on their own by the age of 14 or 15, there are even suggestions that the law should offer legal emancipation and adult status on the circumstances involved (which it does only on rare occasions at this time). The women's liberation movement, the general tendency for females to seek more independence, and even the ERA amendment if passed, may all well have an impact on the concept of the legal age of sexual consent for females. Inasmuch as one of the traditional rationales for sexually protecting young females was the concern with unwanted pregnancies, further improvements in the effectiveness of contraceptive techniques can ultimately remove such concern if the young women can be educated and convinced to use them regularly. Overall, it would appear that young people will increasingly demand and obtain more control over their own lifestyles and personal persuasions. Females will similarly demand and obtain less protection, which is often seen as stifling oppression and independence. Young people are becoming, and will continue to become, more carnally precocious and sexually active. More states will have to modify their statutory rape laws to avoid criminalizing their adolescent males in a discriminatory fashion, and to respond to changes in the social context of youthful sexuality. Similarly, statutory rape laws may also have to be significantly modified or weakened inasmuch as increased sexual activity among the young may also likely involve adults. Statutory rape laws will simply continue to have their functionality eroded, and may become even more dysfunctional in some instances. Ultimately, statutory rape laws may well be lowered to 12 or even younger. In the final analysis, the sexual freedom and sensate quest for carnality of today and tomorrow is, and will continue, to render obsolete old sexual proscriptions and engender new levels of sexual permissiveness. Where sexual virtue has been diluted and, thus, offers little to protect, and the young females increasingly do not cooperate in their own protection, and where the enormity of the task of protecting becomes legally and socially unmanageable, social proscription in regard to such carnal behavior becomes incongruous, if not anachronistic in social context. Such is the prognosis of statutory rape laws.

Because of the extremely abhorrent and pathological way in which incestuous sexual behavior has traditionally been viewed, it would perhaps be logical to anticipate the most minimal shift in social posture in regard to such behavior. There are some recent indications, however, that social proscriptions toward incest may be in the process of being diluted slightly, and the next few years may possibly see some efforts in the direction of "decriminalizing" incest. Certainly, there would appear to be a somewhat more relaxed public stance toward incest than in times past, and where it once carried the ultimate sexual taboo, extending even to discussion of it, there would recently appear to be a somewhat greater degree of tolerance of incest itself. Accounts of incest have become popular entertainment fare, and it is often discussed openly. Sentences for incest would seem in some instances, to be somewhat milder than in the past, and judges not infrequently, are more prone to treat it as a psychiatric problem requiring therapy, rather than a criminal problem requiring punishment. In the area of entertainment, there has been a recent book, that details brother-sister incest, (*Blood Summer* by Don Asher, Putnam), and a prime time, made-for-TV movie, portraying mother-son incest (*Flesh and Blood*), as does another recent film (*Luna*). In the 1920s, there were only six movies about incest; in the 1960s there were 79. Incest is becoming an engaging dramatic theme in modern media.[758]

Furthermore, some authorities are coming out against the public condemnation of incest. Wardell Pomeroy, of the Kinsey research team, has been reported as observing, "Incest between . . . children and adults can sometimes be beneficial." Seymour Parker, an anthropologist at the University of Utah, has been quoted as saying:

> It is questionable if the cost (of the incest taboo) in guilt and uneasy distancing between intimates are necessary or desirable. What are the benefits of linking a mist of discomfort to the spontaneous warmth of the affectionate kiss and touch between family members?[759]

Recently, the *Siecus Report* carried as a lead article, a polemic in favor of incest. The author, in effect, contended that the incest taboo is outdated, and likened contemporary concern with incest to a fear of masturbation a century ago. The article suggests that incestuous sexual behavior is not necessarily perverted or pathological, and the impact of incest not necessarily devastating to the psyche of the participants or to family solidarity. Incestuous behavior may even have redeeming social and psychological benefits, the article concludes.[760] This article, along with other recent pleas for reform and reflection in the area of incest proscriptions have precipitated some social backlash, as evidenced by some editorial rebuttals and journalistic counterattacks in some leading newspapers. Where there is a journalistic dialogue, however, there is an element of social tolerance, and where there is now even a modicum of social tolerance, there is little reason not to expect further erosion of prohibitive incest norms in the future. Sexual gratification, in all of its vagaries, is linked, after a fashion, and a shift in social control policy in regard to one mode not infrequently encourages a shift in another.

It has been said that "overt sexual interaction between adults and children is the least acceptable form of sexual behavior in modern Western society."[761] In spite of rather dramatic shifts in public opinion and social values in regard to sexual behavior and carnal permissiveness, the cultural posture on sexual activity between adult and child remains singularly rigid. In general, adult-child sexual interaction, with the exception of adults masturbating children, is socially proscribed in almost all societies, even the most rudimentary. Interestingly, however, in some primitive and folk societies there is a degree of implicit tolerance of such carnal behavior. Children, for example may have their intial coital experience with an adult, often in the process of crawling into bed at night with some family member or kinsman, in order to stay warm. In industrial societies, on the other hand, the social proscription against sexual activity with a child has not appreciably weakened, even in recent years. Unlike some other forms of sexual deviancy that have remained a criminal offense under law, but are no longer necessarily viewed as manifestations of mental aberrations, sexual activity with a child is still generally seen as psychopathology. Courts, however, are still prone to severely punish such acts rather than have the offender treated as a medical case. Although there are a variety of medical, psychiatric, and psycho-analytic explanations advanced for "pedophilia" and other instances of sexual activity with children, it would appear that, in general, the sexual preference for children tends to grow out of a pattern of arrested psychosexual development (or regression to this stage under stress), with resulting sexual immaturity, or inability or difficulty in relating in an appropriate sexual fashion to adult females. Some researchers have even written "of anxiety evoked by certain kinds of stimulus characteristics of the adult female, which prevents the patient from engaging in adult sexual activity."[762] Causal analysis of adult-child sexual behavior is made more complex by the fact that it can be spontaneous or planned, occur only on one occasion or present a recidivist pattern, involve children of all ages and either sex and, thus, involve a homosexual or heterosexual mode. It can also include only inspection or fondling of the child or actual genital involvement, and may contain an element of voluntary victim precipitation or participation. Sociological researchers have also pointed out that cases of adult-child sexual behavior not infrequently occur when the offender is under the influence of alcohol or drugs, is under stress, or other situations where there is a significant loss of self-control over behavior. Opportunity structure also appears to be a significant contributing factor.[763] Men who obtain carnal gratification from sexual activity with children are, in effect, individuals who, perhaps only in isolated instances, lack or lose adult sexual preference, adult sexual sophistication in relating to adult females, and adult control over their own behavior.

Although it may well be that the apparent increase in the instance of child molesting and assaults in recent years is simply the result of more such cases being officially reported, and more accurate compilation of reports, it is more likely that this kind of offense is actually on the increases and will continue to do so in the future. Opportunity structure for sexual offenses against children is clearly more enhanced today than in the past. Today, children are more mobile than in the past. More often, they go about on their own and are less supervised and chaperoned than was once the case. They are also more active and involved in situations where there is intimate contact with persons outside the family or circle of close acquaintances than in times past. Children are often more sexually precocious, demonstrate more sexual curiosity and desire for sexual experimentation, and less reticence about engaging in potentially sexually oriented interaction with adults. This tendency is likely to continue in the future.

The sexual revolution, women's liberation movement, militancy on the part of many females, the more assertive and independent role of women in general, a demand for better sexual performance from males on the part of some sexually liberated women, the general shift in the traditional sex roles and the posture of male-female relationships, may all contribute to the anxiety, sexual immaturity, and general difficulty in relating to females in an appropriate heterosexual fashion, which some males will undoubtedly experience. From such stress and dissaffection may come a tendency for some males to seek relationships with, and carnal gratification from, children and adolescents.

Whereas child molesting and taking indecent liberties with children was once believed to be the domain of the "dirty old man," at least in the mind of the public, such carnal behavior today appears to be occurring within a wider segment of the population. Local and regional newspapers frequently carry accounts of child molesting and child sexual assaults by people of all ages and socio-economic background.[764] Perhaps more ominous, however, is the general tendency of many child molesters to be more purposive and aggressive in their activities. Once, child molesting was often a spontaneous and isolated incident perhaps preceipitated by a set of unique circumstances; today however, many individuals who seek sexual interaction with children may in some instances work together collectively to recruit children for their carnal purposes. Recently in Rhode Island, for example, police arrested two middle-aged men for having founded and operated a sex club of children. The children were invited to one of the men's apartments for a meeting of "Teen Challenge." There, the adults and the children engaged in homosexual and heterosexual acts. The children, ranging from 9 to 13, were rewarded with points for their sexual performances, and the points, in turn, earned them prizes such as BB guns and bicycles. The kids who received the most points made the "10 Most Wanted List."[765] Although this case can, itself, take some kind of prize for carnal ingenuity, there are numerous incidents across the country today of one or more people actively recruiting children or teenagers for sexual pleasure.[766] Given the seeming widespread audience for kiddie porn, it may well be that the catholic sexual persuasion of some persons is expanding to include sexual activity with children, real or vicarious, as an alternate to more conventional modes of carnal gratification. As people seek to broaden the horizons of their own sexual perversity in the future in an effort to maximize the sensate experience, even the most bizarre forms of carnal behavior, including sexual involvement with children, can become constituent to the carnal repertoire of some.

Researchers have pointed out that often in the instance of child molesters, the offenders deny or disavow the offense, sometimes attempting to rationalize or excuse their behavior by blaming their action on alcohol, and in general rejecting the label of child molester. The general pattern has been for such offenders to view their behavior as pathological and to seek to rid themselves of such sexual preferences if they cannot evade the label. As reported earlier in the discussion, however, this is not always the case. In Europe, members of the Working Group for Pedophilia, established within the framework of the Dutch Association for Sexual Reform, were queried concerning their own sexual preferences for, and sexual experiences with, children. Among other things they were asked if it were possible, would they like to get rid of their pedophilia. A total of 90 percent replied they did not.[767] In some societies, then, sexual activity with children is not only apparently becoming more tolerated, if not accepted, the persons with such a persuasion are coming to view themselves not as individuals with a pathological affliction, but more as people with an unusual but carnally satisfying sexual disposition. In some countries, pedophiles are even becoming militant in regard to their sexual persuasion and are attempting to proselytize their carnal ideology. In England, for example, the Pedophile Information Exchange has been holding public meetings to discuss and advance the cause of child-sex. The public reception to the aims of this group has been somewhat less than charitable, however. The leader of the group, Thomas O'Carroll, attempted to speak at an International Conference on Love and Attraction sponsored by the British Psychological Society at Swansea University, Wales but was ejected from the meeting and escorted off campus. The action was prompted by the school employees' threat to strike if O'Carroll were not removed from the school. The school principal concurred and observed that, "His views on pedophilia, which is really child molestation, are abhorrent. We do not want the sort of person who sympathizes with this sort of thing on our campus."[768] One London paper called for O'Carroll to be fired from his position with the Open University.[769]

Interestingly, there have been other advocates of socially condemned sexual practices, some of whom have been quite vocal in their efforts at legal reform. Lars Ullerstam, a Swedish physician and humanist, has written of "The Erotic Minorities," and contends that persons of unusual sexual appetites whose preferred mode of carnal gratification are blocked by social proscription and sanction are, in effect, discriminated against by the "erotically privileged caste"— those individuals of traditional and conventional sexual persuasion. Ullerstam calls for sweeping legal reform that would permit catering to all socially deviant sexual tastes including pedophilia.[770] In the future, as some individuals of sexually innovative bent attempt to rationalize and legitimate their own taste for sexual vagaries, while yet others press for the loosening of all sexual constraints, there will probably be a continued resistence toward permissiveness in regard to sexual activity with children, even when the social norms proscribing other kinds of carnal behavior have been eroded, if not subverted. Still, there does appear to be an increasing tendency for many individuals to experience difficulty and dissaffection in developing a satisfying, adult heterosexual relationship with persons of appropriate age of the opposite sex. Additionally, the sexual revolution has, in effect, removed much of the mystery and excitement from traditional modes of sexual gratification. The jaded carnal palate and ennui of today's sexual sophistication has led many to the search for new and more perverse forms of sexual endeavors. Given these situations and in the face of accelerating sexual precociousness, even among young children, there is good reason to believe that for some persons of singular sexual persuasion, sexual behavior involving children may become a routinized, if not institutionalized, configuration of carnal gratification.

Similarly, the unattached elderly male may seek sexual liaisons with younger women. The sexual revolution has had its impact on the older generation as well as the young. Perhaps still more sexually reserved than younger people, the elderly are less sexually constrained than in the past and becoming more sexually assertive, especially elderly females. The traditional taboos proscribing romantic and sexual activity between persons of widely disparate ages may have to give way to the exigencies of demographic and sexual pragmatism. Given the much larger percentage of elderly people in the population, it should be anticipated that their political and social influence will be much enhanced. In this regard, it should also be anticipated that social and legal norms concerning sexual behavior that might encompass the elderly may be modified or moderated because of political pressure from the elderly themselves. Some elderly persons, and especially males, may not find heightened heterosexual activity with adult females to be a viable mechanism for the gratification of their carnal desire. For some, sexual interaction with children may be more opportune and satisfying. Accordingly, the incidence of sexual involvement with children, including child molesting involving elderly offenders, will likely increase significantly in the future.

Although the stereotype of the "dirty old man" is essentially erroneous, inasmuch as most child molesting offenders are, in fact, young or middle-aged adults, nevertheless, older individuals sometimes can and do commit offenses of a sexual nature, including sexually interacting with children and young adolescents. Opportunity structure would appear to be a factor, and in this connection it should be recalled that the number and proportion of elderly people in the population will be increasing at a significant rate in the years ahead. There are now 23 million Americans past age 65, but by the turn of the century, there will be nearly 31 million individuals in this age category.

In the subsequent three decades after that, the number of individuals over age 65 will grow to almost 52 million.[771] Traditionally, the elderly have been treated as being asexual—in effect, having no sexual desire or inclination. We now know this to be a totally distorted social error. Elderly people do have a sexual urge and often seek to fulfill it. In many instances to implement such sexual fulfillment, they may encourage sexual interaction with younger persons. The elderly widow, for example, may have little choice other than a male younger than herself.

Although public attitudes, both here and in Great Britain, have moderated considerably in regard to carnal behavior between adults and young people, they have not been totally diluted. In England recently, for example, a 26-year-old, married female school teacher was accused and tried of having sexual relations with an 11-year-old male student, with accompanying public outrage.[772] Ultimately in the court trial the woman was acquitted, but the social stigma associated with residual suspicion remained to brand her as an unpunished sexual offender.

Although the phenomenon of child prostitution is hardly new or of American origin, its manifestation in our society in recent years is particularly ominous from a social standpoint. Historically, child prostitution has been characteristic of societies experiencing the vicissitudes of abject poverty, often in the midst of some even greater social disequilibrium such as war or revolution. Such is not the case in our own society, nor do the child prostitutes of recent years necessarily derive from personal situations of poverty or economic deprivation. For the most part, the young people involved of both sexes appear to be socially, rather than economically, deprived and victims of a profound demoralization process growing out of broken homes, lack of family cohesion, and identity, neglect and abuse, and the inability to relate in an effective way with traditional significant others. In short, they are social castoffs who, lacking a self-image of purpose and worth and without meaningful relationships with others, simply covert their bodies into mechanisms of value and substitute instrumental economic and secondary carnal relationships with sexual clients for effective relationships with loved ones. These young people have become, in effect, sexual machines dedicated to economic, and thus emotional, survival in what they view as a cold, depersonalized, hostile, and totally commercialized world. That there are willing customers for the commercial sexual favors of 13-year-old females suggest that the basic cultural fabric of our society has worn thin and frayed as sexual license and carnal depravity flourish in the face of a diluted, if not extinct, moral order and social control. Sexual interaction with child prostitutes is simply seen by many sexual explorers as another vagary in the search for innovative and fulfilling carnal satisfaction.

The startling appearance and apparent growth of a large population of child and adolescent male prostitutes—estimated to be as high as one third of a million or more—is particularly foreboding, inasmuch as such behavior is in sharp contrast with the traditional male image and role conceptualization.[773] (The female prostitute can, in effect, offend the moral order, but does not contradict the basic cultural image of female role parameters. The male prostitute, however, does. Homosexuality encounters a more hostile reception in Miami than in most large cities, because of the large Cuban population, for whom homosexuality is the cultural antithesis of their concept of machismo.) The abandonment of such a traditional gender posture suggests a measure of social alienation and dissaffection on the part of a segment of the younger male generation greater than at any other time in the past. Furthermore, the presumably large clientele that the young male prostitutes serve is indicative of a homosexual presence in society perhaps far larger than ever imagined and possibly even growing. There is nothing in the immediate social future that would indicate a diminishment of the exodus of alienated young people, of both sexes, from home to the street and from effective social involvement to the exigencies of sexual and commercial instrumentalism. Furthermore, the parade of juvenile prostitutes, of both sexes, will likely encounter a carnal constituency eager for their services in their own quest for sensate gratification, regardless of social repugnance or depravity of their behavior.

The sexual revolution of recent years will have some erosive impact on socially proscriptive norms prohibiting sexual activity between individuals of widely disparate ages, but perhaps not as much as on other sexual norms. Structural conditions facilitating and encouraging such sexual deviancy, however, may engender an increased incidence of all forms of such carnal behavior. The sexual precociousness of children and the new posture of sexual liberation and assertiveness on the part of female adolescents will enhance the opportunity structure for carnal behavior with these populations. The increase in the divorce rate and the greater likelihood of children and adolescents living in the same house with step-parents or their mother's paramour may well contribute to a greater occurrence of legal incest. The aging population in this society will also likely lead to a greater likelihood of romance or sexual interaction between partners of disparate age. Finally, the continuing problem of males who, because of anxiety, role stresses, identity crises, and sexual and social immaturity and ineptitude, may well be exacerbated by the profound changes in male-female role relationships. This can manifest itself in the form of a greater likelihood of such males attempting to engage in carnal behavior, either of heterosexual of homosexual mode with underage adults.

Chapter 11

EROTIC DOMINANCE, SADOMASOCHISM, AND RAPE

Sexual Deviancy in Violent Context

It has been said that love and hate are but two sides of the same coin. In a similar vein, sexual activity and violence are often inextricably interrelated. At the most elemental levels of behavior, certain varieties of animals, birds, and fish will aggressively defend territorial areas. Naturalists who have studied territoriality in such creatures have pointed out that the violent competition among males of the species can be conceptualized as primarily competition for real estate, with sexual access to females on, or who will gravitate to, that real estate as a secondary consideration. The territorial instinct and sexual appetite, however, are "profoundly intermeshed," as Robert Ardrey has pointed out. The studies of naturalists tell us that male animals in their territorial fights are sexually stimulated by the fights themselves. Successfully defended territory tends to enhance sexual desire. Ardrey, for example, quotes one zoologist, who in reporting on one species, asserted that:

> The inspiration of ownership seems necessary to stimulate sexual desire in both males and females. Away from the stamping ground copulation is only rarely attempted and apparently never consummated.[774]

Ardrey, on another occasion, reflects that, "In most but not all territorial species—not in chameleons, for example—the female is

345

sexually unresponsive to an unpropertied male."[775] Male animals
then fight to defend their territory, and constitutent to this territorial
exclusivity, is outlet for sexual gratification. Although it is usually
the males who resort to violence to defend area and mate, in some
instances, the female will become aggressive also. Konrad Lorenz,
for example, gives an example of a female stork who discovered that
a strange female stork was attempting to possess her territoriality
and mate, and violently drove off the usurper.[776] He also has reported instances of male-female pairs of rats defending territoriality,
and viciously attacking unpaired rats in an attempt to establish
territorial boundaries.[777] The territorial fights between males may be
essentially symbolic in some instances, but violent even to death in
others. Some male animals may not even survive a season of such
territorial-sex fights. Male animals may sometimes also be quite
aggressive, to the point of violence, in their mating activities with
their females, and in this regard Lorenz has commented on male
baboons, for example, treating the females of his species somewhat
brutally and dictatorially.[778]

TERRITORIALITY, JEALOUSY, AND VIOLENCE

In humans, territoriality conflicts also occur, although often at
a more subtle level of interaction. Young males may attempt to assert
themselves over other males in an effort to obtain dominance in a
neighborhood or other area, and part of this dominance can include
exclusive access, or at least first choice of females in the area, as
courting or dating partners. Just as little boys may fight for the
attention of little girls, gangs of teen-aged males may fight, sometimes even to the death in defense of "turf" and all on the turf
including eligible females. Grown males may compete symbolically
in the world of business or government, as a means of acquiring
"territory," in terms of status, power and economic privilege, and as
related in fact and fiction, may even derive a kind of sexual stimulation from the conflict.

Not unlike the animal species of which Ardrey spoke, the available female may be more sexually responsive to the more propertied
male, symbolically speaking. Henry Kissinger once observed that
power is a strong aphrodisiac. Territoriality, as reflected in sexual
jealousy has been a significant motivational factor in many crimes of
violence. Jealous males have been known to commit assault, may-

hem, and murder on other males to "protect" their spouses, fiancées, lovers, girlfriends, and, even in some instances, complete strangers. Females have also resorted to violence against other females as a result of sexual jealousy. The killing of a person of the opposite sex caught involved in sexual activity with one's spouse, has been labeled the "unwritten law" by some and constitutes justifiable homocide in some states. Crimes growing out of sexual jealousy have not always only involved others of the same sex. Jealous males have sometimes assaulted or murdered their spouses or lovers, as well as, or in place of, the offending interloper. Women likewise, have sometimes, inflamed by sexual jealousy, slain both adulterous spouse or boyfriend and their female sex object. Nor is all sexual jealousy heterosexual in origin. Homosexuals of both sex have had occasion to do violence to rivals or unfaithful lovers. As a number of penological researchers and writers have pointed out, for example, violence arising out of homosexual jealousies is endemic in most prisons.[779]

COURTING BEHAVIOR AND VIOLENCE.   In courtship, sexual conflict, real or symbolic, is often intermixed with love, affection, and lust. The course of true love is never smooth, it is said, and many couples engage in periodic "lovers quarrels," sometimes to the point of physical violence, which may, in extreme cases, involve beatings, thrown objects, stabbings, and even shootings. Courtship, in our society, can in some instances, occur only under closely monitored and supervised conditions and circumstances, perhaps even mandating chaperones. In other instances, the couple may be left much to their own devices.

The increased sexual permissiveness of recent decades coupled with the general middle-class orientation toward proprietous comportment, especially in the sense of males being "gentlemen" when with a lady, would suggest that at least, couples courting without supervision, would seek some kind of mutual consensus in regard to the level of sexual intimacies which they both desired. Some research, however, points to a different conclusion. A few years ago, two researchers studied male exploitative sexual behavior in dating situations, as perceived by the females and concluded that there was a significant amount of coercion, and offensive force to the point of violence, used by the males in their efforts at sexual activity with the females.[780] The study suggested that there is a progressive pattern of sexual exploitation, ambivalent resistance, and a reluctance to resort to formal authority as a recourse. A sample of 291 college co-eds at one university was queried concerning male sexual aggression on dates, and 55.7% reported that they had been "offended" at least once during the year, at some level of erotic intimacy. These experiences ranged from "necking and petting above the waist" to "attempted intercourse with violence." A significant percentage (20.-9%) said they had experienced forceful attempts at intercourse. A total of 6.2% indicated that they had been offended by "aggressively forceful attempts at sexual intercourse in the course of which menacing threats or coercive infliction of physical pain were employed." These were not single occurrences. The 162 women interviewed reported 1,022 offensive episodes. The data from the study indicated that mild levels of offensive experiences of erotic intimacy tended to occur more frequently with non-involved pairing (i.e., first date, occasional date), while episodes of offensive intimacy at a serious level occurred more with involved pairing (i.e., steady dating, pinned, or engaged). A total of 7 out of 10 of the most violent episodes involved this latter category of males. In a subsequent study of seniors in a high school by the same researchers a similar pattern of sexual exploitation was found. In another study by one of these researchers, it was shown that sexually aggressive males were also more successful sexually than were unaggressive males.[781] Inasmuch as these young people were largely middle class, there is some reason to believe that such male sexual aggression may be more pronounced among young men of the lower socio-economic strata. The findings of such researchers as Kirkpatrick and Kanin would seem to suggest that youthful courtship apparently involves a not inconsiderable amount of wrestling, and some occasional arm twisting, along with the endearments, and whispers of sweet nothings.

MARRIAGE, SEX, AND VIOLENCE

Sexual aggression and violence does not necessarily end with marriage, however. Wifebeating (and husbandbeating for that matter) in addition to more generalized mutual hostility and violence is not uncommon in our society. This pattern of wifebeating, or mutual fighting, is frequently related directly or indirectly to sex. The husband may come home drunk, demand sexual intercourse, be refused by his wife, and at this point physically assault his wife. The beatings in some cases, curiously enough can result from a sexual role reversal situation. One study of the wives of wifebeaters found that the wives were "aggressive, efficient, masculine, and sexually frigid."[782] The husbands in this study were "shy, sexually ineffectual, reasonably hard-working 'mother's boys' with a tendency to drink excessively." The wives assertively controlled the marital relationship and this tended to complement the husband's dependency needs and his subsequent subservient role. Sometimes, after a husband's heavy drinking bout, the husband and wife would effect a role reversal, aided by the alcohol. The husband would become aggressive and beat his wife. This served to "release him momentarily from his anxiety about his uneffectiveness as a man." Many of these fights arose over the wife's rejection of the husband's sexual advances. The resultant beatings gave "his wife apparent masochistic gratification and helped probably to deal with the guilt arising from the intense hostility expressed in her controlling castrating behavior."

Sometimes, wifebeating does not stop at a mere beating. In studies of wife assaulters where there was also an intent to kill, there was a similar pattern of "very masculine, outspoken domineering women," and husbands who played a "generally submissive role."[783] These wives, aware of their husband's passiveness and dependence tended to exploit these weaknesses by witholding affection, sex, or threatening divorce or affairs with other men, all with profit gains in mind." The husbands would hold their hostility in check as long as possible and when they could do so no longer, would react with aggressive outbursts. Thus, they could not properly channelize hostility and frustration growing out of the inappropriate husband-wife relationship and its attendant interaction. Sexual desire generates powerful emotions, and conflicts over opportunity for sexual outlet sometimes erupts into violence, and even murder. In this connection, a number of empirical studies have suggested an interactive relationship between sexual arousal and aggressive behavior.[784]

Contrary to popular belief, wifebeating or abuse is not necessarily more characteristic of the lower socioeconomic levels of society. It would appear that wifebeating is found in all socioeconomic and educational levels, but where the middle or upper class family can more likely keep the intra-family violence secret, the lower class family tends to more often have such violence become "a matter of public accounting and record."[785] Some studies of wifebeating suggest that such family violence is more likely to occur "when the level of education was lower than that of the wife."[786] Also, there appears to be a greater degree of violence associated with the wife having some high school education or a college degree.[787] Not infrequently, wifebeating occurs with couples who have been separated at one time or another, who are separated or divorced, or who are in the process of getting a divorce. Such a context would suggest an element of territoriality or threat of loss of territoriality, and, thus, sexual access, related to such violence.

VIOLENCE AND THE ENHANCEMENT OF CARNAL GRATIFICATION

For some men and women, carnal gratification can only be accomplished and enjoyed within the framework of violence and the infliction of pain on others, even if symbolically. Some men beat their wives because they are sexually aroused by doing so, and their sexual gratification is thus enhanced. Such men may not necessarily even realize the nature of their carnal appetites. Other men, perhaps the latter day disciples of the Marquis de Sade, recognize it all too well and must seek out women who will submit to violence and pain. Some prostitutes specialize in servicing this need and for a handsome fee, plus payment for any necessary medical and dental treatment resulting from the encounter, will permit their clients to beat them up as part of the sexual encounter. Such beatings are known as "dumpings," and while only a few prostitutes offer such a specialized sexual service, there appear to be significant numbers of clients willing to pay the premium price for the privilege of indulging their appetite for sexual violence. Other prostitutes, who may not permit real beatings may humor their customers with violent needs to the extent of letting their customers pretend to beat them, or to beat them with soft rubber sticks or some other harmless instrument. Just as some persons need to inflict pain in order to enjoy sexual gratification, others need to experience it. For this privilege, such men may require the services of prostitutes who will play a "dominant" role.[788] They must abuse the client, possibly beating or burning him, in addition to engaging in such dramaturgics as leading the client around the floor on a leash like a dog, and perhaps kicking him with sharp spiked-heeled shoes. Again, some prostitutes specialize in providing "disciplinary" services as it is known and command high fees for doing so. Such prostitutes may have an elaborate set of whips and "punishment" devices to assist them in rendering carnal pleasure. Females, too, may also require pain and humiliation for satisfactory sexual gratification and women with this particular aberration will often seek out men who are prepared to satisfy their needs. In the opening chapter of *The Anderson Tapes,* it will be recalled that the protagonist encountered such a woman.

Ancillary to sadistic and masochistic sexual appetites is the need for "bondage." Here, the individual may enjoy pain and humiliation as part of the sexual senario, but finds that the carnal experience is enhanced if he is bound and, thus, helpless. Similarly, libertines of sadistic bent can magnify their own sexual gratification where their victim is subject to bondage. In recent years, there has been a significant rise in establishments making and selling "leather" goods and other kind of restraints for the purpose of sexual bondage. Interestingly "bondage" and related activities are becoming, in some instances, component to the repertoire of "normal" sexual practices of some married couples. In Alex Comfort's best selling sex manual *The Joy of Sex,* the author advised couples to experiment with "lighthearted bondage," and many sex-oriented periodicals like *Playboy* have, from time to time, contained letters to the editor from husbands and wives who enthusiastically reveal the details of their own sexual activities which may involve bondage, mutual spankings, and other forms of mild violence as means of adding erotic enhancement to their carnal fantasies and sexual titilation. It has been predicted in some of the sex-oriented magazines that S-M (sadomachochistic) sexual activities will become very much more popular and prevalent as time goes on, as persons with jaded sexual palates, seek erotic variety and sexual unorthodoxy as a means of rejuvenating their carnal exigencies.

Sadomasochism or either of its bifurcated persuasions has been the object of intense preoccupation and discussion by psychopathologists, psychiatrists, psychologists and other therapists for many decades and no totally comprehensive and satisfactory theory of its origin or etiology has ever been advanced.[789] It does appear that it is a learned appetite acquired through various chance encounters and experiences and the attendant casual linkages. Childhood memories and incidents combine to associate carnal gratification with the giving or receiving of pain, and humiliation. Such linkages are reinforced through time and ultimately a convoluted pattern of sexual stimulation and gratification is established and ritualized.

Sadomasochism is not an absolute persuasion, except in the most extreme and compulsive instances. Almost everyone may have a slight, or latent tendency in such directions, and may accordingly, derive carnal gratification from some occasional sadomasochistic episode, real or vicarious. Sexual fantasy moves such as *The Story of O* would seemingly afford some modicum of sexual titilation, for many of its viewers, and assuage curiosities about sadomasochistic practices, if not provide inspiration for subsequent sexual variety, and vicarious carnal gratification. As mentioned above, some recent marriage manuals suggest introducing an element of sadomasochism into a jaded sex life for fun and variety. Furthermore, a non inconsiderable portion of pornographic literature includes some sadomasochistic content.

In the extreme, however, sadomasochism may be considered as a psychopathological perversion which is dysfunctional to the normal mental processes, and psychosocial processes, and its compulsive pattern interruptive to a conventional lifestyle and sexual interaction. Interestingly, there are even sadomasochistic subcultures that involve institutionalized means of seeking partners and acting out the sadomasochistic sexual interaction.[790] Some such sadomasochistic subcultures are homosexually oriented, others bisexually oriented, while some are heterosexual in orientation.

One such type of subculture is the homosexual network that has inculcated a set of institutionalized sadomasochistic norms that involve symbolic acts of dominance and submission rather than the actual infliction of, or experiencing, physical pain. This behavioral configuration has been labeled "leathersex," and its adherents or members are termed "leathermen."[791] The heterosexual sadomasochistic subcultures frequently include "submissive" males who seek "dominant" females. Such females are not, infrequently, prostitutes who specialize in S-M services. These subcultures often have elaborate communication networks that facilitate meeting persons with similar sexual persuasions, and the sharing of information and ideological support.[792] Inasmuch as males appear to a greater likelihood to have a sadomasochistic sexual preference or persuasion than females, this fact not infrequently generates the basic problem of heterosexual male sadomasochists finding accommodating partners. There may well be a fadish dimension to sadomachism and in this connection, it has been suggested that it is becoming more popular and more widespread as a sexual mode of behavior, and that it will become a more prominent component of the sexual repertoire as many seek more variety and inspiration in their carnal gratification.

Carnal appetites that seek violence constituent to sexual gratification may not find spankings or symbolic bondage hearty enough fare, and may seek more extreme forms of sexual violence even to the ultimate form of violence—murder. In this connection, James Prescott has asserted that crime, and interpersonal violence, and even warfare, are all directly related to the repression of sexual gratification such as premarital and extramarital sex, and the "deprivation of body pleasure throughout life-but particularly during the formative periods of infancy, childhood, and adolescence."[793]

SEXUAL VIOLENCE IN CRIME

Crimes of sexual violence have figured prominently in the history of criminality both in this country and abroad. Some of the most infamous have been those crimes where the offender apparently obtained some degree of carnal gratification from the death or violence visited on the victim, or at least enjoyed some neurotic or psychotic pleasure intimately linked to carnal stimulation, from the sexual abuse and violence inflicted on the victim. The grisly story of Bluebeard is so classic that the name itself has become a euphemism for someone who murders a series of spouses. The enigma of Jack the Ripper, perhaps the most infamous of all English sex criminals continues to offer morbid fascination to mystery and crime buffs even today, a century later. This individual it will be recalled, murdered a number of prostitutes in London, and then eviscerated them. Presumably there was a sexual element, even if only symbolic, involved in the psychotic motivation for the bizarre crimes. A relatively recent theory is that a member of the British royal family was actually the murderer and that he had learned his eviscerating skills from watching and assisting in, the butchering of stags at the royal hunting preserves.

Prior to the turn of the century in this country, a particularly infamous, but little known today, sex criminal was Herman Webster Mudgett, who holds the all-time American record for sex murders. In the 1890s, he seduced, slaughtered, and dissected more than 200 young women. He would court the women, promise to marry them, seduce them, and persuade them to sign over their possessions to him and then murder them.[794]

Not long after the end of World War II, Americans were shocked and horrified by a sex crime which attracted national attention and national indignation. In 1946, William Heirens, a 17-year-old University of Chicago student and model church-going son, was arrested for having kidnapped, sexually molested, strangled, and dissected 6-year-old Suzanne Degnan.[795] It also appeared that he had previously committed 24 burglaries, four assaults with intent to murder and one assault and robbery. He had also shot and stabbed two women and after the murder of one of them, scribbled a note in lipstick on the victim's bathroom wall. That read, "For heaven's sake, catch me before I kill more." After he was apprehended, psychiatrists discovered that Heirens was psychotic and had a split personality. His alter ego named George, so William Heirens asserted, was really the person who had done all the bad things of which he was accused.

Perhaps no sex criminal of recent years received more publicity, even international publicity than did Caryl Chessman. Chessman had committed a series of robberies, but also was found guilty of various sex crimes that he allegedly perpetrated as "the Red Light Bandit." His *modus operandi* was to prowl the lover's lanes and outlying areas of Los Angeles in an automobile equipped with a red spotlight. By acting as if he were a policeman, he was able to rob parked couples. On two occasions, he forced women to get out of their cars and into his and then forced them to perform "unnatural sex acts." On another occasion, he forced a 17 year-old girl to submit to "attempted rape." She subsequently developed schizophrenia and was confined to a state hospital for many years. Chessman was convicted on a total of 17 charges including technical kidnapping for robbery with bodily harm, since he had forced the female victims into his car. He was sentenced to death, but managed to evade the gas chamber for many years through a series of legal maneuvers and court appeals. He authored several best-selling books about his ordeal in death row, and people and groups around the world demonstrated in his behalf and made appeals that his life be spared.

If Caryl Chessman was a colorful and even popular sex criminal, George William Rae may well have been the most energetic sex criminal. Rae, the Boston Strangler, as he was known, raped and murdered a number of women before he was apprehended. The exact number of crimes he committed is not known. Rae suggested that he may have raped as many as several hundred women in his criminal career. He confessed to committing several rapes in one day, on occasion. Rae was quite compulsive and would sometimes make the decision to seek a rape victim very suddenly as his mind was "building this image up" as he put it. He was quite violent and often lost control of himself in the midst of a rape murder, sometimes severely biting the victim on her breasts and belly. When he retained some control of himself after the crime, he would frequently be angry at himself. As he phrased it:

> ... I remember she [a rape murder victim] had a big bush and for an old lady she was very well built ... All the way down was these red bite marks, and you see, and I remember looking at them and saying, gee, did I do that? ... and it made me mad, somehow, to see her like that, dead, and with come on her hair and them bites ...[796]

If the Boston Strangler was singular in his sexual endurance and capacity for violent sex crimes, Richard Speck stood apart for the unparalleled savagery of his crime.[797] In July, 1966, Richard Speck, a sometime merchant marine, forced his way into the student nurse quarters of a resident hall of the South Chicago Community Hospital. There, at gunpoint, he tied and gagged nine student nurses, some as they later came into their rooms. Over a period of some hours, Speck carried the bound girls, one by one, to another part of the house; he murdered eight of them. Some were stabbed, some were strangled, and several endured both stabbing and strangling. At least one had been sexually assaulted. Speck had been drinking as well as taking drugs the evening he committed the murders and could not remember his action, and did not know why he killed the girls. Psychiatric authorities did not find Speck insane, but he had contracted syphilis at one time in his life, and had a long standing hostility toward women, a low I.Q., and a variety of psychiatric problems. Speck had a history of violent crimes including a jail term for assaulting women with knives, in addition to a prison term for forgery and burglary. He had also been suspected in the murder of a 33-year old barmaid who was beaten to death and left in an abandoned hog house, and in the case of a 65-year old widow who was bound, robbed, and raped. Speck was almost shocked at the accusation that he was a rapist and claimed that on drugs he was incapable of raping any one. He also could not feature himself as a murderer. His psychiatrist also believed that the real Richard Speck was not a man who wished to kill. As to why he did, the psychiatrist offered the following explanation for his schizoid behavior:

> The essential elements are: a brain damaged human being—impulsive, childish, emotionally labile, racked by headaches; drugs, alcohol and barbiturates which excite him; a basic obsessive-compulsive personality, rigid punitive, Puritanical, sadomasochistic, containing unconscious hostility to females because of a Madonna-prostitute complex; hatred of his wife for suspected infidelity, and for divorcing him.[798]

Violent Homosexual Crime

The victims of violent sex crimes are not always female. One of the biggest sex-related mass murders in recent times involved the death of at least 27 teen-aged boys.[799] In 1973, a 17-year old boy named Elmer Henly turned himself in to the police in Houston, Texas, and confessed that he had shot and killed Dean Allen Corll with his own gun, in self-defense. The subsequent investigation revealed the almost unbelievable facts of the murder of literally dozens of young boys. Corll was a 33-year old bachelor, who lived alone in a Houston suburb. He was also a homosexual with bizarre, carnal appetites. Corll had offered young Henley and his 18-year old friend, David Brooks, a fee of $200 for every boy that they could deliver to him. The two youths became Corll's procurers often picking up teenage hitchhikers and taking them to Corll's house for acrylic sniffing "parties." Once there, the newcomers would be drugged, seized, stripped naked, and handcuffed to a specially constructed plywood board. In a room full of "sado-masochistic gadgetry," the boys would be tortured and sexually abused sometimes over a period of days, and then finally strangled or shot with a .22 caliber pistol. Henley and Brooks not only lured the boys to Corll's house, they also helped Corll later bury the bodies of the victims. The homosexual torture murders might still be going on had it not been for the fact that Corll once tried to make Henley and Brooks his victims also, and Henley had subsequently shot and killed him. Henley and Brooks ultimately led police to a series of grave sites where the murdered boys were buried. There the police found "wall-to-wall bodies." The number of victims rose to 27 but there was reason to believe that there may have been even more. The murdered youths, some as young as 13, had in some instances, been runaways and accordingly, their deaths were unnoticed. Henley told the police that Corll "had a lust for blood," but somehow this was inextricably tied up with his homosexual appetites.

Homosexual violence is perhaps less prevalent than violent heterosexual offenses, but it would appear to be increasing in incidence and brutality. The homosexual rape, for example, is occurring with some frequency today. In Christiansburg, Virginia for example, two men went into a public restroom in a large store in a shopping center. When a 17-year old youth entered the restroom they drew a knife on him and forced him to perform sexual acts at knife point.[800] Where at one time homosexual rape was almost totally restricted to various populations in total institutions such as jails and prisons, it is now beginning to appear as a street crime.

Sexual Murder

In the instances of the murder-sexual crimes, several distinctive elements of the offense suggest themselves. Unlike the more "common" rapes where the offender may be familiar with the victim, the victims of the sex-murder are usually complete strangers to the offenders. Usually, the offender is severely disturbed with a complex psychiatric pathology. At the time of the crime, the offender may "black out," or have some degree of amnesia concerning the incident. They may not even be aware of their crime, or deny it even when confronted by the evidence. The perpetrator of such crimes may even feel remorseful or sorrow at what he had done. Finally, the sexual motivation for the crime may be secondary to some other more deep-seated neurotic or psychotic motivation rather than sexual stimulation. The murder or violence, itself, can be more stimulating than sexual gratification constituent to the crime. The act of violence may permit the acting-out of some internalized and generalized hostility, and the sexual activity involved may even be something of an afterthought. In any event, the sex-murderer often loses complete control over his behavior, and accomplishes to gratify his carnal lust only within the complex framework of primal aggression and violence.

Rape as Modal Sexual Violence

Violent sex crimes involving murder, and particularly those of a more sensational nature, are relatively infrequent in occurrence. Forcible rape is a violent sex crime and occurs with considerable frequency, however. Even a decade ago, official F.B.I. statistics suggested that more than 30,000 forcible rapes per year were reported. This figure may well be extremely misleading, however, inasmuch as many rapes are never reported. Similarly, more recent figures would suggest a significant rise in the number of rapes reported in most years, over the previous years. In 1973, there were 51,000 rapes reported and by the following year, the number of rapes had reportedly increased by 9%.[801] Whether this indicates an actual increase in the number of rapes occurring, a larger percentage of rapes committed being reported to authorities, or simply a better reporting system, is quite debatable. In any event, the official figures on rape do not provide an entirely accurate picture of the crime. It has been estimated that perhaps no more than 30% of all actual rapes are ever reported. Some estimates suggest that only 10% of all rapes are ever reported.[802] Females might refrain from reporting rape for a number of reasons. A woman, for example, might be concerned about possible rejection from her husband or boyfriend, and, thus, prefer to conceal the crime. Some women may not report being raped because they fear retaliation from the rapist or his friends. Sometimes when a child is raped by a stepfather or mother's boyfriend, the women may hide the fact of the rape for fear of losing her husband or paramour. The majority of rape victims who do not report the crime to law enforcement authorities may well do so because of apprehension about the ordeal of police investigation, medical examination, and the embarassment of court room testimony.[803]

RAPE AND THE ELUSIVE OFFENDERS

Not only is rape a crime that is frequently not reported, it is also a crime that is frequently not cleared by arrest. In 1968, for example, 45% of the forcible rapes reported were not cleared by arrest, as opposed to 86% of the criminal homicides which were cleared by arrest.[804] Rapes often occur at times, and in places and circumstances where the victim may not be able to identify or describe her attacker. There may be few clues, and there are seldom any witnesses other than the victim. Thus, many rapists are never apprehended. In some states, at least until recently, the victim's testimony had to be corroborated. Rape has been a traditionally difficult crime to prosecute because of the legal problems of proof and reluctance of juries to convict. Because of the problems of identifying and apprehending the offender, and the difficulty of making a case against the accused person, many rapists are never punished for their crime. Even the repeat rapist may often avoid detection and apprehension. In St. Louis in 1969 one offender named the "Phantom Rapist," terrorized the city for several months with his sex crimes.[805] He was connected with 23 sexual assault cases, but after he was arrested it appeared that he may actually have committed as many as 60 sexual assaults.

In this instance, the "Phantom Rapist" turned out to be a young member of the police force. After arrest, he was released on bond. He soon attempted another rape and was again arrested. His initial apprehension might not have occurred had he not left notes at the scene of his crimes in which he taunted the police for their ineptitute in catching him, and referring to specific officers by name. His familiarity with the police officers by name, in effect, gave him away. The fact of his being a policeman almost successfully shielded him from discovery and apprehension for his crimes.

THE SOCIAL CONTEXT OF RAPE

On superficial examination, rape might appear to be a relatively simple crime. Someone takes by force that which is not freely given. Rape, however, is actually a crime of far more complex dimensions. Rape, for example cannot be said to be a crime growing out of sexual deprivation. Rapists are not infrequently married, or have female acquaintances with whom they enjoy sexual intercourse on a regular basis. It is true, however, that some rapists have reported that they had an unhappy marriage, and some have complained that their wives were not "responsive sexually." Some rapes are committed by men after an argument with their wives.[806] Neither is rape a crime perpetrated by "oversexed" individuals. Rapists are frequently younger men. It was reported, for example, that in 1968, almost 2 out of 3 men arrested for forcible rape were under the age of 25.[807] Negroes constitute a disproportionate percentage of arrested rapists. In 1968, for example, 41% of the persons arrested for rape were Negroes even though they only made up 10.5% of the population.[808] Various studies have also shown extremely high rape rates for Spanish-Americans and blacks in comparison with whites. Blacks also, however, have a disporportionately high rate of rape victimization. Although some researchers have reported that Negroes were more likely to rape white women, other research such as the detailed study of rape in Philadelphia by Amir has suggested that rape was essentially an "intraracial event," i.e., Negro men rape Negro females.[809] Studies of rape both here and abroad have shown that both rape offenders and victims are more likely to be persons of the lower end of the socio-economic scale, than persons from the middle and upper end of the scale. Amir also found that half of the persons arrested in Philadelphia had previous arrest records.[810] Rape would appear to be a crime based partially on circumstances and opportunity structure. Amir's study indicated that rapes occur more frequently on weekends, and between the hours of 8:00 P.M. and 2:00 A.M.[811] These are the times when both offenders and victims are out and about. Thus, there is opportunity for the rapist to see his victim, perhaps meet or contact her, and interact with her. As Amir pointed out, the traditional assumption that rape only occurs between total strangers must be rejected in the face of evidence. In his study, he found that offenders and victims tended to live in the same area, and this fact no doubt allowed them some knowledge of each other. In more than one-third of his cases, the offender and victim knew each other as acquaintances or close neighbors. Also in one-third of the cases he studied, the rapist met his victim at her home or place where she stayed, and in fact, committed the rape there.[812] In some instances, the offender and victim perhaps met in some public place, and left together, and then later the female resisted his sexual advances or refused to submit to sexual intercourse, at which point the male may on impulse have used force to rape her. Such impulsive incidents and comcommitants of rape are in the minority however. In Amir's study, rape was found to be a planned event in approximately three-quarters of the cases. This was especially so where the rape was perpetrated in the victim's home. The offender may select his victim beforehand and carefully monitor her behavior patterns as a means of identifying the most appropriate time for the crime. In this connection, some rapists have gone to extraordinary lengths to obtain the name and address of a particular female, or to follow her about for a time before actually perpetrating the rape. The rapist, however, may select the scene for the rape rather than the victim. He may find a secluded dwelling, or an apartment well located for his access and exit, and the female living there simply becomes his automatic rape victim. In effect, she becomes the rape victim because of where she lives rather than what she looks like. Group rapes also are prone to be planned. In the Philadelphia study, 43% of the cases were multiple-rapes. Group rapists are often younger offenders and the victims are in the same age level.

RAPE AND MOTIVATION

There has been considerable controversy concerning whether rape is committed by normal or aberrant offenders. Some writers, particularly feminist advocates, assert that rape is only exaggerated masculine behavior and "normal" in the sense that it represents a kind of conformity to the expectations of the male role. As one female writer puts it:

> ... Rape can best be undersood as the act of over-conformity by a man trying to fulfill society's expectations of him. The virility mystique exhalts power, dominance, assertiveness, strength and toughness; all attributes highly valued within a competitive, capitalistic social system.[813]

Other authorities, however, are more prone to stress mental pathology as the most significant element in the motivation for rape. Ralph Garofalo, a psychologist at a New England institution for sexual offenders, has studied 100 rapists and has drawn certain conclusions about their motivation.[814] As others have asserted, sexual desire is not the only element of motivation. One category of rapists, he claims, are motivated in rape by their "aggressive feelings" toward women. They tend to overidealize their mothers, but also tend to view most women as "unfaithful, demanding and untrustworthy." When they rape a female they have, in effect, substituted the victim, who may be a complete stranger, for "important women in their lives who have disappointed them." Rapists in this category often rely on violence and brutality as part of their rape behavior. They seek to "humiliate, dirty, and defile the victim." They may beat the victim, mutilate her genitals and/or breasts, and even in some instances, murder her.

A second category of rapists that Garofalo described was those men whose primary motivation was sexual. These offenders may have a history of other sexual crimes such as voyeurism or exhibitionism, and may even have repressed feelings of homosexuality. These men not infrequently had a father that was "uninvolved with his family," and a mother who was "cold and ungiving," and a "harsh disciplinarian" especially in regards to the son's erotic interests. The offender, later in life, may develop a sense of impotence and inadequacy. His rape victim may even be a female that he has involved in his fantasies of skilled love making. The final category of rapists is the variety motivated by both sex and aggression. These men can only "discharge anger best through a sadistic sexual act." The "overpowering hostility" of such persons makes them closest to being psychopathic. Even Garofalo, however, perceives a kind of normal behavior in rape, however, and suggests that most men at one time or another have had sexual desires toward strange women they see or meet. [Former President Jimmy Carter even publicly revealed that, on occasion, he had lust in his heart for other women.] The distinction between the normal male and the rapist is a simple one. The normal man finds "socially acceptable outlet[s] for their desires," while the rapist "loses all sight of moral or legal consideration."

Recent studies conceptualize rape as a "pseudosexual act," i.e., it is an act where needs other than sexual are operating.[815] In this study of rape offenders and victims, the findings suggested that the majority of rapists had heterosexual outlets available to them. The rapists used force without even trying to negotiate consent, and more than one-half had a history of repeated violent assaults. More than one-third of the offenders experienced some type of sexual dysfunction during the rape. Instead of a sexual motivation, the main psychological determinants seemed to be anger and the need to have power over the victim. A substantial percentage of offenders demonstrated some type of personality disorder, and for the majority of the individuals, "the rapes were but another aspect of multiple conflicts with the law both sexual and non-sexual."[816] The researchers concluded that essentially rape represents, "a transient reaction to extraordinary stresses that temporarily overwhelm the individual's psychological resources," and a situation where "the offender's psychological resources are developmentally insufficient to cope with the successive and increasing demands of life."[817] Rape, in effect, grows out of stresses experienced by the offender and certain situational crisis factors that can trigger the actual assault.

There are, of course, exceptions to every rule. Several years ago, it was reported that a former American beauty contestant, in love with a young Mormon missionary, chased him from the United States to England where, with the help of a male friend, she kidnapped the young man.[818] She subsequently took him to a secluded cottage and chained or handcuffed him to a bed for two days. When he refused to have sexual intercourse with her, she chained him hand and foot to the bed, and while he was spread-eagled on the bed and helpless, she forced him to have sex with her, raping him, in effect. In the ensuing trial, it was claimed that the woman had an "all consuming passion" for the young missionary.

RAPE AS ECONOMIC CRIME

Rape as a crime has undergone something of a conceptual metamorphosis over time. At one point in history, and even today in some primitive and folk societies, rape is considered to be essentially an economic crime, or crime against property, if you will. The female wife or daughter represented a fixed economic worth. A daughter raped was a daughter less salable on the market. As "used" or imperfect merchandise she would bring a lesser price in the exchange process attendant to marriage. Among some primitive groups, bride capture still exists. Bride capture is theft and so is rape inasmuch as the violated female may have no marriage ability among her own kind, and, thus, becomes the property of her violator by default, as it were. Brides might be captured or raped and, thus, obtained from outside groups, but in the interest of harmony within the social order, constraints had to be imposed against rape and bride capture. Susan Brownmiller in her elaborate exposition on rape has pointed out, for example, that:

> A payment of money to the father of the house was a much more civilized and less dangerous way of acquiring a wife. And so the bride price was codified, at fifty pieces of silver. By this circuitous route the first concept of criminal rape sneaked its tortuous way into man's definition of law. Criminal rape, as a patriarchal father saw it, was a violation of the new way of doing business. It was, in a phrase, the theft of virginity, an embezzlement of his daughter's fair price on the market.[819]

The parents or kinsmen of a raped female might seek redress or restitution, for the loss to their economy. Ultimately, rape became more of a crime against order and the offender might have to answer to the king or crown through fine or other punishment. Even at this point, however, the female rape victim by agreeing to marry her violater, could spare him the King's punishment and such action might accomplish the consolidation of property and, in effect, placate her kinsmen. It is interesting to note, however, that until quite recently an individual whose spouse was lured away by another man might sue for economic damages in civil court.

Rape had other economic dimensions as well. At one point in history, women were required to marry their rapists. In yet other times, this may have been an option available to the offender in lieu of punishment or economic restitution, as a kind of redemption. In the Middle Ages, women of noble birth might inherit land in the absence of male heirs, but could not marry without the permission of their overlords. Once married, however, the woman's husband acquired title to the land regardless of the objection of the overlord. Through rape, and/or forced abduction and marriage, "adventurous, upward-mobile knights" might acquire property and position by "stealing an heiress."[820]

RAPE IN MILITARY CONTEXT

Prior to contemporary times, military men fought more for economic considerations than for political ideologies. In general, their remuneration was based on victory. To the victor belongs the spoils, and in most cases, the spoils were derived from looting, pillaging, and rape. Women in conquered lands might be enslaved as concubines and later sold, or raped for the carnal gratification of the moment. Rape was even encouraged by some kings, chiefs, and generals as a means of taking revenge on a conquered people, or as an aid in intimidating and thus better subjugating them. Rape, and the subsequent pregnancies and births, also tended to amalgamate conquered peoples and was, thus, functional. From ancient times to the present, fighting men have been compensated economically by allowing them the privilege of rape, and especially of conquered populations. The Golden Horde of Genghis Khan, and the troops of the Byzantine Emperor Alexius in the First Crusade, fought for the privilege of plunder and rape. In more recent centuries when military expeditions were obstensibly more politically than economically motivated, rape and pillage were often explicitly forbidden to troops, but just as often implicitly permitted at an informal level.[821]

It has been reasoned that to encourage rape and plunder would only serve to alienate the enemy populations, and cause them to fight much harder. Since political considerations were foremost such concerns were necessarily taken into account. Troops, however, must be motivated and opportunities for sexual outlet must be made available. Some armies accomplished to provide these outlets in the form of prostitutes and even in some cases, mobile brothels. Inasmuch as some armies like that of the United States could not even openly admit the existence of formerly authorized brothels because of religious and social indignation on the part of our civilian populations, the military had to operate, or at least encourage, the operation of brothels on a more or less clandestine basis. The United States, like most other modern armies, has formerly proscribed rape and plunder, and attempted to enforce such proscriptions with severe sanctions. Both because of the determination of the troops, and the sometimes lax enforcement of such norms, the rape of females in foreign countries, and especially in the enemy population, has been an endemic offense in every one of our wars. George Washington is said to have sentenced one of his revolutionary privates to death for a second conviction of rape. Rape has been punished in all American wars, but at the same time there have been widespread incidences of rape in all of our wars. Other armies in recent wars may have forbidden rape at a formal level, but tacitly permitted it or even encouraged it an an informal level. Some particularly infamous examples of mass rape by the military in recent wars include the capture of Nanking, China, by Japanese troops in 1937, when according to some estimates there were as many as 1,000 rapes a day. Other military campaigns particularly characterized by the brutal mass rape of civilians were the Russian capture of Berlin and their occupation of Vienna, Austria, the Biafran Civil War in Nigeria,[822] as well as the Pakistani campaign in Bangladesh where perhaps more than 200,000 (some claim as many as 400,000) Bengali women were raped by Pakistani soldiers. Inasmuch as Moslem husbands will not live with a wife who has been touched by another man, even a rapist, the rape victims were essentially homeless outcasts.[823] The number of soldiers of any army who are apprehended, convicted, and punished for rape, would seem to be extremely small in relation to the total number of rapes committed. For World War II, for example, the U.S. Army reports 971 convictions for rape by General Courts Martial.[824] The total number of rapes committed must surely have been vastly larger than this. War creates a different social context from peacetime, and the mechanisms of social control are often weaker. War causes men to play unfamiliar roles, sometimes with dysfunctional results. Feminist writers like Brownmiller claim that war and the military causes men to have an exaggerated perspective of maleness and a male-centered world (this last since women are normally not directly involved in the war). This unreal situation, and the power attendant to the military, gives the soldier a sense of superiority, and the opportunity to exercise their masculinity to the fullest. As she puts it, "War provides men with the perfect psychologic backdrop to give vent to their contempt for women." In short, as she sees it, "Men who rape in war are ordinary Joes, made unordinary by entry into the most exclusive male-only club in the world."[825]

RAPE AND MARITAL PROPERTY

Rape has also been viewed in another economic context. The institution of marriage, it has been said, makes a women the "property," or at least the sexual property of her husband. The rapist, in effect, damages the sexual property of the husband. Kasinsky has spoken to this concept and has commented:

> The woman who is "possessed" at the time of the rape by a husband or lover, is often referred to as despoiled, her value as a desirable sexual object being dimished according to her man.[826]

She goes on to document her view by reference to an empirical study of the reactions of a group of husbands to the rape of their wife. The study conducted by Linda Holmstrom,[827] pointed to two common reactions. The first was that the husbands, themselves, had been hurt, and the second was that they should seek revenge on the offenders. In this vein, she quotes a legal authority who in this connection concluded that:

> Rape laws bolster and in turn are bolstered by a masculine pride in the exclusive possession of a sexual object. They focus a male's aggression, based on fear of losing his sexual partner, against rapists rather than against innocent competitors. Rape laws help protect the male from any decrease in the "value" of his sexual possession, which results from forcible violation.[828]

RAPE AND PHYSICAL VIOLENCE

In addition to being conceptualized as an economic crime, rape has always been viewed as a crime of violence against person. In this connection, it is interesting to note that the violence dimension is critical to the social definition. One study of raped women suggested that many do not view themselves as rape victims, especially if there was little violence, and/or if the offender was someone with whom they were acquainted.[829] Similarly, other research has shown that many men and women believe that "it is impossible to rape a woman against her will."[830] Implicitly, this view would indicate that rape necessarily involves significant violence. Much of the legal process attendant to the conviction of rape revolves around questions of consent, degree of resistance, degree of force and violence, and whether the offender was aware of resistance and non-consent. In this connection, until recently, in most states, it was believed that the victim's prior chastity or sex life had a direct bearing on the probability of her consent. Rape victims and many behavioral scientists argue that the preoccupation with violence and force and degree of consent, and especially the concern with past sexual history, all tend to humiliate and degrade the victim. The medical examination, the police interrogation and investigation, the publicity, and the courtroom testimony, so these behavioral scientists claim, in effect put the victim on trial, by inferring that she may have had some degree of responsibility for her own victimization in terms of raising suspicions about the validity of her non-consent. The absence of violence, of course, tends to especially raise the question of force and consent. The customary legal procedures have been criticized by Kasinsky who argues that:

> ... These practices assault and challenge her sense of personal autonomy and integrity, and strip her bare, comparable to the brutality of the rape experience itself.[833]

The type of violence which not infrequently attends rape may assume some unusual modes, however. Beatings, burnings, and knife assaults, even if the victim offers little resistance, are not uncommon. Biting, scratching, or other forms of more animalistic violence are also not unknown. Perhaps, one of the more unusual varieties of rape violence, however, is the so-called "rape by instrumentality." In some rapes, the assailant does not penetrate the victim with his penis, but rather, uses some object to penetrate the victim and thus cause pain and physical damage. In 1979 for example, a Los Angeles composer and record producer, was charged with having "raped" an Academy Award nominated movie actress with the barrel of a revolver.[832] This act was allegedly part of a physical assault incident where the accused came to the home of the actress and beat and pistol-whipped her, culminating with the "rape" by gunbarrel. California had enacted several years earlier, a specific statute which added "rape by instrumentality" to the existing legal code. The new law carried a maximum sentence of five years. The enactment of this law grew out of a case in San Francisco in which a 9 year old girl was raped with a bottle.[833] Interestingly, the assault occurred after the television movie *Born Innocent* portrayed a young girl in a reform school being "raped" with a broom handle by a gang of fellow inmates.[834] Similar incidences in the past are not unknown and it appears that the ultimate aim of such sexual assaults was to destroy the integrity of the victim's hymen, thereby symbolically depriving the victim of the status of virgin.

In a similar but more severe pattern of sexual assault, U.S. soldiers in Vietnam sometimes "raped" captured female prisoners-of-war or suspects with tree limbs or the handle of an entrenching tool.[835]

The etiology of rape suggest strong linkages between the frustration and pathological anger on the part of the perpetrator and the often violent, nature of the sexual offenses.[836] In some instances in recent years, rape and sexual assault have even taken on a cult-like or faddish dimension. In Italy, for example, some young people, usually the offsprings of the new rich and professional status families, have indulged themselves in "murder, torture, and gang rape," with the victims often being young people like themselves. The motive is presumably excitement or perverted amusement. Typical victims are high school aged girls who are kidnapped, tortured, sexually abused, and then clubbed or shot to death.[837]

RAPE AS POLITICAL SUBJUGATION

Largely because of the alleged lack of sensitivity for the feelings of rape victims, and the traumatic experience which attends the prosecution of rape, many feminist writers have begun to conceptualize rape as a kind of political crime, in that it aids males in their domination of women. Kasinsky, for example, contends that rape is the outcome of sexual conflict, "in our competitive, aggressive society justified by the sexist notion that males should control and dominate a woman's sexual being as well as the economic life."[838] Brownmiller has even projected a kind of primal sex struggle between prehistoric male and female. She visualizes a prehistoric rape, possibly even a gang rape by "a band of marauding men," in which male domination over female was established. In this connection, she sees rape as the ultimate weapon in the subjugation of women. According to Brownmiller:

Man's discovery that his genitalia could serve as a weapon to generate fear must rank as one of the most important discoveries of prehistoric times, along with the use of fire and the first crude axe. From prehistoric times to the present, I believe, rape has played a critical function. It is nothing more or less than a conscious process of intimidation by which all men keep all women in a state of fear.[839]

RAPE AND SEXUAL HUMILIATION

Studies of rape support the thesis that rape is not entirely the result of sexual motivation. In a significant number of rape cases, the offender attempts to humiliate the victim by forcing her to engage in various sexual practices classified as "perverted." These practices include fellatio, cunnilingus, anal intercourse, and making the victim masturbate the offender. Amir found that such sexual humiliation occurred in 27% of the rapes he studied.[840] Other studies render similar findings. Such percentages, while not overly large, certainly suggest an element of hostility in the rape. In group-rape events, sexual humiliation occurs in 34% of the cases Amir studied. Some victims in interracial rapes have reported that they were insulted by their assailants, some of whom directed racially derogatory phrases such as "white bitch," and "Have you ever screwed a Negro?," at the victim.[841] Various black militants such as Eldridge Clever spoke of raping white women as "an insurrectionary act," and expressed delight at rape as a means of "defiling his [the white man's] women."[842] Rape then would appear to contain elements of race, class, and sex conflict, in addition to carnal desire.

It would appear that the use of various verbal threats and abusive language by rapists is, in fact, a very important device employed to control and intimidate the victim and thus facilitate the crime in the sense of manipulating the victim and making her compliance more likely, and also to aid in "normalizing" or rationalizing the crime.[843]

RAPE AND DEATH

The rapist may deliberately hurt or even kill his victim because the infliction of pain is requisite to sexual gratification. Some rapists accidentally kill their victims in the process of struggling with them.

Still other rapists kill their victims only as an afterthought as a means of evading arrest and attempting to cover up their crime. Rape may lead to violence and death in ways other than the offender killing the victim. The victim may occasionally kill the rapist or would-be rapist. One such case that attracted widespread attention was that of Joan Little, a black female prisoner in the jail at Washington, North Carolina in August, 1974.[844] It was alleged that the night jailor, Clarence Alligood, attempted to rape her in her cell. She killed him with an ice pick and escaped. Alligood was found dead by multiple stab wounds, and was undressed from the waist down. Ultimately, she surrendered and was prosecuted and tried for murder. Because of the circumstances, the jury acquitted her. A variation of this theme was the Inez Garcia case in which Mrs. Garcia claimed she had been raped, and then 20 minutes later shot and killed a man, she claimed helped to rape her.[845] Because of the 20 minute delay between the rape and the murder, the court believed the murder was premeditated and she subsequently was convicted of second degree murder.

RAPE AND VICTIM PRECIPITATION

In spite of protests to the contrary, studies of rape do suggest an element of victim precipitation.[846] Elements of victim precipitation may have been little more than the female voluntarily putting herself in a "risk situation," but, nevertheless, this was a contributing factor to the crime. In some instances, the victim entered a vulnerable situation by going into dangerous areas, in other cases, the victim may have gone with the rapist to a bar, or in his car, or admitted him to her house or apartment. Some victims have previously used "what could be interpreted as indecent language and gestures or makes what could be taken as an invitation to sexual relations." In some cases, the offender may have believed that the victim had actually agreed to sexual relations, and then retracted her promise before intercourse was consummated. In effect, the victim may have gone into a dangerous situation, and then maximized the chances of being raped by suggestive behavior, and voluntarily accompanying the male who ultimately raped her. The signals and clues she put out may simply have been misinterpreted by the rapist as positive. Many females (and males) and especially advocates of women's liberation take issue with the general concept of victim precipitation and claim that females should not be forced to restrict their latitude of movement or mode of behavior, as a protection from rape. As they see it, a female has the right to engage in sexuality or sexually related behavior without giving implicit permission to have sexual intercourse with her. They maintain that women should have exclusive sexual determination of their bodies regardless of time, place, and circumstances and to this end, have urged, and brought about some reform in the rape laws of various states.

Other significant judicial events concerning rape are also occurring. In July, 1977, for example, a California Court of Appeal unanimously overturned the conviction of a convicted rapist.[847] In this instance, a 23-year-old waitress was hitchhiking, and was picked up by a 32-year-old salesman who subsequently raped her. The Court explained its decision by stating that a woman who enters a stranger's car "... advertises that she has less concern for the consequences than the average female." In Wisconsin, a county judge sentenced a 15-year-old black defendent to a probated sentence for having raped a 16-year-old white girl in a high school stairwell. The judge explained his mild sentence with the comment that, "I'm trying to say to women to stop teasing. There should be a restoration of modesty in dress and elimination from the community of sexual-gratification businesses," and also that, "Whether women like it or not they are sex objects. Are we supposed to take an impressionable person 15 or 16 years of age and punish that person severely because they react to it normally?"[848] Feminists and other groups were outraged and mounted a successful campaign to have a recall election for the judge in the hopes of having him ousted from the bench. He was subsequently defeated at the polls.

The stereotype of rape often incorporates the young, attractive female who dresses or acts in an overly-provocative fashion, who has placed herself in a vulnerable situation, and who accordingly gives out inappropriate and erroneous signals that she is available, to the overly-sexed, perpetuator who is overcome by lust, and mistakenly thinks the victim encouraged him. As so much of the scientific evidence indicates, however, this stereotype is largely mythical. Rapists are seldom, if ever, oversexed, or overcome by lust. Rape victims, in many instances have not placed themselves in vulnerable situations, but are assaulted at home, at work, or on the way to and from. Certainly, they are not necessarily young, attractive, or provocative. Nowhere is this myth more shattered than in the face of the fact that many rape victims are elderly and even sometimes invalids. A 65 to 90 year-old female living quietly along would hardly seem to be a sexually appealing victim or one who was in any way, a participant or precipitant in her own sexual victimization. The existence of the elderly rape victim would seem to underscore the extremely pathological nature of the crime and the non-sexual, aberrant motivation of the perpetrator. There are frequent newspaper accounts of rapes of elderly women all across the country and some defy rational explanation such as the sexual assault of a 69-year-old, blind woman, terminally ill with cancer, in California, by two men who broke into a nursing home in the fall of 1980. There appears to be no upper age limit for rape victimization. In Virginia in 1980, a 24 year old individual was convicted of breaking into the home of an 89 year old widow and raping her, but there have undoubtably been even older rape victims.[849]

RAPE AND LEGAL REFORM

In this connection, pressure to reform all of the police, medical, and judicial procedures surrounding rape have resulted in a number of changes. Many cities now have special police rape squads or teams, often with a female member. The rape squad attempts to investigate the case with maximum sensitivity for the feelings of the victim and to minimize her embarrassment. Medical procedures have also been altered in many instances to accomplish the same thing. Some states have effected extensive legal and judicial reform especially in terms of removing the need for corroboration of the victim's testimony and prohibiting the introduction of testimony concerning the prior sexual activities of the victim.[850]

The reforms have taken a variety of forms including making the rape laws "sex neutral," and simply referring to the act as assault or sexual battery in some legal degree, making penalties more flexible and appropriate to the circumstances of the crime, thus, encouraging juries to convict, and severely restricting the lines of questioning the defense attorney can pursue. Many of these legal reforms have, in fact, acted to make the legal process more efficient. Between 1972 and 1977 in Michigan, where the law was substantiantially revised, for example, rapes reported rose by 30%, arrests for rape were up 62%, and there were 90% more successful prosecutions.[851]

MARITAL RAPE

Recently it was reported that the Labor government in South Australia has proposed legislation that would permit married women to charge their husbands with rape.[852] Australia is not the only instance of laws addressing rape within marriage. Various countries including Israel have legal statutes that prohibit an individual from raping his/her spouse. In recent years, several states including Iowa, Delaware, New Jersey, and Oregon have put marital rape laws on their books. Behavioral scientists are just recently beginning to examine the concept of marital rape, and explore its interactional parameters and social and legal import.[853] With the exception of some instances of alleged rape involving a divorced or legally separated husband and wife, there had never been a case of a husband tried for raping his wife, until the Rideout trial in Oregon.[854] A young married woman, Greta Rideout, accused her husband, John, of raping her after a quarrel. The husband, John, claimed they had voluntary sex after the quarrel as part of "making up." The couple had a history of marital disputes and fights, and subsequent sexual reconciliations. They had a sexual history of unconventional bent. Both admitted exramarital affairs. She admitted having had two abortions, including one for a child fathered by a man other than her husband. She conceded that she had lied at one time, in telling her husband that his stepbrother forced her to have sex. She had also told her husband about her lesbian fantasies (although she denied that she had actually been involved in a lesbian relationship). When the jury sifted all the evidence and information they had heard, and deliberated about the case, they ultimately voted to acquit unanimously. Under English Common Law and U.S. legal tradition, the marriage vows carried implicit sexual consent, but feminists spokespersons have attacked the concept of wife as sexual property in marriage. Had Mrs. Rideout prevailed in court, the case might yet have been overturned on appeal. There will no doubt be other similar cases in the future and the ultimate outcome is difficult to predict given the clash of historical tradition and feminist and liberal social and legal reform.

Before the case was even tried, Mrs. Rideout announced her intention to seek a divorce and after the trial intended to go ahead with the action. She and her husband were subsequently reconciled and reunited and decided to take up their marriage again. After a few weeks, however, marital troubles again erupted and they again indicated that they would move to obtain a divorce.

There have been convictions of individuals for raping their wives where they were divorced or separated. In 1979, a 32 year-old man in Massachusetts was convicted of raping his estranged wife and was sentenced to three to five years in prison.[855]

RAPE IN INSTITUTIONAL CONTEXT

It is difficult to identify a vivid example of a commercial configuration of sexual deviancy within a violent context. There are, as of now, no rape-for-pay establishments. It is possible, as pointed out earlier, however, to hire a prostitute that will permit herself to be beaten up if that affords the customer sexual gratification. Recently, also there has been a burgeoning market for "snuff" films—a new form of stag movies where the females portrayed experience torture, death, and dismemberment—as a new form of male carnal stimulation. Some brothels do provide sadistic services such as whippings and humiliation, for a price, for those who require masochistic stimulation for satisfactory carnal enjoyment. In a similar vein, bondage equipment and literature is widely available on a commercial basis.

As opposed to commercial configurations of rape, per se, however there are widespread institutional contexts within which rape is often endemic, the most notable being prisons and correctional facilities. In such settings, rape victims are not infrequently treated as sexual commodities, sometimes being bought, sold, or traded. In a particularly revealing, and dramatic article published several years ago, the more brutal specifics of violent sex within the context of the prison were detailed.[856] In this instance, the author of the article "Sexual Assaults in the Philadelphia Prison System and Sheriff's Vans," relates the almost unbelievable details of homosexual rape and sexual molestation in jails and in law enforcement vans transporting inmates. The author tells of young prisoners being repeatedly gang raped while being transported to court, and of other young men being sexually assaulted within minutes of being admitted to a detention center. Homosexual rape, according to the account, was systematic and brutal. Allegedly, more than 2,000 such rapes occurred over a two year period. This account is apparently not an isolated set of incidents. In other instances, similar stories have been told, where in some cases, guards and block wardens would "reward" groups of inmates by giving them a young prisoner for homosexual purposes. In yet other situations, the young person might be "sold" to a particular set of inmates. For survival, some young prisoners have had to voluntarily become the habitual victim of sodomy by one individual inmate who would then undertake to protect him from the other inmates.[857] The institutional context of the prison, with its endemic homosexual abuse and violence, cannot help but dehumanize both rape offenders and victims, alienating them further from conventional society, and programming the offender, as it were, to derive carnal gratification, and to vent aggressions and hostilities, through the exercise of sexual violence, and forcing the victim to accept the fact of victimization as an inescapable fact of the exigencies of carnal behavior. Victims of homosexual rape and those coerced into homosexual behavior not only suffer the immediate trauma of violence and brutality, but also often experience long-term residual social stigma and negatively altered self-image.

SUMMARY

Rape may very well continue to increase in incidence in the future. The opportunity structure can enlarge, and the various societal strains that may encourage rape, and especially the conflicts that promote rape as an other than purely sexual crime, may intensify. Inasmuch as investigation and judicial procedures are being reformed, there will certainly be more encouragement for rape victims to come forward and report the crime.

There is a paucity of scientific literature on the crime of rape, and the author of one article on its etiology has called for more scientific inquiry.[858] In the face of the seriousness that society attaches to the crime, the author raises the question as to why rape has been so little studied and why our knowledge of the parameters of the offense is so limited. There are a number of obfuscating factors attendant to rape that may well account for our paucity of insight, however. Compared to other crimes, rape is statistically relatively infrequent, and our figures and data on rape are subject to a number of limitations. There are a number of legal areas surrounding rape that are vague and subject to controversy. Because of the personal and sensitive nature of the crime, it is difficult to obtain adequate information from either offender or victim. Rape is a lurid crime which is often surrounded with emotion, and it is largely this emotional context that has proved to be a handicap to objective progress in establishing the occurrence of the crime, apprehending and convicting the offender, and treating and addressing the social and mental trauma accruing to the victim.

It is interesting to note that the United State Supreme Court recently ruled that rape may never be punished by death because ". . . in terms of moral depravity and of the injury to the person and to the public it does not compare with murder, which does involve the unjustified taking of human life."[859] Thus, having taken the first step in moderating the penalty for rape because the punishment exceeded the cost to the victim, it is not inconceivable that there will be further judicial steps in this direction. At some point in the future, it may be argued, that in the face of liberalized sexual values and behavior, that rape should not be punished on the basis of its sexual, and thus social consequences, but simply as a physical assault. If the ERA Amendment is passed, for example, males may argue that rape of a female equates with the physical assault on a male, and should be punished equally. In the absence of a social rationale that rape goes beyond mere physical trauma, such a judgment may be difficult to evade, and the sexual revolution may well be rapidly eroding that social rationale. It may well be that in time, the very concept of "sex" crime itself will be eliminated from our legal perspective.

Thus, legal procedures are being modified so as to facilitate convictions for rape, and to encourage females to report and prosecute the crime, while other legislation and judicial decisions are reducing the penalties for rape, and, in some instances, formally taking into account the factor of victim precipitation of the crime. In the future, rape may more frequently be prosecuted and convicted, but the seriousness of the crime will likely be decreased as penalties are reduced. In the meanwhile in some states, reformed courtroom procedures are leading to more convictions, but penalties remain severe. In New York, for example, in 1974, shortly after it revised its rape law, a man was sentenced to 12½ to 25 years in prison (he must serve at least 12½ years before he becomes eligible for parole), without the traditional requirement of corroboration by physical evidence of the attempt, and evidence of the victim's lack of consent.[860] Accordingly, some legal authorities are concerned that the rape law reforms may increase the possibility of false accusations, and the likelihood of convicting an innocent person.[859] In the meanwhile, feminist groups and other persons continue to press for further modification of existing rape laws and legal procedures.

Although proponents of reform in all of these various aspects of rape and rape trials have been quite vocal and effective in bringing about changes, there have also been those opponents who hold reservations about the social and legal import of such changes. Some attorneys, for example, have opposed drastic changes in rape prosecution, trial, and evidence procedures in the belief that such changes would be counter-productive and would tend to make convictions more difficult to obtain.[862] Some sociologists have expressed concerns that changes in rape laws concerning evidence, testimony, and judicial procedures might seriously erode our traditional posture in regards to the presumption of innocence and the rights of the accused.[863] In rape cases as with other kinds of crimes, there are instances of mistaken identity, circumstantial evidence, and malicious accusations. There have been cases of persons both falsely accused of rape and falsely convicted.[864]

As pointed out earlier in the discussion, some types of violence are indirectly related to, rather than, a constituent part of carnal behavior. In this connection, wife beating and assaulting appears to be on the increase in this country, or at least surfacing to a greater extent in recent years, especially among the middle and upper-middle class. Inasmuch as wifebeating not infrequently grows out of the problems of sexual role playing and sexual dominance, it should be viewed as a variety of carnal behavior. Like rape, it may satisfy needs to release hostility, anger, and aggression, but it may also operate to serve certain sexually-related needs. Wifebeating is related to a number of factors including the frustrations experienced by the husband in connection with his work and income, his fear of loss of control, and a strained marital relationship. Just as child battering, by parents of both sexes, has tended to increase as social stresses and frustrations experienced by many parents have multiplied, wifebeating also appears to be following this trend. For many of the same reasons discussed in connection with rape, the frustrations, pressures and strains, and role conflicts experienced by husbands will likely accelerate in the future, and it is also likely that the incidence of wifebeating, as a response to these pressures, will become more widespread. Although agencies, and law enforcement groups are increasingly developing mechanisms of intervention, the erosion of the influence of the extended kinship system, increasingly renders the nuclear family atomized and alienated, with the members left to their own resources to deal with problems and pressures on their own.

All sexually-related violence is not involuntary. Sado-masochism provides both inflictor and receiver of pain and humiliation with sexual stimulation and carnal fulfillment. There are those who voluntarily pursue such practices for these purposes. Traditionally viewed as a sexual perversion and aberration of pathological dimensions, sado-masochism would appear to be enjoying, perhaps a greater degree of social toleration, and if not encouragement, in recent years. S-M literature, once suppressed and hidden pornography, is now openly sold and read. Some books, like *The Story of O* have even been made into movies. Many more conventional books and movies have S-M themes and scenes (The opening chapter of *The Anderson Tapes,* for example). "Snuff" films depicting violence and brutality to the point of murder and dismemberment are replacing "stag" films in some quarters. Shops and periodical ads now openly display and sell "leather" and "bondage" equipment and apparel, and apparatus ranging from whips to spanking "harnesses." Much sex humor today, cartoons in "men's" magazines, for example, has an S-M theme. As mentioned earlier in the discussion, best selling sex manuals even recommended S-M behavior in moderated doses, including spanking for erotic purposes, and bondage. There is little doubt that S-M behavior will become much more widespread in the future, and may well even become a relatively common mode of carnal expression in the sexual repertoire of many couples. The sexually-oriented periodicals are predicting a much increased interest in S-M behavior and indicate their intention to respond to this interest with the articles and pictures in their magazines. This may well have the effect of propagandizing on many persons and S-M behavior may be seen in a more legitimate light than in the past. There are finite limits to the sensory pleasures experienced through sexual activity, but in the future, the tendency to try and expand carnal gratification to those limits will doubtless continue. Experimentation in these directions will probably involve more persons, even those of relatively conventional sexual persuasion, to try S-M activity in some form or another. Sexual violence will likely afford some persons, of jaded carnal pallet, expanded horizons of sexual gratification using the convoluted linkages of pain and orgasm. Even in the milder, or more symbolic modes, S-M will probably be used to test role limits, and perhaps serve as a mechanism of temporarily affording a return, through fantasy, to a sexual relationship of more primal and biologically assertive posture.

Rape, however, perhaps more than most other sexual crimes, remains an act of social controversy and behavior still largely misunderstood and subject to contextual obscurity. It is even difficult to say with certainty whether rape, as a crime, is increasing in frequency. Certainly the various governmental statistics would suggest that rape is on the increase, but this may well only be a function of better police-reporting procedures. There is little doubt, however, that in many instances today, a rape may be reported, where in times past the female victim may have been reluctant to come forward and submit to the ordeal of interrogation and trial, and the subsequent sexual stigma. Nevertheless, even with better police reporting efforts, more rape convictions, and a much increased tendency for females to report rape, the available information on the full extent and frequency of the crime would beem to be little more than the tip of the iceberg, so to speak, for rape is still essentially a socially unsanctioned sexual offense.

An uninformed logic might lead to the conclusion that with today's much liberalized sexual attitudes and values, the widespread incidence of premarital and extra-marital sexual behavior, and the presumably large number of females who might voluntarily consent to sexual activity, rape would seem to be an unnecessary, and even anachronistic sexual crime. Why take with force that which may be given freely? Such logic erroneously postulates a rational model of behavior to explain the crime of rape. Rape is far more complex to explain and certainly can be more correctly viewed through the perspective of an irrational act. Even the definition of rape, as commonly perceived by many in society is vague, if not downright murky. As pointed out earlier in the discussion, even women victims of rape do not always view themselves as rape victims, especially if there was minimal violence, or if the offender was an acquaintance. Similarly for many persons, the absence of overt, physical violence in an act of rape, or the involvement of a non-stranger as perpetrator tends to mitigate or obfuscate the offense. Rape is very much a situational crime, and the social definition of the context and its constituent elements is subject to complex variation of perception and interpretation. A number of factors including age and race of victim and perpetrator, the sequence of events leading up to the act, the previous degree of acquaintance and intimacy between the principals, and the perceived physical and social harm suffered by the victim, among others, all contribute to the social delineation of rape. The convoluted complexity of rape has further been traditionally compounded by the fact that at one time or another, rape has been conceptualized as a crime against property, a crime against person, and even a political crime.

Rape has received an inordinate amount of social attention in recent years, largely because of the efforts of various women's rights groups, militant and otherwise. Their educational and lobbying activities have made the public more aware of the problem of rape as a crime, made them more sensitive to the ordeal of the rape victim who elects to report and prosecute the crime, and actually brought about reforms in police, legal, and judicial statutes and procedures. The directions of legal processing of rape are interesting and carry implications for long term change of social values concerning rape.

Legal sanctions for rape have traditionally been severe in this country. In many states, the death penalty, or long terms of imprisonment up to and including life, were often invoked in rape trials. Such penalties were vigorously applied especially in the instance of youthful female victims, and where the offender was black and the victim was white. Severe punishments were supposed to serve as effective deterrents to rape and especially those involving age and racial disparity. The severe penalties were seen as just because of the perceived social enormity of the crime. To the individual victim, the personal and social harm was great. Aside from the expected physiological and psychological trauma of being physically assaulted and violated, there were other considerations. If the victim were a virgin, she had lost her physical and sexual integrity, was sexually "spoiled," and thus less marriageable in the matrimony market. The quality of her life in the future was much diminished, and her prospects for marital and family fulfillment were significantly eroded. Even the parents and relatives were affected by social stigma. Similarly, the married woman also was "spoiled" after rape and her sexual and social adjustment with her husband may have been seriously compromised. Again, even the husband and other members of the family may have experienced residual stigma along with the victim's stigma. Then, too, in an earlier time when the majority of females were virginal before marriage, and after marriage had experienced sexual activity only with their husband, the situation of forced sex with another male was seen as being especially traumatic to the female rape victim and residually harmful to her social and mental well-being. In the face of such irreparable cost to the victim, severe penalties were seen as only just. In the instance of the racial dimension of punishment the severe penalties presumably also served the latent function of enforcing the color bar in interpersonal, and especially sexual activities, between the races. In implementing the rape laws, black rapists with white victims were especially singled out for the most severe legal sanctions.

In deliberating on rape cases, juries considered the past sexual history of the victim, from the standpoint of diminishing the harm of rape. A "spoiled" or unchaste woman would be less victimized by rape than a virginal one, so the cultural reasoning went, and it was precisely this, and similar considerations, that prompted many juries to acquit accused rapists where there was the shadow of suspicion that the female victim may have been even partially willing, and that a sexual history on her part may have rendered her so disposed.

The problem of juries often failing to convict in the face of such severe penalties for rape prompted some women's rights groups and other organizations to press for lower penalties as a more expeditious means of obtaining conviction. These groups also affectively lobbied for changes in courtroom and trial requirements. As a result a number of states including New Jersey, California, Iowa, Connecticut, Ohio, Michigan, and Florida, to name some, have made important changes in their rape statutes. In some of these states, testimony concerning previous sexual experience may no longer be introduced in evidence. In other states, corroborating medical evidence is no longer required, and in some, the distinction between consensual and forced sexual activity has been legally refined.[865] The penalties for rape are also being reduced drastically and, often applied proportionally to the degree of severity of the rape act, i.e., "staircasing the sexual offenses." In some states, the penalty may now be no greater than several years in prison with possibility of earlier parole.

In the face of the revised courtroom and legal dimensions of rape investigations and trials, women seem more inclined to report rapes, district attorneys appear to be more willing to prosecute, and juries appear to be more potentially disposed to convict accused rapists, especially in light of the much reduced sentences in some states. The prognosis for rape convictions may, however, be more complex in the future, and the legal reforms may be viewed from other perspectives than that of successful lobbying by women's groups. The reduced penalties may be initially functional in getting juries to convict, but over time they may tend to dilute the public image of rape as a heinous crime. An offense that carries a maximum penalty no greater than many minor property crimes, may well come to be seen as a minor crime against person in the minds of many people in society. Furthermore, the reduced penalties may, in time, come to be socially interpreted in other ways. Sex surveys, for example, now reveal a much increased percentage of non-virgins before marriage, a greater frequency of young unmarried females having a history of sexual activity with multiple partners, and a much increased incidence of married women having extra-marital affairs. The sexual freedom and sexual activity more characteristic of today's young women may tend to remove the social "halo" traditionally assigned to women on the assumption of their sexual virtue.

If penalties for rape become relatively minimal, in comparison with past times, it may come to be believed that the less severe punishment simply reflects the less seriousness of the offense and the eroded social and physical cost to the individual victim. In short, the minimum sentences for rape conviction may well come to be seen as maximum punishments for what is less and less perceived to be a serious crime inasmuch as a generation of sexually active women may be viewed as having relatively less to lose from rape than their more virtuous sisters of yesteryear. Furthermore, the "staircasing" of sexual offenses, and especially the defining of various degrees of severity in rape cases, while it may aid prosecution and conviction in the immediate future, could under some circumstances be dysfunctional to that purpose in the future. The delineation of a number of degrees of severity in rape, based on various factors constituent to the offense, may well tend to complicate and hinder prosecution and facilitate legal defense on technicalities, just as the various degrees of homicide sometimes makes prosecution more difficult. Different degrees of criminal culpability raises the question of different degrees of guilt, which in turn, engenders plea bargaining and increases the likelihood of legal compromises, and fosters degrees of doubt concerning degrees of guilt in regard to degrees of severity of the crime.

In the future, over and above the question of increased likelihood to report, prosecute, and convict for rape, the actual incidence of rape may well increase. It may increase in spite of the fact of the increased availability of carnal outlets, and especially females willing to consent to coitus. As discussed earlier, rape is, generally speaking, not the result of sexual deprivation, and is not "normal" or even rational behavior. Curiously rape, although classified as a crime, is not officially listed as a sexual deviation, and is only recently beginning to be viewed informally in that light.

Stresses and conflicts, alienation and a sense of powerlessness, and a frustration growing out of the inability to control our social situation, are all endemic to contemporary society. These stresses and frustrations may well be accelerating. Even the female liberation movement may be a contributive factor to such stress in some men, in that it represents a disequilibrium of traditional male-female relationships and erodes or dilutes some males' self images and attendant roles. This shift in women's rights and roles may cause some males to experience even more difficulty in appropriately relating to females, on an interpersonal basis, according to the new standards, and especially in terms of sexually relating to them. The fact that the new generation of sexually liberated women are said to be demanding a higher level of sexual performance from their male partners, as well as insisting on autonomy and equality may well compound the problem. Thus, the type of males who experience a social impotency around, and difficulty in relating to, women may have their insecurities and their hostilities exacerbated by the militancy and independence of women in the future. Rape is an act of violence and such males may increasingly act out their frustrations and anger toward females through rape. It is the violent dimension of rape that the offender enjoys. One researcher has reported that rape, as an act of intense violence, often occurs after a man has been sexually rejected. She went on to say, "typically, the rapist gets little kick from the assault if the woman does not provoke him to violence," and "the more the woman fights the more the rapist likes it."[866] As another author phrased it, rape is a "crime of aggression toward women marked by the need to degrade and abuse."[867] The future may hold an increase in the number of males with this need, and, thus, an increase in violent assaults and rape.

Another significant factor which may well portend ill in the prognosis for rape is opportunity structure. Opportunity structure for rape continues, and will continue to enlarge. More women live alone. More young females who are students or work will live alone or with friends rather in the supervision of home or dormitory. An increasing divorce rate will mean more divorced women living alone. Women will continue to be more mobile in the sense of moving more, traveling more, and going to more places such as restaurants, bars, resorts, etc., either alone or with other females. All of these tendencies will place women in a more vulnerable situation in terms of rape. She will be more exposed to the possibility of assault and rape. Even the trend for women to increasingly move into traditional forms of male employment will enlarge the opportunity structure for rape inasmuch as male occupations are usually more vulnerable to the danger of assault, in terms of routine, location, time, etc. The male labor force with which these women will be working, may even represent a greater potential threat of rape. Overall, there is every reason to believe that the structural factors facilitating rape will be even more opportune in the future, and various societal trends may well encourage or increase the motivation for rape. It is doubtful that the increased likelihood of arrest, prosecution, and conviction for rape will serve as an effective deterrent, and the changes in judicial procedures, and reduced sentences may even serve to prompt a further increase in rape.

In this connection, it is interesting to note that for some reasons basically similar to those associated with female rape, the incidence of homosexual rape is apparently increasing. Cases of homosexual assault, and forcing the male victim to perform sexual acts under threat of force or violence are becoming relatively common.[868] Also, homosexual rape and sexual abuse have become an almost endemic problem in correctional institutions. This fact has encouraged some states to alter their rape laws to permit males, who are victims of homosexual assault, to charge and prosecute for rape.[869] In spite of such legal reforms, homosexual rapes may also increase in the future as a result of increased opportunity structure, and perhaps the growing militancy of homosexuals generally, which may in turn, motivate those homosexual individuals with personality disorders to become bolder in their homosexual encounters, to the point of violence and rape.

We live in a social world of violence with that propensity constituent to much of the fabric of our cultural life. Violence permeates our behavior, even sexual, and often dictates the parameters of our social relationships within the sphere of carnal fulfillment. The social context of sexual behavior includes the dimension of social dominance and hostility as an integral part of biological gratification.

NOTES

[1]Many venerable and ancient cliches and shibbolethes are redolent of the perception of such non-existent causal linkages. An example might be the old saw that "where there is smoke, there is fire."

[2]Quoted in Greer Litton Fox, " 'Nice Girl': Social Control of Women Through a Value Construct," *Signs: Journal of Women in Culture and Society,* 2(4) (Summer, 1977):810.

[3]Ibid.

[4]Ibid.

[5]Ibid.

[6]Ibid.

[7]Ibid.

[8]Ibid.

[9]In regard to this, in July, 1977, a California Court of Appeal unanimously overturned the conviction of a convicted rapist on the basis of the victim having been hitchhiking when the offender picked her up. In the decision, the Court explained that by hitchhiking and entering a stranger's car a woman ". . . advertises that she has less concern for the consequences than the average female." See "Rape and Culture: Two Judges Raise the Question of the Victim's Responsibility," *Time,* September 10, 1977, p. 41.

[10]For a detailed exposition on the dramaturgical parameters of a gynecological examination, see Joan P. Emerson, "Behavior in Private Places: Sustaining Definitions of Reality in Gynecological Examinations," in Hans P. Dreitzel (ed.), *Recent Sociology No. 2.* (New York: Macmillan Co., 1969), 74–97.

[11]Jacqueline Boles and Albeno P. Garbin, "The Strip Club and Stripper Customer

Patterns of Interaction," *Sociology and Social Research,* 58(2)(January, 1974): 141.

[12]Marilyn Salutin, "Stripper Morality," *Transaction,* 8(8)(June, 1971):12–22.

[13]Clifton D. Bryant, *Deviant Behavior: Occupational and Organizational Bases* (Chicago: Rand McNally College Publishing Co., 1974), p. 272.

[14]For a particularly insightful report on the sexual stereotyping of stewardesses see Paula Kane and Christopher Chandler, *Sex Objects in the Sky: A Personal Account of Stewardess Rebellion* (Chicago: Follett Publishing Co., 1974).

[15]Reported in Jay David, *Sex and the Single Stewardess* (Chicago: Playboy Press, 1976), p. 3.

[16]Kane and Chandler, p. 156.

[17]See "Never on Monday," *Time,* November 6, 1972, p. 69.

[18]For a detailed history of anti-Catholic prejudice in the United States see Ray Allen Billington, *The Protestant Crusade 1800–1860.* (New York: Macmillan, 1938).

[19]Scipio de Ricci, *Female Convents: The Secrets of Nunneries Disclosed.* New York: Appleton, 1934). This volume was originally published in London in 1829.

[20]See J. R. Chaplin, "The 'Secrets' of the Nunnery," *Rumor, Fear, and the Madness of Crowds* (New York: Balantine Books, 1959), pp. 13–29.

[21]See Morton Hunt, *The World of the Formerly Married* (Greenwich, Conn: Fawcett Publications, Inc., 1967), esp. pp. 92–117.

[22]Ibid., p. 107.

[23]Ibid., p. 109.

[24]Ibid.

[25]Charles M. Smith, "Selecting the Clerical Wife," *How To Become a Bishop Without Being Religious* (Garden City, N.Y.: Doubleday and Co., Inc., 1965), p. 21.

[26]Frederick E. Whiskin, "Delinquency in the Aged," *Journal of Geriatric Psychiatry,* 1(2) (Spring, 1968):250.

[27]Frederick E. Whiskin, "The Geriatric Sex Offender," *Geriatrics,* 22 (October, 1967):168–9.

[28]Whiskin, "Delinquency in the Aged," pp. 249–250.

[29]For an insightful commentary on the social disvaluement of sexual conduct in the elderly, see Gerhard Falk and Ursula A. Falk, "Sexuality and the Aged," *Nursing Outlook,* 28(1)(January, 1980):51–55.

[30]Clifton D. Bryant and George R. Gross, "The Scarlet Plumbing Fixture: The Bidet and Sexual Stigmatization, in Clifton D. Bryant (ed.), *Sexual Deviancy in Social Context* (New York: Franklin Watts, Inc., 1977), pp. 13–25.

[31]This is an old con in the carnival business, but for a particularly charming version of it see, Arthur L. Lewis, *Carnival* (New York: Trident Press, 1970), pp. 38–39.

[32]See Associated Press, "Sexually Suggestive Mail Investigated: Three Operations Halted," *Roanoke (Va.) Times and World News,* 10 July 1979, sec. A, p. 4.

[33]See Lloyd Shearer, "Slave Trade," *Parade,* November 13, 1977, p. 12.

[34]Lawrence K. Hong, William Darrough, and Robert Duff, "The Sensuous Rip-Off: Consumer Fraud Turns Blue," *Urban Life and Culture,* 3(4)(January, 1975): 464–470.

[35]Leonard Blank, "The Impulse to Look and to Show," *The Journal of Sex Research,* 3(3)(August, 1967):226.

[36]There appears to be a near universal cultural mandate to conduct sexual activities within a context of social privacy. Cross-cultural surveys have only been able to identify few primitive societies that did not prescribe sexual activities to be conducted privately in a situation of privacy and seclusion. See Clellan S. Ford and Frank A Beach, *Patterns of Sexual Behavior* (New York: Harper, 1951), pp. 68–72. It is interesting to note, too, that in very recent years, this norm is being violated in some instances. Referred to here are instances of "swinging," group sex, and the sex spa establishments where more than one couple may be engaged in coitus in the same room at the same time.

[37]The practice of bare-breasted females in Bali as in other areas of Oceania and Southeast Asia, has allegedly been much curtailed in recent decades, presumably due to the influence of Christian missionaries, the diffusion of Western culture, and the constituent values concerning public nudity, as well the new attitudes that have attended the nationalistic movements in these areas with the new concern for a "civilized" image. Reports from anthropological informants and some pictorial expositions in periodicals such as *National Geographic* suggest that in Bali, and in some of the other Southeast Asian and Oceanic countries, especially in remote villages or away from the scrutiny of outsiders, the older customs of semi-nudity still prevail.

In an earlier day, the semi-nudity of the native women on Bali was implicitly advertised as a tourist attraction. In recent years, Bali continues to have large numbers of tourists (100,000 in 1977) especially from Australia, New Zealand, France, West Germany, and the United States. It has been reported, however, that some of the female tourists in Bali are swimming in the nude and, accordingly, the tourists have "become their own leading attraction." See "Intelligence Report: Bali Topless," in *Parade,* 25 December, 1977, p. 4. It is interesting to note that at about the same time many third world countries were moving vigorously to cover up the breasts of their female citizens, in the United States there were significant changes in cultural modesty norms concerning the female breast. Although the "topless" trend in entertainment, such as exotic dancers and performers, in some bars and supper clubs was the most evident indication, even if confined essentially to certain locales, there were also other more general trends in this regard. These included clothing fads such as the topless bathing suit (and the earlier abbreviated top portions of bikinis), "peek-a-boo" and see-through blouses, and the "natural" or "braless" look. There was also more toplessness and other forms of female semi-nudity (and in some instances, male also) in advertising, theater and films, and in pictorial coverage in many periodicals. Exposure of the female breast even became something of a game or spectator sport in the form of wet T-shirt contests popular at many college and university settings. All such activities and departures from traditional modest norms in recent decades suggest a rather dramatic shift from an earlier era in terms of social values and the public posture of permissiveness toward female nudity as well as a curious anachronistic emphasis on the breast.

[38]For an engaging dramatization of such an episode, hear "The Isle Is Full of Voices," Program 11 of The Way of Mankind, Vol. II (an LP record series produced by the National Association of Educational Broadcasters, Urbana, Ill.).

[39]It has been reported that there is a real problem in Paris growing out of the fact

that large numbers of voyeurs who frequent "parks and open spaces" come to observe couples who are engaged in lovemaking. These voyeurs, not infrequently, then rob the couples. See R. Spencer Smith, "Voyeurism: A Review of Literature," *Archives of Sexual Behavior,* 5(6)(November, 1976):586.

[40]See Edward Sagarin, "Power to the Peephole," *Sexual Behavior,* 3(2)(February, 1973):2–7.

[41]Ibid., p. 3.

[42]Such a pasttime and, presumably even its latent, vicarious sexual function, is well-known, wide-spread, and popularly accepted as an innocent recreational diversion. In Great Britain, it is known as "bird watching," and in the United States, it might be recalled that a popular 1950s song began with the line, "Standing on the corner watching all the girls go by." A popular vicarious sexual sport enjoyed by many pubescent males is that of "shooting squirrel," i.e., striving for glimpses of pubic hair, or the crotch region of females as accidently exposed when they carelessly bend over, sit down, cross their legs, or otherwise engage in anatomical contortions.

[43]Sagarin, p. 7.

[44]See Tom Burnam, *The Dictionary of Misinformation* (New York: Thomas Y. Crowell, 1975), p. 131.

[45]For an illustration of this painting and a commentary on it, see *American Painting: 1900–1970* (New York: Time-Life Books, 1970), pp. 72–73.

[46]Ibid., p. 72.

[47]See James G. Cozzens, *Guard of Honor* (New York: Harcourt, Brace and Co., 1948), pp. 214–218.

[48]Ibid., p. 215.

[49]See Myron Brenton, *The Privacy Invaders* (Greenwich, Conn.: Fawcett Publications, Inc., 1964), p. 165.

[50]Scientific sex research of recent years has maintained the laboratory machine-rigor tradition of the Masters and Johnson studies. Some studies of sexual arousal, however, have involved the use of strain gauges attached to the penises of the male subjects to monitor the degree of erection, and also special devices to measure changes in the blood flow in the vaginas of the female subjects. See, for example, Daniel Goleman and Scherida Bush, "The Liberation of Sexual Fantasy," *Psychology Today,* October, 1977, pp. 48–53, 104–107.

[51]See William A. Nolen, *The Making of a Surgeon* (New York: Random House, Inc., 1970).

[52]Catherine S. Chilman, *Adolescent Sexuality in a Changing American Society: Social and Psychological Perspectives* (Washington, D.C.: U.S. Government Printing Office, 1978), p. 93.

[53]Ibid., p. 98.

[54]S. L. Halleck, "Voyeurism and Exhibitionism in Adolescence," *Human Sexuality,* 9(5)(May, 1975):75–76.

[55]Ibid., p. 75.

[56]Chilman, p. 94.

[57]Ibid.

[58]Halleck, p. 76

[59]See Amanda Stewart, *Sex Therapist: My Story* (New York: Ace Books, 1975), esp. pp 7–8; 131–137.

[60]For a detailed and accurate account of carnival "kootch" shows, and especially "strong" ones, see Lewis, pp. 219–227 and pp. 262–277; for another particularly vivid exposition (both pictorial as well as narrative) on "kootch" shows see Susan Meiselas, *Carnival Strippers.* (New York: Farrar, Strauss and Giroux, 1979).

[61]Lewis, p. 224.

[62]Ibid., p. 225.

[63]Ibid., p. 267.

[64]Ibid., p. 272.

[65]See Anatole Broyard, "Woman as Stud: An Inquiry into Feminine Literature," *Mademoiselle,* July, 1974, pp 98–99+, and pp. 117–118.

[66]Ibid., p. 98

[67]See A. C. Kinsey, W. B. Pomeroy, C. E. Martin et al., *Sexual Behavior in the Human Female* (Philadelphia: Saunders, 1953).

[68]Havelock Ellis, quoted in Sagarin, pp. 3–4.

[69]Sagarin, p. 4.

[70]For an interesting account of such activities, see Sara Harris, "Money or Time No Object, but Couples Must Love Animals," *The Puritan Jungle: American's Sexual Underground* (New York: G. P. Putnam's Sons, 1969), pp. 139–163.

[71]See William Feigelman, "Peeping: The Pattern of Voyeurism Among Construction Workers," *Urban Life and Culture,* 3(1)(April, 1974):35–49.

[72]Angela Fox Dunn, "The Dark Side of Erotic Fantasy," *Human Behavior,* 7(11)(November, 1978):18.

[73]"Is Sex Neurotic,?" *Time,* January 3, 1977, p. 76.

[74]Ibid.

[75]"Bedroom Battle," *Time,* June 4, 1979, p. 64.

[76]Robert J. Stoller, "Sexual Excitement," *Archives of General Psychology,* 33(8)(August, 1976):900.

[77]Ibid., p. 904.

[78]Ibid., p. 903. Robert J. Stoller has also written on perversion in detail and especially the relationship of hostility and sexual activity. For a complete exposition, see his *Perversion: The Erotic Form of Hatred* (New York: Pantheon Books, Div., Random House, 1975).

[79]Idem., p. 903.

[80]Ibid.

[81]For a review of some of these opposing views, see Dunn.

[82]See Irvin D. Yalom, "Aggression and Forbidingness in Voyeurism," *Archives of General Psychiatry,* 3(September, 1960):305–319.

[83]Ibid., p. 308.

[84]Ibid., p. 310.

[85]Ibid.

[86]Ibid.

[87]Eustace Chesser, *Strange Loves: The Human Aspects of Sexual Deviation* (New York: William Morrow and Co., Inc., 1971), p. 236.

[88]Spencer R. Smith, "Voyeurism: A Review of Literature," *Archives of Sexual Behavior,* 5(6)(November, 1976):585–609.

[89]Ibid., p. 593.

[90]Ibid., p. 594.

[91]Ibid., p. 596.

[92]Ibid., p. 598.

[93]Ibid., p. 599.

[94]Ibid., p. 602.

[95]Ibid., p. 603

[96]Ibid., pp. 603–605.

[97]Ibid., p. 607.

[98]For a detailed exposition of porno movie houses and the vicarious thrills they offer, see Joseph Slade, "Pornographic Theaters Off Times Square," *Transaction,* 9(1,2)(November–December, 1971):35–43+.

[99]Ibid., p. 38.

[100]Ibid., p. 39.

[101]Charles A. Sundholm, "The Pornographic Arcade: Ethnographic Notes on Moral Men in Immoral Places," *Urban Life and Culture,* 2(1) (April, 1973): 85–104.

[102]John Lindquist and Howard L. Cane, "Myths and Realities of Dirty Book Buyers," *Free Inquiry in Creative Sociology,* 7(1)(May, 1979):51.

[103]Slade, (1971) p. 38.

[104]See Goleman and Bush, pp. 48–53+; 104–107.

[105]Studies have shown, however, that there are attitudinal limits to the degree of sexual explicitness in public entertainment that will be tolerated by adult audiences. One such study indicated, for example, divided patrons in categories of "occasional" and "regular," and "non participants" and "curiosity-seekers," in terms of frequency of attendance. The persons who exhibit the most permissive posture toward sexually explicit behavior and male/female nudity were the "occasional" and "regular" participants as opposed to "non participants" and "curiosity-seekers." In the instance of all categories of persons, however, there was a tendency to believe that actual intercourse should not be permitted in films or on stage, and to a lesser degree among some of the participants, that simulated intercourse should not be portrayed. See Kyle Knowles and Houshang Poorkaj, "Attitudes and Behavior on Viewing Sexual Activities in Public Places," *Sociology and Social Research,* 58(2)(January, 1974):130–135.

[106]Kinsey, Pomeroy, Martin et al. Some research in recent years has tended to dilute, if not negate, Kinsey's findings. Findings of several studies have indicated that "any sex difference in response to erotica is only slight and for some types of erotica women are more aroused than men." See H. J. Eyseneck, and K. D. B. Nias, *Sex, Violence, and the Media* (New York: St. Martin's Press, 1978), p. 222. Furthermore, some recent and detailed explorations of female sexual fantasy reveal scenarios of rich, erotic complexity. See, for example, Karen Shanor, *The Fantasy Files: A Study of the Sexual Fantasies of Contemporary Women* (New York: Dial Press, 1977); another insightful examination of sexual mental imagery in females is Nancy Friday, *My Secret Garden: Women's Sexual Fantasies* (New York: Trident Press, 1973).

[107]See Susan Fraker, William J. Cook, Dewey Gram et al., "Crackdown on Porn," *Newsweek,* February 28, 1977, pp. 21–27.

[108]See "Blacking Out Blue," *Time,* June 7, 1976, p. 63.

[109]See Harry F. Waters and Janet Huck, "The Lewd Tube," *Newsweek,* December 29, 1975, p. 60.

[110]See Joseph W. Slade, "Recent Trends in Pornographic Films," *Society,* 12(6)(September/October, 1975): 77–84.

[111]See Slade (1975), p. 78–79.

[112]Walker Sachs, "Sex Machine: No Business Like Show Business," *Business and Society Review,* 10(20) (Winter, 1976–177):24.

[113]See H. J. Eysenck and K. K. B. Nias, p. 274.

[114]Sexual fantasy and the attendant carnal gratification can involve children, adults, animals, or objects. The theatrical scenarios of sexual fantasy can invoke all manner of plots, backdrops, and actors. Deriving sexual stimulation and vicarious gratification from juvenile pornography would not necessarily make one a pedophile although there is likely a strong, connecting relationship. Clinicians have even reported that fantasy involving incest is not uncommon. They are referring to fantasy on the part of the child or juvenile involving sexual activity with parents or relatives. See Alvin A. Rosenfeld, Carol C. Nadelson, and Marilyn Krieger, "Fantasy and Reality in Patients Reports of Incest," *Journal of Clinical Psychiatry,* 40(4) (April, 1979):159–167; 164–172. Sexual arousal can even be accomplished by viewing masturbation. One study involving both males and females watching films of male and female individuals masturbating indicated that males are much more highly aroused by viewing females masturbate than males, but females tend to be sexually aroused about equally by both. See Donald L. Mosher and Paul R. Abramson, "Subjective Sexual Arousal to Films of Masturbation," *Journal of Consulting and Clinical Psychology,* 45(5) (October, 1977): 796–807.

[115]See, for example, Fraker et al., pp. 21–27.

[116]See Morris Fraser, "Child Pornography," *New Statesman,* 95(2448) (February 17, 1978): 213.

[117]See "Kid's Stuff," *The Economist,* 263(6981) (June 18, 1977): 51–52.

[118]See Merill Sheils and Anthony Marro, "The Memphis Smut Raker," *Newsweek,* April 5, 1976, pp. 62–63.

[119]See Fraker et al., p. 21.

[120]Associated Press, "Anti-pornography Groups Bomb Adult Store: Man Dazed," *The* (Jackson, Miss.) *Clarion Ledger,* 25 August 1977, p. 10.

[121]See "War on Pornography Begins in Earnest," *U.S. News & World Report,* September 13, 1976, pp. 75–76.

[122]"Pornography Controls Imperative," *Intellect,* 103(2362) (January, 1975): 219.

[123]Harold B. Kuhn, "The 'Right to Leer,'" *Christianity Today,* 21(3) (November 5, 1976): 90.

[124]Slade, (1971), p. 43.

[125]Ibid., p. 41.

[126]Ibid., p. 43.

[127]Ibid., p. 79.

[128]"X-rated Expletives," *Time,* May 20, 1974, p. 72–73.

[129]Ibid., p. 73.

[130]Ibid.

[131]Ibid.

[132]See Ashley Montagu, *The Anatomy of Swearing,* (New York: The Macmillan Co.), 1967, p. 86. Although this was the case, it would appear that women, in

general, are increasingly making use of swear words in their language repertoire. Again, Montagu comments:

> ... Hence we perceive that until recently swearing in women was
> negatively sanctioned as unfeminine and bypassed by the resort to
> emotional expression through weeping. With the growing emancipa-
> tion of women from her inferior status she has now altogether aban-
> doned the privilege of swooning and has reduced the potential oceans
> of tears to mere rivulets. Today, instead of swooning or breaking into
> tears, she will often swear and then effectively do whatever is in-
> dicated. . . . (p. 87)

Montagu then goes on to say ". . . many modern women have grown to be ashamed
of tears and quite belligerently proud of swearing." (p. 87) On the assumption
that younger females are more apt to be "liberated" than those in earlier
generations, it also seems that the younger females are the ones most likely to
use swear words. Certainly this stereotype, valid or not, is promoted by fictional
characters such as Jenny in Erich Siegel's *Love Story.* See also *Time,* May 20,
1974, p. 73.

[133]Ibid., p. 72.

[134]Ibid., p. 72.

[135]Ibid.

[136]See Herbert Freed, "Nudity and Nakedness," *Sexual Behavior,* 3(1) (January, 1973): 7.

[137]See *Time,* May 20, 1974, p. 73.

[138]Reported in William N. Stephens, *The Family in Cross-Cultural Perspective* (New York: Holt, Rinehart and Winston, Inc., 1963), p. 94.

[139]Ibid., p. 98.

[140]Denali Crest, "Those Four-letter Words of Love: Why We Use Them," *Sexology,* 41(1) (August, 1974): 16–17.

[141]Ibid.

[142]Myron Brenton, *Sex Talk* (New York: Stein and Day, 1972), pp. 76–77.

[143]Crest, p. 18.

[144]Ibid.

[145]See Beverley T. Mead, "Coping with Obscene Phone Calls," *Medical Aspects of Human Sexuality,* 9(6) (June, 1975) 127–128. The remarks in the following paragraphs about obscene phone callers draws heavily on this article. For additional insights into the pathology of obscene phone callers, see R. P. Nadler, "Approach to Psychoanalysis of Obscene Telephone calls," *New York State Journal of Medicine,* 68 (1968): 521–526.

[146]Mead, p. 127.

[147]Ibid.

[148]Ibid.

[149]Ibid.

[150]The increasing sophistication of telephone call tracing equipment and procedures is making obscene phone calls much more hazardous for the offender. There is equipment, for example, that can be attached to the victim's phone line and when an obscene telephone call comes, the victim simply does not hang up and

goes to another phone and calls the phone company. As long as the victim does not hang up, the caller's phone number is "locked into that of the victim," and can easily be traced. See Dick Hammerstrom, "Equipment Can Trace Obscene Calls," 13 November 1977, *Roanoke* (Va.) *Times and World News.*

[151]This discussion on telephone masturbators is largely based on Gene W. Brockopp and David Lester, "The Masturbator," *Crisis Intervention,* 1 (1969): 10–13.

[152]See David Lester, "Telephone Counseling and the Masturbator: A Dilemma," *Clinical Social Work Journal,* 1(4) (April, 1973) 257–260.

[153]Brockopp and Lester, p. 10.

[154]Clifton D. Bryant and C. Eddie Palmer, "Massage Parlors and 'Hand Whores:' Some Sociological Observations," *The Journal of Sex Research,* 11(3) (August, 1975): 237.

[155]See "Dirty-Story Time," *Parade,* July 4, 1976, p. 20.

[156]Ibid.

[157]See Associated Press, "Teen-Ager's Poem Too Rough," *Roanoke* (Va.) *Times and World News,* 6 November 1977, sec. A, p. 6.

[158]Associated Press, "Hung Jury Ends Trial on Obscenity," *Roanoke* (Va.) *Times and World News,* 18 November 1977, sec. A, p. 2.

[159]See Rudy Maxa, "New-found Faith Keeps Flynt Hustling," *Roanoke* (Va.) *Times and World News,* 8 January 1878, sec. A, p. 10.

[160]Nathaniel Sheppard, Jr, "Bar Group Debates Pornography and Effects That It Has on Society," *The New York Times,* 30 October 1977, p. 26.

[161]Landmark News Service, "Pornographer Attacks Norfolk Ordinance," *Roanoke* (Va.) *Times and World News,* 21 January 1978, sec. C, p. 3.

[162]See Sachs, p. 24.

[163]See Gary Wills, "Measuring the Impact of Erotica," *Psychology Today,* August, 1977, pp. 30–76.

[164]William E. Mitchell, "The Baby Disturbers: Sexual Behavior in a Childhood Contraculture," *Psychiatry,* 29 (4) (February, 1966): 367–377.

[165]Terrance L. Stocker, Linda W. Dutcher, Stephen M. Hargrove et al., "Social Analysis of Graffiti," *Journal of American Folklore,* 85(338) (October–December, 1972): 356.

[166]Ibid.

[167]Lee Sechrest and A. Kenneth Olson, "Graffiti in Four Types of Institutions of Higher Education," *The Journal of Sex Research,* 7(1) (February, 1971): 65.

[168]Ibid., p. 67.

[169]Ibid., p. 68.

[170]Ibid., p. 70.

[171]Curtis Ingham, "Graffiti: The Soap-Box of the Seventies," *Ms. Magazine,* September, 1975, p. 66.

[172]See Jim Hougan, "Kilroy's New Message," *Harper's Magazine,* November, 1972, pp. 20–26.

[173]Alan Dundes, "Here I Sit—A Study of American Latrinalia," *Kroeber Anthropological Society Papers,* 34(1966): 102–104.

[174]Jack Horn, "Gang Graffiti-Spray-Can Boundaries," *Psychology Today,* February, 1976, p. 100.

[175]"An Identity Thing," *Time,* March 13, 1972, p. 44.

[176]A recent, insightful exposition on the pornography industry is Carolyn See, *Blue Money* (New York: David McKay Co., Inc., 1974).

[177]For a fuller discussion of Twain's *1601*, see Ralph Ginsburg, *An Unhurried View of Erotica* (New York: Ace Books, Inc., 1958), especially pp. 73–76.

[178]Ibid., p. 75.

[179]Ibid., p. 76.

[180]Ibid.

[181]Ibid., pp. 19–20.

[182]Quoted in Ibid., pp. 21–22.

[183]Harris's *My Secret Life* is discussed in great detail in Stephen Marcus, *The Other Victorians: A Study of Sexuality and Pornography in Mid-Nineteenth Century England* (New York: Basic Books, 1966).

[184]For an elaborate exposition on pornography in the United States, see "The Porno Plague," *Time*, April 5, 1976, pp. 58–63. The discussion here heavily draws on this article.

[185]Ibid., p. 58.

[186]See Ron Sproat, "The Working Day in a Porno Factory," *New York Magazine*, March 11, 1974, pp. 37–40.

[187]Ibid., p. 40.

[188]Thomas H. Van De Velde, *Ideal Marriage: Its Physiology and Technique* (New York: Random House, 1930).

[189]"J," *The Sensuous Woman* (New York: Dell Publishing Co., Inc., 1971).

[190]Ibid., pp. 110–111.

[191]Alex Comfort, *The Joy of Sex: A Cordon Bleu Guide to Lovemaking* (New York: Crown Publishers, 1972).

[192]David P. Reuben, *Everything You've Ever Wanted to Know About Sex But Were Afraid to Ask* (New York: David McKay Co., 1969). Reuben's book was not without its share of detractors. After a slow start, the book became something of a national best seller and book-club selection in a number of book clubs. Some of the critics and reviews, however, viewed the book as humorous as much as medically instructive. *Life*, for example, called it "howling funny." Another reviewer in *Look* termed it, "psychiatrically naive, perhaps dangerous, for anyone to get the idea that reading a book will solve real sexual difficulties." Ultimately, some critics pointed out that Reuben's book had numerous errors, inaccuracies, and even dangerous advice. It was, overall, a publishing success, but according to some critics such as Dr. Pomeroy (a former Kinsey researcher) the book had "a lot of junk in it." See J. J. Fenstermaker, "Dr. Reuben Meets the Press," *Illinois Quarterly*, 41(2) (Winter, 1978): 26–36.

[193]See E. M. Palmegiano, "The Propaganda of Sexuality: Victorian Periodicals and Women," *Victorians Institute Journal*, 6 (1977): 21–30.

[194]See Bob Greene, " 'X-Rated' Catalog Embarrasses Staid Company," *Roanoke* (Va.) *Times and World News*, 10 February 1980, sec. E, p. 8.

[195]Ginsburg, p. 81.

[196]*Time*, April 5, 1976, p. 61.

[197]Ibid.

[198]See Waters and Huck, *Newsweek*, December 29, 1975, p. 60. Also, "Blacking Out Blue," *Time*, June 7, 1976, p. 63.

[199]See John C. Carlin, "The Rise and Fall of Topless Radio," *Journal of Communication,* 26(1) (Winter, 1976): 31–37.

[200]C. Eddie Palmer, "Filthy Funnies, Blue Comics, and Raunchy Records: Dirty Jokes and Obscene Language as Public Entertainment," in Clifton D. Bryant (ed.), *Sexual Deviancy in Social Context,* pp. 82–101.

[201]For a detailed account of Bruce's career see Albert Goldman, "What Lenny Bruce Was All About," *The New York Times Magazine,* June 27, 1971, pp. 121–131.

[202]See Mark Goodman, "George Carlin Feels Funny," *Esquire,* December, 1974, pp. 122–125.

[203]Quoted in Blank, p. 223.

[204]Traditionally, a tourist attraction of some third world countries was the nudity or semi-nudity of the native women. Bali, where the females, until recently, were naked from the waist up, was a case in point. More recently, it is sometimes the tourists who are providing the spectacle for the natives. Female tourists from Europe, Australia, and New Zealand often swim in the nude in Bali. A similar phenomenon is also occurring in other parts of the world. In some areas, such as Antigua, some female tourists, who come with sailboat and yacht owners, often go topless or swim in the nude inviting the stares of other tourist sightseers.

[205]See Marvin Opler, "Absence of Clothes Doesn't Mean Absence of Morality," *Sexual Behavior,* 3(1) (January, 1973): 6.

[206]Martin S. Weinberg, "Sexual Modesty, Social Meanings, and the Nudist Camp," *Social Problems,* 12(3) (Winter, 1965): 313.

[207]See Freed, p. 3.

[208]For an insightful exposition on streaking, see James M. Toolan, Murray Elkins, Paul D'Encarnacao et al., "The Significance of Streaking," *Medical Aspects of Human Sexuality,* 8(7) (July, 1974): 152–165.

[209]Ibid., p. 157.

[210]See William A. Anderson, "The Social Organization and Social Control of a Fad," *Urban Life,* 6(2) (July, 1977): 221–240.

[211]Ibid., p. 221.

[212]Ibid.

[213]Ibid., p. 232.

[214]Ibid., p. 236.

[215]Ibid.

[216]Toolan et al., pp. 159–165.

[217]Ibid., p. 157.

[218]Ibid.

[219]For a detailed discussion of nudist ideology, see Weinberg, pp. 311–318. For an early statement on the nudist ideological posture, see also, Maurice Parmelee, *Nudism in Modern Life* (New York: Alfred A. Knopf, new rev. ed., 1931).

[220]American Sunbathing Assn., "Sunbathers, Ahoy!" in Charles H. McCaghy, James K. Skipper, Jr., and Mark Lefton (eds.), *In Their Own Behalf: Voices from the Margin* (New York: Appleton-Century-Crofts, 1968), p. 7.

[221]Weinberg, p. 315.

[222]American Sunbathing Assn. in McCaghy, Skipper, and Lefton, (eds.), p. 7.

[223]See "San Diego Nude Beach Lures Tourists," *The New York Times,* 13 June 1976, p. 31. There has been at least one detailed sociological study of naked swimmers at the public beach, which addressed the participants, their ideological posture, and the attendant social context. See Jack D. Douglas, Paul K. Rasmussen with Carol Ann Flanagan, *The Nude Beach* (Beverly Hills, Calif.: Sage Publications, 1977).

[224]C. Lasègne, "Les Exhibitionistes," *Paris, L'Union Medicale,* 23(1977):703.

[225]N. K. Rickles, *Exhibitionism* (Philadelphia: Lippincott, 1950).

[226]See David, pp. 122–123.

[227]See Halleck, pp. 75–76.

[228]Ibid., p. 76.

[229]Melitta Schmideberg, "On Treating Exhibitionism: Some Implications," *International Journal of Offender Therapy and Comparative Criminology,* 16(2) (1972): 130.

[230]See Halleck, p. 76.

[231]James L. Mathis, "The Exhibitionist," *Medical Aspects of Human Sexuality,* 3(6) (June, 1969): 93.

[232]Ibid., pp. 93–95.

[233]Ibid., p. 95.

[234]See Donald H. Russell, "Treatment of Adult Exhibitionists," *International Journal of Offender Therapy and Comparative Criminology,* 16(2) (1972): especially 121–122.

[235]Miller and Haney, for example, have reported the case of an exhibitionist who had a lengthy career in correctional and mental institutions because of having exposed his genitals to female children on several occasions. He was eventually cured through therapy. See Howard Miller and John R. Haney, "Behavior and Traditional Therapy Applied to Pedophiliac Exhibitionist: A Case Study," *Psychology Report,* 3(2) (December, 1976) 1119–1124.

[236]Mathis, p. 95.

[237]Schmideberg, p. 132.

[238]Russell, p. 122.

[239]Schmideberg, p. 133.

[240]Ibid, p. 133.

[241]Blank, pp. 223–224.

[242]Irving Barnett, "The Successful Treatment of an Exhibitionist: A Care Report," *International Journal of Offender Therapy and Comparative Criminology,* 16(2) (1972): 126.

[243]Observations in this paragraph are largely drawn from Mathis, p. 97.

[244]See Alex K. Gigeroff, J. W. Mohr, and R. C. Turner, "Sex Offenders on Probation: The Exhibitionists," *Federal Probation,* 32(2) (September, 1968): 21.

[245]See James L. Mathis and Mabelle Collins, "Mandatory Group Therapy for Exhibitionists," *American Journal of Psychiatry,* 126(8) (February, 1970): 1162–1166. For other reports on group therapy, see Amorette Lee Freese, "Group Therapy with Exhibitionists and Voyeurs," *Social Work,* 17(2) (March, 1972): 44–52.

[246]Jim Stevenson and Ivor H. Jones, "Behavior Therapy Techniques for Exhibitionism," *Archives of General Psychiatry,* 27 (December, 1972): 839.

[247]Gigeroff, Mohr, and Turner, pp. 19–20.

[248]Mathis, p. 95.

[249]Harold Levitan, "An Exhibitionist," *The Psychoanalytic Quarterly,* 32 (1963): 246.

[250]Freese, p. 49.

[251]For some detailed discussion of the therapy and treatment of exhibitionism while on probation, see Arnold Veraa, "Probation Officer Treatment for Exhibitionists," *Federal Probation,* 40(1) (March, 1976); also, Mathis and Collins; Freese; and, Gigeroff, Mohr, and Turner.

[252]William L. McWhorter, "Flashing and Dashing: Notes and Comments on the Etiology of Exhibitionism," in Clifton D. Bryant (ed.) *Sexual Deviancy in Social Context,* pp. 101–110.

[253]See Sharon Kantorowski Davis and Phillip W. Davis, "Meaning and Process in Erotic Offensiveness," *Urban Life,* 5(3) (October, 1976): 377–396.

[254]"And Now Bring On the Boys," *Time,* August 6, 1979, p. 69.

[255]For a detailed exposition on the use of sex in advertising, see Vance Packard, *The Hidden Persuaders* (New York: Pocket Books, Inc., 1958).

[256]James K. Skipper and Charles H. McCaghy, "Stripteasers: The Anatomy & Career Contingencies of a Deviant Occupation" Social Problems 17 (3)(Winter 1970):394.

[257]Skipper and McCaghy, p. 397.

[258]See "Morganna Perpetuates Mystique," *Roanoke* (Va.) *Times and World News,* 30 September 1979, sec. E, p. 1.

[259]The legal battle over toplessness has continued for some time in the United States without legal resolution. In Tulsa, Okla., for example, two city ordinances were enacted to prohibit bare-breasted women from serving food, this effectively outlawing topless waitresses. A Municipal Court Judge, however, ruled that the ordinances were unconstitutional because, among other things, they violated new sexual discrimination guidelines by specifying "females." See Associated Press, "Law Prohibiting Topless Waitresses Ruled Discriminatory," *Roanoke* (Va.) *Times and World News,* 8 December 1977, sec A, p. 2.

[260]Richard G. Ames, Stephen W. Brown, and Norman L. Weiner, "Breakfast with Topless Barmaids," in Jack D. Douglas (ed.) *Observations of Deviance* (New York: Random House, 1970), p. 45.

[261]There is a considerable amount of literature on stripping as an occupational specialty. See, for example, Jacqueline M. Boles and Albeno O. Gabrin, "The Choice of Stripping for a Living: An Empirical and Theoretical Explanation," *Sociology of Work and Occupations,* 1(1) (February, 1974): 4–17; also, James K. Skipper and Charles H. McCaghy, "The Stripteaser," *Sexual Behavior,* 1(3) (June, 1971): 78–88; and Clifton D. Bryant, "Epidermal Exposure and Ecydysiastic Eroticism," *Deviant Behavior: Occupational and Organizational Bases,* pp. 270–274.

[262]See, "Now Bring on the Boys," *Time,* p. 69. See also Mary Bland Armistead, "Turning the Tables: The Guys Take It Off," *Roanoke* (Va.) *Times and World News,* 30 January 1980, sec C, p. 1.

[263]"And Now Bring on The Boys," *Time,* p. 69.

[264]Ibid.

[265]Ibid.

[266]See "Stripping Sailor Angers Brass," *Roanoke (Va.) Times and World News,* 28 February, 1980.

[267]"And Now Bring on the Boys," *Time,* p. 69.

[268]Skipper and McCaghy, p. 392.

[269]Marilyn Salutin, "Stripper Morality," *Transaction: Social Science and Modern Society,* Vol. 8, No. 8, Whole No. 68 (June, 1971), p. 13.

[270]See Ann Terry D'Andre, "An Occupational Study of the Strip-Dancer Career," Paper delivered at the Pacific Sociological Association Annual Meeting held in Salt Lake City, Utah (April 22–24, 1965).

[271]Sandra Harley Carey, Robert A. Peterson, and Louis K. Sharpe, "A Study of Recruitment and Socialization Into Two Deviant Female Occupations," *Sociological Symposium,* 11 (Spring, 1974): 11–24.

[272]Salutin, p. 18.

[273]Boles and Garbin, 1974, pp. 136–144.

[274]Will Grimsley, "Stripper Laments Nudity in Films," *The Nashville Tennessean,* 13 October 1969, p. 21.

[275]See Associated Press, "Nude Therapy Used by Church," *Roanoke (Va.) Times and World News,* 7 January 1977.

[276]See Associated Press, "Bake Shop Goodies Feature Risque Art," *Roanoke (Va.) Times and World News,* 12 November 1977, sec. C, p. 6.

[277]See Associated Press, "First Blue Movies, Now—Blue Cakes?" *Roanoke (Va.) Times and World News,* 28 December, 1976, p. 1.

[278]See "Hours of Waiting to Fill the Tank," *Time,* July 2, 1979, p. 20.

[279]See Associated Press, "ABC Board Bans X-rated Puppets; Publicity Profitable," *Roanoke (Va.) Times and World News,* 11 July 1980.

[280]See Waters and Huck, p. 60; and "Blacking Out Blue," p. 63.

[281]See Stephens, pp. 376–377.

[282]For an interesting description of this genital mutilization, found in a fictional but well-researched novel, see Richard Llewellyn, *A Man in a Mirror* (New York: Pocket Books, Inc., 1961) especially pp. 52–53. As Llewellyn had his protagonist portray the operation, "They split almost the length," Jim said. "They put the muscular tissue through the outer tube. They cut all the connecting tissue. Then they cut away a piece on each side of the tube . . . When the healing is over, a flap of pupice remains." The speaker goes on to comment that, "After two years there is still great tenderness" . . . [and there are] . . . "Three or four years before there is no pain."

The practice of genital mutilation among preliterate and folk peoples is not confined to males only. Among the Gikuyu people of Kenya, *irua* or the ritual circumcision of young people of both sexes is carried on even in recent times. In the instance of females, the circumcision involves the surgical amputation of the tip of the clitoris. Females are forbidden to masturbate as children, even though males are not prior to the time of their own puberty rites and circumcision. The trimming of the clitoris apparently serves to desensitize the clitorial area and prevents them from having localized sexual feelings in that area. This, in turn, helps enforce the proscription against female masturbation and encourages females to seek sexual gratification through genital coitus in marriage. For a detailed ethnographic account of clitoridectomy among the Gikuyu, see Kenyatta Jomo, *Facing Mount Kenya: The Tribal*

Life of the Gikuyu (New York: Vintage Books) 1965, especially pp. 125–156.

For a very recent and detailed analysis of female circumcision among contemporary Egyptian females, see Assaad, Marie, "Female Circumcision in Egypt: Social Implications, Current Research, and Prospects for Change," *Studies in Family Planning,* 11(1) (January, 1980): 3–16. In this study, the author points out that in Egypt and in other parts of the Arabic world, female circumcision may involve surgical trimming of the labia minora and the labia majora as well as excision of the clitoris. The practice is usually performed relatively early in a girl's life, often between the ages of six and 10, before reaching puberty. The function of female circumcision is manifold, but includes among reasons, "the attentuation of sexual desire, this protecting the woman against her own oversexed nature" (pp. 5–6). By desensitizing the clitorial area, females are prevented from being an oversexed wife, and more importantly, female modesty and chastity are better insured, as is the "impeccability of the hymen" protected (p. 5). Females who are circumcised are also better able to establish their feminine ability. Presumably female circumcision also discourages masturbation, which might endanger the hymen and encourage excess sexuality.

[283]For an insightful account of these practices, see William Clive's fictional, but historically detailed and accurate account, of the battle of Isandhlwana during the Zulu Wars, *The Tune That They Play* (New York: Simon and Schuster), 1973, especially Chapter 2.

[284]See Helen A. Gibney, "Masturbation: An Invitation for an Interpersonal Relationship," *Perspectives in Psychiatric Care,* 10(3) (July–September, 1972): 128–134.

[285]In the *King James Bible,* Book of Genesis 38:8–9, Onan is instructed by Judah, to marry his dead brother's wife and impregnate her in the name of his brother. Onan did not carry out these instructions, however. The passage tells that

> ... and Onan knew that the children should not be his; and it came to pass, when he went unto his brother's wife, that he spilled it on the ground, lest that he should give seed to his brother.

The Douay version of Genesis describing Onan's action is essentially the same, differing only slightly in some phraseology. It reveals that

> He knowing that the children should not be his, when he went into his brother's wife, spilled his seed upon the ground, lest children should be born in his brother's name.

The spilling of seed was interpreted by some as masturbation, although it is now generally conceded by biblical scholars, and especially according to Roman Catholic interpretation, that Onan's "sin" was *coitus interruptus,* not masturbation. Most dictionaries, however, still list two definitions of onanism, one meaning uncompleted coition, and the other, masturbation. See Tom Burnam, *The Dictionary of Misinformation* (New York: Thomas Y. Cowell Company, 1975), pp. 171–172.

[286]Mentioned in Gibney, p. 129, with the source cited as Jacques Elliot, "Miscomprehensions of Parents Concerning Child Health and Behavior," *American Journal of Orthopsychiatry,* 12(2) (1942): 204.

[287]See Gerhert S. Schwarz, "Devices to Prevent Masturbation," *Medical Aspects of Human Sexuality,* 7(5) (May, 1973): 141.

[288]See Gibney, p. 129.

[289]See Schwarz, p. 142.

[290]Ibid., p. 143.

[291]Ibid.

[292]Ibid., p. 141.

[293]Ibid., p. 143.

[294]See Ibid., p. 149.

[295]See William R. Miller and Harold I. Lief, "Masturbatory Attitudes, Knowledge and Experience: Data from the Sex Knowledge and Attitude Test (SKAT)," *Archives of Sexual Behavior,* 5(5) (September, 1976): 456–457.

[296]Gibney, p. 129.

[297]For a detailed exposition on the social and medical history of masturbation, see R. R. Newman, "Masturbation, Madness, and the Modern Concepts of Childhood and Adolescence," *Journal of Social History,* 8(3) (Spring, 1975): 1–27.

[298]Ibid., p. 9.

[299]Ibid., p. 11.

[300]Ibid., p. 15.

[301]See B. G. Jefferis and J. L. Nichols, *Light on Dark Corners, A Complete Sexual Science & Guide to Purity Containing Advice to Maiden, Wife, & Mother How to Love, How To Court, How To Marry,* &c. &c. by B. G. Jefferis and J. L. Nichols. To Which Has Been Added *The Story of Life* by Ozora S. Davis Ph.D., President of Chicago Theological Seminary, and Dr. Emma F. A. Drake, Editor, Idaho *WCTU White Ribboner.* Abridged by Milton Klonsky, with Additional Counsel on Jealousy; The Curse & Cure from Dr. Foote's *Home Cyclopedia of Popular Medical, Social, & Sexual Science.* Grove Press. $5. New York, 1967). For a detailed and humorous review of this book's reprint, see William Styron, "The Vice that Has No Name," *Harpers Magazine,* February, 1968, pp. 97–100. A book similar in theme was A. T. Schofield and Percy Vaughn-Jackson's *What a Boy Should Know* (London and New York: Cassell and Co., 1913). In this book, the authors wrote of the masturbating boy as one who "will probably look pale and pasty," and who would probably have indigestion, constipation, spots and pimples, and "be more easily tired." He would, they wrote, "not have so good 'an eye' for games."

[302]See Walt Sheldon, *Troubling of a Star* (Chicago: Sears Readers Club, 1953), p. 77.

[303]William H. Masters and Virginia E. Johnson, *Human Sexual Inadequacy* (Boston: Little, Brown, and Co., 1970), p. 96.

[304]Philip Roth, *Portnoy's Complaint* (New York: Random House, Inc., 1969).

[305]Philip Roth, "Whacking Off," *Partisan Review,* 34(7) (Winter, 1967): 385–399.

[306]See Alfred Kinsey, Wardell B. Pomeroy, and Clyde E. Martin, *Sexual Behavior in the Human Male* (Philadelphia: W. B. Saunders Co., 1948), pp. 507–508.

[307]Warren J. Gadpaille, "Masturbation by Married Individuals," *Medical Aspects of Human Sexuality,* 8(11) (November, 1974): 63–64.

[308]Hannah Stone and Abraham Stone. *A Marriage Manual* (New York: Simon and Schuster, 1952), pp. 221–223.

[309]See Wardell B. Pomeroy, *Boys and Sex* (New York: Delacorte Press, 1968), pp. 53–55.

[310]Jacqueline Kasun, "Turning Children into Sex Experts," *Public Interest,* 55 (Spring, 1979): 3–4.

[311]Ibid., p. 4.

[312]Robert C. Sorensen, *Adolescent Sexuality in Contemporary America: Personal Values and Sexual Behavior Ages Thirteen to Nineteen* (New York: World Publishing Co., 1973).

[313]Chilman, p. 95.

[314]Ibid., pp. 144–145.

[315]Ibid., p. 95. Masturbation is still the object of considerable anxiety, conflict, and personal distress among some young people. For a detailed value on the place of masturbation in human development, see Irvin M. Marcus and John J. Francis, *Masturbation: From Infancy to Senescence* (New York: International Universities Press, Inc., 1975).

[316]Morton Hunt, *Sexual Behavior in the 1970s* (New York: Dell Publishing Co., Inc., 1975), p. 77.

[317]Ibid., pp. 84–85.

[318]Ibid., p. 86.

[319]Ibid., p. 83.

[320]Schwarz, p. 143.

[321]Hobart H. Sewell, "Sexual 'Norms' in Marriage," *Medical Aspects of Human Sexuality,* 8(10) (October, 1974): 84.

[322]Gadpaille, p. 64.

[323]Ibid.

[324]Masters and Johnson, p. 373.

[325]Hans Hessellund, "Masturbation and Sexual Fantasies in Married Couples," *Archives of Sexual Behavior,* 5(2) (March, 1976): 133–147.

[326]C. J. Bennett, "Female Masturbation—More Common Than We Think," *Medical Times,* 99(3) (March, 1971): 181.

[327]Alfred C. Kinsey, Wardell B. Pomeroy, Clyde E. Martin et al., "Sexual Behavior in the Human Female," in Martin S. Weinberg (ed.) *Sex Research: Studies from the Kinsey Institute* (New York: Oxford University Press, 1976), p. 83.

[328]Hunt, 1975, p. 76.

[329]Ibid., p. 77.

[330]See Robert J. Levin and Amy Levin, "Sexual Pleasure: The Surprising Preferences of 100,000 Women," *Redbook,* September, 1975, pp. 56–57.

[331]Masters and Johnson, p. 342.

[332]Ruth Clifford, "Development of Masturbation in College Women," *Archives of Sexual Behavior,* 7(6) (November, 1978): 559–573.

[333]Bennett, pp. 181–189.

[334]Ibid., p. 185.

[335]Sandra Coyner, "Women's Liberation and Sexual Liberation," in Roger W. Libby and Robert N. Whitehurst (eds.). *Marriage and Alternatives: Exploring Intimate Relationships.* (Glenview, Ill.: Scott, Foresman and Co., 1977), p. 223.

[336]Levin and Levin, p. 56.

[337]Hunt, 1975, p. 81.

[338]Ibid., pp. 97–98.

[339]Ibid., p. 97.

[340]Shere Hite, *The Hite Report: A Nationwide Study of Female Sexuality* (New York: Dell Publishing Co., Inc., 1976).

[341]Ibid., p. 59.

[342]See George Mazzei, *Good Vibrations: The Vibrator Owner's Manual of Relaxation, Therapy, and Sensual Pleasure.* (New York: Hawthorne Books, 1977).

[343]Betty Dodson, *Liberating Masturbation* (New York: Bodysex Designs, 1974).

[344]Anne Koedt, "The Myth of the Vaginal Orgasm," in S. Firestone and Anne Koedt (eds.), *Notes From the Second Year: Major Writings of the Radical Feminists* (New York: Radical Feminism, 1970).

[345]Quoted in Barbara Cady, "Self-Sexuality: A New Frontier," *Playgirl,* July, 1977, p. 33.

[346]Ibid.

[347]Ibid., p. 60.

[348]Coyner, p. 223.

[349]Ibid.

[350]Claire Safran, "Plain Talk About the New Approach to Sexual Pleasure," *Redbook,* March, 1976, p. 86.

[351]Quoted in Ibid., p. 88.

[352]Virginia E. Johnson, "What's Good and Bad About the Vibrator," *Redbook,* March, 1976, p. 136.

[353]Correspondence with Arizona Legislative Council, and various materials pertaining to the Second Regular Session of the 34th Legislature of the House of Representatives of the State of Arizona and related legislative proposals supplied by that organization.

[354]Cited in Hunt, 1975, pp. 133–136.

[355]Ibid., p. 136.

[356]Ibid., p. 137.

[357]Ibid., p. 109.

[358]Robert Ruark, *The Honey Badger* (Greenwich, Conn.: Fawcett Publications, Inc., 1965), p. 235.

[359]See Lester, pp. 257–60.

[360]Brockopp and Lester, p. 10.

[361]One study of massage parlor patrons indicated that two-thirds of the customers wanted "extras" (sexual services in addition to a massage), but only 42 percent of the customers actually received "extras." Of those customers who received sexual services, 14 percent received intercourse, 7 percent received oral sex, and 79 percent received masturbation. Whether one can obtain sexual services in addition to massage, and the particular kind of sexual services received, is a function of the particular massage parlor. See Edward G. Armstrong, "Massage Parlors and Their Customers," *Archives of Sexual Behavior,* 7(2) (March, 1978): 117–125.

[362]Mary Simpson and Thomas Schill, "Patrons of Massage Parlors: Some Facts and Figures," *Archives of Sexual Behavior,* 6(6) November, 1977): 524.

[363]Bryant and Palmer, pp. 227–41. For additional perspectives on such establishments, see Albert J. Velarde, "Becoming Prostituted: The Decline of the Mas-

sage Parlor Profession and the Masseuse," *British Journal of Criminology,* 15(3) (July, 1975): 251–263.

[364]Paul L. Rasmussen and Lauren L. Huhn, "The New Masseus: Play for Pay," *Urban Life,* 5(3) (October, 1976): 277.

[365]Ibid., p. 291.

[366]Ibid., p. 290.

[367]See, for example, Julia Heiman, Leslie Lo Piccolo, and Joseph Lo Piccolo, *Becoming Orgasmic: A Program of Sexual Growth for Women* (Englewood Cliffs, N.J.: Prentice Hall, 1976).

[368]For some samples of such literature, see Lonnie Garfield Barbach, *For Yourself: The Fulfillment of Female Sexuality* (New York: Doubleday and Co., Inc., 1976); and Georgina Kline-Graber and Benjamin Graber, *Woman's Orgasm: A Guide to Sexual Satisfaction* (Indianapolis: The Bobbs-Merrill Co., Inc., 1976).

[369]"J," *The Sensuous Woman* (New York: Dell Publishing Company, 1971), p. 39.

[370]Coyner, p. 222.

[371]Ibid.

[372]Trudy Willis, "Doctor-Author Views Homosexuality as a 'Disorder,' " *Roanoke* (Va.) *Times and World News,* 30 September 1976, p. 29. Interestingly, the United States Surgeon General announced that homosexuality would "no longer be considered a 'mental disease or defect.' " In a similar vein, the Immigration and Naturalization Service issued an order to its agents to stop preventing foreign homosexuals from entering the country." See *The New York Times,* 19 August 1979, sec. E. p. 9.

[373]George Weinberg, *Society and the Healthy Homosexual* (Garden City, N.Y.: Doubleday and Co., Inc., 1973), p. 22.

[374]Ibid., p. 23.

[375]Cited in Ibid., pp. 28–29. The original source is Thomas Szasz, *The Manufacture of Madness* (New York: Harper and Row, 1970).

[376]See Gerald Herman, "The 'Sin Against Nature' and Its Echoes in Medieval French Literature." *Annual Mediaevale,* 17 (1976): 87.

[377]Ibid., p. 70

[378]Ibid.

[379]A. D. Harvey, "Prosecutions For Sodomy in England at the Beginning of the Nineteenth Century," *The Historical Journal,* 21(4) (December 1978): 939.

[380]Ibid., p. 946.

[381]Ibid.

[382]See David R. Greenberg and Marcia H. Bystryn, "Social Sources of the Prohibition Against Male Homosexuality," Paper presented at the Annual Meeting of the Society for the Study of Social Problems, September 1978.

[383]See Geoff Robertson, "The Abominable Crime," *New Statesman,* 88 (November 1, 1974): 611.

[384]Some studies have suggested that personal style may be a more significant factor in why homosexuals are disliked than sexual preference. See Mary Riege Laner and Roy H. Laner, "Personal Style or Sexual Preference? Why Gay Men Are Disliked," *International Review of Modern Sociology,* 9(2) (July–December, 1979): 215–228. Laner and Laner, for example, observe that:

It appears that in matters of clothing style, manner, and interests, conformity to the norm has the best chance of acceptance in a predominately heterosexual world (p. 225).

They also comment that even in terms of the attribution of dangerousness, ". . . low homophobia among heterosexuals is related to the degree to which heterosexuals believe that homosexuals are conventional persons, at least in outward appearance." (pp. 225–226).

[385]See "The Homosexual: Newly Visible, Newly Understood," *Time,* October 31, 1969, p. 61.

[386]Albert J. Reiss, Jr., "The Social Integration of Queers and Peers," *Social Problems,* 9(2) (Fall, 1961): 108.

[387]See Ibid., pp. 102–119.

[388]Ibid., p. 117.

[389]Robert Trumbull, "Australia Issue: Homosexuality," *The New York Times,* October 1973.

[390]S. Bobys and Mary Riege Laner, "On the Stability of Stigmatization: The Case of Ex-Homosexual Males," *Archives of Sexual Behavior,* 8(3) (1979): 256.

[391]*Time,* October 31, 1969, p. 61.

[392]Ibid.

[393]Charles H. McCaghy and James K. Skipper, Jr., "Lesbian Behavior as an Adaption to the Occupation of Stripping," *Social Problems,* 17(2) (Fall, 1969): 159.

[394]Ibid., p. 162.

[395]Ibid., p. 163.

[396]See Charles Winick, and Paul M. Kinsie, *The Lively Commerce: Prostitutes in the United States* (New York: The New American Library, 1972), pp. 215–216.

[397]See C. A. Tripp, *The Homosexual Matrix* (New York: McGraw-Hill Book Co., 1975), pp. 222–223.

[398]Arthur N. Gilbert, "The Africaine Courts-Martial: A Study of Buggery and the Royal Navy," *Journal of Homosexuality,* 1(1) (1974): 111.

[399]Colin J. Williams and Martin S. Weinberg, "The Military: Its Processing of Accused Homosexuals," *American Behavioral Scientist,* 14(2) (November/ December, 1970): 203. For a fuller exposition, see Colin J. Williams and Martin S. Weinberg, *Homosexuals and the Military: A Study of Less Than Honorable Discharge* (New York: Harper and Row, 1971).

[400]Williams and Weinberg (1970), 203.

[401]Ibid., p. 216.

[402]See "Vice Scandal," *Parade,* August 8, 1976, p. 13.

[403]For a detailed exposition on the Matlovic case, see Martin Duberman, "The Case of the Gay Sergeant," *The New York Times Magazine,* 9 November 1975, pp. 16–17+; 58–71. Although Sgt. Matlovich was ultimately forced out of the armed services, he was later vindicated on appeal and ordered reinstated by the courts.

[404]See "Second Sergeant Comes Out," and " 'Unfit' Wacs Going to Court," *The Advocate,* August 13, 1975.

[405]See David L. Aiken, "Pentagon Retreats on Security Clearance Issues," *The Advocate,* August 27, 1975.

[406]Greshman M. Sykes, *The Society of Captives: A Study of Maximum Security Prisons* (New York: Atheneum, 1965), pp. 72; 95–99.

[407]See Edward Sagarin, "Prison Homosexuality and Its Effect on Post-Prison Sexual

Behavior," *Psychiatry,* 39(3) (August, 1976), pp. 245–257.

[408]Columbus B. Hopper, "Conjugal Visiting at the Mississippi State Penitentiary," *Federal Probation,* 29(2) (June, 1965): 39–46.

[409]One study of homosexual behavior in female correctional institutions, for example, concluded that, "The results of this study give no support to explanations based on deprivation . . ." See Allice M. Propper, "Lesbianism in Female and Coed Correctional Institutions," *Journal of Homosexuality.* 3(3) (Spring, 1978): 272.

[410]Gene Kassenbaum, "Sex in Prison," *Sexual Behavior,* 2(1) (January, 1972): 39.

[411]John H. Gagnon and William Simon, "The Social Meaning of Prison Homosexuality," *Federal Probation* 32(1) (March, 1968): 23–29. See also, Rose Giallombardo, *Society of Women: A Study of a Woman's Prison* (New York: John Wiley and Sons, Inc., 1966).

[412]See Alice M. Propper, "Make-believe Families and Homosexuality Among Imprisoned Girls," paper read at the annual meeting of the American Society of Criminology, November 9, 1979.

[413]Kassebaum, pp. 40–41. Comments here on based on this source.

[414]For a detailed description of this "con," see, Robert J. Kelly, "Acquiring a Protector," *Sexual Behavior,* 2(1) (January, 1972): 41.

[415]For a detailed exposition on such involuntary sexual activity in correctional institutions, see, Daniel Lockwood, *Prison Sexual Violence* (New York: Elsevier North Holland, Inc., 1980).

[416]Alan J. David., "Sexual Assaults in the Philadelphia Prison System and Sheriff's Vans," *Transaction,* 6 (December, 1968): 8–16.

[417]This comment was cited in Linda Charlton, "The Terrifying Homosexual World of the Jail System," *Sexual Behavior,* 2(1) (January, 1972): 44.

[418]Ibid.

[419]Kassenbaum, p. 45.

[420]George L. Kirkham, "Violence Accompanies Sex," *Sexual Behavior,* 2(1) (January, 1972): 42.

[421]Azmy Ishak Ibrahim, "Deviant Sexual Behavior in Men's Prisons," *Crime and Delinquency,* 20(1) (January, 1972): 40. Also see Charlton, p. 44.

[422]See, "How Gay Is Gay? Homosexual Men and Women Are Making Progress Toward Equality," *Time,* April 23, 1979, pp. 72–78. Also see Robert G. Meyer and Riddick, Flynn, and Associates, "Legal and Social Ambivalence Regarding Homosexuality," *Journal of Homosexuality,* 2(3) (1977): 281–287. Also see Stephen A. Mitchell, "Psychodynamics, Homosexuality, and the Question of Pathology," *Psychiatry,* 41(3) (August, 1978): 254–263; also, Steven Goldberg, "What Is 'Normal?' Logical Aspects of the Question of Homosexual Behavior," *Psychiatry,* 38(3) August, 1975): 227–243.

[423]*Time,* October 31, 1969, p. 56.

[424]See, "Homosexuals: Spiraling Toward Acceptance?" *The New York Times,* 7 October 1973.

[425]John Kifner, "Lesbian Won Votes with Candor," *Roanoke* (Va.) *Times and World News,* 19 November 1974.

[426]"The Lavendar Panthers," *Time,* October 8, 1973, p. 73.

[427]Ibid.

[428]See, "Homosexual Wins Fight to Take Bar Examination in Minnesota," *The New York Times,* 7 January 1973.

[429]Martin Arnold: Homosexuals: Not Exactly a Banner Day for Gay Lib," *The New York Times,* 13 February, 1972.

[430]"Foster Care of Youths by Homosexuals Tried," *Roanoke* (Va.) *Times and World News,* 8 May 1974.

[431]For a detailed exposition on this phenomenon, see Ronald M. Enroth and Gerald E. Jamison, *The Gay Church* (Grand Rapids, Mich.: William B. Erdmans Publishing Co., 1974).

[432]See Jack Star, "The Homosexual Couple," *Look,* January 26, 1971, pp. 69–71.

[433]Jill Gertson, "Goals Set Forth by Homosexuals," *The New York Times,* 1 December 1974, p. 74.

[434]Cited in Gene D. Phillips, "The Homosexual Revolution," *America,* 123(15) (November 14, 1970): 406.

[435]For a detailed account of the political efforts to redefine homosexuality, see Malcolm Spector, "Legitimizing Homosexuality," *Society,* 14(5) (July/August, 1977): 52–56.

[436]See Jane E. Brody, "More Homosexuals Aided to Become Heterosexual," *The New York Times,* 28 February 1971, pp. 1, 47.

[437]See Gerald C. Davison, "Homosexuality: The Ethical Challenge," *Journal of Consulting and Clinical Psychology,* 44(2) (April, 1976): 157–162; and Irving Bieber, "A Discussion of 'Homosexuality': The Ethical Challenge," *Journal of Consulting and Clinical Psychology,* 44(2) (April, 1976): 163–166.

[438]See, for example, Merle Miller, "What It Means to Be a Homosexual," *The New York Times,* 17 January 1971, pp. 9–11.

[439]Joseph Epstein, "Homo/Hetero: The Struggle for Sexual Identity," *Harpers Magazine,* September, 1970, pp. 37–51.

[440]Hunt, 1974, p. 305.

[441]Ibid., 311.

[442]Ibid.

[443]See Fred Klein, *The Bisexual Option: A Concept of One-Hundred Percent Intimacy* (New York: Arbor House, 1978).

[444]See John Money, "Bisexual, Homosexual, and Heterosexual: Society, Law, and Medicine," *Journal of Homosexuality* 2(3) (Spring, 1977): 229–233.

[445]Phillip W. Blumstein and Pepper Schwartz, "Bisexuality: Some Social Psychological Issues," *Journal of Social Issues,* 33(2) (Spring, 1977): 30–45.

[446]See Laud Humphreys, "Tearoom Trade: Impersonal Sex in Public Places," *Transaction,* 7(3) (January, 1970): 10–25; also, Jay Corzine and Richard Kirby, "Cruising the Truckers: Sexual Encounters in a Highway Rest Area," *Urban Life,* 6(2) (July, 1977): 171–192.

[447]Phillip W. Blumstein and Pepper Schwartz, "Bisexuality in Men," *Urban Life,* 5(3) (October, 1976): 339–357.

[448]See "The Bisexual and the Navy," *Time,* February 2, 1976, p. 49.

[449]"Bisexual Chic: Anyone Goes," *Newsweek,* May 27, 1974, p. 90.

[450]Quoted in Ibid.

[451]Quoted in Ibid.

[452]See, for example, Michele Matto, "The Transsexual in Society," *Criminology,* 10(1) (May, 1972): 85–109. Remarks here are primarily derived from this source.

[453]For a detailed exposition on the process of transsexual conversion, see Janice G. Raymond, *The Transsexual Empire: The Making of the She-Male* (Boston: Beacon Press, 1979); For another description of transsexualism with a psychiatric and psychological perspective, see Harry Brierley, *Transvestism: A Handbook with Case Studies for Psychologists, Psychiatrists, and Counsellors* (New York: Pergamon Press, 1979); For another discussion of transsexual behavior and lifestyle, see Deborah Heller Feinbloom, *Transvestites and Transsexuals: Mixed Views* (New York: Dell Publishing Co., 1977).

[454]"School Teacher Fired After Sex Change Operation," *Roanoke* (Va.) *Times and World News,* 19 October 1976, p. 2.

[455]Matto, p. 104.

[456]Thomas Kando, "Passing and Stigma Management: The Case of the Transsexual," *The Sociological Quarterly,* 13 (Fall, 1972): 475–483.

[457]"The Transsexuals," *Newsweek,* November 22, 1976, pp. 104–105.

[458]See David Holden, "James and Jan: A Remarkable Explorer in the Passage From One Sex to Another," *New York Times Magazine,* March 17, 1974, pp. 18+; see also, "Across the Frontiers of Sex," *Newsweek,* April 8, 1974, pp. 74–76.

[459]See Ray Kennedy, "She'd Rather Switch—and Fight," *Sports Illustrated,* September 6, 1976, pp. 17–19.

[460]Robert L. Munroe, John W. M. Whiting, and David J. Holly, "Institutionalized Male Transvestism and Sex Distinctions," *American Anthropologist,* 71(1) (February, 1969): 87.

[461]See Andrew Kopland, "The King/Queen of Drag," *New Times,* January 9, 1978, pp. 76–80.

[462]Ibid., p. 76.

[463]For a detailed exposition on such practices, see Laud Humphreys, *Tearoom Trade: Impersonal Sex in Public Places* (Chicago: Aldine Publishing Co., 1970).

[464]Cited in Neil R. Coombs, "Male Prostitution: A Psychosocial View of Behavior," *The American Journal of Orthopsychiatry,* 44(5) (October, 1974): 782–789.

[465]See "A Transvestite Prostitute Horde Plaging Manhattan Plaza Area," *The New York Times,* 2 September 1979, p. 41.

[466]Ibid.

[467]Ibid.

[468]Cited in Coombs, "Male Prostitution: A Psychosocial View of Behavior," especially pp. 787–788. Some of the traditional studies of the etiology of homosexuality have been challenged by new research findings. See Jane E. Brody, "Kinsey Study Finds Homosexuals Show Predisposition," *The New York Times* (August 23, 1981). pp. 1, 30.

[469]See Robert W. Deiser, Victor Eisner, and Stephen I. Sulzgacher, "The Young Male Prostitute," *Pediatrics,* 43(6) (June, 1969): 936–941.

[470]See Robin Lloyd, *For Money or Love: Boy Prostitution in America* (New York: Vanguard Press, Inc., 1976).

[471]See David J. Pittman, "The Male House of Prostitution," *Transaction,* 8(5,6) (March/April, 1971): 21–27.

[472]James P. Driscoll, "Transsexuals," *Transaction,* 8(5,6) (March/April, 1971): 25–28+.

[473]K. N. Ginsburg, "The Meat Rack: A Study of the Male Homosexual Prostitute," *American Journal of Psychotherapy,* 21(2) (April, 1967): 170–185.

[474]See George Lee Seward, "On First Being A John," *Urban Life and Culture,* 1(3) (October, 1972): 269.

[475]For a detailed exposition on the delivery of this kind of recreational sex, see Bryant and Palmer.

[476]More recently, this is not always the case. In some communities, law enforcement authorities, frustrated in their efforts to put massage parlors out of business, have begun harrassing the clientele. There have been instances of recording the automobile license plate numbers of customers and threatening calls to their wives. In other cases, customers have been arrested and carried to court where they are embarrassed by the publicity. In at least one instance, the judge ordered a massage parlor customer to have a psychiatric examination before he pronounced sentence. In a similar vein, New York City Mayor Edward Koch in 1980 used City-owned television station to publicize the names of johns.

[477]In many massage parlors, the masseuses are efficient to the point of assembly-line speed. One article reported that the motto of a particular parlor was, "Get 'em in, get 'em up, get 'em off, and get 'em out." See Bryant and Palmer, 1975, p. 137.

[478]Humpreys, 1970, pp. 10–13.

[479]Ibid., p. 13.

[480]Ibid.

[481]Ibid.

[482]See Martin S. Weinberg, and Colin J. Williams, "Gay Baths and the Social Organization of Impersonal Sex," *Social Problems,* 23(2) (December, 1975): 124–136.

[483]Ibid., p. 124.

[484]Ibid., p. 127.

[485]Ibid., p. 132.

[486]Franklyn N. Judson, Kenneth G. Miller, and Thomas R. Schaffnit, "Screening for Gonorrhea and Syphyllis in the Gay Baths—Denver, Colorado," *American Journal of Public Health,* 67(8) (August, 1977): 740–742.

[487]Ibid., 740.

[488]Corzine and Kirby, "Cruising the Truckers," pp. 171–192.

[489]Ibid., p. 178.

[490]Ibid., p. 189.

[491]Ibid., p. 185.

[492]Ibid., pp. 190–191.

[493]See, for example, Wardell Pomeroy, 1968, pp. 53–55. Also, Wardell Pomeroy, *Girls and Sex* (New York: Delacorte Press, 1969), p. 130.

[494]"J," p. 51.

[495]"M," *The Sensuous Man* (New York: Dell Publishing Co., Inc., 1972), pp. 45–62.

[496]See Hunt, 1975, especially Chap. 2, pp. 65–105.

[497]Sorensen, p. 145.

[498]Hunt, 1975, p. 85.

[499]Stephens, pp. 376–377.

[500]Ibid., p. 376.

[501]Reported in Ibid., p. 378.

[502]Ibid., p. 377.

[503]Chilman, p. 93.

[504]Ibid., p. 98.

[505]Larry Lister, "Adolescents," in Harvey L. Gochras and Jean S. Gochras (eds.), *The Sexually Oppressed* (New York, Associated Press, 1977), pp. 41–53.

[506]Cited in Ibid., p. 44.

[507]Ibid., p. 42.

[508]Hunt, 1975, pp. 131–132.

[509]Vern L. Bullough, *Sexual Variance In Society and History* (New York: John Wiley and Sons, 1976), p. 285.

[510]Hunt, 1975, p. 132.

[511]See Pamela Swift, "Keeping Up . . . With Youth: Chastity Reborn," *Parade,* October, 27, 1974, p. 15.

[512]Hunt, 1975, p. 132

[513]See Eugene J. Kanin, "Male Aggression in Dating-Courtship Relations," *American Journal of Sociology,* 63(2) (September, 1957): 197–204: also, Clifford Kirkpatrick and Eugene Kanin, "Male Sex Aggression on a University Campus," *American Sociological Review,* 22(1) (February, 1957): 52–58; and Eugene J. Kanin, "An Examination of Sexual Aggression as a Response to Sexual Frustration," *Journal of Marriage and the Family,* 29(3) (August, 1967): 428–433. For a more recent study of courtship and violence see: Mary Riege Laner "Abuse and Aggression in Courting Couples," *Deviant Behavior* vol. 3, no 2 (Jan.-March, 1982). pp. 42–62.

[514]Cited in Hunt, 1975, p. 133. The original source is Kinsey, Pomeroy, Martin et al., pp. 239–244; 273–275.

[515]Hunt, 1975, p. 136.

[516]Ibid., p. 135.

[517]L. M. Terman, *Psychological Factors in Marital Happiness* (New York: McGraw-Hill Book Co., 1938).

[518]W. W. Ehrmann, *Premarital Dating Behavior* (New York: Henry Holt Publishing Co., 1959).

[519]Mervin B. Freedman, "The Sexual Behavior of American College Women: An Empirical Study and an Historical Survey," *Merrill-Palmer Quarterly,* 2(1) (January, 1965): 33–48.

[520]See Kinsey, 1948 and 1953.

[521]Kinsey, 1948, p. 293.

[522]Kinsey, 1953, p. 330.

[523]Hunt, 1975, pp. 150–152.

[524]Ibid.

[525]Levin and Levin, p. 38. For a complete report and exposition on the study, see Carol Tavris and Susan Sadd, *The Redbook Report on Female Sexuality: 100, 000 Married Women Disclose the Good News About Sex* (New York: Dell Publishing Co., Inc., 1975).

[526]Chilman, p. 113.

[527]Ibid.

[528]David Gelman, Diane Weathers, Lisa Whitman, et al., "The Games Teen-Agers Play," *Newsweek,* September 1, 1980, p. 48.

[529]Cited in Ibid.

[530]Cited in Ibid.

[531]See Arno Karlen, "The Unmarried Married on Campus," *The New York Times Magazine*, January 26, 1969. pp. 28+, 77–80.

[532]Bell, p. 55.

[533]Hunt, 1975, pp. 154–155.

[534]Chilman, p. 123

[535]Melvin Zelnik, Kim Young, and John Kantner, "Probabilities of Intercourse and Conception Among U.S. Teenage Women, 1971 and 1976," *Family Planning Perspectives* 11(3) (May/June, 1979): 177–183

[536]Cited in Gelman, Weathers, Whitman, et al., p. 53.

[537]Ibid., p. 152.

[538]See Joyce R. Starr and Donald E. Carns, "Singles in the City," *Society*, 9(4) (February, 1972): 43–48; also, "Games Singles Play," *Newsweek*, July 16, 1973, pp. 52–58; also, Mary Alice Kellogg, "Singles in the Suburbs, Or You Can Go Home Again," *Saturday Review*, June 24, 1972, pp. 16–18; and Susan Jacoby, "49 Million Singles Can't All Be Right," *The New York Times Magazine*, February 17, 1974, pp. 12, 41+.

[539]"Church for Singles," *Newsweek*, June 12, 1972, p. 73.

[540]"Games Singles Play," p. 52.

[541]Ibid.

[542]Cynthia Proulx, "Sex as Athletics In the Singles Complex," *Saturday Review of the Society*, April 21, 1973, p. 73.

[543]Ibid., p. 61.

[544]Kellogg, p. 18.

[545]"Games Singles Play," p. 57.

[546]"Humanizing the Meat Market," *Society*, 11(1) (November/December, 1973), p. 11.

[547]Marion Meade, "Sex in Singles Bars," *Sexology*, 39(12) (July, 1973); 15–19.

[548]Ibid., p. 16.

[549]"Games Singles Play," p. 57.

[550]Proulx, pp. 61–66.

[551]Ibid.

[552]Ibid., p. 65.

[553]See Jerald W. Cloyd, "The Market-Place Bar: The Interrelations Between Sex, Situation, and Strategies in the Pair Ritual of *Homo Ludens*," *Urban Life*, 5(3) (October, 1976): 293.

[554]See Julian Roebuck and S. Lee Spray, "The Cocktail Lounge: A Study of Heterosexual Relations in a Public Organization," *American Journal of Sociology*, 72(4) (January, 1967): 388–395.

[555]Ibid., p. 393.

[556]See Ibid., p. 393

[557]Ibid.

[558]See David Shaw, "Rentagirl: A Look at Escort Agencies," *Forum: The International Journal of Human Relations*, 1 (September, 1972): 50–53.

[559]Ibid.

[560]See Bryant and Palmer for a detailed analysis of self-perceptions of masseuses and their patrons.

[561]Anna K. and Robert T. Francoeur, *Hot & Cool Sex: Cultures in Conflict* (New York: Harcourt Brace Jovanovich, 1974), p. 11.

[562]See Stephens, especially pp. 5–10.

[563]Ibid.

[564]Kinsey, Pomeroy, and Martin, in Weinberg, 1976, (ed.), pp. 73–74.

[565]Cited in Ibid., p. 73.

[566]Americans were not the only population that was sexually unsophisticated. Several years ago, a survey of the sexual habits of the French revealed that, unlike their image, they were remarkably "conservative and less imaginative in their lovemaking" than had been hitherto suspected. Close to 70 percent of the husbands and 90 percent of the wives reported that they had never been unfaithful. The great majority of the respondents indicated that they had sex at night before they went to sleep and overwhelmingly favored the classical position. Only 19 percent of the women reported that they had ever masturbated and only 73 percent of the men. In general, the French were simply not as innovative or sophisticated in their sexual behavior as were most Americans. See "Never on Monday," *Time,* November 6, 1972, p. 69.

[567]Kinsey, Pomeroy, and Martin, in Weinberg, 1976, (ed.), p. 69.

[568]Ibid., p. 74.

[569]Kinsey, Pomeroy, and Martin, in Weinberg, 1976, (ed)., p. 77.

[570]Reported in Vance Packard, *The Sexual Wilderness: The Contemporary Upheaval in Male-Female Relationships* (New York: David McKay Co., Inc., 1968), p. 271.

[571]One particular case of this kind, several years later became something of a landmark case, and was interesting because of its intricacies. In 1969, a married couple in Virginia met with a male friend in the bedroom of their home. The wife performed fellatio on the male friend and later on her husband, with the friend observing. Photographs of these activities were made. At a later date, one of the couple's daughters carried to school a photograph of the wife and the friend sitting nude on the sofa. School officials found the photograph and summoned police and welfare authorities. The police obtained a search warrant, searched the home and uncovered "thousands" of obscene photographs including the ones portraying the wife committing fellatio on her husband. The police also found a large amount of other obscene and sexually explicit material. The husband and wife were subsequently tried and convicted of committing sodomy with each other under Virginia's "crimes against nature" statute. The wife was also tried in a separate hearing and convicted of engaging in sodomy with the male friend. She received the maximum sentence of three years. There were a series of appeals and a petition for a writ of habeas corpus. In general, courts previously had held that married couples enjoyed a right of privacy in consenting sexual matters, but in this case, the third party being present and the photographs, tended to dilute their right to privacy. As the court phrased it, "by permitting an onlooker in the marital bedroom, the (couple) could have no reasonable expectation of privacy and, therefore, no constitutional protection." One of the judges who dissented observed that, "to the majority, sodomy was 'so odious that not even the constitution may be successfully interposed to protect a husband and wife so despicably disposed.' "

See Joseph L. Koplin, "Constitutional Law—Marital Right of Privacy—The Marital Right of Privacy Does Not Protect a Husband and Wife Performing Sodomy in the Presence of a Third Person," *The George Washington Law Review,* 45(4) (May, 1977): 848–850.

[572]See Levin and Levin, pp. 51–58. For the complete report, see Tavris and Sadd.

[573]"Sex Practices Tied to Death of Woman," *Roanoke* (Va.) *Times and World News,* 24 March 1973, p. 3.

[574]See Tavris and Sadd, p. 131.

[575]Ibid., p. 133.

[576]Another national survey of female sexuality suggested that females were experiencing a more enhanced appreciation of sex and were engaging in a wider range of sexual activities than were females in the Kinsey era. In this survey, sex practices such as cunnilingus appeared to be efficious for the women who experienced them. The study reported that while only approximately 30% of the women could orgasm regularly from intercourse, 42% orgasmed regularly during oral stimulation (p. 229 & p. 359). The women also appeared to be more comfortable with practices such as masturbation and oral sex than were the case at the time of the Kinsey study. Still, many of the respondents expressed cynical attitudes about the so-called "sexual revolution" feeling that the position of women in the sexual exchange process has not changed that much, and that the sexual revolution had, in fact, been dysfunctional to women in some ways. See Hite.

[577]Hunt, 1975, pp. 181–182.

[578]Cited in Ibid., p. 186.

[579]There are some studies that suggest perhaps many males are adjusting relatively well to the sexual revolution. In one national survey of male sexuality, it was reported that although most males considered the best sex life to be that of marriage with only one sex partner, they also spoke of preferring variety in their sex life such as different sexual positions and oral sex. Unlike the stereotypical myth of American males, the respondents in this study indicated that they received significant pleasure during foreplay, and especially liked "kissing and caressing," even without intercourse. The men seemed to have real concern for their partner's sexual needs and reported "feelings of deep distress if a partner fails to achieve orgasm." Almost one-half said they never cheat on their wives or steadies. In short, this study indicated that males were quite comfortable with today's sexual context as well as with many traditional values. See Anthony Pietropinto and Jacqueline Simenauer, "Beyond the Male Myth," *Cosmopolitan,* April, 1978, pp. 227–229; 314–318, also, Anthony Pietropinto and Jacqueline Simenauer, *Beyond the Male Myth* (New York: Time Books, 1977). For another insightful exposition on the male in today's context, see Bernie Zilbergeld, *Male Sexuality* (Boston: Little, Brown, and Co., 1978).

[580]See United Press International, "U.S. Judge Threatens to Imprison Woman for Illegitimate Births," *The New York Times,* 17 June 1979,

[581]See Sharon Johnson, "Two Pioneer Programs Help Unwed Teen-age Fathers Cope," *The New York Times,* 5 March 1978, p. 54; see also, Erdwin H. Pfuhl, Jr., "The Unwed Father: A 'Non-Deviant' Rule Breaker," *The Sociological Quarterly,* 19(1) (Winter, 1978): 113–128.

[582]The so-called "menstrual taboos," are "very common the world over." See *The Family in Cross-Cultural Perspective* (New York: Holt, Rinehart, and Winston, Inc., 1963), p. 403.

[583]Traditional medical views in this regard are being moderated somewhat during recent years. See Elisabeth Bing and Libby Colman, *Making Love During Pregnancy* (New York: Bantam Books, 1977); see also, Geraldine Carro, "Sex During Pregnancy," *Ladies Home Journal,* March, 1978, pp. 74, 149.

[584]The voluntarily childless couple being pressured by parents and peers to have children and thus, becoming "deviants" of a sort for the failure to do so is a common theme in soap operas such as "Dallas." Even having "too many" children could prove to be socially stigmatizing in some instances. In the tongue-in-cheek book, *How To Be A Bishop Without Being Religious* (New York: Doubleday and Co., Inc., 1965) pp. 24–25, author Charles Merrill Smith points out that a successful minister must never convey the image of excessive carnality, and that he lead his congregation to believe that ". . . he really didn't enjoy the procedure essential to this end very much [fathering children]." One might conclude, therefore, that a large number of children might implicitly erode the desired image.

[585]See Associated Press, "Sterilized Men Can Wed, Says Pope," *Roanoke* (Va.) *Times and World News,* 6 August 1977.

[586]See Associated Press, " 'Prophet' Sought in Polygamy War," *Roanoke* (Va.) *Times and World News,* 29 September 1977, sec A., p. 16. Also, Associated Press, "By Sects and Giant Families Polygamy Grows in the West," *The New York Times,* 9 October 1977, p. 1; see also, Mally Ivins, "Polygamy, Growing in the U.S. West, Is Encountering Little Opposition," *The New York Times,* 9 October 1, 1977, p. 1.

[587]See Levin and Levin, pp. 38–42; 190–192.

[588]Hunt, 1975, p. 259.

[589]Ibid., p. 261.

[590]Ibid., p. 264.

[591]Linda Wolfe, "How Three Wives Justify Their Love Affairs," *Redbook,* May, 1973, p. 90.

[592]See Harold Greenwald, "Sex Away from Home," *Sexual Behavior,* 1(6) (September, 1971): 6–14.

[593]Wolfe, p. 90.

[594]See Ralph E. Johnson, "Some Correlates of Extramarital Coitus," *Journal of Marriage and the Family,* 32(3) (August, 1970): 449–456.

[595]See Clifton D. Bryant, "The Subversion of Sexual Comportment," *Deviant Behavior,* esp. pp. 20–21.

[596]See James A. Peterson, "The Office Wife," *Sexual Behavior,* 1(5) (August, 1971): 2–10; see also, Lawrence Lipton, *The Erotic Revolution: An Affirmative View of the New Morality* (Los Angeles: Sherbourne Press, Inc., 1965), especially chapter 3, pp. 52–71.

[597]Bryant has addressed this possible causative linkage in some detail. See Clifton D. Bryant, *Deviant Behavior: Occupational and Organizational Bases* (Chicago: Rand McNally Publishing Co., 1974), especially pp. 20–22.

[598]Warren Weaver, Jr., "Washington Sex: Always Available," *The New York Times,* 20 June 1976. "Sexual Politics" is hardly new in United States history. See

"Mix of Sex, Politics Has Spiced U.S. History," *Roanoke* (Va.) *Times and World News,* 6 June 1976, sec. A., pp. 1, 8.

[599]For a detailed, descriptive account of extra-marital sexual activity among factory workers see Donald Roy, "Sex in the Factory: Informal Heterosexual Relations between Supervisors and Work Groups," in Clifton D. Bryant (ed.), *Deviant Behavior,* pp. 44–66.

[600]Jerry M. Lewis, "Promiscuous Women," *Sexual Behavior,* 1(8) (November, 1971): 77.

[601]For an interesting set of case study vignettes of sexual affairs from the female standpoint, see Linda Wolfe, *Playing Around: Women and Extramarital Sex* (New York: William Morrow and Co., Inc., 1975).

[602]See Associated Press, "Adultery Behind Most Problems in Marriages," *Roanoke* (Va.) *Times and World News,* 11 April 1977, sec. C, p. 8.

[603]Quoted in Wendy James, and Susan Jane Kedgley, *The Mistress.* (London: Albelard-Schuman Ltd., 1973), p. 39.

[604]Quoted in Ibid., p. 35.

[605]See Rhoda Amon, "Mistresses Form Self-Help Group," *Roanoke* (Va.) *Times and World News,* 24 April 1977, sec. E, p. 1, 13.

[606]Levin and Levin, p. 42.

[607]See Duane Denfeld and Michael Gordon, "The Sociology of Mate Swapping: Or the Family that Swings Together Clings Together," *Journal of Sex Research,* 7(2) May, 1970): 35–99; see also, William Breedlove and Jerrye Breedlove, *Swap Clubs: A Study in Contemporary Sexual Mores* (Los Angeles: Sherbourne Press, 1964); Charles Paulson and Rebecca Paulson, "Swinging in Wedlock," Transaction: Social Science and Modern Society. *Society,* 9(4) (February, 1972): 23–34; Gilbert D. Bartel, "Group Sex Among Mid-Americans," *The Journal of Sex Research,* 6(2) (May, 1970): 113–130; George C. O'Neill and Nena O'Neil, "Patterns in Group Sexual Activity," *The Journal of Sex Research,* 6(2) May, 1970): 101–112; and Robert R. Bell, " 'Swinging': The Sexual Exchange of Marriage Partners," *Sexual Behavior* 1(2) (May 1971): 70–79.

[608]See Charles Remsberg and Bonnie Remsberg, "Weird Harold and the First Swingers' Convention," *Esquire,* December, 1970, pp. 189; 270–274.

[609]See Duane Denfeld, "How Swingers Make Contact," *Sexual Behavior,* 2(4) (April, 1972): 60–63.

[610]Denfeld and Gordon, p. 95.

[611]Gilbert D. Bartell, "A Single Sexual Standard," *Sexual Behavior,* 1(8) (November, 1971): 79.

[612]Harris, pp. 139–163. Although bestiality as a sexual variant is presumably not widespread, it is not, however, necessarily infrequent. There are, of course, anthropological references to human-sexual contact in other cultures, but there has also been a persistant presence of bestiality practices in this society. Kinsey reported a not insignificant percentage of rural males having had sexual contact with an animal. His data indicated, for example, that between 40 percent and 50 percent of farm boys had sexual contact with animals, and in Western areas, the figure rose to 65 percent. Rural youths apparently sometimes engage in sexual intercourse with livestock on an experimental basis, particularly their sexual initiation. In Jerzy Kosinski's book, *The Painted Bird,* he describes some Polish peasants and their sexual activities with goats. In one instance a peasant

girl, Ewka, has intercourse with a buck goat. See Jerzy Kosinski, *The Painted Bird.* (New York: The Modern Library, 1970), p. 151. Bestiality, otherwise, has tended to be more associated with single, often isolated adults such as the gold miner or prospector and his ubiquitous jenny, or the spinster and her large dog. Such sexual activity is generally a function of social (or special) isolation and the absence of an appropriate human sexual partner or outlet. Bestiality as component of a marital or other mixed sex dyadic relationship is unusual and suggest a particularly neurotic need for carnal gratification of bizarre variation. Interestingly, pornography involving bestiality has not enjoyed an inordinate degree of popularity among clientele of such material. In fact, pornography involving such subject matter does not appear to erotically stimulate some persons. In one trial of a defendent who was charged with being a wholesaler of obscene films and specifically films portraying bestiality, the jury acquitted with the explanation that the films in question were "too disgusting and repulsive to appeal to the prurient interest of average people." The two films mentioned, "Man's Best Friend," and "Every Dog Has His Day," portrayed two men involved in sexual activity with a German Shepherd. The jurors reluctantly acquitted the defendant because they believed "the films did not appeal to the 'prurient interest' of 'ordinary adults' because they did not create any feeling of longing or desire." The judge agreed that "if you're not aroused, it's not obscene." See Leslie Maitland, "Bestiality Found of Little Appeal, Jury Acquits Movie Wholesaler," *The New York Times,* 18 December 1977, p. 72.

[613]See Richardson, pp. 82–89.

[614]This practice receives a detailed exposition in Fernando Henriques, *Stews and Strumpets: A Survey of Prostitution: Primitive, Classical, and Oriental,* (London: MacGibbon and Kee, 1961), pp. 121–122.

[615]"Bring Back the Brothels," *Time,* November 19, 1970, p. 30.

[616]See "Prostitution Prospers Along Alaskan Pipeline," *Roanoke* (Va.) *Times and World News,* 12 May 1974, pp. 3–14.

[617]Winick and Kinsie, especially pp. 225–233.

[618]Quoted in Ibid., p. 233.

[619]Ibid., pp. 215–216.

[620]Ibid., p. 217.

[621]See Lloyd Shearer (ed.), "Rehabilitating Lost Women," *Parade,* January 2, 1972, p. 4.

[622]Winick and Kinsie, p. 49.

[623]Ibid., p. 58.

[624]Ibid.

[625]Ibid.

[626]"Suburbia: The Call Wives," *Newsweek,* February 17, 1964, p. 18.

[627]See Clifton D. Bryant, and J. Gipson Wells (eds.), *Deviancy and the Family* (Philadelphia: F. A. Davis Co., 1973), p. 244.

[628]Bryant and Palmer, pp. 227–241.

[629]Bell, Charles W., "The Prostitution Boom in Italy." *The Washington Post,* (Sunday, August 13, 1972): p. H14.

[630]See Lorano O. Sullivan, "Love for Sale: Firm Operating Brothels Looks for Investors," *The Wall Street Journal,* 31 December 1971, pp. 1, 13.

[631]See Lesley Oelsner, "Prostitute Neighbors Vexing Tenants, Especially in Luxury Units," *The New York Times,* 22 August 1971, p. 46.

[632]Eric Pace, "Operation Eros Seeks Eviction of Prostitutes," *The New York Times,* 23 January 1972.

[633]Some have acquired such fame that in some instances, the madames of such establishments have penned their memoirs, which have subsequently become best sellers. For such an example, see Paul Tabor, *Pauline's: Memoirs of the Madam on Clay Street* (Louisville, Ky.: Touchstone Publishing Co., 1970); For another perhaps better known book about a madame and her life and career, see Polly Adler, *A House Is Not A Home.* (New York: Popular Library), 1953; for a more recent similar book, see Xaviera Hollander, *The Happy Hooker.* (New York: Dell Publishing Company, Inc.), 1972.

[634]A particularly engaging and insightful pictorial account of Storyville prostitutes is found in Lee Friedlander, *Bellocq: Storyville Portraits* (New York: The Museum of Modern Art, 1971).

[635]Winick and Kinsie, p. 163.

[636]Ibid.

[637]Ibid., pp. 143–145.

[638]For an elaborate exposition of the process see, Diana Gray, "Turning Out: A Study of Teenage Prostitution," *Urban Life and Culture* 1(4) (January, 1973): 401–426.

[639]See James H. Bryan, "Apprenticeships in Prostitution," *Social Problems,* 12(3) (Winter, 1965), 287–297; see also, Barbara Sherman Heyl, "The Madam as Teacher: The Training of House Prostitutes," *Social Problems,* 24(5) (June, 1977): 545–555.

[640]Bryan, p. 293.

[641]Ibid., p. 291.

[642]For a detailed discussion of the brothel as a work system, see Barbara Sherman Heyl, "The Madam as Entrepreneur," *Sociological Symposium,* (11) (Spring, 1974): 61–82.

[643]The role set of the call girl is described in some detail in Mary Gray Riege, "The Call Girl and the Dance Teacher," *Cornell Journal of Social Relations,* 4(1) (Spring, 1969): 58–71.

[644]Maxine Atkinson and Jacqueline Boles, "Prostitution as an Ecology of Confidence Games: The Scripted Behavior of Prostitute and Vice Officers," in Clifton D. Bryant (ed.), *Sexual Deviancy in Social Context,* (New York: New Viewpoints, 1977) pp. 219–231.

[645]Winick and Kinsie, p. 75.

[646]Ibid., p. 59.

[647]Ibid., pp. 58–59.

[648]See Ann Blackman, "As GI's Leave, Bar Girls Suffer," *Roanoke* (Va.) *Times and News World,* 3 November 1972, p. 14.

[649]Winick and Kinsie, p. 172.

[650]Winick and Kinsie, pp. 183–184.

[651]Bryant, *Deviant Behavior: Occupational and Organizational Bases* p. 370.

[652]Winick and Kinsie, p. 185.

[653]Virginia McManus, *Not For Love* (New York: Dell Publishing Co., 1971), p. 149.

[654]See Weaver.

[655]See "Government-Supervised Brothels," Parade, June 9, 1974.

[656]"Call Girls' Clientele Mainly Executives," *The Roanoke* (Va.) *Times and World Report,* 14 May 1976.

[657]Norman R. Jackman, Richard O'Toole, and Gilbert Geis, "The Self-Image of the Prostitute," *The Sociological Quarterly,* 4(2) (Spring, 1963): 151.

[658]Associated Press, "Prostitutes' Customers 'Disgraced' by Arrests," *The Charlotte* (S.C.) *Observer,* 6 December 1977, sec. A, p. 3.

[659]Associated Press, "Mass Arrest Brings Suicide," *Roanoke* (Va.) *Times and World News,* 30 September 1977, sec. A, p. 20.

[660]Quoted in James C. Mills, "Why Nice Men Go to Prostitutes," *Redbook,* March, 1977, p. 103.

[661]Charles Winick, "Prostitutes' Clients' Perception of the Prostitutes and of Themselves," *International Journal of Social Psychiatry,* 8(4) (Autumn, 1962): 296.

[662]See Marilyn Ellias "Stand-In for Eros," *Human Behavior,* 6(3) (March, 1977): 17–23.

[663]"All About the New Sex Therapy," *Newsweek,* November 27, 1972, p. 71. After the publicity about the sexual surrogate therapy appeared, a number of "expose" books purportedly written by former sex therapists appeared. See, for example, Heather Hill (with John Austin), *Sexual Surrogate: Notes of a Therapist* (Chicago: Henry Regenry Co., 1976); and Amanda Steward, *Sex Therapist: My Story.* (New York: Ace Books, 1975).

[664]Susan Greene, "Resisting the Pressure to Become a Surrogate: A Case Study," *Journal of Sex and Marital Therapy,* 3(1) (Spring, 1977): 40-49.

[665]David R. Mace, "Delinquent Sex and Marriage Counselors," *Sexual Behavior,* 1(3) (June, 1971): 40.

[666]See Carol Tavris and Susan Sadd, *The Redbook Report on Female Sexuality* (New York: Dell Publishing Co., Inc.) p. 165.

[667]Weaver, 1976.

[668]See Judy Flanders, "Prostitutes Don't See Themselves as Criminals," *Roanoke* (Va.) *Times and World News,* 11 January 1973.

[669]For a detailed socio-political exposition on the legal aspects of miscegenation statutes, see Robert J. Sickels, *Race Marriage and the Law* (Albuquerque: University of New Mexico Press, 1972).

[670]See Pearl S. Buck, *The Hidden Flower* (New York: J. Day Co., 1952), and Sinclair Lewis, *Kingsblood Royal* (London: J. Cape, 1948).

[671]For an analysis of interracial dating and the attendant social sanctions and personal stresses experienced by the participants, see Frank A. Petroni, "Teenage Interracial Dating," *Transaction,* 8(11) (September, 1971): 54–59.

[672]Quoted in John M. MacDonald, *Rape: Offenders and Their Victims* (Springfield, Ill.: Charles C. Thomas Publishing Co., 1971), p. 246.

[673]Susan Brownmiller, *Against Our Will: Men, Women, and Rape* (New York: Simon and Schuster, 1975), p. 370.

[674]MacDonald, pp. 246–247.

[675]Ibid., p. 250.

[676]Ibid., p. 249.

[677]"Children: Innocent Till When?" *The Economist,* 264(6993) (September 10, 1977): 47–48.

[678]MacDonald, p. 302.

[679]Melinda Beck, Jerry Buckley, and Tenley-Ann Jackson, "A Law That Makes Sex Legal at 13," *Newsweek,* May 7, 1979, p. 36.

[680]Ibid.

[681]Ibid.

[682]Ibid.

[683]Ibid.

[684]Le Roy G. Schultz, "The Child as a Sex Victim: Socio-legal Perspectives," *Rape Victomology* (Springfield, Ill.: Charles C. Thomas Publishing Co., 1975), pp. 257–258. Remarks in this paragraph are heavily drawn from this source.

[685]Cited in Schultz, p. 258.

[686]Rene T. S. Brant and Veronica B. Tisza, "The Sexually-Misused Child," *American Journal of Orthopsychiatry,* 47(1) (January, 1977): 81.

[687]Ibid.

[688]Ibid., p. 87.

[689]Ibid., p. 82.

[690]Macdonald, p. 111.

[691]Schultz, pp. 260–261.

[692]Ibid., p. 259.

[693]Macdonald, pp. 115–117.

[694]Matti Virkkumen, "Victim Precipitated Pedophilia Offense," *British Journal of Criminology,* 15(2) (April, 1975): 179.

[695]Ibid., p. 175.

[696]MacDonald, pp. 114–115.

[697]For a classic, detailed discussion of this topic, see Leslie A. White, "The Definition and Prohibition of Incest," *American Anthropologist,* 50(3, Pt. 1) (July–September, 1948): 416–435; see also, Edward Sagarin, "Incest: Problems of Definition and Frequency," *The Journal of Sex Research,* 13(2) (May, 1977): 125–135; for a legal statement on the subject, see Ralph Slovenki, "Incest," in the Legal Briefs Section of *Siecus Report,* 7(5) (May, 1979): 4–5.

[698]Ibid., p. 256.

[699]Schultz, p. 256.

[700]Alvin A. Rosenfeld, Carol C. Nadelson, and Marilyn Krieger, "Fantasy and Reality in Patients' Reports of Incest," *Journal of Clinical Psychiatry,* 40(4) (April, 1979): 159–164.

[701]Ibid., p. 163.

[702]See Susan Forward and Craig Buck, *Betrayal of Innocence: Incest and Its Devastation* (Los Angeles: J. P. Tarcher, 1978).

[703]Unfortunately, many of these books are based on woefully inadequate or questionable data. A number of such books have obviously been directed toward the trade market and have something of a sensational nature. They are generally based on a very small number of interviews selected on an unscientific sampling basis. In some instances, only a small and selected number of the interview cases are presented and the rationale for the particular selection is not given. As polemics, they are interesting but add little to our scientific knowledge about incest. Because of their unsubstantiated inference that incest is nearly endemic to our family and kinship system, such books promote a distorted image of parents as highly potential sexual abusers of their children. A good example of this genre (as evidenced by its dramatic title), is *Kiss Daddy*

Goodnight (New York: Hawthorn Books, 1978); for another recent book with a sensational flavor (as labeled by one book reviewer in *Siecus Report,* May, 1979, p. 11), see Sandra Butler, *Conspiracy of Silence: The Trauma of Incest* (San Francisco: New Glide Publications, 1978).

[704]Henry Giarretto, "Humanistic Treatment of Father-Daughter Incest," *Journal of Humanistic Psychology,* 18(4) (Fall, 1978): 59–76.

[705]Ibid., p. 74.

[706]Alvin A. Rosenfeld, "Endogamic Incest and the Victim-Perpetrator Model," *American Journal of Diseases of Children,* 133 (April, 1979): 406.

[707]Ibid., p. 407.

[708]Ibid., p. 407.

[709]Ibid., p. 408.

[710]Ibid., p. 409.

[711]Ibid., p. 410.

[712]For a detailed exposition on this topic see Middleton, "Brother-Sister and Father-Daughter Marriage in Ancient Egypt," *American Sociological Review,* 27(5) (October, 1962): 603–611.

[713]Katherine N. Dixon, L. Eugene Arnold, and Kenneth Calestro, "Father-Son Incest: Underreported Psychiatric Problem?" *American Journal of Psychiatry,* 135(7) (July, 1978): 838.

[714]Ibid., p. 837.

[715]Ibid.

[716]Ibid., p. 835.

[717]See "Son, Mother Charged with Incest," *Roanoke* (Va.) *Times and World News,* 17 August 1979, sec. B, p. 1.

[718]See "Incest Probation Violated; Mom, Ex-Marine Jailed," *Roanoke* (Va.) *Times and World News,* 5 June 1980, sec. B, p. 3.

[719]See "Touch of Incest: More Than Brother and Sister," *Time* (July 2, 1979): p. 76; see also "Brother and Sister Convicted of Incest," *Roanoke* (Va.) *Times and World News,* 2 August 1979, sec. A, p. 5.

[720]"I Married My Sister," *Newsweek,* July 2, 1979, p. 36.

[721]Bryan Strong, "Toward a History of the Experimental Family: Sex and Incest in the Nineteenth-Century Family," *Journal of Marriage and the Family,* 35(3) (August, 1973): 457–466.

[722]Ibid., p. 460.

[723]Ibid.

[724]Within this decade, a Czechoslovakian researcher has conducted a detailed, scientifically controlled study of 161 children born to women who had been involved in sexual relationships with their fathers, brothers or sons, and 95 children born to these same women as a result of sexual relations with men to whom they were not related. On the basis of the study data, the researcher concluded that there is an "unmistakable effect of inbreeding on infant mortality, congenital malformations, and intelligence level." "Children of Incest," *Newsweek,* October 9, 1972, p. 58.

[725]See Clifton D. Bryant, "Inappropriate Family Role Behavior," in Clifton D. Bryant and J. Gipson Wells (eds.), *Deviancy and the Family* (Philadelphia: F. A. Davis Co., 1973), especially pp. 32–34. Remarks here heavily draw on this material.

[726]See Yvonne M. Formes, *Child Victims of Incest* (Denver: The American Humane Association Children's Div., n.d.) p. 5.

[727]See, for example, Noel Lustig, John W. Dresser, Seth W. Spellman et al., "Incest: A Family Group Survival Pattern," *Archives of General Psychiatry,* 14(1) (January, 1966): 31-40; Irving B. Weiner, "Father-Daughter Incest: A Clinical Report," *Psychiatric Quarterly,* 36(1962): 607–632; Hector Cavallin, "Incestuous Fathers: A Clinical Report," *American Journal of Psychiatry,* 122(10) (1966): 1132–1138; also, Irving Kaufman, Alice L. Peck, and Consuelo K. Tagiuri, "The Family Constellation and Overt Incestuous Relations Between Father and Daughter," *American Journal of Orthopsychiatry,* 24(2) (April, 1954): 266–277.

[728]Bruno M. Cormier, Miriam Kennedy, and Jadwiga Sangowicz, "Psychodynamics of Father-Daughter Incest," *Canadian Psychiatric Association Journal,* 7 (1962): 203–217.

[729]Bryant, 1973, p. 34.

[730]See Paul H. Gebhard and John H. Gagnon, "Male Sex Offenders Against Very Young Children," *American Journal of Psychiatry,* 121 (6) (December, 1964): 576–579.

[731]Ibid., p. 578.

[732]Ibid., p. 579.

[733]For an example of such behavior, see "Boy 17, Charged in Molesting Case," *Roanoke* (Va.) *Times and World News,* 25 April 1980, sec. B, p. 3.

[734]See, for example, Charles H. McCaghy, "Child Molesting," *Sexual Behavior,* 1(5) (August, 1971): 16–24. This portion of the commentary is primarily based on this source.

[735]Ibid., p. 24.

[736]See Jaffy Hermann, "The Lolita Complex: Men Who Love Luscious Little Girls," *Cosmopolitan,* April, 1978, pp. 246–276.

[737]MacDonald, p. 302.

[738]Charles H. McCaghy, "Drinking and Deviance Disavowal: The Case of Child Molesters," *Social Problems,* 16(1) (Summer, 1968): 43–49.

[739]Ibid., p. 44.

[740]Ibid., pp. 45–48.

[741]Frederic Bernard, "An Inquiry Among a Group of Pedophiles," *The Journal of Sex Research,* 11(3) (August, 1975): 242–255.

[742]Ibid., p. 254.

[743]Frederick E. Whiskin, "The Geriatric Sex Offender," *Geriatrics,* 22 (1967): 168.

[744]Ibid., p. 169.

[745]"Child's Garden of Perversity," *Time,* April 4, 1977, p. 55.

[746]See Fraker et al., "Crackdown on Porn," *Newsweek,* February 28, 1977, pp. 21-27. See also, Myra McGherson, "Booming Porn Sideline Cashes in on Photos of Children," *The Roanoke* (Va.) *Times and World News,* 30 January 1977, sec. A, p. 6.; and Morris Fraser, "Child Pornography," *New Statesman,* 95(2448) (February 17, 1978): 213.

[747]Ibid., see also, Associated Press, "Undercover Agent Catches Pornographers," *Roanoke* (Va.) *Times and World News,* 8 February 1977.

[748]Hugo Beigel, "Children Who Seduce Adults," *Sexology,* 40(5) (February, 1974): 40.

[749]"Youth for Sale on the Streets," *Time,* November 28, 1977, p. 23.

[750]See Donald J. Shoemaker, "The Teeniest Trollops: 'Baby Pros,' 'Chickens,' and Child Prostitution," in Clifton D. Bryant (ed.) *Sexual Deviancy in Social Context.* (New York: New Viewpoints, 1977), pp. 241-253.

[751]For a detailed exposition on this new form of sexual exploitation see Robin Lloyd, *For Money or Love: Boy Prostitution in America* (New York: Vanguard Press, Inc., 1976).

[752]Marion Meade, "She's 40, He's 20—: Still Taboo?" *Sexology,* 40(5) (December, 1973): 40.

[753]"Island Teacher Who Wed Student Gets Settlement after Suspension," *The New York Times,* 15 January 1978.

[754]See Associated Press, "Grandson Makes Plans to Marry Grandmother," *Roanoke* (Va.) *Times and World News,* 10 December 1977, sec. A., p. 3.

[755]Associated Press, "Decline Recorded in Teen-age Birth Rate," *Roanoke* (W. Va.) *Times and World News,* 26 November 1976, p. 19.

[756]Robert Veit Sherwin, "The Law and Sexual Relationships," *The Journal of Social Issues,* 22(2) (April, 1966): 109–122.

[757]Celeste MacLeod, "Street Girls of the '70s," *The Nation,* April 20, 1974, pp. 486–488.

[758]"Attacking the Last Taboo: Researchers Are Lobbying Against the Ban on Incest," *Time* April 14, 1980, p. 72.

[759]Ibid.

[760]James W. Ramey, "Dealing With the Last Taboo," *Siecus Report,* 7(5) (May, 1979): 1-7.

[761]J. W. Mohr, R. E. Turner, and M. B. Jerry, *Pedophilia and Exhibitionism* (Toronto: University of Toronto Press, 1964), p. 12.

[762]Ibid.

[763]It is interesting to note that individuals accused, tried, and convicted of sexual offenses against children and juveniles, not infrequently are persons who are involved with children and juveniles on an intimate basis in the course of their work or avocation. See, for example, Associated Press, "Tennessee Priest Convicted of Homosexual Crimes," *Roanoke* (Va.) *Times and World News,* 4 June 1977; and Associated Press, "Police Charge Scout Leaders in Morals Case," *Roanoke* (Va.) *Times and World News,* 11 September 1976, sec. A, p. 2.

[764]As a typical example, a local newspaper carried an account of a 20-year-old man who was convicted of having committed oral sodomy on a 3½-year-old boy. See Roy Reed, "Child Molester Given 3-Year Term," *Roanoke* (W. Va.) *Times and World News,* 27 September 1977.

[765]See Associated Press, "Police Break Up R.I. Sex Club," *Roanoke* (Va.) *Times and World News,* 17 February, 1977, p. 24; for other similar reports of male homosexual clubs that victimized children, see Associated Press, "At Least 15 Arrested in Child Sex Ring," *Roanoke* (Va.) *Times and World News,* 9 December, 1977, sec. A, p. 6; also Associated Press, "Sex Ring Story Worries School," *Roanoke* (Va.) *Time and World News,* 11 December 1977, sec. A, p. 16; and Craig Waters, "Gentlemen Prefer Boys: 24 Men Indicted for Abuse of 70 Boys in Boston Hired-Sex Ring," *New Times,* January 23, 1978, p. 21.

[766]See, for example, Dick Hammerstrom, "Man Convicted in Morals Case Involving Boys," *Roanoke* (Va.) *Times and World News,* 18 May, 1977.

[767] Bernard, p. 253.

[768] Geoffrey Lakeman, "Child Sex Chief 'Kicked Out' of Love Conference," *The (London) Daily Telegraph,* 8 September 1977; see also, "Yes, Virginia, There is PIE," *National Review,* 29(39) (October 8, 1977): 1221–1222.

[769] Lawrence Turner, "Child-Sex Men Won't Keep Quiet," (London) *Sunday Mirror,* 28 August 1977, p. 5.

[770] See Lars Ullerstam, *The Erotic Minorities* (New York: Grove Press, Inc., 1966).

[771] See Allan J. Mayer et al., "The Graying of America," *Newsweek,* February 28, 1977, pp. 50–64.

[772] See Victor Knight, Gordon Gregor, and Jean Carr, "Tarnished for Life, (London) *Sunday Mirror,* September 4, 1977, p. 1.

[773] Robin, p. 226.

[774] Quoted in Robert Ardrey, *The Territorial Imperative: A Personal Inquiry into the Animal Origins of Property and Nations* (New York: Dell Publishing Co., 1966), p. 52. The original source given is Helmut K. Buechner, "Territorial Behavior in the Uganda Kob," *Science,* 133 (1961); 698–699.

[775] Ardrey, p. 3.

[776] Konrad Lorenz, *On Aggression* (New York: Bantam Books, 1967), pp. 146–147.

[777] Ibid., pp. 152–153.

[778] Ibid., p. 131.

[779] See Davis, 1968; Charlton, 1972; Lockwood, 1980; see also Peter L. Nacci, "Sexual Assault in Prison," *American Journal of Corrections,* 40(1) (January–February, 1978): 30–31. This has even been seen as a theme in several prison movies such as *The Glass House,* starring Alan Alda.

[780] See Clifford Kirkpatrick and Eugene Kanin, "Male Sex Aggression on a University Campus," *American Sociological Review,* 22(1) (February, 1957): 428–433.

[781] Eugene Kanin, "An Examination of Sexual Aggression as a Response to Sexual Frustration," *Journal of Marriage and the Family,* 29(3) (August, 1967): 428–433.

[782] See John E. Snell, Richard J. Rosenwald, and Robey Ames, "The Wife-beater's Wife: A Study of Family Interaction," *Archives of General Psychiatry,* 11 (August, 1964): 107–113.

[783] See Leroy G. Shultz, "The Wife Assaulter," *Corrective Psychiatry and Journal of Social Therapy,* 6(1960): 103–11.

[784] For a brief survey of such literature, see Ann Frodi, "Sexual Arousal, Situational Restrictiveness, and Aggressive Behavior," *Journal of Research in Personality,* 11(1) (March, 1977): 48–58.

[785] John P. Flynn, "Recent Findings Related to Wife Abuse," *Social Casework,* 58(1) (January, 1977): 17.

[786] Ibid.

[787] Ibid.

[788] For a detailed exposition of such prostitution services, see Monique Von Cleef (with William Waterman). *The House of Pain: The Strange World of Monique Von Cleef, The Queen of Humiliation.* (Secaucus, N.J.: Lyle Stuart, Inc., 1973).

[789] For some detailed expositions on the subject, see, Robert L. Sack and Warren Miller, "Masochism: A Clinical and Theoretical Overview," *Psychiatry,* 38(August, 1975): 244–257; also, Gertrud Lenzer, "On Masochism: A Contribution to the History of Phantasy and Its Theory," *Signs: Journal of Women*

in Culture and Society, 1(2) (Winter, 1975): 277–324; and Gerald Green and Caroline Green, *S-M: The Last Taboo* (New York, Grove Press, 1974).

[790]See Andreas Spengler, "Manifest Sadomasochism of Males: Results of an Empirical Study," *Archives of Sexual Behavior,* 6(6) (November, 1977): 441–456.

[791]For an elaborate description of this type of S & M subculture, see G. W. Levi Kamel, "Leathersex: Meaningful Aspects of Gay Sadomasochism," *Deviant Behavior: An Interdisciplinary Journal,* 1(2) (January–March, 1980): 171–191.

[792]See for example, Thomas S. Weinberg and Gerhard Falk, "The Social Organization of Sadism and Masochism," *Deviant Behavior: An Interdisciplinary Journal,* 1(3–4) (April–September, 1980): 379–393; also see, Thomas S. Weinberg, "Sadism and Masochism: Sociological Perspectives," *Bulletin of the American Academy of Psychiatry and the Law,* 6(0) (XYZ, 1978): 284–295.

[793]See James W. Prescott, "Body Pleasure and the Origins of Violence," *The Bulletin of the Atomic Scientist,* 31(9) (November, 1975): 14.

[794]See "Texas: Fly Now, Pay Later," *Newsweek,* August 27, 1973, p. 22.

[795]"Bill & George," *Time,* July 29, 1946, pp. 18–19.

[796]For a detailed exposition of his criminal memoirs, see George William Rae, *Confessions of the Boston Strangler* (New York: Pyramid Publications, 1967). This quote is taken from a brief selection from the book which was included in Charles H. McCaghy, James K. Skipper Jr., and Mark Lefton (eds.), *In Their Own Behalf: Voices from the Margin.* p. 198.

[797]See Jack Altman and Marvin Ziporyn, "Born to Raise Hell: The Mind of a Murderer" *Saturday Evening Post,* July 1, 1967, pp. 27–31, 39–40, 44–48, 70. See also, "Crime: One by One," *Time,* July 22, 1966, p. 19; and "Crime: 24 Years to Page One," *Time,* July 29, 1966, pp. 15–17.

[798]Altman and Ziporyn, p. 48.

[799]"The Nicest Person," *Newsweek,* August 20, 1973, p. 32; Arthur Bell, "The Fate of the Boys Next Door," *Esquire,* March 1, 1974, pp. 96–99, 174–176; "The Houston Horrors," *Time,* August 20, 1973, p. 24; and "Texas: Fly Now, Pay Later," *Newsweek;* see also Clifford L. Linedecker, *The Man Who Killed Boys* (New York: St. Martin's Press, 1980).

[800]For a news account of this incident, see "Arrest Made Tuesday in Sodomy Assault," *The* (Va.) *Blacksburg-Christianburg New Messenger,* 9 September 1976, p. 1.

[801]"Rape: Motive for Murder," *The Economist,* 255(6868) (April 12, 1975): 71.

[802]See Susan Griffin, "Rape: The All-American Crime," in Leroy G. Schultz (ed.), *Rape Victomology,* p. 20.

[803]See Macdonald, pp. 26–27.

[804]Ibid., p. 28.

[805]"St. Louis Return of the 'Phantom,'" *Newsweek,* July 14, 1969, p. 24.

[806]Macdonald, p. 73.

[807]Ibid., p. 54.

[808]Ibid., p. 51.

[809]Menachem Amir, *Patterns in Forcible Rape* (Chicago: University of Chicago Press, 1970), p. 366.

[810]Ibid., p. 340.

[811]Ibid., p. 339.

[812]Ibid., p. 341.

[813]Renee Goldsmith Kasinsky, "Rape: A Normal Act?" *Canadian Forum,* 55 (September, 1975): 18.

[814]"Portrait of a Rapist," *Newsweek,* August 20, 1973, pp. 67–68. Comments here are heavily drawn on this material; see also A. Nicholas Groth and H. Jean Birnbaum, *Men Who Rape: The Psychology of the Offender* (New York: Plenium Publishing Co., 1979).

[815]See Nicholas Groth and Ann Wolbert Burgess, "Rape: A Sexual Deviation," *American Journal of Orthopsychiatry,* 47(3) (July, 1977): 400. Rape is not included among the various types of sexual deviations listed in the American Psychiatric Association's *Diagnostic and Statistical Manual of Mental Disorders* (DSM-II) or in the World Health Organization's *International Classification of Diseases.*

[816]Ibid., p. 405.

[817]Ibid.

[818]See Associated Press, "Court Told Boyfriend Pursued by Lover," *Roanoke* (Va.) *Times and World News,* 24 November 1977.

[819]Brownmiller, p. 18.

[820]Ibid., p. 24.

[821]For an interesting discussion of this topic, see Brownmiller, Chap. 3, "Wars," pp. 31-113. Comments here are heavily drawn on this material. See also the detailed exposition on crimes, including rape committed by military personnel against civilians in, Clifton D. Bryant, *Khaki-Collar Crime: Deviant Behavior in the Military Context* (New York: The Free Press, 1979), especially Chap. 7.

[822]John Blashill, "What Follows War," *Time,* February 2, 1970, pp. 17–18.

[823]Brownmiller, pp. 79–80.

[824]Ibid., p. 77.

[825]Ibid., p. 32.

[826]Kasinsky, p. 20.

[827]For the details of this study, see Lynda Lytle Holmstrom, "Rape: An Indicator of Women's Family Role." Paper presented at I.S.A. Meetings, August, 1974, Toronto, Canada.

[828]Cited in Kasinsky. The original source is given as Camille Le Grande, "Rape and Rape Laws: Sexism in Society and Law 61," *California Law Review,* 919(921) (1973) for estimates of rapes in various states.

[829]Kasinsky, p. 20.

[830]Ibid.

[831]Ibid.

[832]See Associated Press, "Musician Faces Rape Hearing," *Roanoke* (Va.) *Times and World News,* 10 October 1979, Sec. A, p. 3.

[833]Ibid.

[834]Ibid.

[835]See Clifton D. Bryant, 1979, p. 213.

[836]See Leslie Maitland, "Rape: Newly Discovered Motives are Linked to Sexual Violence," *Roanoke* (Va.) *Times and World News,* 29 July 1974, p. 2; also, A. Nicholas Groth, Ann Wolbert Burgess, and Lynda Lytle Holmstrom, "Rape: Power, Anger, and Sexuality," *American Journal of Psychiatry,* 134(11) (November, 1977): 1239–1243.

[837]See Associated Press, "Italy Shudders: Young Rich Embracing Sadism," *Roanoke* (Va.) *Times and World News,* 2 April 1976, p. 9.

[838]Kasinsky, p. 21.

[839]Brownmiller, pp. 14–15.

[840]Amir, pp. 160–161.

[841]Ibid., p. 21.

[842]Ibid., p. 51.

[843]See Lynda Lytle Holstrom, and Ann Wolbert Burgess, "Rapists' Talk: Linguistic Strategies to Control the Victim," *Deviant Behavior: Interdisciplinary Journal,* 1(1) (October–December, 1979): 101-125.

[844]See "Rape: Motive for Murder," *The Economist,* 255(6868) (April 12, 1975): 71.

[845]Ibid.

[846]See Amir, chap. 15, "Victim-Precipitated Forcible Rape," pp. 259–276; 346–347.

[847]Quoted in "Rape and Culture: Two Judges Raise the Question of the Victim's Responsibility," *Time,* September 12, 1977, p. 41.

[848]Ibid.

[849]See "Man Convicted of Raping 89-Year-Old," *Roanoke* (Va.) *Times and World News,* 30 May 1980, Sec. A, p. 6.

[850]See, for example, Jan Ben Dor, "Justice After Rape: Legal Reform in Michigan," in Marcia J. Walker and Stanley L. Brodsky (eds.) *Sexual Assault: The Victim and the Rapist* (Lexington, Mass: D. C. Health and Co., 1976), pp. 149–168.

[851]"A Revolution in Rape: Keeping a Woman's Past Sexual Life Out of Court," *Time,* April 2, 1979, p. 50.

[852]See Lloyd Shearer, "Rape in Marriage," *Parade,* September 26, 1976, p. 6.

[853]See Richard J. Gelles, "Power, Sex, and Violence: The Case of Marital Rape," *The Family Coordinator,* 26(4) (October, 1977): 339–347.

[854]See Peter Bonuentre, "Was It Rape?" *Newsweek,* January 1, 1979, p. 55; also, "Rape: No: A Wife Loses," *Time,* January 8, 1979, p. 61; and Jerrold K. Footlick, "Beating the Rape Rap," *Newsweek,* January 8, 1979, p. 41.

[855]See "Husband-Rapist Sentenced," *Roanoke* (Va.) *Times and World News,* 25 September 1979.

[856]Davis, pp. 8–16; for a particularly detailed report on such offenses, see Peter C. Buffum, *Homosexuality in Prisons (Washington, D. C.: Government Printing Office, 1972).*

[857]The phenomenon of "selling" young, sexually appealing inmates to other inmates for homosexual purposes, guards rewarding groups of prisoners by "giving" them such inmates, and the process of a young inmate voluntarily becoming a homosexual partner of an older inmate for protection purposes are widespread in correctional institutions, and well documented in the literature. Such behavior has been shown or mentioned in a number of very authentic movies such as *Scared Straight, Squires of San Quentin,* and *The Glass House.*

[858]Norman S. Goldner, "Rape as a Henious but Understudied Offense," *The Journal of Criminal Law, Criminology, and Police Science,* 63(3) (September, 1972): 402–407.

[859]Associated Press, "Supreme Court Bans Death Penalty for Rape," *Roanoke* (Va.) *Times and World News,* 30 June 1977, sec. A, p. 7.

[860]See Caroline Rand Herron and Donald Johnston, "A Rape Law Conviction," *The New York Times,* 1 December 1974, sec. E, p. 10.

[861]See Linda Wolfe, "New Rape Laws Ending the Anti-Victim Bias," *The New York Times,* 1 December 1974, p. 10E. For a detailed discussion of this exigency, see John M. McDonald, "False Accusations of Rape," *Medical Aspects of Human Sexuality,* 7(May, 1973): 170–193.

[862]See Melville Carico, "Some Lawyers Oppose New Rape Trial Approach," *Roanoke* (Va.) *Times and World News,* 7 February 1980, sec. B, p. 11.

[863]See, for example, Edward Sagarin, "Forcible Rape and the Problem of the Rights of the Accused," *Intellect,* 103(1975): 515–520.

[864]See Mark Barabak, "Falsely Accused of Rape. He Lost Job, Savings, Almost His Wife." *San Francisco Examiner and Chronicle,* 9 November 1980. Sec. E, p. 2.

[865]See Wolfe, p. 10E.

[866]Associated Press, "Resistance Excites Rapist," *Roanoke* (Va.) *Times and World News,* 9 May 1975, p. 9.

[867]Leslie Maitland, "Rape: Newly-discovered Motives are Linked to Sexual Violence," *Roanoke* (Va.) *Times and World News,* 29 July 1974, p. 2.

[868]Accounts of such assaults are relatively common in many local newspapers. See, for example, "Arrest Made Tuesday in Sodomy Assault," *The* (Va.) *Blacksburg-Christiansburg News Messenger,* 9 September 1976, p. 1.

[869]See "Law for Male Rape Victims," *The New York Times,* 7 July 1974.

SUBJECT INDEX

NAME INDEX

Harlan
COBEN

Tylko jedno spojrzenie

Z angielskiego przełożył
ZBIGNIEW A. KRÓLICKI

ALBATROS

Wydawnictwo
A. Kuryłowicz

WARSZAWA 2008

Tytuł oryginału:
JUST ONE LOOK

Redakcja: Beata Słama
Ilustracja na okładce: Jacek Kopalski
Projekt graficzny okładki i serii: Andrzej Kuryłowicz

ISBN 978-83-7359-227-8

Dystrybucja
Firma Księgarska Jacek Olesiejuk
Poznańska 91, 05-850 Ożarów Maz.
t./f. 022-535-0557, 022-721-3011/7007/7009
www.olesiejuk.pl

Sprzedaż wysyłkowa – księgarnie internetowe
www.merlin.pl
www.empik.com
www.ksiazki.wp.pl

WYDAWNICTWO ALBATROS
ANDRZEJ KURYŁOWICZ
Wiktorii Wiedeńskiej 7/24, 02-954 Warszawa

Wydanie V
Skład: Laguna
Druk: B.M. Abedik S.A., Poznań

*Dziecino, nawet twoje najlepsze wspomnienia
z czasem zblakną jak atrament.*

Trawestacja chińskiego przysłowia zawarta w tekście
piosenki Jimmy X Band *Wyblakły atrament*
(napisanej przez Jamesa Xaviera Farmingtona, wszystkie prawa zastrzeżone)

Scott Duncan siedział naprzeciwko zabójcy.

W pokoju bez okien, o ścianach koloru burzowej chmury, panowało niezręczne milczenie, jak w chwili, gdy muzyka zaczyna grać i nikt z obecnych nie wie, jak to się tańczy. Scott spróbował niezobowiązującego kiwnięcia głową. Zabójca, ubrany w więzienny pomarańczowy drelich, tylko się na niego gapił. Scott splótł dłonie i położył je na metalowym blacie stołu. Zabójca — z akt wynikało, że nazywa się Monte Scanlon, ale z pewnością nie było to jego prawdziwe nazwisko — być może zrobiłby to samo, gdyby nie był skuty.

Dlaczego tu przyjechałem?, ponownie zadał sobie pytanie Scott.

Specjalizował się w oskarżaniu skorumpowanych polityków, więc w swoim rodzinnym New Jersey nie narzekał na brak zajęcia, ale trzy godziny temu Monte Scanlon, spełniający kryteria każdej definicji seryjnego zabójcy, w końcu przerwał milczenie i czegoś zażądał.

Czego?

Prywatnego spotkania z zastępcą prokuratora, Scottem Duncanem.

Było to dziwne z wielu powodów, z których dwa najważniejsze to po pierwsze, zabójca nie miał prawa niczego żądać, a po drugie, Scott nigdy nie spotkał Monte Scanlona ani nawet o nim nie słyszał.

7

— Chciałeś się ze mną widzieć? — przerwał ciszę Scott.

— Tak.

Scott skinął głową i czekał. Nie doczekał się.

— Co mogę dla ciebie zrobić?

Monte Scanlon nadal uważnie mu się przypatrywał.

— Wiesz dlaczego tu siedzę?

Scott omiótł spojrzeniem pokój. Oprócz ich dwóch, znajdowały się w nim jeszcze cztery osoby. Prokurator Linda Morgan podpierała ścianę, z udawaną swobodą Sinatry opierającego się o latarnię. Za więźniem stali dwaj potężni, niemal identyczni strażnicy więzienni z ramionami jak pniaki i torsami jak beczki. Scott spotkał ich już wcześniej i widział, jak wykonują swoją robotę z pogodą ducha instruktorów jogi. Jednak teraz, w obecności tego skutego więźnia, nawet oni byli lekko spięci. Adwokat Scanlona, łasicowaty i cuchnący tandetną wodą kolońską, był czwarty. Wszyscy spoglądali na Scotta.

— Zabiłeś ludzi — odparł Scott. — Wielu.

— Byłem, jak to się mówi, cynglem. Byłem... — Scanlon odczekał moment — zabójcą do wynajęcia.

— Nie zajmowałem się żadnym z tych zabójstw.

— To prawda.

Ten dzień zaczął się dla Scotta zupełnie zwyczajnie. Przygotowywał pozew sądowy dla członka zarządu firmy zajmującej się utylizacją odpadów, który przekupił burmistrza pewnego miasteczka. Rutynowa sprawa. Codzienność w Garden State, jak nazywano stan New Jersey. Było to zaledwie... No ile, godzinę czy półtorej godziny temu? Teraz siedział przy jednym stole z człowiekiem, który, według szacunkowego wyliczenia Lindy Morgan, zabił setkę ludzi.

— Dlaczego więc chciałeś zobaczyć się ze mną?

Scanlon wyglądał jak podstarzały playboy, który w latach pięćdziesiątych podrywał siostrę Gabor. Był mały i chuderlawy. Siwiejące włosy miał zaczesane do tyłu, zęby pożółkłe od nikotyny, skórę niezdrową od nadmiaru słońca i zbyt wielu długich nocy w zbyt wielu ciemnych klubach. Nikt z obecnych nie wiedział, jak naprawdę nazywa się ten człowiek. Został